·*Good Food*·
CLASSICS

· Good Food · CLASSICS

Published by Consumers' Association

Which? Books are commissioned and researched by The Association for
Consumer Research, and published by Consumers' Association,
2 Marylebone Road, London NW1 4DF

British Library Cataloguing-in-Publication Data
A catalogue record for this book is available from the British Library

ISBN 0 340 59655 4

Typeset by Litho Link Ltd, Welshpool, Powys
Printed and bound in Great Britain by Bath Press Colourbooks, Glasgow

Typographic and cover design: Paul Saunders
Text illustrations: Ann Savage

Photography: Philip Dowell
Home economist: Ann Page-Wood
Stylist: Carolyn Russell

Cookery consultant: Jacqui Hine

Contributors:

Sonia Allison	Sallie Morris
Lizzie Boyd	Sri Owen
Moira Buxton	Claudia Roden
Anna Del Conte	Yan-kit So
Gail Duff	Meera Taneja
J Audrey Ellison	John J Tovey
Bernice Hurst	Rosemary Wadey
Elisabeth Lambert Ortiz	Kathie Webber
Prue Leith	

The publishers would also like to thank David Mellor
who loaned many of the props.

Contents

Introduction

Good Food Classics presents classic recipes from all over the world, to suit all occasions – everyday meals as well as celebrations – and to appeal to all tastes. Like good novels, classic recipes are those to which we return time and time again, and which always somehow surprise and please. The word 'classic' has long ceased to be applicable only to the set-pieces of international restaurant menus and to traditional dishes like moules à la marinière and fruit fools (although you will find such favourites in these pages). Over the past forty years travel, technology, the proliferation of restaurants representing any number of national and regional cuisines, and a revolution in food retailing have broadened our expectations immeasurably. Pasta, stir-fries, ratatouille, kormas and kebabs are now just as much classics as roasts, puddings and cakes – and are frequently much healthier because of their greater reliance on fresh fruit and vegetables, and their use of vegetable oils rather than hard fats.

To compile what we hope will become a classic in its own right we have called on the expertise of top food specialists covering the world's greatest cuisines. Between them they have contributed more than 400 recipes – from the simplest combination of ingredients, where the whole is much more than the sum of its parts, like kichri on page 126 (with little more than rice, lentils and cheese), to surprises like paper-wrapped pork on page 80, which is a little fiddly to prepare and needs marinating but eminently justifies the effort. In fact, throughout the book are recipes with a twist – simple and effective creations that you will quickly come to regard as classic standbys. Vegetarians will find masses of recipes, all marked clearly with a ⓥ at the head of the ingredients list, but equally there are plenty of ideas for meat- and fish-eaters to explore.

Interspersed among the main sections for soups, fish, vegetables, puddings, bread and cakes and so on you will find eight features to provide inspiration: easy and appetising breakfasts to start off the day, perfect Sunday brunches, picnics and barbecues that go far beyond the soggy sandwich and sausage-and-steak routine. For evening entertaining there are some excitingly different approaches in the shape of two sumptuous Indian dinner party menus (one traditional, one modern), a Dutch/Indonesian rijsttafel (a feast of exotic tastes – none of them difficult to achieve), and an Italian dinner party, like the best of classic Italian fashion, full of understated elegance.

The precepts of healthy eating pervade the book. Even recipes which might sound rather wicked have been adapted accordingly (see overleaf). Often, it isn't the dish itself that's the culprit but the way it is served – by itself it may be relatively innocuous, but when loaded up with chips and vegetables swimming in butter the meal becomes a less-than-healthy prospect.

THE RECIPES

Fat, sugar and salt content have been taken into consideration during the development of these recipes and the minimum quantities necessary have been used without compromising flavour or texture. When frying, use just enough oil necessary to prevent the food from sticking to the pan and always drain it well on kitchen paper.

Use a vegetable oil whenever possible except in baking, when a hard fat is normally required. Butter and margarine contain about the same number of calories but margarine contains significantly less saturated fat. White vegetable fat can be used for shallow-frying and baking.

Semi-skimmed milk has been used in the recipes instead of full-fat but skimmed milk may be substituted if you like, which will reduce the total fat rating. Instead of single cream we have used low-fat plain yogurt. Wholemilk Greek yogurt makes an excellent substitute for double cream. Experiment with different yogurts but take care when adding them to hot food in case they separate.

Where an alternative ingredient is given in brackets the nutritional information is given for the first ingredient and not that in the bracket.

Unusual ingredients are explained in the glossary of food terms at the back of the book, and there is plenty of guidance on how and with what to serve a dish.

NUTRITIONAL FACTBOXES

After each recipe in the book you will find a nutritional factbox, which indicates how many calories are in a single serving, as well as a breakdown of the most important elements that should be considered when following a healthy diet. Here is an example.

Curried parsnip and potato soup

KILOCALORIES	200	SUGARS	8g
TOTAL FAT	8g	SODIUM	100mg
SATURATED FAT	–	FIBRE	6g

Kilocalories

The amount of energy that food provides is measured in kilocalories. Our daily intake of calories needs to be balanced against our age, sex, body build and the amount of energy we use in our daily routine. Unused calories are laid down as body fat.

Fats

The total amount of fats in a dish is given first, with the amount of saturated fat within that total given underneath. Saturated fats, found mainly in animal and dairy products, should be kept low in order to keep down blood cholesterol levels, which put some people at risk of heart disease. Healthy eating recommendations are that on average men should limit their daily intake of total fat to 95g, women to 70g.

Sugars

Sugars are found naturally in most vegetables and fruits in varying quantities but in a form which is difficult to digest in large quantities. Refined sugar has no nutritional value except to provide pure energy but it is easy to consume in large amounts. Refined sugar is used widely in the food industry to add bulk and flavour to most products, including savoury ones. These are often referred to as 'hidden sugars' and should be taken into consideration when looking at the overall daily consumption of sugars. Excess sugar can result in obesity and dental decay. The sugar content calculated in these recipes is the total amount in the foods and not just the added refined sugar. Healthy eating recommendations are that we should limit our average intake of sugars to around 60g a day.

Sodium

High sodium (salt) intake can raise blood pressure and lead to heart and kidney disease as well as strokes. Like sugar, it is found naturally in many foods and care should therefore be taken when adding salt to recipes. Salt is referred to as sodium on the nutritional labels on food – 1g salt = 390mg sodium. Healthy eating recommendations are that we should limit our daily sodium intake to 2300mg, i.e. around 6g salt. In this book the quantity of sodium given after each recipe is the amount per head from all sources in the dish and not just the added refined salt. Many classic recipes from countries with a warm climate contain considerably more salt than those from more temperate regions so if you are following recipes in other books you may wish to adjust the salt content accordingly. Likewise, if you are using stock cubes or garlic or onion salt don't add extra salt to the recipe.

Fibre

Fibre aids the digestion and rids the body of waste material. On average we need 18g of fibre a day. This can easily be achieved by eating five portions of vegetables and fruit (including the skins if possible), having wholemeal bread every day and pasta or brown rice at least once a day.

The figures in the nutritional factboxes are rounded up when necessary to the nearest whole figure. If a dash appears after a nutrient rather than a figure it means that the total amount present in the recipe is nil, or less than 0.5g (or less than 5mg in the case of sodium).

What you won't find in the boxes

- Protein – irrelevant to most general nutritional information in the developed countries as we eat far more protein than we need.

- Carbohydrates – we should aim to take half our calorie intake from complex carbohydrates (found in fruit and vegetables, particularly potatoes, as well as bread, rice and cereals).

- Vitamins and minerals – most of us get all the vitamins and minerals we need from a healthy and varied diet without the need to take supplements.

A Good Start to the Day

A good breakfast made with wholesome ingreddients will set you up for the day and will help prevent mid-morning hunger pangs.

Time is usually short in the mornings but with a little organisation it need not be time-consuming to give the family something wholesome: healthy ingredients are as easy to serve up as convenience foods, and many breakfast dishes can be prepared the night before and need only a quick final cook in the morning.

Cereals are easy to serve, and should preferably be the wholegrain types, which contain vital vitamins, minerals and fibre; add dried fruits or honey rather than spoonfuls of sugar to give sweetness. Sugar-free muesli, with plenty of dried fruits and nuts and served with chopped fresh fruit and yogurt or milk, is one of the healthiest breakfasts; for a hot cereal dish such as porridge, try adding chopped dried figs and apricots and a few raisins before cooking.

Fresh fruit – half a grapefruit, some grapes or an apple – is a marvellous starter, served plainly or topped with natural yogurt, sunflower seeds and a sprinkling of wheatgerm.

There is little to compare with the smell or flavour of fresh hot toast. Make it from a wholemeal loaf and spread it with marmalade, honey or sugar-free jam. Wholemeal rolls, biscuits and crispbreads can be served instead of toast for a Continental breakfast or with eggs in some form: boiled, poached, coddled, scrambled or made into a savoury custard.

If breakfast is not breakfast without bacon, grill it instead of frying it and serve it with apple rings or tomatoes and wholemeal toast. In Scandinavia, Germany and Eastern Europe cheese and cold meats as well as delicate chicken liver pâtés are popular: choose low-fat hard cheeses or mild-cured lean ham and serve with tomatoes and wholemeal bread.

Oily fish gives a healthy start to the day. It is rich and only small quantities need be served: poach or grill kipper fillets, grill whole or filleted herrings, coated with oatmeal, or serve smoked mackerel fillets either grilled or cold.

Waffles and pancakes are favourite breakfast treats in America: for health reasons, make them with wholemeal flour and serve plain ones with yogurt and honey, savoury ones with grilled bacon and tomatoes.

People who really cannot face eating first thing in the morning could try orange brose: mix together 75 g medium oatmeal (pre-soaked in 150 ml water and pressed through a fine sieve), 275 ml unsweetened orange juice, 1 banana and ½ teaspoonful of dried brewers' yeast, then liquidise till smooth. Or perhaps a yogurt drink: mix equal amounts of yogurt and pure fruit juice, sweeten to taste with honey if desired and blend in a liquidiser.

Right *(clockwise from top) Muesli, fruit compote, cheesy pancakes, egg and mushroom custards, smoked mackerel and tomato patties, wholewheat waffles and hot bacon baps*

HOT BACON BAPS

——— • ———

The baps can be filled and wrapped ready for the oven the night before and stored in the fridge.

SERVES 4

175–225 g/6–8 oz lean bacon rashers, derinded
1–2 tbsp chutney
4 wholemeal baps (or soft rolls)
1 small or ½ medium-sized cooking apple, peeled,
cored and sliced

Grill the bacon until cooked through but not crisp; cut it into small strips and mix with the chutney. Split the baps in half and place a quarter of the bacon and chutney mixture on the bottom half of each bap, cover with apple slices and replace the bap tops.

Put the baps, two at a time, into roasting bags (or foil) and seal them. Place them on a baking sheet. To cook, bake the baps for 10–12 minutes in an oven preheated to 200°C/400°F/gas 6.

KILOCALORIES	275	SUGARS	3g
TOTAL FAT	12g	SODIUM	1460mg
SATURATED FAT	4g	FIBRE	3g

SMOKED MACKEREL AND TOMATO PATTIES

——— • ———

The patties are best made in advance and chilled in the fridge overnight.

SERVES 4

450 g/1 lb potatoes
1 medium-sized onion, thinly sliced
4 tbsp semi-skimmed milk
3 tbsp parsley, finely chopped
pinch cayenne pepper
1 tbsp tomato purée
125 g/4 oz smoked mackerel fillet
3–4 tomatoes
25 g/1 oz bran
4 tbsp vegetable oil
8 small parsley sprigs

Scrub but do not peel the potatoes. Cut them into even chunks and steam them with the onion until tender.

Peel the potatoes and mash them with the onion and milk. Leave to cool before mixing in parsley, cayenne pepper and tomato purée.

Skin, bone and flake the mackerel. Cut two of the tomatoes into eight slices, skin and finely chop the rest. Mix the mackerel and the chopped tomatoes into the potatoes. Shape the mixture into eight round flat cakes and coat them with bran. (Brush the patties with a little beaten egg beforehand to help the bran to stick.) Chill in the fridge.

Brush the patties with oil and set them on a foil-lined grill pan. Grill them under high heat for 3 minutes; turn them over carefully, brush with oil before topping each with a tomato slice, and cook for a further 2 minutes. Serve hot, garnished with parsley.

KILOCALORIES	315	SUGARS	6g
TOTAL FAT	19g	SODIUM	100mg
SATURATED FAT	2g	FIBRE	4.5g

EGG AND MUSHROOM CUSTARDS

——— • ———

The mushrooms can be cooked the previous night and the egg mixture prepared, but do not mix the two until ready to use.

SERVES 4 Ⓥ

125 g/4 oz button mushrooms
25 g/1 oz butter (or margarine)
4 eggs
150 ml/¼ pt semi-skimmed milk
4 tbsp parsley, finely chopped
black pepper

Wipe the mushrooms clean and chop them finely. Melt the butter or margarine in a frying-pan over low heat, add the mushrooms and cook for 2 minutes. Set them aside to cool. Beat the eggs with the milk, then add the parsley, a good grinding of pepper and the mushrooms.

Divide the mixture between four lightly greased ramekins or individual soufflé dishes. Stand these on a baking sheet and heat through in the oven, preheated to 190°C/375°F/gas 5, for 20 minutes. Serve hot with wholemeal toast.

KILOCALORIES	335	SUGARS	2g
TOTAL FAT	27g	SODIUM	280mg
SATURATED FAT	12g	FIBRE	0.5g

FRESH AND DRIED FRUIT COMPOTE

— • —

Serve the compote cold, topped, if liked, with low-fat plain yogurt, for a high-fibre start to the day.

SERVES 4 Ⓥ

12 prunes
12 dried whole apricots
25 g/1 oz dried apple rings
300 ml/½ pt unsweetened orange (or pineapple) juice
1 pink grapefruit
2 large oranges
2 rings fresh pineapple (or canned in natural juice)

Put the dried fruits in a saucepan with the fruit juice, bring them slowly to the boil, remove from the heat and leave them to soak in the juice overnight.

Cut the rind and pith from the grapefruit and oranges; cut the flesh lengthwise into quarters and thinly slice them. Dice the pineapple. Mix the fresh and dried fruits.

KILOCALORIES	180	SUGARS	42g
TOTAL FAT	1g	SODIUM	30mg
SATURATED FAT	–	FIBRE	6.5g

CHEESY PANCAKES

— • —

The batter (which is rather thicker than ordinary pancake batter) can be made the night before and stored in the fridge.

MAKES 8 Ⓥ

125 g/4 oz fromage blanc, curd or ricotta cheese
2 eggs, beaten
50 g /2 oz wholemeal flour
½ tsp bicarbonate of soda
½ tsp mustard powder
6 tbsp semi-skimmed milk
oil for frying

Cream the cheese in a bowl and gradually beat in the eggs. Mix the flour with the bicarbonate of soda and mustard powder and fold it into the cheese mixture, followed by the milk. Alternatively, mix all the ingredients in a liquidiser. Beat the batter thoroughly before cooking, adding if necessary a few more drops of milk.

Heat a ½ tablespoonful of oil in a small frying-pan over medium heat; add 2 teaspoonfuls of the batter and tilt the pan to spread it. Cook until the underside of the pancake has browned and the top is bubbling and almost set; turn it over to cook the other side. Slide the pancake from the pan and keep it hot while cooking the remaining batter. Serve the pancakes at once, on their own or with grilled bacon and/or grilled tomatoes.

KILOCALORIES	160	SUGARS	2g
TOTAL FAT	12g	SODIUM	70mg
SATURATED FAT	2g	FIBRE	0.5g

SPECIAL MUESLI MIX

— • —

Once mixed, this muesli will keep up to two months stored in an airtight container in a cool dry place.

Ⓥ

225 g/8 oz rolled oats
175 g/6 oz rolled wheat
175 g/6 oz rolled barley
175 g/6 oz rolled rye
225 g/8 oz raisins
125 g/4 oz stoned dates, finely chopped
125 g/4 oz dried whole apricots, finely chopped
50 g/2 oz toasted flaked coconut
50 g/2 oz banana chips, broken
125 g/4 oz shelled hazelnuts
125 g/4 oz shelled brazil nuts, roughly chopped
50 g/2 oz sunflower seeds

Allow about 50 g/2 oz of the mix for each person, soak it overnight in milk or yogurt, or flavoured with a little fruit juice. The muesli can be eaten as it is or with chopped or grated apple, chopped orange or halved and deseeded grapes. Soaked dried fruits, such as prunes, apricots or apple rings, can also be added.

KILOCALORIES	215	SUGARS	9g
TOTAL FAT	10g	SODIUM	20mg
SATURATED FAT	2g	FIBRE	3g

Ⓥ This symbol denotes a recipe suitable for vegetarians.

BREAKFAST DISHES

GRANOLA

This crunchy cereal mixture contains a good selection of nutrients and can be stored for several weeks in an airtight container in the fridge.

450 g/1 lb rolled oats
250 g/9 oz wholemeal flour (wheat, rye, barley or a mixture)
175 g/6 oz flaked almonds
225 g/8 oz sunflower seeds
150 g/5 oz brown sugar
1 tsp salt
300 ml/½ pt (approx) unsweetened orange (apple, pineapple or grapefruit) juice
2–3 tsp vanilla essence

Thoroughly blend all the dry ingredients in a large mixing bowl; stir in the fruit juice and vanilla essence to moisten and clump the mixture together.

Spread the granola on two or three deep baking sheets or roasting tins, taking care not to pack it too tightly. Bake at 120°C/250°F/gas ½ for about 2 hours, stirring the mixture every 30 minutes to ensure it crisps throughout. Cool thoroughly before storing.

Serve the granola with plain yogurt or with hot or cold milk.

Variation: Consider adding chopped nuts, dates or desiccated coconut. Granola also makes a pleasant topping for fruit salads, compôtes and purées.

[Nutritional values are per average 75 g/3 oz portion.]

KILOCALORIES	285	SUGARS	10g
TOTAL FAT	12g	SODIUM	110mg
SATURATED FAT	1g	FIBRE	4g

Please see the introduction for a full explanation of the nutritional factboxes.

TOMATO AND HAM RAREBITS

These rarebits can also be served as a snack, even as a lunch or supper dish with a large bowl of crisp salad.

SERVES 4

25 g/1 oz butter (or margarine), softened
1 tsp mild ready-made English mustard
225 g/8 oz Cheddar cheese, grated
75 g/3 oz lean ham, chopped
½ tsp Worcestershire sauce
1 tbsp tomato purée
2 tbsp semi-skimmed milk
pinch salt, pepper
4 large slices wholemeal bread
parsley sprigs

Mix the butter or margarine with the mustard, cheese, ham, Worcestershire sauce, tomato purée and milk. Season to taste with salt and pepper.

Lightly toast the bread, then spread the slices with the rarebit mixture. Brown under a hot grill for about 5 minutes or until the cheese is bubbly; serve garnished with parsley sprigs.

KILOCALORIES	400	SUGARS	2g
TOTAL FAT	28g	SODIUM	1070mg
SATURATED FAT	16g	FIBRE	2g

WHOLEWHEAT WAFFLES

Waffles – or wafers – were known in England as early as the twelfth century. The design of the waffle iron, which Elizabethan settlers took with them to America, has barely changed over 500 years. Wholewheat flour enhances the flavour and retains useful fibre, B vitamins, calcium and iron.

MAKES 6 Ⓥ

125 g/4 oz wholewheat flour
1½ tsp baking powder
1 tbsp soft brown sugar (optional)
1 egg, separated
150 ml/¼ pt semi-skimmed milk
25 g/1 oz butter, melted
pinch salt
oil for greasing

Sift the flour and baking powder into a bowl and stir in the husks from the sieve. Add the sugar and the egg yolk. Gradually mix in the milk to form a smooth batter, and stir in the butter. Whisk the egg white with the salt until stiff, then fold it carefully into the batter.

Grease the waffle iron well and heat to near smoking point over medium heat. Spoon in sufficient batter (about 1 tablespoonful in each compartment), close the waffle iron and cook for 2–3 minutes on each side, turning the iron over once.

Serve with plain yogurt and honey, blueberry purée, date butter (see page 16) or marmalade (see below), or as a savoury (omit the sugar from the batter) with grilled tomatoes and mushrooms.

KILOCALORIES	145	SUGARS	6g
TOTAL FAT	6g	SODIUM	190mg
SATURATED FAT	3g	FIBRE	2g

MARMALADE
—— • ——

Unlike citrus marmalades, which need a high proportion of sugar in order to gel and store for any length of time, this nutritious spread derives its natural sweetness from sun-dried fruits. However, its storage life is short: only one week in a covered container in the fridge. Keep in the freezer for two or three months.

Ⓥ

225 g/8 oz dried apricots
225 g/8 oz dried prunes
225 g/8 oz dried peaches (or pears)
250 g/9 oz can crushed pineapple
1 tbsp honey (optional)

Wash the dried fruits and leave them to soak overnight in about 600 ml/1 pt of water or just enough to soften the fruit. Remove the apricots and peaches (or pears) and cook the prunes in the soaking water over gentle heat until soft enough for the stones to separate from the flesh. Cool the prunes and remove the stones.

Reduce the apricots, prunes and peaches to a purée in a food processor. Fold in the drained pineapple, mixing it thoroughly; if necessary, sweeten to taste with honey.

The marmalade can also be folded into plain yogurt and used to flavour and sweeten milk puddings.

[Nutritional values are per average spread, roughly 15 g/½ oz.]

KILOCALORIES	10	SUGARS	2g
TOTAL FAT	–	SODIUM	–
SATURATED FAT	–	FIBRE	–

WHOLEWHEAT PANCAKES
—— • ——

Soya milk is a good alternative for those allergic to cow's milk.

SERVES 4 Ⓥ

50 g/2 oz rolled oats
50 g/2 oz finely milled wholemeal flour
225 ml/8 fl oz soya milk (or cow's milk)
2 tbsp vegetable oil
1 tsp brown sugar
100 ml/4 fl oz water (or semi-skimmed milk)
pinch salt
oil for frying (optional)

Mix the oats and wholemeal flour with the 8 fl oz of soya milk and set the batter aside in the fridge for about 8 hours or overnight. Just before cooking the pancakes, put the batter in the liquidiser with the oil, sugar, water (or second quantity of milk) and salt.

Blend the mixture until it has the consistency of single cream. Heat a small frying-pan, greased lightly with oil if necessary. Spoon about 2 tablespoonfuls of the batter into the pan, tilting it so that the batter covers the bottom of the pan evenly. Cook over gentle heat until the edges of the pancake begin to brown, turn it carefully and cook the other side until golden.

Stack the cooked pancakes on a plate and keep them hot while using up the remaining batter.

Serve with unsalted peanut butter or apple sauce.

KILOCALORIES	175	SUGARS	2g
TOTAL FAT	9g	SODIUM	220mg
SATURATED FAT	–	FIBRE	2g

SCRAMBLED TOFU

Soya bean curd, also known as tofu, is a classic ingredient in many Chinese stir-fried dishes and is rich in protein; it is sold in blocks and is available from health food shops and supermarkets.

SERVES 4 (V)

450 g/1 lb block tofu
2–3 tbsp vegetable oil
1 bunch spring onions, chopped
2 tbsp soya sauce
¼ tsp turmeric
¼ tsp ground coriander

Drain the tofu through a strainer for about 20 minutes, then cut it into small cubes. Heat the oil in a heavy-based pan and add the tofu, spring onions, soya sauce and spices. Cover the pan with a lid and simmer the mixture over gentle heat until the liquid is absorbed. Serve on wholewheat toast.

KILOCALORIES	180	SUGARS	1g
TOTAL FAT	15g	SODIUM	10mg
SATURATED FAT	2g	FIBRE	0.5g

OEUFS EN COCOTTE

Baked eggs – oeufs en cocotte – are part of the French culinary repertoire and make a change to the traditional British fry-up of bacon and eggs.

SERVES 4

4 large slices wholemeal bread
100 g/4 oz bacon rashers, derinded
40 g/1½ oz butter (or margarine), melted
8 small eggs
150 ml/5 fl oz single cream
pinch salt, pepper
2 tbsp parsley, finely chopped

Toast the bread, cut it into small cubes and set them aside. Chop the bacon finely and fry it in its own fat until crisp; pour off the fat and drain the bacon thoroughly on kitchen paper.

Cover the base of a lightly greased, shallow ovenproof dish (25 × 20 cm/10 × 8 in) with the toast cubes. Trickle the melted butter over them and top with the bacon. Set the oven to 180°C/350°F/gas 4.

Break the eggs, one at a time, into a saucer and slide them carefully on top of the bacon. Spoon a little cream over each egg and sprinkle with salt and pepper.

Stand the dish in a large roasting tin and pour in hot water to come halfway up the sides of the dish. Bake, uncovered, just above the centre of the oven for 7–12 minutes – the yolks should be set and the whites firm. If not, flash the dish under a hot grill for a couple of minutes to solidify the whites without overcooking the yolks.

Serve at once, sprinkled with parsley and accompanied with wholemeal bread and grilled or baked mushrooms.

KILOCALORIES	400	SUGARS	2g
TOTAL FAT	27g	SODIUM	1080mg
SATURATED FAT	14g	FIBRE	2.5g

DATE BUTTER

Breakfast spreads need not be restricted to marmalade, honey and yeast extracts. Date butter is an easily prepared alternative – a high-energy food rich in carbohydrates and potassium.

(V)

175 g/6 oz stoned dates, chopped
150 ml/¼ pt water

Put the dates in a heavy-based saucepan, add the water and bring to the boil over gentle heat. Simmer, stirring constantly, for about 8 minutes or until the mixture is smooth.

Cool the date butter and store it in a covered container in the fridge. Use as a spread on bread, toast and crackers.

[Nutritional values are per average spread, roughly 15 g/½ oz.]

KILOCALORIES	12	SUGARS	3g
TOTAL FAT	–	SODIUM	–
SATURATED FAT	–	FIBRE	–

 This symbol denotes a recipe suitable for vegetarians.

SOUPS AND SAUCES

The basis for good, nourishing soups and stews is a stock. Brown stock is made from bones as well as fresh meat simmered slowly for several hours and given additional flavour by vegetables, herbs and spices.

White stocks are obtained from leftovers and trimmings such as chicken and game carcases, giblets and skins. Stocks can be frozen for 2–3 months before being used; if fresh, use within two days.

A pressure cooker is ideal for making stocks and soups as it reduces the cooking time by up to a third. Less liquid is required, so always follow the manufacturer's instructions.

WHITE STOCK (VEGETABLE)

MAKES 2.5 litres/4 pt (approx) Ⓥ

1 large onion, chopped
1 large leek, incl green part, chopped
1 kg/2 lb mixed vegetables and/or trimmings
1 large bouquet garni
6 peppercorns
salt to taste

Most types of vegetables are suitable, though potatoes tend to make the stock cloudy and should be omitted. Clean and trim the vegetables but do not peel. Place in a large pan with 2.5 litres/4 pt cold water, bouquet garni, peppercorns and salt. Bring to the boil over gentle heat, cover the pan and simmer gently for 1½–2 hours, topping up with water occasionally. Strain the stock through muslin or a fine sieve.

Bouquet garni The classic French herb flavouring for stocks, sauces and soups consists of sprigs of fresh parsley, thyme and a bay leaf tied together in a bunch; other aromatic herbs – basil, chervil, tarragon and rosemary – can be added to taste. Remove the bouquet before serving the dish.

WHITE STOCK (CHICKEN)

MAKES 2.5 litres/4 pt (approx)

1 large chicken, incl giblets
1 medium-sized onion, roughly chopped
2 medium-sized carrots, roughly chopped
2 celery sticks, roughly chopped
1 bouquet garni
6 black peppercorns
salt to taste

Place the cleaned chicken and giblets in a large pan with the vegetables, bouquet garni and peppercorns. Add 2.5 litres/4 pt of cold water and bring to the boil over a gentle heat; remove any scum, cover the pan with a lid and simmer for 1½–2 hours or until the chicken is tender. Top up with hot water as necessary.

Remove the chicken and use the meat for other recipes. Strain the stock and leave to cool before removing the surface fat. Reheat and season to taste.

WHITE STOCK (FISH)

MAKES 2.5 litres/4 pt (approx)

1 kg/2 lb white fish trimmings
salt to taste
1 medium-sized onion, thinly sliced
6 parsley stalks (or 1 large leek (white part only)
and 2 celery sticks, chopped)
1 bay leaf
2 tsp lemon juice

Put the cleaned trimmings in a pan with 2.5 litres/4 pt of cold water; bring slowly to the boil and remove all scum before adding a seasoning of salt, the onion, parsley stalks (or prepared vegetables), the bay leaf and lemon juice. Bring back to the boil, cover and simmer gently for 30 minutes. Strain the fish stock through a muslin.

STOCK CUBES

Stock cubes are often heavily salted although they are excellent as store-cupboard emergencies. Good vegetable cubes are available which contain no salt.

SOUP

Soups can be thickened by the roux method of mixing butter with flour or by adding cornflour near the end of the cooking process. They can also be thickened using cereals, pasta and pulses. Creamed soups are enriched by the careful addition of milk or yogurt and, as the name suggests, they are white and creamy in colour so the foundation stock should always be white.

AVOCADO SOUP

The avocado pear contains more protein than any other fruit and is a good source of vitamins A and B.

SERVES 4 (V)

2 celery sticks, finely sliced
300 g/11 oz potatoes, diced
1 litre/1¾ pt semi-skimmed milk
1 medium-sized avocado
1 tbsp chopped chives

GARNISH
low-fat plain yogurt (optional)
chives

Cook the celery and potatoes in lightly salted water until tender; strain and reduce the vegetables to a purée in a food processor, moistening it with a little of the cooking liquid.

Peel and stone the avocado, cut it into chunks and blend in a liquidiser. Mix the potato and avocado purées, return to a pan and gradually stir in the milk; simmer over gentle heat and just before the soup comes to the boil, stir in the chives and season to taste.

Serve hot or chilled, garnished if liked with more chives or with a swirl of yogurt. Chilled, the soup has a more pronounced flavour.

KILOCALORIES	240	SUGARS	14g
TOTAL FAT	11g	SODIUM	210mg
SATURATED FAT	4g	FIBRE	2.5g

CARROT SOUP

Carrots have a natural affinity with dill: it gives attractive colour to the orange-golden soup, and its sharpness complements the sweetness of young carrots.

SERVES 4 (V)

250 g/9 oz carrots, sliced
1 small onion, finely chopped
4 tbsp flour
1 tbsp butter (or margarine)
pinch salt, pepper
½ tsp dried dill weed
750 ml/1¼ pt semi-skimmed milk, scalded
1 tbsp parsley, finely chopped

Put the carrots and onion in a pan of boiling water and simmer, covered, for about 10 minutes or until tender. Strain the vegetables and purée them in a liquidiser.

Blend the flour into the carrot purée and return it to the saucepan; add the butter, salt and pepper to taste, and the dill weed. Gradually blend in the scalded milk, stirring constantly over gentle heat. Remove the pan from the heat as soon as the soup reaches boiling point.

Serve with chopped parsley.

Note: As an alternative to the flour and butter method of thickening, use 250 g/9 oz diced potatoes. Simmer them in water with the carrots and onions; season and flavour the puréed vegetables and blend in the milk.

KILOCALORIES	230	SUGARS	13g
TOTAL FAT	9g	SODIUM	350mg
SATURATED FAT	5g	FIBRE	2.5g

WATERCRESS SOUP

Summery in colour, delicate in flavour and rich in vitamin A, this soup is a quick and easy starter for a dinner party.

SERVES 4 (V)

1 bunch of watercress
2 celery sticks, finely chopped
325 g/12 oz potatoes, diced
1 litre/1¾ pt semi-skimmed milk
1 tbsp chives, chopped
pinch salt, pepper

Cook the celery and potatoes in lightly salted water until tender; strain and purée them in a food processor.

Rinse the watercress, picking off bruised leaves and most of the stalks. Put two-thirds of the watercress in a pan, cover with boiling water and simmer over gentle heat until just soft (about 3 minutes). Cool slightly, then blend the cooked watercress to a smooth purée in the liquidiser.

Mix the two purées together, put them in a pan and gradually stir in the milk; bring the soup to the boil over gentle heat and stir in the chives. Season to taste.

Serve, garnished with the remaining sprigs of watercress and accompanied with a bowl of crisp wholemeal bread croûtons.

KILOCALORIES	180	SUGARS	14g
TOTAL FAT	4g	SODIUM	310mg
SATURATED FAT	2.5g	FIBRE	1.5g

CELERIAC SOUP

A nourishing winter soup. Over-large celeriac can be tough and woody; the best buys are small-to-medium roots which should be peeled thickly.

SERVES 4 Ⓥ

450 g/1 lb celeriac
lemon juice
25 g/1 oz butter (or margarine)
1 medium-sized onion, roughly chopped
1 litre/1¾ pt white stock (see page 17)
1 bouquet garni (see page 17)
pinch salt, pepper
1 tbsp plain flour
5 tbsp semi-skimmed milk

Cut root and top ends off the celeriac, peel them thickly and cut into large cubes; drop these into cold water with a little lemon juice to prevent discoloration. Melt the butter in a large, heavy-based pan and fry the onion gently for 3 minutes or until transparent. Drain the celeriac thoroughly, add to the onions and sauté, covered, for 10 minutes.

Add the stock, the bouquet garni, salt and pepper; bring to the boil and lower the heat. Cover the pan with a lid and simmer for 1½ hours or until the celeriac is very soft. Stir occasionally.

Let the soup cool slightly, then blend it in a liquidiser. Mix the flour to a smooth liquid with the

milk. Stir it into the soup and cook through, stirring continuously, until the soup comes gently to the boil and thickens; correct the seasoning. Simmer for 5 minutes more.

KILOCALORIES	135	SUGARS	13g
TOTAL FAT	4g	SODIUM	300mg
SATURATED FAT	2g	FIBRE	5g

JERUSALEM ARTICHOKE SOUP

This soup is also known as Potage Palestine, which further compounds the mistaken belief that these small knobbly tubers have anything to do with Jerusalem – or artichokes. Sweet of flavour and nutty of texture, these artichokes go well with almonds and/or ginger.

SERVES 4 Ⓥ

675 g/1½ lb Jerusalem artichokes
lemon juice (or vinegar)
25 g/1 oz butter (or margarine or 2 tbsp vegetable oil)
1 medium-sized onion, thinly sliced
1 litre/1¾ pt white stock (see page 17)
pinch salt, pepper
150 ml/¼ pt semi-skimmed milk
2 tbsp ground almonds
2 tbsp parsley, finely chopped

Scrub the artichokes; peel them thinly and drop them into a bowl of cold water with a little lemon juice or vinegar added to prevent discoloration. Melt the butter in a large, heavy-based pan and fry the onion for a few minutes until transparent. Pat the artichokes dry on kitchen paper, a few at a time, slice them thinly and add them to the pan. Sauté gently in the butter until well coated, but do not let them brown. Pour the stock over the artichokes, bring it to the boil, then simmer, covered, for about 20 minutes or until the artichokes are tender; season to taste.

Let the soup cool slightly, then blend in a liquidiser. Reheat the soup and stir in the milk without letting the soup boil again.

Serve hot in individual bowls, topped with ground almonds and chopped parsley.

KILOCALORIES	170	SUGARS	6g
TOTAL FAT	9g	SODIUM	170mg
SATURATED FAT	4g	FIBRE	7g

MUSHROOM AND WATERCRESS SOUP

— • —

A light, refreshing and quickly made soup, good on chilly summer and autumn evenings. Watercress should be bought and used absolutely fresh.

See illustration page 23.

SERVES 4 Ⓥ

225 g/8 oz mushrooms, thinly sliced
1 large bunch watercress
1.25 litres/2 pt white stock (see page 17)
1 medium-sized onion, quartered and thinly sliced
pinch salt, pepper

Bring the stock slowly to the boil. Meanwhile, strip the watercress of its stalks, remove any bruised leaves and wash the remainder carefully. Add the onion to the stock and simmer for 2 minutes before adding the mushrooms; continue cooking for 1 minute. Stir in the watercress, season, and heat the soup through.

Serve hot, accompanied with brown Melba toast or wholemeal cracker biscuits.

KILOCALORIES	30	SUGARS	1g
TOTAL FAT	1g	SODIUM	470mg
SATURATED FAT	–	FIBRE	1g

CURRIED PARSNIP AND POTATO SOUP

— • —

This is a winter soup to satisfy large appetites. The curry flavouring will complement the sweetness of parsnips.

SERVES 6 Ⓥ

2–3 tbsp vegetable oil
1 large onion, thinly sliced
1–2 tbsp curry powder
500 g/1¼ lb parsnips, sliced
500 g/1¼ lb potatoes, sliced
1.25 litres/2 pt white stock (see page 17)
pinch salt, pepper
150 ml/¼ pt semi-skimmed milk
chopped coriander or parsley

Heat the oil in a large, heavy-based pan and fry the onion for 5 minutes until soft, then stir in the curry

powder and fry for a further 1–2 minutes. Add the sliced parsnips and potatoes, stirring over gentle heat.

Pour the stock into the pan, bring it slowly to the boil and season. Cover the pan with a lid and simmer gently until the vegetables are soft and tender, for 30–40 minutes.

Remove the pan from the heat, let the soup cool slightly, then blend it in a liquidiser. Return the soup to the pan, stir in the milk and heat through.

Serve, sprinkled with freshly chopped coriander or parsley and with wholemeal bread or croûtons.

KILOCALORIES	200	SUGARS	8g
TOTAL FAT	8g	SODIUM	100mg
SATURATED FAT	–	FIBRE	6g

CHICKEN, MUSHROOM AND BARLEY SOUP

— • —

This soup originates from Eastern Europe. Use chicken stock or buy chicken pieces on the bone, cover with water and bring to the boil. Simmer until the chicken is tender and use both the pieces and the stock.

SERVES 4

1 litre/1¾ pt chicken stock (see page 17)
1–2 tbsp pearl barley
175 g/6 oz cooked chicken, skinned and diced
2 medium-sized potatoes, diced
1 small carrot, sliced (or 1 tbsp cooked peas
or chopped beans)
pinch salt, pepper
100 g/4 oz mushrooms, thinly sliced
1 tbsp parsley, finely chopped

Soak the barley in the chicken stock for 15 minutes, then bring to the boil over gentle heat; cover the pan with a lid and simmer for 1 hour or cook in a pressure cooker.

Stir in the diced chicken and potatoes, and the carrot if used; season to taste and continue to cook, covered, over gentle heat until the potatoes are soft. Add the mushrooms and the peas or beans and simmer gently for another 5 minutes. Spoon the soup into bowls, sprinkle with parsley and serve.

KILOCALORIES	150	SUGARS	2g
TOTAL FAT	3g	SODIUM	330mg
SATURATED FAT	1g	FIBRE	2g

FISH SOUP

— • —

This chunky fish soup can be made with a variety of fish: coley, cod, haddock, whiting, halibut. Shellfish can also be replaced with similar amounts of firm white fish.
See illustration page 23.

SERVES 4

350 g/12 oz each of two types of white fish
(total 700 g/1½ lb)
100–125 g/4 oz shelled mussels (or prawns)
2–3 tbsp vegetable oil
1 large onion, finely chopped
1 large leek, thinly sliced
1–3 garlic cloves, finely chopped (optional)
1 large carrot, thinly sliced
1 large celery stick, thinly sliced
2 large potatoes, diced
900 ml/1½ pt fish stock (see page 17)
1 can (400 g/14 oz) tomatoes, roughly chopped
2 tbsp dry cider (or white wine)
pinch salt, pepper
2 tbsp parsley, finely chopped

Wash, skin and bone the fish and cut into bite-sized pieces. Rinse the shellfish and set both aside.

Heat the oil in a large, heavy-based saucepan, add the onion, leek and garlic and cook over gentle heat for 7 minutes, stirring occasionally. Mix in the carrot, celery and the potatoes; cook gently for another 3 minutes. Stir in the fish stock, the chopped tomatoes with their juice, the cider or wine, and pepper. Simmer, covered, for 15 minutes.

Blend half the parsley and the white fish into the soup and simmer for another 10 minutes; add the shellfish. Correct the seasoning, stir in the rest of the parsley and cook for another 5 minutes.

Serve with fresh wholemeal bread.

KILOCALORIES	365	SUGARS	8g
TOTAL FAT	12g	SODIUM	710mg
SATURATED FAT	–	FIBRE	4g

CURRIED HADDOCK SOUP

— • —

Smoked haddock is good value for money; here curry emphasises its flavour, toasted coconut its texture.

SERVES 4

175 g/6 oz smoked haddock fillet
450 ml/¾ pt semi-skimmed milk
450 ml/¾ pt water
1 bay leaf
2 tbsp vegetable oil
25 g/1 oz plain flour
1 tbsp mild curry powder
1 tbsp lemon juice
pinch salt, pepper
1½ tbsp unsweetened desiccated coconut

Rinse the haddock and put it in a pan with the milk, water and bay leaf; cook over gentle heat, uncovered, until the flesh is tender, after about 10 minutes. Strain through a sieve, reserving the cooking liquid and discarding the bay leaf. Remove skin and any bones from the haddock and flake the flesh.

Heat the oil in a saucepan, stir in the flour and curry powder and cook this roux for 2 minutes, stirring constantly. Gradually blend in the reserved haddock liquid, stirring all the time over gentle heat until it comes to the boil and thickens slightly.

Add the lemon juice and haddock to the soup. Season to taste; cover the pan with a lid and heat through over low heat for 5 minutes. Meanwhile, toast the coconut for a few minutes until it is golden-brown. Spoon the soup into individual bowls and sprinkle the coconut on top.

KILOCALORIES	200	SUGARS	6g
TOTAL FAT	11g	SODIUM	720mg
SATURATED FAT	2g	FIBRE	1.5g

LETTUCE SOUP

— • —

Prettily pale green in colour and light in texture, this soup is ideal for a chilly summer evening.

SERVES 4 Ⓥ

2 round lettuces (Webb's)
pinch salt, pepper
25 g/1 oz butter (or margarine or 1 tbsp vegetable oil)
1 garlic clove, crushed
25 g/1 oz plain flour
450 ml/¾ pt semi-skimmed milk
450 ml/¾ pt water
large pinch of grated nutmeg
raw carrot, finely grated

Remove any bruised and damaged outer leaves from the lettuces, wash the heads and shake them dry. Shred the leaves coarsely and put in a pan, adding boiling water to the depth of 2.5 cm/1 in and a little salt. Bring to the boil; cover the pan with a lid and simmer gently for 10 minutes. Drain the lettuce, let it cool slightly, then reduce it to a smooth purée in a liquidiser.

Melt the butter in a heavy-based pan, add the garlic and stir-fry gently for 3 minutes; mix in the flour and cook to a roux over low heat for 2 minutes, stirring all the time. Gradually blend in the milk mixed in the water, stirring until smooth. Add the lettuce purée and season to taste. Cook, stirring continuously, until the soup comes to the boil and thickens slightly; simmer for 5 minutes.

Serve the soup hot, sprinkled with grated carrot, with wholemeal cheese crackers.

KILOCALORIES	150	SUGARS	10g
TOTAL FAT	8g	SODIUM	220mg
SATURATED FAT	5g	FIBRE	2g

CHILLED LEEK AND POTATO SOUP

This delicate soup is also known as vichyssoise but in spite of its French name it originated in the USA: it is said that the French chef at the New York hotel, where the soup was first presented, used Vichy water instead of plain tap water for the basic chicken stock.

SERVES 4 (V)

6 leeks (approx 675 g/1½ lb), white parts only, finely sliced
4–5 medium-sized potatoes, finely sliced
50 g/2 oz unsalted butter
1 litre/1¾ pt white stock (see page 17)
pinch salt, pepper
pinch grated nutmeg
3 tbsp parsley, finely chopped
300 ml/½ pt semi-skimmed milk
chopped chives

Melt the butter over gentle heat in a large heavy-based saucepan; add the leeks, cover the pan with a lid and cook gently for 15–20 minutes or until the leeks are soft, stirring them from time to time. Add the potatoes and stir-fry for another 5 minutes.

Pour the stock over the vegetables, and add salt, nutmeg and parsley. Bring the soup to the boil, stirring constantly; cover the pan with a lid and simmer for 30–40 minutes.

Let the soup cool slightly, then blend it in a liquidiser. Correct the seasoning. Leave the soup to cool thoroughly, then stir in the milk. Chill, covered, in the fridge for several hours.

Serve in chilled bowls and sprinkle with chopped chives.

KILOCALORIES	310	SUGARS	12g
TOTAL FAT	11g	SODIUM	250mg
SATURATED FAT	6g	FIBRE	5g

CLEAR VEGETABLE SOUP

Clear vegetable soups are best made from good white stock; at a pinch use vegetable stock cubes.

SERVES 4 (V)

2 tbsp vegetable oil (or 25 g/1 oz butter or margarine)
2 tsp paprika
350 g/12 oz onion, thinly sliced
1 large turnip, diced
1 large red pepper, deseeded and diced
1 large green pepper, deseeded and diced
1.25 litres/2 pt white stock (see page 17)
pinch salt, pepper

Melt the butter in a large pan, stir in the paprika and cook for 1 minute. Add the prepared vegetables and toss in the butter for 5 minutes over gentle heat until coated and soft. Stir in the stock, bring to the boil, cover the pan with a lid and simmer for 20–25 minutes. Season to taste, adding more paprika if necessary.

Serve with brown bread croûtons.

KILOCALORIES	85	SUGARS	6g
TOTAL FAT	6g	SODIUM	470mg
SATURATED FAT	3g	FIBRE	2.5g

Right (clockwise from top right) Bean soup, lentil and spinach soup, mushroom and watercress soup, fish soup and corn chowder. In the centre is Indonesian chicken soup and in the tureen at the back vegetable soup.

LENTIL AND SPINACH SOUP

—— • ——

This soup is a meal in itself, with protein from the
lentils, and essential vitamins, calcium and iron.
  See illustration page 23.

SERVES 4 Ⓥ

225 g/8 oz lentils, golden or green
600 ml/1 pt boiling water
1.25 litres/2 pt white stock (see page 17)
450 g/1 lb fresh spinach or
225 g/8 oz frozen leaf spinach
2 tbsp vegetable oil
1 large onion, thinly sliced
pinch salt, pepper, cayenne
low-fat plain yogurt

Put the lentils in a large saucepan and cover with the
boiling water. Leave to soak for 1 hour, then add the
stock; bring to the boil, cover and simmer over gentle
heat until the lentils are cooked, usually after ¾–1 hour.
  Meanwhile, wash the fresh spinach, drain it and
shred it finely; or drain and shred the thawed spinach.
Heat the oil in a pan and fry the onion over medium
heat for 8–10 minutes or until golden; stir in the
spinach and let the mixture simmer, covered, until the
spinach is cooked.
  Add the spinach mixture, which will have exuded a
fair amount of liquid, to the lentils; season to taste,
stirring gently. Add a little water if necessary.
  Put a spoonful of yogurt in each bowl before ladling
in the soup. Serve with brown bread or wheaten soda
bread.

KILOCALORIES	185	SUGARS	7g
TOTAL FAT	8g	SODIUM	480mg
SATURATED FAT	1g	FIBRE	5g

SPINACH OR SORREL SOUP

—— • ——

In Tudor England, sorrel was a common vegetable,
cooked and eaten like spinach, served as a sauce with
fish or made into soups with a distinctive sharp
flavour. It is no longer grown commercially, but keen
gardener-cooks may wish to grow it. It should be
added to soups at the final stage, to preserve its
flavour, and should only be prepared with stainless-
steel utensils.

SERVES 4 Ⓥ

225 g/8 oz spinach leaves (or sorrel or a mixture)
1–2 tbsp vegetable oil
1 large onion, diced
450 g/1 lb old potatoes, diced (peeled weight)
1 litre/1¾ pt white stock (see page 17)
pinch salt, pepper
150 ml/¼ pt semi-skimmed milk

Strip the leafy parts from the stalks of the spinach or
sorrel and wash them in several changes of cold water.
Leave in a colander to drain.
  Heat the oil in a large pan and fry the onion for 5
minutes or until soft but not brown. Add the potatoes,
stir-fry them for 1–2 minutes, then pour in the stock.
Bring to boil and season to taste; cover the pan and
simmer for 30 minutes or until the potatoes are quite
tender. Remove the lid, return the soup to the boil and
add the spinach or sorrel, cooking for another minute.
  Remove from the heat; leave to cool slightly, then
blend in a liquidiser or press through a sieve. Return
the soup to the heat, stir in the milk and heat through
without boiling.
  Serve at once with chunks of fresh bread.

KILOCALORIES	180	SUGARS	5g
TOTAL FAT	8g	SODIUM	210mg
SATURATED FAT	–	FIBRE	3g

MINESTRONE

—— • ——

This classic soup from Italy differs from region to
region, although the Genoese claim credit for its
invention. It is nearly always served with grated
Parmesan; Cheddar is cheaper and slightly less rich.

SERVES 4 Ⓥ

1 large leek, including the green part, sliced
1 medium-sized onion, coarsely chopped
1–2 carrots, thinly sliced
1–2 celery sticks, sliced
100–125 g/4 oz spring greens, shredded
100–125 g/4 oz runner beans, thinly sliced
50 g/2 oz haricot beans, soaked overnight
1 can (400 g/14 oz) tomatoes, roughly chopped
1 litre/1½ pt white stock (see page 17)
pinch salt, pepper
1 tbsp parsley, finely chopped
50 g/2 oz short-cut wholewheat macaroni
Cheddar cheese, grated, to garnish (optional)

Drain the haricot beans and place them in a large pan covered with water, and rapid boil for 10 minutes. Add the vegetables, stock, the tomatoes with their juice, a pinch of salt and the parsley.

Bring the contents to the boil over medium heat, stirring frequently. Lower the heat and cover the pan with a lid; simmer gently for 1½–2 hours or until the haricot beans are tender. Season to taste. Stir in the macaroni and cook for a further 15 minutes.

Serve with grated cheese and crusty brown bread.

KILOCALORIES	80	SUGARS	8g
TOTAL FAT	1g	SODIUM	360mg
SATURATED FAT	–	FIBRE	5g

MUSSEL SOUP

Popular in English cooking since the Middle Ages, mussels are in season from September to March. Imports of packed, frozen mussels can be bought throughout the year, pre-cooked and shelled, or cleaned and ready for cooking.

SERVES 4

450 g/1 lb frozen mussels, shelled
1–2 tbsp vegetable oil
1 medium-sized onion, finely chopped
2 garlic cloves, crushed
2 large potatoes, diced
1 can (400 g/14 oz) tomatoes, roughly chopped
600 ml/1 pt fish stock (see page 17)
150 ml/¼ pt dry cider
pinch salt, pepper

Rinse the mussels in a colander under cold water. Heat the oil in a large, heavy-based pan, add the onion and garlic and cook over gentle heat for 5–8 minutes until the onion turns transparent. Add the potatoes and stir-fry for 5 minutes, then blend in the tomatoes with their juice, the fish stock and cider; bring to the boil, cover the pan with a lid and simmer until the potatoes are just tender. Stir in the mussels and heat through without boiling; season to taste.

Serve with wholemeal or French bread.

KILOCALORIES	265	SUGARS	6g
TOTAL FAT	9g	SODIUM	380mg
SATURATED FAT	1g	FIBRE	2.5g

SOTO AYAM
Indonesian chicken soup

Beautifully golden and mildly spiced, this soup is substantial enough as a main course, served with a bowl of freshly boiled rice and a spicy-hot sambal.

See illustration page 23.

SERVES 6–8

1 small chicken (1.5 kg/3 lb approx)
1.5 litres/2½ pt boiling water
pinch salt, pepper
2 tbsp corn oil
75 g/3 oz prawns, peeled and finely chopped
6 shallots, finely chopped
3 garlic cloves, finely chopped
1 tbsp ground ginger
¼ tsp turmeric
½ tsp chilli powder (optional)

GARNISH
1 tbsp coriander leaves
1 tbsp spring onion, chopped
50 g/2 oz bean sprouts (optional)
thin lemon slices

Cut the chicken in halves or quarters, and clean and wash them thoroughly. Place in a large pan with the boiling water, and season; bring back to the boil, remove any scum, then cover the pan with a lid and simmer for 40 minutes or until the chicken is tender.

Strain the stock through a fine sieve and set it aside; cut the chicken into small cubes, discarding skin and fat but not the bones. Heat half the oil in a large pan, add the prawns, half the shallots and all the garlic and fry for 1 minute. Stir in the ginger and turmeric and half the reserved stock; add the chicken bones. Bring to the boil, cover with a lid and simmer for 15 minutes. Strain the mixture through a fine sieve.

Fry the remaining shallots in a large pan until golden-brown; add chilli powder if used. Stir in the liquid in which the prawns and bones were cooked, with the remaining stock; bring back to the boil and simmer for a further 5 minutes.

Add the chopped chicken and simmer for another 5 minutes. Pour over the rinsed and drained bean sprouts. Float coriander leaves, spring onions and lemon slices on top, and serve.

KILOCALORIES	405	SUGARS	1g
TOTAL FAT	18g	SODIUM	300mg
SATURATED FAT	5g	FIBRE	0.5g

PIGEON SOUP

Pigeon has a mildly gamey flavour and is excellent for a main course. The only worthwhile meat is the breast, but the legs and carcases make good stock for a soup.

SERVES 6–8

*4–6 pigeon carcases
2 tbsp vegetable oil
2 large onions, roughly chopped
3 large carrots, roughly chopped
2 celery sticks, chopped
2 leeks, sliced
parsley stalks
12 peppercorns
1 bay leaf
1 tsp lemon juice
2 litres/3 pt water
pinch salt, pepper
1–2 tbsp sweet sherry or port (optional)*

Heat the oil in a large heavy-based pan and stir-fry the vegetables over medium heat for 10–15 minutes, until they begin to colour. Break the pigeon carcases into pieces and wrap them in a piece of muslin. Add them to the pan with the parsley, peppercorns, bay leaf and lemon juice.

Add the water, bring to the boil and remove any scum from the surface. Cover with a lid and simmer very gently for 3 hours.

Strain the stock through a fine sieve or muslin, reserving the vegetables. Retain any decent meat from the pigeon carcases. Blend the vegetables with the stock to a smooth purée in a liquidiser.

Return the soup to the pan, add the meat and reheat. Correct the seasoning, adding lemon juice, salt and pepper to taste; stir in the sherry or port if used. If necessary, thicken the soup with a little cornflour.

Serve hot with crusty bread.

KILOCALORIES	315	SUGARS	9g
TOTAL FAT	17g	SODIUM	190mg
SATURATED FAT	–	FIBRE	3.5g

SPLIT PEA SOUP

Split peas do not need soaking before cooking, but the cooking time varies according to type and age. They tend to lose their flavour if overcooked.

SERVES 4 (V)

*200 g/7 oz split peas (yellow, red or green)
1 litre/1¾ pt water
1 medium-sized onion, grated
2 bay leaves
1 tsp dried or 2 tsp fresh basil
2 large sprigs parsley
pinch salt, pepper
grated raw carrot (optional)*

Wash the peas carefully. Put them and the water in a large saucepan and bring to a fast boil; add the onion and bay leaves, reduce the heat, and cover the pan with a lid. Simmer gently until the peas are tender, after 35–40 minutes, or cook in a pressure cooker. Add the basil and parsley and season; simmer the soup for another 10 minutes.

Remove the pan from the heat and let the soup cool slightly; remove the bay leaves and blend the soup to a purée in a liquidiser. Return the soup to the pan, heat it through, adding a little more water if necessary.

Serve, sprinkled with freshly grated carrot and accompanied with a bowl of crisp bread croûtons.

KILOCALORIES	80	SUGARS	4g
TOTAL FAT	1g	SODIUM	110mg
SATURATED FAT	–	FIBRE	2.5g

LENTIL SOUP WITH TOMATOES

Potage made from good stock, thickened with dried lentils or beans and flavoured with vegetables and herbs and sometimes supplemented with small amounts of meat, has always been the mainstay of farming communities throughout the world.

SERVES 4 (V)

*100 g/4 oz orange lentils
2 tbsp vegetable oil
1–2 carrots, grated
1 medium-sized onion, grated
1 small turnip, grated
1 medium-sized potato, diced
1 celery stick, thinly sliced
1 litre/1¾ pt white stock or water
1 bouquet garni (see page 17)
pinch salt, pepper
2 tomatoes, skinned and chopped
4 tbsp low-fat plain yogurt*

Wash the lentils in a colander and leave them to drain. Heat the oil in a large heavy-based pan. Add all the prepared vegetables; cover the pan and sweat the vegetables over gentle heat for 12–15 minutes or until they are just beginning to turn pale golden. Stir in the lentils, add stock or water and the bouquet garni.

Bring the soup to the boil, stirring frequently. Cover the pan and simmer over low heat for 1 hour or until the lentils and vegetables are soft and almost mushy. Season to taste with salt and pepper after the first 30 minutes. Stir occasionally to prevent sticking.

Discard the bouquet garni and spoon the soup into bowls. Float a tomato piece on each, then top with a little yogurt.

KILOCALORIES	165	SUGARS	8g
TOTAL FAT	7g	SODIUM	360mg
SATURATED FAT	–	FIBRE	3g

BEAN SOUP

Green flageolet beans, kidney beans and black-eyed beans require eight hours' soaking and ten minutes' rapid boiling before being added to the other ingredients (see also page 123).
See illustration page 23.

SERVES 6 (V)

50 g/2 oz yellow split peas
50 g/2 oz green flageolet beans
50 g/2 oz red kidney beans
50 g/2 oz green lentils
50 g/2 oz black-eyed beans
1 can (400 g/14 oz) tomatoes, roughly chopped
2.5 litres/4 pt water
1 large onion, finely chopped
2 green peppers, deseeded and diced
2 medium-sized potatoes, finely chopped
1 tsp cinnamon
1/2 tsp turmeric
1/2 tsp ground ginger
pinch salt, pepper
bunch of coriander, finely chopped (optional)
bunch of parsley, finely chopped
few sprigs of fresh mint, finely chopped or
1 tbsp dried mint
bunch of watercress, coarsely chopped

Drain and rinse the beans after soaking and boiling; rinse the dried peas and lentils in a colander under cold running water. Put them all in a large pan with the

tomatoes and their juice, the prepared vegetables, the spices and the water. Do not add salt at this stage as this will toughen the pulses. Bring the soup to the boil, cover the pan and simmer for about 1 hour or until the beans are tender; season with salt after 45 minutes.

Stir in the chopped coriander, if used, the parsley, mint and watercress and simmer for 5 minutes, adding a little more water if the soup is too thick. Correct the seasoning and serve hot with crusty bread.

KILOCALORIES	125	SUGARS	5g
TOTAL FAT	2g	SODIUM	140mg
SATURATED FAT	–	FIBRE	3.5g

VEGETABLE SOUP

This is a thick, chunky and colourful soup that is ideal for a winter meal.
See illustration page 23.

SERVES 4–6 (V)

2 tbsp yeast extract
1 litre/1 3/4 pt vegetable stock
1 small raw beetroot, grated
2 small carrots, diced
1 medium-sized potato, cubed
1 medium-sized onion, roughly chopped
125 g/4 oz fresh or frozen green beans (or peas)
175 g/6 oz courgettes, diced
1 large handful chopped spinach (or cabbage)
1 large tomato, skinned and roughly chopped
1 can (225 g/8 oz) chickpeas, rinsed
50 g/2 oz barley
2 bay leaves
2–3 parsley sprigs
1/2 tsp dried marjoram
1/2 tsp garlic powder
pinch salt, pepper

Dissolve the yeast extract in the stock. Prepare all the vegetables and put them in a large pan with the water, the chickpeas and the barley. Add the herbs and garlic powder, bring to the boil, cover the pan and simmer for about 1 hour or until the contents are tender. Correct the seasoning and remove the bay leaves.

Serve hot, with warm wholemeal bread.

KILOCALORIES	160	SUGARS	4g
TOTAL FAT	2g	SODIUM	1230mg
SATURATED FAT	–	FIBRE	5g

CORN CHOWDER

Chowders are a kind of thick soup-cum-stew, traditional in American cookery. The Mid-West, with its huge maize fields, specialises in sweetcorn chowders.
See illustration page 23.

SERVES 4 Ⓥ

4 large corn cobs or 225 g/8 oz frozen
or canned sweetcorn kernels
600 ml/1 pt white stock (see page 17)
pinch salt, pepper
2–3 tbsp vegetable oil
1 large onion, finely chopped
3 celery sticks, finely sliced
1 green pepper, deseeded and diced (optional)
1/2 tsp sugar
1 tbsp lemon juice
300 ml/1/2 pt semi-skimmed milk
Tabasco sauce
2 tsp cornflour
6 tbsp semi-skimmed milk
2 tsp made mustard
parsley, finely chopped

Rinse the corn cobs thoroughly, then cut and scrape the kernels off the cobs on to a plate, removing as much pulp and milky liquid as possible. Put the cob stalks in a large pan with the stock and a pinch of salt; simmer, covered, for 15 minutes. Strain the liquid through a fine sieve and set it aside.

Melt the butter in a large, heavy-based pan and fry the onion, celery, pepper (if used) and corn kernels with the sugar until the onion softens (about 10 minutes). Season fresh and previously frozen kernels with a little salt, canned kernels hardly at all. Add the lemon juice and the strained stock, bring to the boil, then cover the pan and simmer for 15 minutes before stirring in the 1/2 pint of semi-skimmed milk, and Tabasco sauce to taste. Bring the soup back to the boil, stirring continuously.

Blend the cornflour and milk, stir in a few spoonfuls of the hot soup, then stir this mixture into the soup. Heat it through without boiling, and correct the seasoning with salt, pepper and mustard.

Just before serving, stir in the parsley.

KILOCALORIES	235	SUGARS	14g
TOTAL FAT	13g	SODIUM	325mg
SATURATED FAT	1g	FIBRE	2g

SAUCES

Salads achieve their particular character as much from the sauce or dressing as from the ingredients themselves (though sauces can double the calorific value of a recipe, so remember to go easy on them). Herbs, spices, seeds and nuts give specific flavours and the choice of oil and vinegar is of the greatest importance. Olive and walnut oils are considered the finest in flavour.

Semi-solid dips are perfect with a selection of raw vegetables, cocktail biscuits and wholemeal crackers, pitta bread or chunks of bread.

The best toppings for puddings are purées, made from fresh or dried fruits, or low-fat plain yogurt (see also **Sweets and puddings** chapter).

A simple white sauce (savoury or sweet) is made from equal amounts, by weight, of fat and flour mixed with a liquid (usually milk) to the required consistency by one of the following methods:

ROUX

The fat is melted in a small heavy-based pan, the flour added and stirred continuously until it forms a smooth ball which leaves the sides and base of the pan cleanly. The liquid is then added gradually, the sauce being whisked constantly to prevent lumps, and brought to the boil between each addition of liquid.

QUICK METHOD

All the ingredients (cut-up fat, flour, liquid) are put into the pan together and cooked over a medium heat whilst being constantly whisked.

BLENDING METHOD

The flour is mixed to a paste with a little of the cold liquid, the remainder is boiled and poured over the flour paste and the mixture cooked over gentle heat until thickened.

MICROWAVE

Blend the flour to a paste with a little of the measured liquid, gradually stir in the remainder and add the cut-up fat. Cook on high for 3–4 minutes, stirring every minute until the sauce has thickened. Use a large bowl to accommodate the rising milk as it boils.

A healthier savoury sauce can be made by replacing some of the flour with wholewheat flour and substituting half the milk with stock or cooked vegetable water. Use polyunsaturated margarine, but only use oil if strong flavours are to be added to compensate for the bland flavour.

BASIC WHITE SAUCE
——— • ———

MAKES 300 ml/½ pt Ⓥ

1½ tbsp butter (or margarine)
2 tbsp plain flour
300 ml/½ pt semi-skimmed milk, scalded

Melt the butter in a small, heavy-based pan, without letting it brown; stir in the flour and beat it to a smooth ball with a wooden spoon over gentle heat. Cook and beat this mixture for 2–3 minutes.

   Gradually beat in the milk, stirring as the ingredients mix; let the mixture thicken and come to the boil between each addition of milk. When all the milk has been added, let the smooth sauce simmer gently for about 5 minutes. Season, or use as the basis for a more flavoursome sauce.

[Nutritional values are for the full 300 ml/½ pt.]

KILOCALORIES	390	SUGARS	15g
TOTAL FAT	25g	SODIUM	350mg
SATURATED FAT	16g	FIBRE	1g

PARSLEY AND LEMON SAUCE
——— • ———

Serve this simple sauce with steamed or grilled fish, poultry or vegetable dishes.

SERVES 4 Ⓥ

300 ml/½ pt basic white sauce
juice and finely grated peel of ½ lemon
1 tbsp parsley, finely chopped
pinch salt, pepper

Make up the white sauce (see above), mix in the lemon peel and juice and the parsley. Reheat the sauce for 1 minute and correct the seasoning.

KILOCALORIES	90	SUGARS	4g
TOTAL FAT	5g	SODIUM	270mg
SATURATED FAT	3g	FIBRE	0.5g

BLUE CHEESE AND CHIVE SAUCE
——— • ———

Best made with a strong, ripe blue cheese and good for mixing into freshly cooked pasta to serve as a lunch or supper dish.

SERVES 4 Ⓥ

300 ml/½ pt basic white sauce
50–75 g/2–3 oz blue cheese, diced
2 tbsp chives, chopped
pinch salt, pepper

Make up the white sauce (see left). Blend in the cheese and stir over low heat until it has melted. Fold in the chives, season to taste and pour over drained, hot pasta. Toss thoroughly and serve at once.

KILOCALORIES	165	SUGARS	4g
TOTAL FAT	12g	SODIUM	450mg
SATURATED FAT	8g	FIBRE	–

HOT TARTARE SAUCE
——— • ———

This is reminiscent of but less rich than cold tartare sauce, and just as suitable with all types of fish.

SERVES 4 Ⓥ

300 ml/½ pt basic white sauce
1 tbsp lemon juice
1 tbsp parsley, finely chopped
1 tbsp drained capers, finely chopped
2 tsp drained gherkins, finely chopped
pinch salt, pepper
1 small egg yolk
2 tbsp semi-skimmed milk

Prepare a basic white sauce (see left) and keep it simmering over low heat; mix in the lemon juice, parsley, capers and gherkins. Correct the seasoning. Beat the egg yolk with the milk and add a little of the hot sauce. Stir this mixture back into the sauce, heat it through without boiling. Serve at once.

KILOCALORIES	110	SUGARS	4g
TOTAL FAT	7g	SODIUM	330mg
SATURATED FAT	4g	FIBRE	–

FRUITY CURRY SAUCE

This sauce, which goes well over hard-boiled egg halves served with brown rice, can be mild or spicy according to taste.

SERVES 4 (V)

25 g/1 oz butter or *margarine*
1 large dessert apple, peeled and grated
25 g/1 oz plain or *wholewheat flour*
1 tbsp curry powder
450 ml/³⁄₄ pt lukewarm semi-skimmed milk
1 tbsp tomato purée
pepper

Melt the butter or margarine in a small, heavy-based pan; add the apple and fry over gentle heat until it turns golden and softens slightly. Stir in the flour and curry powder to form a roux and cook for 2 minutes, stirring continuously.

Gradually blend in the milk, stirring briskly and letting the sauce come to the boil between each addition. When the sauce has thickened, simmer it gently for 2 minutes, stir in the tomato purée, season and heat through.

KILOCALORIES	145	SUGARS	11g
TOTAL FAT	7g	SODIUM	140mg
SATURATED FAT	5g	FIBRE	2g

FRENCH MUSTARD SAUCE

A simple and piquant sauce.

SERVES 4 (V)

300 ml/¹⁄₂ pt basic white sauce
2 tsp made French mustard

Prepare the basic white sauce (see page 29). Blend a little with the mustard, then return to the main sauce. Heat gently before serving. Alternatively, use dry mustard powder. Add 1 teaspoon of powder to the flour when making the basic white sauce.

KILOCALORIES	90	SUGARS	4g
TOTAL FAT	6g	SODIUM	180mg
SATURATED FAT	3g	FIBRE	–

BROWN BREAD SAUCE

This variation on the traditional bread sauce has a distinctly nutty flavour and warm colour.

SERVES 4 (V)

4 cloves
1 medium-sized onion, peeled but left whole
1 bouquet garni
300 ml/¹⁄₂ pt semi-skimmed milk
50 g/2 oz fresh brown breadcrumbs
15 g/¹⁄₂ oz butter
pinch salt, pepper

Stick the cloves halfway into the onion. Put it in a pan with the bouquet garni, add the milk and bring just to boiling point over gentle heat. Remove the pan, cover it with a lid and leave the milk and onion to infuse for 1 hour.

Strain the milk into a pan, stir in the breadcrumbs and butter and cook the sauce over low heat until it is smooth and has thickened; season to taste.

KILOCALORIES	110	SUGARS	5g
TOTAL FAT	4g	SODIUM	260mg
SATURATED FAT	3g	FIBRE	0.5g

HORSERADISH AND BEETROOT SAUCE

A bright pink, piquant sauce to serve with roast beef, boiled silverside or brisket or grilled sausages.

SERVES 4 (V)

300 ml/¹⁄₂ pt basic white sauce
1 tbsp creamed horseradish
50 g/2 oz pickled horseradish
50 g/2 oz pickled beetroot, drained and grated
pinch salt, pepper

Prepare the white sauce (see page 29). Mix in the creamed horseradish and beetroot, then season to taste. Simmer gently for 2 minutes before serving.

KILOCALORIES	105	SUGARS	5g
TOTAL FAT	6g	SODIUM	290mg
SATURATED FAT	4g	FIBRE	0.5g

CHEESE SAUCE

— • —

This sauce is particularly good with pork and bacon.

SERVES 4 Ⓥ

300 ml/½ pt basic white sauce
75 g/3 oz mature Cheddar cheese, grated
pinch French mustard
pinch salt, pepper

Prepare the white sauce (see page 29) but do not season it; stir in the cheese and mustard. Season to taste with salt and pepper. Thin the sauce with a little cold milk and reheat if necessary.

KILOCALORIES	165	SUGARS	4g
TOTAL FAT	12g	SODIUM	400mg
SATURATED FAT	8g	FIBRE	–

GOOSEBERRY AND WATERCRESS SAUCE

— • —

Gooseberry sauce is traditional with mackerel and herring. This version of the old English recipe also marries well with grilled pork chops. It can be stored in the freezer for up to one month.

SERVES 4 Ⓥ

325 g/12 oz gooseberries, topped and tailed
3 tbsp warm water
1–2 tsp lemon peel, grated
15 g/½ oz butter
1 tbsp sugar
small bunch of watercress, finely chopped
pinch salt

Wash and drain the gooseberries, put them in a pan with the warm water and cover with a lid. Bring the gooseberries to the boil, lower the heat and simmer until the fruit is soft.

Add the lemon peel, butter, sugar and watercress and stir over low heat until the sugar has dissolved. Season lightly with salt before serving hot or cold.

KILOCALORIES	65	SUGARS	7g
TOTAL FAT	3g	SODIUM	130mg
SATURATED FAT	2g	FIBRE	2g

CUCUMBER AND CORIANDER SAUCE

— • —

Light and summery in taste and perfect with poultry and fish.

SERVES 4 Ⓥ

100–125 g/4 oz cucumber, peeled and thinly sliced
300 ml/½ pt basic white sauce
1 tbsp fresh coriander, finely chopped
pinch salt, pepper

Wring out the cucumber slices in a cloth to remove as much liquid as possible; chop them finely and set aside.

Make up the white sauce (see page 29), fold in the chopped cucumber and coriander, and correct the seasoning if necessary. Simmer very gently for 5 minutes before serving.

KILOCALORIES	90	SUGARS	4g
TOTAL FAT	5g	SODIUM	270mg
SATURATED FAT	3g	FIBRE	0.5g

FRENCH DRESSING

— • —

In spite of its name this salad dressing is an American/British corruption of the French *sauce vinaigrette*, to which are added mustard and other seasoning.

MAKES 150 ml/¼ pt Ⓥ

6 tbsp oil
2 tbsp vinegar
1–2 tsp made mustard
pinch salt, pepper

Whisk or shake together the oil, vinegar and mustard; season to taste. The dressing can be further flavoured with crushed garlic, finely chopped herbs, onion, tomato purée, Worcestershire or Tabasco sauce, and vinegar can be replaced with fresh lemon or grapefruit juice.

KILOCALORIES	70	SUGARS	–
TOTAL FAT	8g	SODIUM	40mg
SATURATED FAT	1g	FIBRE	–

MAYONNAISE

Mayonnaise is a cold emulsion of egg yolks, oil and acid which takes on the consistency of thickish cream. Use a polyunsaturated oil such as sunflower or soya. For best results, all ingredients and equipment should be at room temperature.

If mayonnaise does curdle, it can often be rescued by beating a fresh egg yolk and gradually whisking in the curdled mixture, or by slowly beating another 150 ml/ 5 fl oz oil into the original mixture. Although high in calories, only a small quantity is required. It can be mixed with low-fat plain yogurt to reduce calories.

MAKES 150 ml/5 fl oz Ⓥ

1 large egg yolk
pinch salt
pinch dry mustard
pinch caster sugar
pinch white pepper
150 ml/5 fl oz oil (olive, vegetable or a mixture)
3 tsp vinegar
2 tsp lemon juice
2 tsp warm water

Put the egg yolk in a bowl and beat it thoroughly with the salt, mustard, sugar and a good pinch of white pepper. Gradually add the oil, drop by drop, beating steadily all the time with a whisk or fork. As soon as the mayonnaise begins to thicken, add 2 teaspoonfuls of the vinegar.

Continue to beat in the oil, still drop by drop, until about two-thirds has been incorporated and the mayonnaise is thick and glossy. Beat in the remaining vinegar, followed by the last of the oil which should be added in a thin, continuous trickle, under steady whisking.

Stir in the lemon juice, then fold in the warm water which prevents a mayonnaise separating. Spoon the mayonnaise into a dish, cover it and chill. It will store in the fridge for up to one week.

Garlic mayonnaise (aïoli). Crush or pound 2–3 garlic cloves, add the egg yolk and proceed with the recipe for Mayonnaise. Serve as a dip, with avocado pears, roast beef or any cold, plainly cooked vegetable.
[Nutritional values are per average 30 g/1 oz portion.]

KILOCALORIES	280	SUGARS	–
TOTAL FAT	31g	SODIUM	80mg
SATURATED FAT	5g	FIBRE	–

COCKTAIL SAUCE

Cocktail sauce is *the* classic dressing for prawn cocktail. It also teams well with other seafood, such as crab, lobster, canned tuna fish or red salmon.

SERVES 4 Ⓥ

150 ml/5 fl oz reduced calorie mayonnaise
1 tbsp tomato purée
1 tsp horseradish relish
½ tsp German mustard
2 tsp strained lemon juice
½ tsp Worcestershire sauce

Mix all the ingredients thoroughly and leave the sauce to chill, covered, in the fridge. It keeps there for up to 1 week.
Note: Alternatively, replace half the mayonnaise with low-fat plain yogurt.

KILOCALORIES	120	SUGARS	3g
TOTAL FAT	11g	SODIUM	370mg
SATURATED FAT	–	FIBRE	–

TARTARE SAUCE

The classic accompaniment to grilled and fried fish of all types. It is also good with lamb steaks and chops.
See illustration page 74.

SERVES 4–6 Ⓥ

150 ml/5 fl oz reduced calorie mayonnaise
1½ tbsp gherkins, finely chopped
1 tbsp capers, drained, finely chopped
1 heaped tbsp parsley, finely chopped

Mix together the mayonnaise, gherkins, capers and parsley, blending thoroughly. Serve the tartare sauce chilled. It will store, in a covered container, for up to 1 week in the fridge.
Note: Alternatively, replace half the mayonnaise with low-fat plain yogurt.

KILOCALORIES	90	SUGARS	1g
TOTAL FAT	8g	SODIUM	380mg
SATURATED FAT	–	FIBRE	0.5g

THOUSAND ISLAND DRESSING

A basic mayonnaise transformed into a colourful and tempting dressing for green salads, cold chicken, hard-boiled eggs and seafood.

SERVES 4 (V)

150 ml/5 fl oz reduced calorie mayonnaise
1 medium-sized egg, hard-boiled and chopped
(optional)
2 tbsp tomato ketchup
1 tbsp stuffed olives, finely chopped
1 tbsp parsley, finely chopped
2 tsp onion, finely grated
Tabasco sauce

Mix together the mayonnaise, chopped egg, tomato ketchup, olives, parsley and onion. Season to taste with Tabasco sauce. Spoon into a covered dish and leave to chill in the fridge. The dressing will store for up to 1 week.
  Note: Alternatively, replace half the mayonnaise with low-fat plain yogurt.

KILOCALORIES	155	SUGARS	5g
TOTAL FAT	13g	SODIUM	710mg
SATURATED FAT	1g	FIBRE	–

CELERY SEED DRESSING

A completely fat-free dressing for all types of vegetable and green salads.

SERVES 4–6 (V)

175 ml/6 fl oz unsweetened pineapple juice
1½–2 tbsp honey
½ tsp celery seeds
2 tbsp lemon juice
2 tsp cornflour

Put the pineapple juice, honey and celery seeds in a pan. Blend the lemon juice with the cornflour and stir this into the other ingredients. Bring the mixture to boiling point over gentle heat, stirring constantly. Simmer for 3–5 minutes. Cool and chill before use.

KILOCALORIES	95	SUGARS	25g
TOTAL FAT	–	SODIUM	10mg
SATURATED FAT	–	FIBRE	–

CUCUMBER DRESSING WITH YOGURT AND MINT

This dressing goes well with tomatoes, cooked green beans and pulse salads.

SERVES 4 (V)

1 cucumber, peeled
pinch salt, pepper
4 tbsp oil
1 tbsp red wine vinegar
150 ml/5 fl oz low-fat plain yogurt
1 garlic clove, crushed
2 tbsp fresh mint, finely chopped or 1 tbsp dried mint

Cut the cucumber into very thin slices, spread them on a flat dish and sprinkle them lightly with salt to draw out the liquid. Leave them for 30 minutes, then rinse in a colander under cold running water. Dry the cucumber on kitchen paper, then chop coarsely.
  Beat the oil and vinegar into the yogurt, add the garlic and mint and fold in the cucumber; or blend in the liquidiser. Season to taste before chilling.

KILOCALORIES	145	SUGARS	4g
TOTAL FAT	13g	SODIUM	30mg
SATURATED FAT	2g	FIBRE	0.5g

YOGURT DRESSING

For a dressing of even fewer calories, omit the mayonnaise and replace it with tomato purée.

SERVES 4 (V)

100 ml/4 fl oz low-fat plain yogurt
4 tbsp reduced calorie mayonnaise
or green dressing (see page 34)
1 tbsp lemon juice
1–2 tbsp chives or parsley, finely chopped or
1–2 tsp dill or chervil, finely chopped

Beat the yogurt with the mayonnaise until smooth, stir in the lemon juice and the chopped herbs. Cover the dressing and chill in the fridge; eat within 2 days.

KILOCALORIES	100	SUGARS	3g
TOTAL FAT	9g	SODIUM	400mg
SATURATED FAT	–	FIBRE	–

VINAIGRETTE

This traditional French sauce is used to dress raw and cooked vegetables.

MAKES 150 ml/¼ pt ⓥ

6 tbsp oil (olive, vegetable or a mixture)
2 tbsp vinegar
pinch salt, pepper

Whisk or shake the oil and the vinegar in a screw-top jar. The vinegar will influence the final flavour and may be wine, cider, malt or herb-flavoured. Season the dressing to taste and pour it over the salad just before serving.

A scant tablespoonful of fresh, finely chopped herbs – parsley, tarragon, chervil or chives – or finely chopped onion or crushed garlic may be added to the vinaigrette dressing.

KILOCALORIES	70	SUGARS	–
TOTAL FAT	8g	SODIUM	40mg
SATURATED FAT	1g	FIBRE	–

SUNFLOWER AND YOGURT DRESSING

Yogurt is an ideal low-calorie base for dressings to go with vegetable and rice salads.

SERVES 4 ⓥ

2–3 tbsp sunflower seeds
225 ml/8 fl oz low-fat plain yogurt
1–2 tbsp chopped chives (or the green part of spring onions)
pinch sea salt (or powdered kelp)

Toast the sunflower seeds in a dry pan over gentle heat for a few minutes until they release their aroma; do not brown. Grind them to a powder in a liquidiser.

Blend the other ingredients until the dressing is smooth and chill in the fridge before use.

KILOCALORIES	95	SUGARS	4g
TOTAL FAT	5g	SODIUM	140mg
SATURATED FAT	1g	FIBRE	1g

GREEN DRESSING

Quickly made in a liquidiser, this can accompany all types of vegetables and will keep for about a week in the fridge. This version is also suitable for vegans as it is made with soya milk instead of eggs.

MAKES 300 ml/½ pt (approx) ⓥ

4 tbsp soya milk powder
8 tbsp water
pinch salt
6–8 tbsp corn oil
4 tbsp lemon juice (approx)
4 tbsp spring onions, chopped
4 tbsp parsley (or watercress), freshly chopped
2–3 tsp tarragon, freshly chopped

Blend the soya milk powder, water and salt in a liquidiser until smooth; while the machine is still running, slowly pour the oil through the top and continue to blend at high speed until the mayonnaise has thickened. Spoon the mayonnaise into a bowl and mix in half the lemon juice.

Fold the spring onions, parsley or watercress and tarragon into the mayonnaise; sharpen it to taste with more lemon juice. Cover and chill in the fridge.

KILOCALORIES	100	SUGARS	–
TOTAL FAT	11g	SODIUM	40mg
SATURATED FAT	2g	FIBRE	–

AVOCADO DIP

—— • ——

Serve as a first course with Melba toast, crackers or crudités or as a sauce with shellfish and poached cold salmon.

SERVES 4–6 Ⓥ

2 avocado pears
75 g/3 oz cashew nuts
350 ml/12 fl oz water
1 small onion, finely chopped
2 tbsp lemon juice
pinch salt

Cut the pears in half, remove the stones (and reserve) and scoop out the flesh. Put the cashew nuts and the water in a liquidiser and blend until smooth. Add the avocado flesh, onion, lemon juice and salt and blend thoroughly.

Spoon the dip into a serving bowl, place the stone in the middle to prevent discoloration, cover, and chill in the fridge. Stir gently before serving.

KILOCALORIES	200	SUGARS	2g
TOTAL FAT	19g	SODIUM	80mg
SATURATED FAT	4g	FIBRE	3g

NUT BUTTER

—— • ——

A home-made version of peanut butter, but made with a variety of nuts and flavoured with nutritious seeds.

MAKES 225 g/8 oz Ⓥ

150 g/5 oz each shelled peanuts, hazelnuts,
blanched almonds, walnuts
2 tbsp sesame (or sunflower seeds)
150 ml/5 fl oz water

Heat a heavy-based saucepan and dry-roast the sesame or sunflower seeds for 2–3 minutes or until the aroma rises.

Put the nuts, seeds and water in a liquidiser and blend until the mixture has the consistency of butter. Spoon the butter into a container and store in the fridge for up to two weeks.

KILOCALORIES	105	SUGARS	1g
TOTAL FAT	10g	SODIUM	–
SATURATED FAT	1g	FIBRE	1g

HUMMUS DIP

—— • ——

The chief ingredients for this Arab dip are tahini (sesame paste) and chickpeas.

SERVES 4 Ⓥ

225 g/8 oz canned chickpeas
1–2 garlic cloves, crushed
2–3 tbsp tahini
lemon juice
pinch salt, pepper
pinch paprika

Drain the chickpeas and rinse them in cold running water. Put the chickpeas and garlic in a liquidiser and blend to a smooth purée, adding enough water to prevent the machine clogging. Add 2 tablespoonfuls of the tahini and blend thoroughly. Taste the mixture before adding the last tablespoonful of tahini.

Spoon the dip into a bowl, season with lemon juice, salt and pepper. Cover and chill in the fridge for at least 1 hour. Sprinkle with paprika before serving.

KILOCALORIES	65	SUGARS	–
TOTAL FAT	2g	SODIUM	220mg
SATURATED FAT	–	FIBRE	2.5g

FISH

ish provide a marvellous choice of nutritious food, being a valuable source of protein and minerals, especially iodine. Fish are also versatile: they can be eaten raw, fresh or smoked, served plain or with various sauces. Of course, price and availability both vary not only according to the season but also to weather conditions. The majority of fresh fish is frozen at sea and subsequently defrosted by the fishmonger, which results in much fresher fish than that formerly packed in ice boxes. Where possible, ask the fishmonger to do the job of gutting and filleting the fish.

Smoked fish tend to be extremely salty, as part of the preparation process involves them being immersed in a brine solution. Canned fish is a good buy for the store cupboard: those in brine or tomato will keep for at least 12 months, those in oil for several years.

OILY FISH

Examples include herring, mackerel, mullet, salmon, trout and eel. All should have clear shiny eyes, bright gills and a glossy look. **Herring** is the most valuable from a nutritional point of view and is at its best in late summer and autumn. **Kippers** are split herrings put into a brine solution and smoked. **Whitebait**, the tiny fry of herrings, are usually sold frozen and can be bought all year round.

Mackerel, once known as the poor man's trout, comes close behind herring in nutritional value, and is often less expensive. It should be cooked and eaten on the day of purchase. Chill it in the fridge before cooking.

There are two kinds of **mullet**, grey and red, unrelated other than in name. The larger grey mullet is the more common and less expensive; red mullet is chiefly imported frozen – supplies are scarce and expensive.

Most **rainbow trout** are reared on fish farms and are available all year round. **Salmon**, too, is farmed, ensuring uniformity in price and availability all year round.

WHITE FISH

White fish store oil in the liver while the flesh is lean and fat-free. Choose fish with firm, tightly packed scales. **Cod** is a good source of protein and minerals. Whiteness of the flesh denotes freshness. **Haddock** has firm, more delicately favoured flesh than cod. **Whiting**, which looks like a small cod, has soft flaky flesh but deteriorates rapidly.

Flatfish range from small dabs to large halibuts and turbots. **Plaice** is the most common, and fresh examples are recognised by bright brown and orange spots on the upper side. **Halibut** is the most nutritious of all white fish.

PREPARATION

Most fishmongers will gut and fillet fish on request. Once home, all fish should be unwrapped and stored, covered, in the fridge.

Round fish Scale by using the blunt edge of a knife and working from tail to head. Trim off fins with scissors. Make a slit in the belly and remove the guts. The head and tail may be left intact or snipped off, though remember to remove the gills. Rinse inside and out and pat dry. To bone the fish, continue the belly slit to the tail, open the fish out flat and press down upon the backbone to loosen it. Use the knife to dislodge it. Again, rinse and pat dry. Fillet the fish by pulling the skin from the head towards the tail and easing it away with a knife.

Flat fish Make a slit just behind the head on the upper darker side to open up the cavity in which the entrails lie. Snip off the fins, and the head and tail if liked. To fillet the fish, slit it along the backbone from head to tail, but do not cut through the bone. Cut away the four fillets by edging the knife outwards and downwards. To skin the fillets, slit the skin just above the tail and gripping it firmly, work a sharp knife along the fillet close to the skin.

COOKING

Steaming is suitable for fillets, rolled up or left flat, and other thin cuts. The fish should be cooked over simmering water for about 15 minutes and may be seasoned with lemon juice, fennel or tarragon. When **poaching** (simmering in a small amount of liquid), loss of nutrients is kept to a minimum. This method is suitable for all types and cuts of fish.

Baking preserves and enhances the natural flavours. The fish can be placed on foil, seasoned with salt and pepper, lemon juice and fresh herbs; then pinch the foil to create a seal. Set the parcels in an ovenproof dish. Alternatively, arrange the fish in a lightly buttered ovenproof dish, sprinkle with seasoning, make three slashes through the flesh of the fish and bake at 180°C/350°F/gas 4, allowing 30 minutes for whole fish and 20 minutes for steaks and fillets.

When either **shallow** or **deep-frying**, the fish needs some kind of coating or binding agent to prevent it from breaking up. Fillets, steaks and whole small fish are usually coated with batter for deep frying or with seasoned flour or beaten egg and breadcrumbs for shallow frying. The fish absorbs less fat if the oil is heated to 190°C/375°F (a moderately hot temperature) before frying.

Grilling preserves the true flavour of the fish. Brush white fish lightly with a little oil or melted butter (oily fish need no fat addition) and set them on a foil-lined grill pan preheated to medium; fillets take 5 minutes, thick steaks and whole fish 15 minutes (turning once).

IKAN BUMBU ACAR

Red snapper in sweet-and-sour sauce

— • —

Ikan is Indonesian for fish. Red snapper from the Atlantic, which comes close to the local fish used in this Indonesian recipe, has a high protein and mineral content and is very low in fat.

SERVES 4

2 medium-sized or *4 small red snappers
(approx 1 kg/2 lb in weight)*

MARINADE
*2 tbsp tamarind water (or lime juice)
½ tsp each chilli powder and ground ginger
1 tsp ground coriander
½ tsp salt
2 garlic cloves, crushed*

SAUCE
*1 small pineapple (or 440 g/15½ oz can pineapple cubes, unsweetened)
5 blanched almonds (or 3 kemiri)
2 garlic cloves
2 shallots
½ tsp each turmeric and ground ginger
2 tbsp vegetable oil
2 green chillis, deseeded and sliced
3 tbsp white vinegar
½ tsp dry mustard
300 ml/½ pt water
1 red and 1 green pepper, deseeded and diced
1–2 tsp brown sugar*

Clean and gut the fish and remove the coarse scales with the blunt edge of a knife, working from the tail towards the head. Trim tails and fins, leaving the heads on or cutting them off; wash the fish thoroughly and pat them dry. Blend the marinade ingredients, pour over the fish and leave them to marinate for 1 hour, turning them once or twice.

Peel and core the pineapple and cut it into small cubes; or drain the canned pineapple. Pound or grind the almonds or kemiri, garlic and shallots to a smooth paste and stir in the turmeric and ground ginger. Heat the oil in a wok or heavy-based pan. Stir-fry the prepared paste for 1 minute, then add the chillis, vinegar, mustard, a little salt and the water. Simmer the sauce gently.

Meanwhile, bring a large pan of water to a rapid boil; lift the snappers from the marinade and steam them, covered, for 10–15 minutes, depending on size, or until they are tender.

Stir the peppers into the sauce, simmer for 3 minutes, then add the pineapple chunks and sugar to taste. Serve the snappers on a bed of rice with the sauce poured over them.

KILOCALORIES	390	SUGARS	21g
TOTAL FAT	13g	SODIUM	530mg
SATURATED FAT	–	FIBRE	2.5g

Kemiri Also known as candlenuts, these are rich in an oil so volatile that it burns readily, hence the name. The flavour is somewhat tart; the nuts are available shelled, canned or vacuum-sealed.

STUFFED BAKED HERRINGS

——— • ———

This fish remains great value for money. Even more important, herrings are a rich source of vitamins and essential minerals.

SERVES 4

4 medium-sized herrings
50 g/2 oz cracked wheat
¼ small cucumber, peeled
1 tbsp each coriander and mint, finely chopped
1 tbsp parsley, roughly chopped
lemon juice
pepper
1 can (400 g/14 oz) plum tomatoes

Clean and gut the herrings, remove heads, tails and fins and carefully ease out the backbones without breaking the skin. Wash and dry thoroughly.

Meanwhile, leave the cracked wheat to soak and swell in cold water for at least 20 minutes, then drain it well and squeeze it as dry as possible. Finely chop the cucumber and add it to the cracked wheat with the herbs, lemon juice and freshly ground black pepper to taste. Mix well and divide the stuffing between the herrings. Secure the openings with wooden cocktail sticks.

Preheat the oven to 180°C/350°F/gas 4. Arrange the fish in a shallow ovenproof dish that will comfortably take them in a single layer. Mash the tomatoes and their juice to a chunky sauce and pour it over the fish. Correct the seasoning and bake, covered, in the centre of the oven, for about 30 minutes or until cooked through. Serve with a green vegetable or a salad.

KILOCALORIES	340	SUGARS	3g
TOTAL FAT	22g	SODIUM	120mg
SATURATED FAT	4g	FIBRE	1g

ENGLISH KEDGEREE

——— • ———

Kedgeree, an Anglo-Indian dish dating from the days of the Raj, was – and is – a popular breakfast or high-tea dish, and is just as good for lunch or supper.

SERVES 4

175 g/6 oz brown rice
450 ml/¾ pt water
1 tsp salt
225 g/8 oz smoked haddock
225 g/8 oz fresh haddock (or cod) fillet, skinned
semi-skimmed milk
25 g/1 oz butter (or margarine), melted
2 medium-sized hard-boiled eggs, chopped
mild curry powder (or nutmeg) to taste
pepper
juice of ½ lemon
2 tbsp parsley, chopped

Wash the rice thoroughly and put it in a large saucepan with the water and salt. Bring it to the boil, lower the heat, cover the pan and simmer for ¾–1 hour or until the rice grains are tender and have absorbed all the moisture. Remove the pan from the heat, take off the lid and cover the rice with a folded tea towel; leave to stand for 10 minutes.

Meanwhile, poach the fresh and smoked haddock for about 8 minutes in enough milk to cover them. Lift out the fish, remove skin and bones and flake the flesh; reserve the poaching liquid. Fold the fish into the rice, with the butter, chopped eggs and 4 tablespoonfuls of the poaching liquid. Season to taste with curry powder or nutmeg, pepper and lemon juice. Heat through gently, stirring with a fork.

Serve the kedgeree hot, garnished with the parsley.

KILOCALORIES	250	SUGARS	–
TOTAL FAT	10g	SODIUM	1330mg
SATURATED FAT	4g	FIBRE	0.5g

PARSLEYED SALMON OR SEA TROUT

Sea trout in aspic is an excellent summer party dish, less expensive than poached salmon and pretty to look at. You can use tail pieces rather than the expensive middle cuts if you wish, or substitute fresh haddock instead.

SERVES 4–6

1 kg/2 lb salmon (sea trout or haddock)
1 onion, sliced
1 small leek (green top removed), sliced
1 large bunch parsley
juice of 1 lemon
pinch salt, pepper
1 packet powdered gelatine
6 coriander berries, crushed
3 fresh tarragon sprigs
lemon and cucumber slices

Heat the oven to 160°C/325°F/gas 3. Skin, fillet and wash the fish; cut the fillets into 10 cm/4 in pieces. Wash the fish heads and bones for the stock, put them with the skins in a large pan, cover with water and add the onion, leek, parsley stalks (not the leaves), lemon juice and a seasoning of salt and pepper. Bring to the boil, cover the pan with a lid and simmer gently for 30 minutes.

Lay the fillets in a fish kettle or ovenproof dish, strain the fish stock over them and cook for about 8 minutes. Lift the fish out and keep them covered whilst cooling.

Strain the fish liquid through a double layer of muslin. Boil it over high heat until it has reduced to about 600 ml/1 pt.

Meanwhile, sprinkle the gelatine on to 50 ml/2 fl oz of water in a cup and leave it to soak. When it is spongy, add it to the hot stock and allow it to dissolve. Add the coriander berries and season if necessary.

Chop the parsley leaves finely, strip the tarragon leaves from the sprigs and mix the two herbs. Wet a jelly mould or a pudding basin, terrine dish or loaf tin that will take the fish comfortably (about 1 litre/1½ pt size). Layer the fish pieces in the mould, scattering the chopped herbs between each layer; pour the aspic over the fish, and chill the mould for several hours until the aspic has set.

Turn out the mould, garnish with lemon and cucumber, and serve with a bowl of mayonnaise.

KILOCALORIES	360	SUGARS	2g
TOTAL FAT	22g	SODIUM	260mg
SATURATED FAT	5g	FIBRE	1g

COD WITH BACON

The combination of cod and bacon is a happy inspiration for a fish which can sometimes be insipid. As well as contributing flavour, the bacon bastes the dryish fish.

SERVES 4

625 g/1½ lb cod fillets, skinned
15 g/½ oz butter
pepper
175 g/6 oz streaky bacon, rinds removed

Preheat the oven to 190°C/375°F/gas 5. Wash the cod and wipe it dry; cut the fillets into serving pieces and arrange them in a lightly buttered ovenproof dish large enough to hold them in a single layer. Pepper them lightly.

Lay the bacon rashers on a board and stretch them with a broad knife blade to almost double their size; cut them in half and lay them over the cod to cover the fillets completely in order to prevent them drying out during cooking. Dot with any remaining butter.

Bake the cod and bacon, uncovered, near the top of the oven for about 30 minutes, or until the cod is tender and flaky and the bacon crisp.

KILOCALORIES	330	SUGARS	–
TOTAL FAT	21g	SODIUM	810mg
SATURATED FAT	9g	FIBRE	–

HERRING ROES WITH CRUMBLE TOPPING

With a topping of wholemeal breadcrumbs and nuts, protein-rich roes are turned into a delicious lunch or dinner dish.

SERVES 4

750 g/1½ lb herring roes (soft or hard)
150 ml/5 fl oz low-fat plain yogurt
semi-skimmed milk (optional)
175 g/6 oz fresh wholemeal breadcrumbs
100 g/4 oz grated cheese
1 tbsp parsley, finely chopped
2 tbsp mixed chopped nuts
pinch salt, pepper
grated lemon rind
paprika

Preheat the oven to 190°C/375°F/gas 5. Remove any discoloured parts and arrange the roes in a large, shallow ovenproof dish. Beat the yogurt, thinning it with a little milk if necessary. Pour it over the roes.

Mix the breadcrumbs with the cheese, parsley, nuts, salt and pepper. Cover the roes with the crumble mixture, smoothing the top. Bake in the centre of the oven for about 40 minutes.

Sprinkle grated lemon rind and paprika over the topping and serve the roes with a vegetable purée or a crunchy salad.

KILOCALORIES	475	SUGARS	4g
TOTAL FAT	19g	SODIUM	650mg
SATURATED FAT	6g	FIBRE	1.5g

HADDOCK AND TOMATO BAKE

Vary the topping and double the fibre content by using crushed wholewheat cereal instead of the cheese crackers.

SERVES 4

450g/1 lb haddock fillet, skinned
300 ml/½ pt tomato sauce (see page 44)
100 g/4 oz cheese crackers
(or crushed wholewheat cereal)
1 small onion, finely chopped
1 garlic clove, crushed
½ tsp Worcestershire sauce

grated rind of ¼ lemon
50 g/2 oz butter (or margarine), melted
2 tbsp parsley, finely chopped

Preheat the oven to 190°C/375°F/gas 5. Remove any bones from the fish, wash and wipe it dry and cut it into 2.5 cm/1 in strips. Arrange them in a lightly buttered, shallow ovenproof dish and cover with the tomato sauce. Cover with foil or a lid and bake for 20 minutes.

Put the cheese biscuits (or cereal) in a bag and crush them coarsely. Combine them with the onion, garlic, Worcestershire sauce and lemon rind, and stir in the melted butter. Sprinkle this topping over the fish and bake, uncovered, for a further 10–15 minutes.

Garnish with parsley and serve immediately with green noodles or floury potatoes and boiled spinach.

KILOCALORIES	400	SUGARS	8g
TOTAL FAT	23g	SODIUM	470mg
SATURATED FAT	12g	FIBRE	2g

FRIED TROUT WITH CUCUMBER AND TARRAGON SAUCE

Trout and cucumber make a perfect summer combination, and tarragon is a classic herb flavouring for fish.

SERVES 4

4 trout, gutted
½ cucumber, coarsely grated
pinch salt

SAUCE
25 g/1 oz butter (or white vegetable fat)
25 g/1 oz flour
450 ml/¾ pt fish stock
(see page 17)
generous squeeze of lemon juice
pepper
4–6 tbsp vegetable oil
2 tbsp seasoned wholemeal flour
lemon wedges
few sprigs tarragon,
coarsely chopped

Rinse the cleaned trout thoroughly and pat them dry. Sprinkle the cucumber with salt and leave it for 20 minutes; rinse in cold water, drain it thoroughly and squeeze out as much water as possible.

For the sauce, melt the butter or white fat in a small pan, stir in the flour and cook the roux for a couple of minutes. Remove the pan from the heat, and stir in fish stock to make a smooth sauce. Return to the heat, stirring constantly until the sauce thickens. Season to taste.

Heat the oil in a large frying-pan. Coat the trout in the seasoned flour, then fry them for about 4 minutes on each side. Arrange on a warmed serving dish and garnish with lemon wedges and sprigs of tarragon.

Reheat the sauce, add the cucumber and chopped tarragon and serve at once with tiny new potatoes, boiled in their skins.

KILOCALORIES	280	SUGARS	1g
TOTAL FAT	11g	SODIUM	400mg
SATURATED FAT	3g	FIBRE	2g

IKAN WOKU
Baked and grilled marinated fish

This recipe from Menado in Indonesia uses grey mullet; red snapper will do as well, and mackerel is even more nutritious. Choose small fish, whose flesh is firm in texture and more delicate in flavour than that of large, coarse fish.

SERVES 4

1 kg/2 lb red snapper (or grey mullet or mackerel)
3 red chillies, deseeded
5 blanched almonds (or 3 kemiri)
2.5 cm/1 in piece root ginger, peeled
1 large ripe tomato, skinned, deseeded and chopped
½ tsp turmeric
juice of 1 lime (or ½ lemon)
2 tbsp mint, chopped
4 tbsp spring onion, chopped
½–1 tsp coarse salt

Gut, scale and wash the fish, then wipe them dry. In a food processor, grind the chillies, almonds or kemiri and ginger to a paste. Add all the other ingredients and rub this marinade on to the fish, inside and out. Wrap the fish in a loose foil packet and leave to marinate for at least 30 minutes.

Transfer the fish, in the foil parcel, to a shallow roasting dish and bake in a preheated oven (190°C/375°F/gas 5) for 25–30 minutes. Just before serving, unwrap the parcel and place the fish under a hot grill for 5 minutes, turning them once.

Serve the fish hot with the cooking juices poured over them, and accompanied with boiled rice or sauté potatoes and a green vegetable.

KILOCALORIES	260	SUGARS	3g
TOTAL FAT	6g	SODIUM	770mg
SATURATED FAT	–	FIBRE	0.5g

OVEN-BRAISED COD

At its best from autumn until spring, cod combines well with the strongly flavoured seasonal vegetables. The dish is suitable for freezing without the garnish.

SERVES 4

675 g/1½ lb cod fillets, skinned
225 g/8 oz leeks
50 g/2 oz butter (or margarine)
3 celery sticks, roughly chopped
1 small can (225 g/8 oz) tomatoes, chopped
1 tsp brown sugar (or honey)
pinch salt
325 g/12 oz cold cooked potatoes, sliced
2 tbsp parsley, finely chopped
1 tbsp roasted, unsalted peanuts, finely chopped

Wash and wipe the cod fillets dry; cut them into four even-sized pieces. Trim the leeks, leaving on some of the green part. Slit them lengthways and wash and drain thoroughly before cutting into narrow slices.

Melt three-quarters of the butter in a frying-pan; add the leeks and chopped celery and fry them gently, stirring occasionally, for about 10 minutes or until soft and golden. Keeping back most of the juices, mix in the tomatoes and add the sugar or honey and salt to taste. Spread the vegetables over the base of a shallow, well-greased ovenproof dish.

Heat the oven to 190°C/375°F/gas 5. Arrange the sliced potatoes on top of the vegetables and add the cod in a single layer. Melt the rest of the butter and spoon it over the fish. Bake, uncovered, for 25–30 minutes.

Spoon the fish and vegetables on to warm plates and serve hot, sprinkled with parsley and peanuts.

KILOCALORIES	343	SUGARS	6g
TOTAL FAT	15g	SODIUM	360mg
SATURATED FAT	8g	FIBRE	3g

with the fish in a shallow serving dish. Scatter the marjoram over the top and pour the wine over. Cover the dish and leave in the fridge to marinate for 2 days.

Serve chilled, with bowls of black olives, lemon wedges and chunks of French bread.

KILOCALORIES	490	SUGARS	5g
TOTAL FAT	24g	SODIUM	350mg
SATURATED FAT	–	FIBRE	1.5g

FISH FILLETS EN PAPILLOTE

The French developed the 'papillote' method of cooking whereby food is sealed and cooked in an airtight parchment parcel. Traditionally, the papillotes are served straight from the oven, for each diner to open his or her own parcel.

SERVES 4

675 g/1½ lb fish fillets, skinned
40 g/1½ oz butter (or margarine)
1 large leek, white part only, finely shredded
2 small carrots, finely shredded
75 g/3 oz mushrooms, thinly sliced
1 tbsp tarragon (fennel or dill), finely chopped
pinch salt, pepper
oil
lemon juice
1–2 tbsp white wine

Preheat the oven to 250°C/475°F/gas 9. Cut out four circles of greaseproof paper, each 38 cm/15 in in diameter.

Melt two-thirds of the butter and gently sauté the leek and carrots, without browning, for 5 minutes; add the mushrooms and cook for another minute. Stir in the chopped herbs and season to taste.

Wipe the fish fillets clean, then cut them, diagonally, into about 16 slices. Brush one side of each paper round with a little oil, leaving a 2.5 cm/1 in clear border all round. Divide the vegetable mixture between the four papillotes, spooning it on to one half only. Lay the fish slices on top of the vegetables, squeeze a few drops of lemon juice over the fish and spoon over the wine. Dot with butter and season lightly.

Fold the empty paper half over the filling to make a parcel. Close the edges by twisting them hard to make an airtight seal. Brush a baking sheet lightly with oil, then carefully transfer the papillotes on to it. Bake for

FISH IN A PICKLE

This recipe has its origins in Italy and is a delicious way of preparing fresh sardines or sprats.

SERVES 4–6

1 kg/2 lb sprats (or sardines)
6–8 tbsp vegetable oil
50 g/2 oz flour
4 medium-sized onions, thinly sliced
450 ml/¾ pt dry white wine
few strips lemon rind
2–3 stems marjoram

Remove the heads and gut the fish; rinse them and pat dry. Heat half the oil for deep-frying to 190°C/375°F. Toss the fish in the seasoned flour, shake off any excess and fry them in small batches for 2–3 minutes or until they are golden-brown, turning them carefully; drain on kitchen paper and leave to cool.

Pour 1–2 tablespoonfuls of fresh oil into a frying-pan and fry the onions for 2–3 minutes, without browning them. Add the wine and lemon rind and cook this marinade for no more than 2–3 minutes.

Lift the onions from the marinade and layer them

12 minutes, until the parcels have puffed up and are brown.

Bring the papillotes straight from the oven to the table, accompanied with tiny parsleyed potatoes.

For chicken en papillote, use skinned, boned breast and slash it deeply to speed up cooking, which will take about 17 minutes.

KILOCALORIES	250	SUGARS	2g
TOTAL FAT	13g	SODIUM	310mg
SATURATED FAT	6g	FIBRE	1g

Sodium (salt) is found naturally in many foods and therefore care should be taken when adding salt to recipes. Many classic recipes from countries with a warm climate contain considerably more salt than those from more temperate regions and these should be adjusted accordingly. If using stock cubes or garlic or onion salt don't add extra salt to the recipe.

MOROCCAN SPICY FISH

—— • ——

Aromatic spices and herbs are typical of North African dishes, frequently complemented and softened with the addition of honey, raisins, dates and prunes. Use spices to give a delicious touch to any white, firm-fleshed fish, such as cod, monkfish, sea bass, turbot or conger eel.

SERVES 4

675 g/1½ lb fish, boned and skinned
4 tbsp vegetable oil
2–3 garlic cloves, crushed
1 tsp each paprika and cumin
½ tsp ground ginger
good pinch of cayenne
large bunch of fresh coriander (or parsley)
coarsely chopped

Wash and dry the fish and cut it into bite-sized chunks. Heat the oil in a large frying-pan over medium heat and fry the garlic for a few minutes until the aroma rises. Stir in the paprika, cumin, ginger and cayenne and mix well. Add the herbs and the fish and fry carefully over medium heat for about 5 minutes, stirring and turning the pieces until the flesh just begins to flake.

Spoon the spicy fish mixture on to a flat warm dish and serve at once with plain boiled rice and a green side-salad.

KILOCALORIES	245	SUGARS	–
TOTAL FAT	14g	SODIUM	130mg
SATURATED FAT	–	FIBRE	–

FISH PIE

—— • ——

For this pie use any white fish, such as coley, cod or haddock; as a variation sprinkle a little grated cheese over the potato topping, or lay skinned, sliced tomatoes or sliced hard-boiled eggs over the fish.

SERVES 4

450 g/1 lb fish fillets
450 ml/¾ pt semi-skimmed milk
pinch salt, pepper
50 g/2 oz butter (or margarine)
40 g/1½ oz flour
lemon juice
2 tbsp parsley, chopped
700–900 g/1½–2 lb potatoes, cooked

Wash the fish fillets and put them in a pan with the milk and the salt and pepper; poach them for about 7 minutes over gentle heat. Lift out the fish, remove skin and any bones and reserve the poaching liquid.

Heat the oven to 190°C/375°F/gas 5. In a small pan melt 40 g/1½ oz of the butter or margarine, stir in the flour and cook gently for a few minutes. Gradually add the poaching milk to this roux to make a smooth sauce. Add lemon juice to taste and fold in the parsley and the flaked fish. Transfer the mixture to a 1 litre/1½ pt ovenproof dish. Mash the cooked potatoes with the remaining butter and a few tablespoonfuls of milk or any remaining poaching liquid.

Cover the fish with the mashed potatoes and bake for about 40 minutes. Serve hot with carrots or sweetcorn.

KILOCALORIES	445	SUGARS	7g
TOTAL FAT	14g	SODIUM	390mg
SATURATED FAT	8g	FIBRE	3g

FISH-CAKES WITH TOMATO SAUCE

—— • ——

Home-made fish-cakes are infinitely preferable to the pre-packaged variety. They can be frozen when shaped and breaded and cooked from frozen if time is short, though they are better thawed first.

MAKES 8–10

450 g/1 lb cod (or haddock) fillet
300 ml/½ pt semi-skimmed milk
pinch salt, pepper
450 g/1 lb freshly boiled potatoes
1 tbsp tomato ketchup
1 tbsp chopped parsley (or dill)
1 tbsp lemon juice
2 eggs, beaten
25 g/1 oz flour
100 g/4 oz oven-toasted wholemeal breadcumbs
oil for frying

SAUCE

1 small onion, finely chopped
1 clove garlic, crushed
25 g/1 oz butter (or margarine)
1 tsp brown sugar
1 can (400 g/14 oz) tomatoes, chopped
pinch salt, pepper
1 tsp basil (optional)
1–2 tbsp parsley, chopped

Wash the fish thoroughly and put it in a pan with the milk (or half milk and water), salt and pepper. Bring to the boil over gentle heat and poach the fish, uncovered, for about 10 minutes. Lift from the pan and leave to cool before removing skin and bones. Flake the cooked flesh finely.

Mash the potatoes, then add them with the tomato ketchup, herbs and lemon juice to the fish. Correct seasoning if necessary. Bind the mixture with some of the beaten egg and leave it to firm in the fridge.

Divide the fish mixture into eight or ten equal portions and shape each into a round flat cake. Dip them in the flour before covering them in the beaten egg, coat them with breadcrumbs and leave in the fridge for about 30 minutes.

Fry the onion and garlic in the hot butter until they are soft and transparent. Add the sugar and tomatoes, keeping back most of the juices. Season to taste with salt and pepper. Cook the sauce over medium heat for 10–15 minutes. Let it cool slightly, then purée it or rub it through a sieve to get rid of the tomato pips. Return the sauce to the pan, stir in the basil and parsley and heat it through just before serving the fish-cakes.

Heat a little oil in a large frying-pan over medium heat and fry the fish-cakes for 6–8 minutes or until golden on both sides. Alternatively, grill them.

Serve with the hot tomato sauce and a crisp, green salad.

KILOCALORIES	195	SUGARS	6g
TOTAL FAT	5g	SODIUM	330mg
SATURATED FAT	2g	FIBRE	1.5g

IKAN ASAM MANIS
Fish in a sweet-and-sour sauce

———— • ————

The large freshwater fish, *gurami*, traditionally used for this dish is unknown outside its home-waters. Dover sole most closely resembles it in texture and flavour.

SERVES 4

2 Dover sole
2 tbsp white malt vinegar
2 garlic cloves, crushed
1 tsp sea salt
1 tsp ground coriander
½ tsp chilli powder
½ tsp turmeric
2–3 tbsp vegetable oil

SAUCE
600 ml/1 pt tamarind water (see method)
2 tbsp vegetable oil
5 cm/2 in piece root ginger, peeled and finely chopped
2 garlic cloves, crushed
2 tsp brown sugar
½ tsp chilli powder
pinch salt
lemon juice (optional)

GARNISH
2 tbsp gherkins, sliced
2 tbsp coriander (or mint), chopped

Ask the fishmonger to skin the sole on both sides. Alternatively, make a cut above the tail, ease the skin loose with the point of a knife and pull it away towards the head. Cut off the fins, heads and remove the guts from the pockets; rinse and dry thoroughly. Mix the vinegar with the garlic, salt and spices and spoon this marinade over the fish in a shallow dish. Allow to stand for 1 hour.

Prepare the tamarind water from 50 g/2 oz tamarind pulp and 600 ml/1 pt warm water. Strain it into a small saucepan and boil over high heat until it has reduced by half.

In a wok (or frying-pan) heat the oil, sauté the ginger and garlic over medium heat for about 1 minute or until they are golden; stir in the sugar, chilli powder and salt. Pour the tamarind water into the wok, blend thoroughly and heat the sauce through. Adjust the seasoning and, if necessary, a little lemon juice, to achieve a good sweet-and-sour balance.

Heat the oil in a wiped wok, lift the fish from the marinade, cut each sole into two equal halves and fry them for about 5 minutes on each side. Put them on a warmed serving dish, quickly heat the sauce through and pour it over the fish. Garnish with sliced gherkin and chopped coriander or mint.

KILOCALORIES	225	SUGARS	3g
TOTAL FAT	17g	SODIUM	760mg
SATURATED FAT	2g	FIBRE	–

Tamarind Also known as asam or asem, the hard seed pods of the tamarind tree are much used in Indonesian cookery and impart a sour-fruity flavour. Tamarind pulp is sold in sticky blocks which must be softened to extract the juice.

PROVENÇAL FISH CASSEROLE

Provençal cooking uses generous amounts of garlic. Any firm-fleshed fish can be used for this dish.

SERVES 4

4 fish steaks (approx 675 g/1½ lb), skinned
2–3 tbsp olive oil
2 large onions, roughly chopped
2 garlic cloves, roughly chopped
2 tbsp parsley, coarsely chopped
450 g/1 lb tomatoes, skinned and roughly chopped
100 ml/4 fl oz dry white wine
1 tsp fresh or ½ tsp dried marjoram
pinch salt, pepper
100 g/4 oz black olives
1 tbsp tomato purée (optional)
lemon juice, parsley (for garnish)

Heat the oil in a large pan or flameproof casserole and gently fry the onions, garlic and parsley over low heat for 5–8 minutes. Add the tomatoes. Mix well, then stir in the wine, marjoram, black pepper and salt. Simmer, uncovered, for about 20 minutes.

Bury the fish pieces in the sauce and add the olives. Stir in tomato purée and finish the cooking without the lid. Cook on top of the stove or in an oven, preheated to 190°C/375°F/gas 5, for about 20–25 minutes.

KILOCALORIES	345	SUGARS	9g
TOTAL FAT	19g	SODIUM	810mg
SATURATED FAT	3g	FIBRE	3.5g

RED-BRAISED GREY MULLET

Red-braised dishes, originally a Shanghai speciality, obtain their pleasing colour from a combination of thick soya sauce, sugar and Shao-hsing wine.

SERVES 4

1 large or 2 small grey mullet (or red snapper),
about 1 kg/2 lb
8 medium-sized dried Chinese mushrooms
50–75 g/2–3 oz lean pork
½ tsp salt
plain flour
100 ml/4 fl oz (approx) groundnut (or vegetable oil)
6 spring onions, sliced (keep green and
white parts separate)
4 cm/1½ in fresh ginger root,
peeled and shredded
1½ tbsp Shao-hsing wine (or medium-dry sherry)

MARINADE
2 tsp thin soya sauce
½ tsp sugar
white pepper
1 tsp Shao-hsing wine (or medium dry sherry)
½ tsp potato flour (or cornflour)
½ tbsp water
1 tsp groundnut (or vegetable oil)

SAUCE
150 ml/¼ pt mushroom liquid
2½–3 tbsp thick soya sauce
1 tsp brown sugar

Gut, scale and rinse the fish, but leave the heads on. Soak the mushroom caps in boiling water for about 20 minutes. Squeeze out excess water, cut the mushrooms into slivers and reserve the liquid.

Cut the pork into matchstick pieces and mix with the marinade ingredients. Set aside for 15–20 minutes. Prepare the sauce by blending the mushroom liquid with the soya sauce and sugar.

Make two or three diagonal slashes through the thick part on both sides of the fish, and rub them inside and out with a little salt. Dust them lightly on both sides with flour.

Set a heavy-based frying-pan over high heat until smoking hot. Add 3 tablespoonfuls of the oil and fry the fish on both sides for about 3 minutes. Remove them from the wok and pour away the oil. Reheat the wok over high heat, pour in the remaining oil, add the ginger and, as soon as it sizzles, stir in the white spring onion, followed by the mushrooms. Stir well, then add the pork strips and the marinade. Stir and toss for about 1 minute.

Lower the heat, push the ingredients to the sides and place the fish in the centre. Heap some of the pork mixture on to it and turn up the heat. Splash the wine or sherry around the side of the pan, and when the sizzling subsides pour in the prepared sauce. Bring to the boil, lower the heat, cover with a lid and simmer gently for 20–25 minutes.

At the end of cooking time the sauce should have reduced considerably; otherwise remove the lid, turn up the heat and boil briskly.

Lift the fish carefully on to a warm serving dish. Add the green spring onion to the sauce and spoon it over the fish.

KILOCALORIES	600	SUGARS	3g
TOTAL FAT	33g	SODIUM	720mg
SATURATED FAT	1g	FIBRE	0.5g

SOUFFLÉ OF COLEY WITH MUSTARD SAUCE

———— • ————

Coley becomes a luminous white when cooked. It is a highly nutritious fish, much better value for money than the related, more expensive cod.

SERVES 4

450 g/1 lb coley fillet
pinch salt, pepper
1 small onion, finely chopped
1 tbsp parsley, finely chopped
75 g/3 oz butter (or margarine)
75 g/3 oz plain flour
300 ml/½ pt fish stock (see page 17)
150 ml/¼ pt semi-skimmed milk
3 large eggs, separated
25 g/1 oz Cheddar cheese, finely grated
2 small cartons low-fat plain yogurt
2–3 tsp mustard powder

Heat the oven to 180°C/350°F/gas 4. Rinse the fish and simmer it in a little water with a pinch of salt for 5–6 minutes or until the fish will flake. Lift out the fish, remove skin and any bones and flake the flesh. Reserve the cooking liquid. Mix the chopped onion and parsley with the fish, and leave it to cool.

Melt the butter or margarine, stir in the flour, and cook the roux for a few minutes. Gradually stir in most of the fish liquid and the milk to form a thick white sauce. Fold in the flaked fish, beat in the egg yolks and season to taste.

Whisk the egg whites until they are stiff but not dry. Beat 4 tablespoonfuls into the soufflé mixture to soften it, then fold in the rest with a metal spoon. Turn the mixture into a well-greased 18 cm/7 in soufflé dish, sprinkle with the cheese and bake the soufflé on the middle shelf of the oven for 1 hour or until golden-brown and well risen.

Five minutes before the end of cooking time, spoon the yogurt into a small pan; add the mustard mixed to a thin paste with cold water. Heat through without boiling. Season to taste.

Serve at once, with a sauce and a green vegetable or a side salad.

KILOCALORIES	420	SUGARS	7g
TOTAL FAT	24g	SODIUM	490mg
SATURATED FAT	13g	FIBRE	0.5g

BAKED MACKEREL WITH LEMON AND PARSLEY SAUCE

———— • ————

Mackerel is especially rich in oil and bakes to perfection in the oven.

SERVES 4

4 mackerel
butter (or margarine) for greasing
few sprigs rosemary and parsley
pinch salt, pepper

SAUCE
2 tbsp cornflour
rind and juice of ½ small lemon
450 ml/¾ pt fish stock (see page 17)
1 tbsp chopped parsley

Gut and clean the mackerel, and remove tails, heads and fins; wash the fish and dry them thoroughly inside and out. Slash them two or three times on each side. Preheat the oven to 200°C/400°F/gas 6.

Lightly grease a shallow ovenproof dish that will comfortably hold the fish, scatter the bottom with rosemary and parsley sprigs and lay the mackerel on top; season lightly with salt and pepper. Set the dish in the centre of the oven and bake for 30–35 minutes or until the fish are cooked through.

Blend the cornflour to a paste with the lemon juice; pour on the hot stock, stirring all the time, then return the sauce to a pan and allow it to come just to the boil. Stir in the lemon rind and chopped parsley. Serve the sauce in a bowl, to accompany the baked mackerel, with new potatoes and a green vegetable.

KILOCALORIES	405	SUGARS	–
TOTAL FAT	27g	SODIUM	460mg
SATURATED FAT	7g	FIBRE	–

WHITING WITH SEVILLE ORANGE SAUCE

—— • ——

Whiting is a small member of the cod family, less expensive but similarly rich in protein and essential minerals, and available all year round.

SERVES 4

4 medium-sized whiting
100 ml/4 fl oz dry white wine
2 tsp white wine vinegar
ground nutmeg, salt, pepper

SAUCE
25 g/1 oz butter (or margarine)
25 g/1 oz plain flour
1 medium-sized Seville orange
1 large egg yolk
2 tbsp single cream

Preheat the oven to 180°C/350°F/gas 4. Clean the fish, rinse and wipe dry, and arrange them in a shallow ovenproof dish. Pour the wine and vinegar into a pan with a little nutmeg, salt and pepper and simmer for 5 minutes. Pour the liquid over the fish, cover the dish with a lid or foil and bake for about 15 minutes or until the fish is tender and beginning to flake. Strain off the liquid, and make it up to 300 ml/½ pt with cold water. Keep the fish warm.

For the sauce, melt the butter or margarine in a small pan, stir in the flour and cook the roux for 2 minutes over low heat. Gradually stir in the fish liquid to make a smooth sauce. Finely grate the rind from half the orange, and squeeze out and strain all the juice. Add the orange rind and juice to the sauce and correct seasoning to taste. Beat the egg yolk with the cream, beat in a little of the hot sauce, then return this mixture to the pan, stirring all the time until it thickens. Heat the sauce through, but do not let it boil; pour it over the fish and serve immediately with boiled potatoes and a green vegetable.

KILOCALORIES	225	SUGARS	4g
TOTAL FAT	9g	SODIUM	290mg
SATURATED FAT	5g	FIBRE	1g

BAKED MACKEREL FILLETS

—— • ——

Mackerel, like herring, is a good source of calcium and vitamin D. Its flavour is quickly lost, so mackerel should always be bought absolutely fresh, when the blue-green skin is shiny, and cooked on the same day. Available throughout the year, mackerel is at its best in winter and spring.

SERVES 4

2 large mackerel
vinegar
2–3 tbsp seasoned flour
2–3 tbsp vegetable oil
1 medium-sized onion, coarsely chopped
1 small green pepper, deseeded and coarsely chopped
2 large tomatoes, skinned and chopped
150 g/5 oz mushrooms, sliced
4 tbsp dry white wine (or apple juice)
2 tsp chopped fresh basil (or 1 tbsp chopped parsley)
(optional)
pinch salt, pepper

Clean and gut the mackerel, cut off heads, tails and fins: remove the backbones and divide each mackerel into two fillets. Rinse them carefully (the coarse flesh flakes easily) in a bowl of cold water with a dash of vinegar and pat them dry with kitchen paper. Coat the fillets with seasoned flour.

Preheat the oven to 220°C/425°F/gas 7. Heat the oil in a frying-pan and brown the fillets quickly over high heat, turning them once. Transfer the fillets to an ovenproof dish that holds them comfortably in a single layer. Sauté the onion in the pan for 5 minutes, until soft but not browned. Add the green pepper, tomatoes and mushrooms; mix thoroughly, and cook for a further 1–2 minutes. Pour the wine or apple juice over the vegetables, stir in the herbs if used, and simmer for a few minutes; correct seasoning with salt and pepper.

Pour the vegetable mixture over the fillets, cover the dish with a lid or foil and bake in the oven for 15–20 minutes. Serve the mackerel with boiled new potatoes.

KILOCALORIES	420	SUGARS	3g
TOTAL FAT	27g	SODIUM	620mg
SATURATED FAT	5g	FIBRE	2g

Please see the introduction for a full explanation of the nutritional factboxes.

SASHIMI
Raw fish Japanese-style
———— • ————

Many people find the idea of eating raw fish quite off-putting, yet it is a revelation of contrasting tastes and textures. Japanese sashimi consists of thin slices of filleted fish, arranged in an attractive pattern with a few leaves of a fresh and sharp herb, which is dipped in condiments and a light soya sauce at the table.

Practically all saltwater fish and shellfish are suitable for sashimi, including tuna, turbot, sea bream, sea bass, brill, salmon, crab, lobster and scallop.

It is essential that the fish is absolutely fresh. Ask the advice of a reputable fishmonger and tell him that the fish is for eating raw. Bright eyes, red gills, flesh firm to the touch and with a thin layer of slime on the body are all indications of freshness.

SERVES 4

350 g/12 oz fish, skinned (filleted weight)
few sprigs of watercress, (or flat-leaved parsley or coriander)
15 g/½ oz Japanese horseradish powder (optional)
100 g/4 oz white radish (see below)
4 tbsp light Japanese soya sauce

Rinse and dry the fish carefully and cut into slices about 6 mm/¼ in thick. Remove the cooked shellfish from claws, tails and shells and cut them into similar small chunks. Arrange in an attractive pattern on a dish and decorate with the green herb sprigs; allow space for the condiments.

Mix the Japanese horseradish powder to a smooth paste with a few drops of water and shape it into a couple of small pyramids set among the fish slices. Grate the white radish and arrange it in a heap at one corner of the dish. Serve the soya sauce in one or two small bowls or saucers.

To eat sashimi, best done with chopsticks, crumble a little horseradish paste into the soya sauce, then dip a piece of fish and a few strands of grated radish in the sauce.

Note: white radish, also sold as mooli, is milder than the common red radish. It is a much larger vegetable, shaped like a cylindrical carrot or parsnip. However, if white radishes are unavailable, the common red types can be used, either grated or cut into thin slices.

SPICY FISH CURRY
———— • ————

In the following recipe, from Sri Lanka, fish is cooked with coconut milk to give it a subtle nutty flavour.

SERVES 4

675 g/1½ lb haddock (or cod) fillet, skinned
coconut milk made from 175 g/6 oz desiccated coconut and 425 ml/14 fl oz water
1 small onion, finely chopped
1–2 garlic cloves, crushed
2.5 cm/1 in piece fresh root ginger, peeled and finely chopped
1–2 red chillies (or 1 tsp chilli powder)
1–2 tbsp vegetable oil
fresh coriander leaves (or flat parsley)

Wash and dry the fillets. Place them in the freezer for 20 minutes to firm, then cut into 2.5–4 cm/1–1½ in cubes. Prepare the coconut milk.

Put the onion, garlic, ginger and two-thirds of the chillies (or all the chilli powder) in a food processor. Heat the oil in a heavy-based pan and fry the paste for 2–3 minutes without browning. Stir in the coconut milk and bring it slowly to the boil. Simmer for 5 minutes. Add the fish and cook for 5–10 minutes.

Serve the curry garnished with the remaining sliced red chilli and coriander or parsley, accompanied by a bowl of rice.

KILOCALORIES	220	SUGARS	7g
TOTAL FAT	8g	SODIUM	320mg
SATURATED FAT	–	FIBRE	0.5g

KILOCALORIES	135	SUGARS	1g
TOTAL FAT	6g	SODIUM	90mg
SATURATED FAT	1g	FIBRE	–

SHELLFISH

Nutritionally, shellfish compare favourably with other types of seafood, with similar protein values, a slightly higher polyunsaturated fat content than white fish and much lower levels than oily fish. They are a good source of calcium, phosphorus and some, such as clams and oysters, are also rich in iron. All shellfish are low in calories, but high in cholesterol.

TYPES OF SHELLFISH

Cockles, whelks and winkles are available throughout the year. They are sold cooked and shelled, fresh and frozen, and also in brine solution. **Shrimps**, too, are sold cooked and are more expensive; those in their shells may appear to be cheaper, but the shells account for much wastage. They are also available frozen, canned and potted. **Prawns** are merely large shrimps.

Dublin Bay prawns are the scampi and langoustines of more exotic-sounding recipes; they are sold cooked, shelled or unshelled.

Crabs are also boiled before sale. Prices vary according to season and demand, but crab is best and cheapest during the summer months. It is often sold 'dressed' in the shell ready for eating on the day of purchase. Crab meat, labelled white or brown, is also available frozen, canned and potted.

Scallops are sometimes marketed in their distinctive shells, opened to display the creamy-white flesh and bright coral tongue, but are usually sold by weight, shelled and frozen. Fresh, they are in season from September to March.

British mussels are in season from September till the end of March and are sold live by weight; they need thorough scraping to rid them of sand, grit, beards and barnacles (see right). They can be cleaned and plumped up by putting them in a bucket of water with a handful of porridge oats for a couple of hours. Imported mussels are available all year.

Lobster remains a luxury food. The flesh is contained in the body shell and in the claws. The female lobster is larger in the body (though smaller in the claw department) than the male and possesses the edible coral part.

Oysters tend to occupy the same place as lobster for sheer luxury and are consequently outside most household budgets.

Clams are similar to, but smaller than, oysters. They make passable substitutes in compound seafood dishes. They are sometimes available fresh, but more often are sold frozen or canned in brine.

Squid is tender and sweet. Sold fresh or frozen, the body can be up to 20 cm/8 in long, with tentacles fanning out from the head. The translucent membrane covering the body should be removed, together with the head, the ink bag and the pen-like cartilage in the body. Frozen squid is often rubbery.

PREPARATION

Ready-cooked, fresh or frozen shellfish need a minimum of preparation. Rinse and drain them thoroughly. Shellfish sold live, such as mussels and scallops, and those already boiled but still in their shells, such as shrimps and prawns, need more thorough preparation (see right).

Prawns and shrimps can be shelled by twisting off the long tail section, then the head, and finally by peeling away the soft body shell.

Lobsters, once boiled, become bright red. To prepare them, twist off the claws, crack open the large ones and extract the meat. Discard the gelatinous membrane. Split in half lengthways and remove the black vein that runs the length of the body, the gills and the stomach sac just behind the head. Retain the greenish-cream liver in the head and the coral-red spawn in the tail. Remove the meat from the rest of the body, the tail and the large feeler claws; wash and dry the empty shells and pile the meat back in them. Serve with an appropriate sauce or grill them ungarnished.

Crabs should have their two large pincer claws and the small feeler claws twisted off. Crack open with a hammer and remove the white meat with a skewer. Place the crab on its back, push down on the pointed flap and pull the body out from the shell. The stomach behind the head and the poisonous feathered gills, known as 'dead men's fingers', must also be discarded. Reserve the brown meat from the body. Season the white meat with salt, pepper and lemon juice; mix the brown meat with breadcrumbs, seasoning, lemon juice and parsley and replace in the cleaned shell. Arrange the white meat on either side.

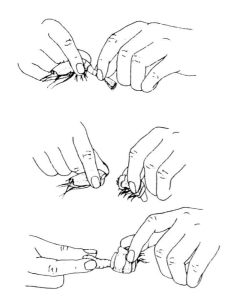

Shelling shrimps
Cooked shrimps and prawns differ in size only, shell them by twisting off first the long tail section, then the head, and finally peel away the soft body shell.

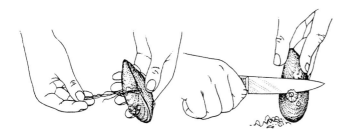

Cleaning mussels
Scrub live mussels thoroughly with a stiff brush, discarding any with broken or open shells. Pull off the beards and scrape away barnacles.

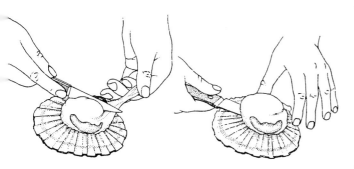

Preparing scallops
Remove the filmy membrane and the black intestinal thread before easing away the white and coral flesh.

SEAFOOD PASTA ORIENTAL

—— • ——

The oriental flavourings of ginger and tamarind bring a delicious new dimension to the usual seafood salad.

SERVES 6–8

½ large or 1 medium-sized monkfish
1 kg/2 lb assorted shellfish
2–3 tbsp olive oil
1 large onion, chopped
2 cloves garlic, crushed
½–¾ tbsp tamarind paste (concentrated)
1½ tsp sugar
2.5 cm/1 in piece fresh root ginger, peeled
pinch salt, pepper
450 g/1 lb ripe tomatoes, skinned and cut into large pieces
large bunch parsley (or coriander), chopped
450 g/1 lb pasta (spaghetti or tagliatelle)
1–2 tbsp butter (or margarine)
2 tbsp pine nuts, roasted

Prepare the fish, washing and drying the monkfish (a large tail piece is the best cut) and cutting it across the bone into 5 cm/2 in chunks. If using mussels, prepare them (see left), then steam them, covered, in a heavy-based pan for about 5 minutes until they open. Simmer scallops in lightly salted boiling water for 2–3 minutes. Cut each scallop into two or three pieces.

Heat the oil in a large, heavy-based pan and fry the onion for about 5 minutes until golden; add the garlic and when the aroma rises, stir in the tamarind and sugar. Add the ginger, finely grated, or the juice squeezed out in a garlic press, with a seasoning of salt and pepper. Mix thoroughly, then add the prepared monkfish, stir-frying it carefully for no more than a couple of minutes before adding the rest of the prepared and cooked fish and shellfish.

Stir the contents of the pan thoroughly; add the tomatoes and parsley. Simmer until the tomatoes have softened slightly and the fish is tender.

Meanwhile, cook the pasta in rapidly boiling water until *al dente*. Drain it thoroughly, place in a serving bowl and toss it in the butter as it melts. Spoon the seafood into a serving dish and sprinkle the roasted pine nuts on top.

KILOCALORIES	435	SUGARS	5g
TOTAL FAT	25g	SODIUM	820mg
SATURATED FAT	7g	FIBRE	2g

MOULES À LA MARINIÈRE

The large British mussel has an especially rich and creamy texture. They are now farmed in many areas of the UK, including Scotland, Norfolk and North Wales, and are usually slightly bigger than those found in the sea.

SERVES 4

1.75 kg/4 lb fresh mussels
2 medium-sized onions, finely chopped
2 shallots, finely chopped
1 garlic clove, crushed
200 ml/7 fl oz dry cider (or white wine)
pinch salt, pepper
40 g/1½ oz butter
2 tbsp chopped parsley

Plunge the mussels into a large bucket of fresh water as soon after buying them as possible. Discard any with broken shells and any which remain open when given a sharp tap – they are not fresh. Scrub the mussels under cold running water, scraping away any barnacles on the shells with a sharp knife and removing the beards with a sharp pull. Rinse the mussels thoroughly in plenty of cold water. Mussels should be cooked and eaten on the day of purchase; cleaned, they can be kept for a few hours, wrapped in a damp cloth in a bucket of water, or at the bottom of the fridge.

Place the onions, shallots, garlic, cider or wine, salt and black pepper in a large, heavy-based pan. Let the contents come to the boil, then tip in the mussels and cook them, covered, over high heat for 5 minutes, shaking the pan gently and frequently until all the shells have opened. Transfer the mussels with a slotted spoon to a warm, deep serving dish, throwing away any which have remained closed. Empty shell halves can be discarded at this stage.

Strain the cooking liquid through muslin or a coffee filter into a small pan, whisk in the butter and adjust the seasoning if necessary. Pour the liquid over the mussels and sprinkle them with the chopped parsley.

Serve immediately with crusty bread and provide finger bowls, and a plate for the empty shells.

KILOCALORIES	320	SUGARS	3g
TOTAL FAT	13g	SODIUM	700mg
SATURATED FAT	6g	FIBRE	0.5g

MUSSELS WITH POTATOES AND LEEKS

Mussel stews are popular all along the Atlantic seaboard; the following is a pleasant combination of textures and flavours, suitable as a main course, or in smaller portions as a starter.

SERVES 4

1.5 kg/3 lb mussels
450 g/1 lb floury potatoes
2 medium-sized leeks, trimmed
3 tbsp vegetable oil
1 tsp cumin (or ½ tsp nutmeg)
225 ml/8 fl oz water (or light chicken stock)
pepper
3–4 tbsp parsley, chopped

Plunge fresh mussels into plenty of cold water as soon as possible after buying them. Discard any with broken shells and any which remain open when given a sharp tap – they are not fresh. Scrub the mussels under cold running water, scraping away any barnacles on the shells with a sharp knife and removing the beards with a sharp pull. Rinse the mussels several times in cold water until all traces of sand have disappeared.

Cut the prepared potatoes and leeks into 6 mm/¼ in slices. Heat the oil in a heavy-based saucepan large enough to hold all the mussels comfortably. Add the vegetables and sauté them for about 5 minutes. Lower the heat, stir in cumin or nutmeg and add the water or stock. Let the vegetables simmer until the potatoes are cooked and breaking up.

Add the mussels to the pan, cover with a lid and let them steam for 2–3 minutes, shaking the pan from time to time. As soon as all the mussels have opened (discard any that remain shut), remove the pan from the heat, grind in pepper to taste, and stir in the chopped parsley.

Spoon the mussel stew into a large, heated dish and serve it at once, accompanied with crusty bread.
Note: Clams, when available, may be used instead of mussels.

KILOCALORIES	335	SUGARS	2g
TOTAL FAT	14g	SODIUM	370mg
SATURATED FAT	1g	FIBRE	3g

COQUILLES AUX CHAMPIGNONS

These molluscs are delicate of flavour, rich in nutrients and handsome nestling in their open shells.

SERVES 4

8 scallops
225 ml/8 fl oz stock (or dry white wine)
3 tbsp butter (or margarine)
2–3 shallots, finely chopped
175 g/6 oz button mushrooms, thinly sliced
1 tbsp flour
pinch salt, paprika
2–3 tsp lemon juice
2 tbsp parsley, finely chopped
6 tbsp brown breadcrumbs
lemon wedges for garnish

Scallops are usually sold cleaned (otherwise, see page 53). Use a knife to ease the scallops from the shells and rinse gently in cold water. Leave frozen scallops to thaw, covered in the fridge for 6–8 hours.

Cut each scallop, including the bright coral, into 2.5 cm/1 in slices and put them in a pan with the stock. Bring to the boil over gentle heat, cover and poach gently for about 4 minutes. Drain, and reserve the cooking liquid.

Melt half the butter in a shallow pan and sauté the shallots and mushrooms for 3 minutes; stir in the flour, cook through for 2 minutes before stirring in enough of the reserved liquid to give the sauce the consistency of thick cream. Season to taste and stir in half the parsley. Fold in the scallops and heat them.

Heat the oven to 200°C/400°F/gas 6. Lightly butter four scallop shells or four ramekin dishes. Spoon the mixture into the shells. Melt the remaining butter and lightly fry the rest of the parsley before adding the breadcrumbs; continue frying until crisp. Sprinkle the crumb mixture over and bake for about 15 minutes.

KILOCALORIES	465	SUGARS	1g
TOTAL FAT	26g	SODIUM	700mg
SATURATED FAT	17g	FIBRE	1.5g

Indian Dinner Parties

Meera Taneja

Indian cooking is different from most other cuisines in a number of ways. Above all, it is the use of spices which gives this cuisine its special character: rice, vegetables (both fresh and dried), meat, poultry, fish, legumes, yogurt, fruits, sweets and sweetmeats are rarely cooked without spices of some kind. Spices are used not merely to enhance colour, taste and aroma, but also for their medicinal, preservative and digestive properties.

The traditional cooking methods of India, including regional techniques such as tandoori and dum cooking, also help to impart a distinctive identity to the food. Tandoori dishes, in which food is cooked over charcoal in an unglazed clay oven (tandoor) sunk in the ground, are favoured in particular by the Punjabis; for Moghul dum cooking, food is steamed slowly in a dough-sealed pot.

More than 25 different spices are commonly used in Indian cookery, the basic eight being chilli (red and green), turmeric, cumin, black pepper, mustard, ginger, coriander and fenugreek. Spice mixes such as garam masala (see page 64) use these in different combinations.

Classic Indian cookery is based on distinctive cultural and regional influences: the Aryans, Ancient Greeks, Moghuls, British and other European cultures have all made their contributions. These, combined with regional, geographic and climatic influences, make it difficult to classify Indian cuisine, though it is popularly described as Moghulai, Tandoori, North, South, East, Central and Western Indian. Specific classifications within the regions, such as Goan or Parsi food, also exist.

Traditional cookery is characterised by a large number of spices, liberal use of ghee (clarified butter) or oil, large amounts of water, a limited range of marinades, and generally longish cooking times. As a contrast to the rich, heavy meals of classic cookery, new Indian cookery includes lighter dishes cooked in the minimum of fat or water, allowing vegetables, meat or poultry to cook in their own juices. It is also distinguished by marinades of fruit juices, honey and seeds which create new flavours, by shorter cooking times, whereby crispness and texture of vegetables are retained, and by modern cooking methods such as stir-frying and oven-cooking.

A typical meal might consist of parathas (breads), rice, meat and/or poultry, dal (pulses), vegetables, plain or flavoured yogurt (raita) and possibly a sweet. A traditional meal is always served as a composite course of three, four or more dishes, but in new Indian cookery there is a preference for serving the meal in four or more courses.

The following party menus, both of which are intended for four people, consist of a classic Indian meal chosen from several regions and a dinner menu on new Indian principles, with each course served separately.

CLASSIC MENU

KHADE MASALE KA GOSHT
Meat cooked in whole spices

— • —

An Indian bouquet garni of spices tied in muslin imparts a mild flavour to the meat and its sauce.

SERVES 4

450 g/1 lb boned lamb (or beef)
pinch salt
600 ml/1 pt water
1 tsp coriander seeds
2 black cardamoms
1 tsp white cumin seeds
4 small red chillies, dried
6 whole black peppercorns
2 bay leaves
2.5 cm/1 in piece cinnamon stick
½ tsp aniseed
4 whole cloves
2 tbsp vegetable oil (or ghee)
2 medium-sized onions, finely chopped
2 garlic cloves, crushed
1 tbsp coriander leaves, chopped

Wipe the meat clean and remove any excess fat before cutting it into 4 cm/1½ in pieces. Place in a large, heavy-based pan with the salt and water. Tie all the spices in a piece of muslin and add to the pan. Bring to the boil over gentle heat and remove any scum from the top. Cover the pan tightly, reduce the heat and simmer until the meat is almost done (about 40 minutes). Lift out the meat and leave to drain on kitchen paper; set the stock aside and discard the spices.

Heat the oil or ghee in a heavy-based saucepan and fry the onions and garlic to a rich golden colour. Add the meat and cook over medium heat until it is rich brown; blend in the stock and correct the seasoning. Cover the pan with a tight-fitting lid, reduce the heat and simmer for another 15 minutes. Transfer to a hot dish, sprinkle with coriander leaves and serve.

KILOCALORIES	365	SUGARS	6g
TOTAL FAT	24g	SODIUM	320mg
SATURATED FAT	7g	FIBRE	1.5g

BATATA VADA
Spiced potato and gram-flour balls

— • —

This is a quick and easy dish to prepare and should be served while still warm.

SERVES 4 Ⓥ

450 g/1 lb potatoes
1 tbsp vegetable oil
1 tsp white cumin seeds
1 medium-sized onion, finely chopped
2.5 cm/1 in piece fresh ginger, peeled and
finely chopped
1 garlic clove, finely chopped
2 fresh green chillies, deseeded and finely chopped
few sprigs of coriander leaves, finely chopped
pinch salt
½ tsp garam masala (see page 64)

BATTER
100 g/4 oz gram flour
good pinch of turmeric
¼ tsp chilli powder
pinch salt
150 ml/¼ pt water (approx)
vegetable oil for frying

Boil the potatoes in their skins, peel and mash them thoroughly. Heat the oil in a frying-pan and add the cumin seeds; as soon as they pop, add the onion, ginger, garlic, chillies and coriander. Stir-fry over high heat for about 1 minute or until the onion is soft. Remove the pan from the heat and add the mixture to the potatoes, with the salt and garam masala. Mix thoroughly and leave the mixture to rest.

Sift the gram flour into a bowl, and add the turmeric, chilli powder and salt. Mix with water to the consistency of thick pancake batter. Let it rest for about 10 minutes, and beat again before use.

Divide the potato mixture into 20–24 walnut-sized pieces and shape them into smooth balls. Heat the oil in a deep-fryer. Using a fork, carefully dip the balls, one at a time, into the batter, coating them completely, then lower them into the hot fat. Fry until crispy and golden; lift out and drain on kitchen paper. Serve whilst warm and crisp.

[Nutritional value is per ball.]

KILOCALORIES	320	SUGARS	4g
TOTAL FAT	17g	SODIUM	270mg
SATURATED FAT	–	FIBRE	5g

SAADI MOONG DAL
Plain moong dal

— • —

A Gujarati version of a simple dish with a distinctive spicy garnish or *tarka*. Use skinless (huskless) split moong beans to reduce the cooking time.

SERVES 4 Ⓥ

225 g/8 oz split moong dal (skinless), washed and
soaked for 30 minutes
450 ml/¾ pt water
½ tbsp vegetable oil (or ghee)
1 tsp mustard seeds
½ tsp white cumin seeds
¼ tsp asafoetida
1 medium-sized onion, finely chopped
1 ripe tomato, finely chopped
1 tsp adoo mirch
3 curry leaves
½ tsp turmeric
½ tsp salt
½ tsp brown sugar
1 tbsp coriander leaves, finely chopped

Bring the water to the boil in a large saucepan; meanwhile, drain the moong dal, wash and drain it again before adding it to the boiling water. Boil for 10 minutes. Reduce the heat, cover the pan and simmer briskly for about 30 minutes.

Heat the oil or ghee in a small, heavy-based frying-pan; add the mustard and cumin seeds and as soon as they pop, stir in the asafoetida, onion and tomato. Stirring frequently, fry for about 5 minutes, or until the onion is soft but not coloured. Add the adoo mirch and curry leaves and, still stirring, the turmeric, salt and sugar. Blend well.

Pour the sizzling *tarka* over the cooked dal; blend and cook, uncovered, over low heat for another 5–7 minutes. Serve hot, sprinkled with coriander leaves.

KILOCALORIES	85	SUGARS	3g
TOTAL FAT	2g	SODIUM	250mg
SATURATED FAT	–	FIBRE	0.5g

AALOO MATTAR
Spiced potatoes and peas

— • —

Popular throughout India, this simple dish can be made at any time of year with fresh or frozen peas.

SERVES 4 Ⓥ

450 g/1 lb potatoes, peeled and cut into
4 cm/1½ in cubes
2 medium-sized onions, roughly chopped
2.5 cm/1 in piece fresh ginger, peeled and
roughly chopped
1 garlic clove
1 green chilli, deseeded and roughly chopped
2 tbsp vegetable oil
½ tsp each white cumin and mustard seeds
1 tsp ground coriander
½ tsp ground turmeric
¼ tsp chilli powder
½ tsp salt
2 large ripe tomatoes, chopped
100 g/4 oz shelled peas, fresh or frozen
300 ml/½ pt water
1 tbsp coriander leaves, finely chopped

Leave the potatoes to soak in cold water; meanwhile, mix the onions, ginger, garlic and chilli to a smooth paste in a blender.

Heat the oil in a large, heavy-based pan and add the cumin and mustard seeds – they should pop and splutter at once. Blend in the onion paste and stir-fry the mixture for about 10 minutes to a deep golden colour, adding a spoonful of water from time to time to prevent the spice mixture from sticking. Add the remaining spices and the salt and continue frying for a few minutes before adding the tomatoes. Stir-fry the mixture for 10–15 minutes.

Drain the potatoes and add them with peas to the pan; stir well and cook for 2–3 minutes. Mix in the measured water and reduce the heat; cover the pan and simmer for 25–30 minutes. Serve at once, sprinkled with coriander leaves.

KILOCALORIES	185	SUGARS	5g
TOTAL FAT	7g	SODIUM	260mg
SATURATED FAT	1g	FIBRE	4g

Right Classic Indian menu *(clockwise from top right)* Vermicelli pudding, spiced fish Bengali-style, plain moong dal, gram-flour dumplings, spiced potato and gram-flour balls, spiced potatoes and peas, pullao rice, meat in whole spices, tangy spiced aubergines above a bowl of pomegranate chutney. In the centre is chicken in piquant sauce.

CHAWAL KA PULLAO
Pullao rice
———— • ————

Rice forms the staple diet of the vast majority of people in India. It is cooked and served in countless ways, from rich and substantial dishes to simple accompaniments.

SERVES 4 Ⓥ

275 g/10 oz basmati rice
1½ tbsp vegetable oil (or ghee)
1 tsp white cumin seeds
6 black peppercorns
1 black (or 4 green) cardamoms
6 whole cloves
2.5 cm/1 in piece cinnamon stick
1 bay leaf, crushed
1 medium-sized onion, finely chopped

Wash the rice thoroughly in several changes of water and leave it to soak in clear water for 25–30 minutes before finally draining it.

Heat the oil or ghee in a heavy-based saucepan, sprinkle in the cumin seeds and as soon as they pop add the rest of the spices. Stir-fry these for a few seconds, add the onion and, stirring frequently, fry them to a rich golden colour. Stir in the rice, level it and pour in enough water to come about 2.5 cm/1 in over the top.

Reduce the heat to a low setting, cover the pan with a tight-fitting lid and let the rice cook undisturbed for about 20 minutes. Remove the pan from the heat and let the rice rest for a few minutes before removing the lid. Gently fluff up the rice with a fork and serve it at once.

KILOCALORIES	160	SUGARS	1g
TOTAL FAT	7g	SODIUM	–
SATURATED FAT	–	FIBRE	0.5g

BOONDI KA RAITA
Gram-flour dumplings in yogurt
———— • ————

These small batter dumplings, added to yogurt, become a refreshing side dish.

SERVES 4 Ⓥ

75 g/3 oz gram flour
150 ml/¼ pt water (approx)
vegetable oil for deep frying

600 ml/1 pt low-fat plain yogurt
½ tsp garam masala (see page 64)
½ tsp chilli powder
¼ tsp black pepper
pinch salt

Sift the gram flour, gradually add the water and beat to a smooth and thick batter (add less or more water as necessary). Set aside for a few minutes.

Heat the oil to smoking point in a deep-fryer. Press the batter, a little at a time, through the holes in a perforated spoon or slice, letting it drop into the hot oil. If the batter does not pass through easily, tap the spoon gently against the side of the fryer.

The batter drops will start to fry at once and rise to the top of the oil; use a clean perforated spoon to turn them until they are pale golden. Lift them out and leave to drain and cool on kitchen paper before mixing them with yogurt or storing them.

To serve, soak the dumplings in warm water to soften them; lift out a handful at a time and gently squeeze out the water, taking care not to break them up. Fold them into the yogurt, along with the spices and salt, and mix thoroughly. Alternatively, the spices can be sprinkled in a decorative pattern over the yogurt and dumplings.

KILOCALORIES	365	SUGARS	12g
TOTAL FAT	27g	SODIUM	380mg
SATURATED FAT	1g	FIBRE	2g

MURGHI MASALEDAR
Chicken in piquant sauce
———— • ————

A traditional dish from the Punjab region, prepared by the *bhoona* method whereby the spicy mixture is cooked very slowly and gradually browned. Prepare a day in advance.

SERVES 4

8–10 chicken pieces (drumsticks/thighs), skinned
450 g/1 lb onions, coarsely chopped
2 garlic cloves, coarsely chopped
2.5 cm/1 in piece fresh ginger, peeled and coarsely chopped
1 green chilli, deseeded and coarsely chopped
2 tbsp vegetable oil
4 green cardamoms
6 whole cloves
8 black peppercorns

2.5 cm/1 in piece cinnamon stick
2 bay leaves
1 tsp white cumin seeds
2 tsp ground coriander
3/4 tsp chilli powder
1/2 tsp ground turmeric
1 1/4 tsp salt
225 g/8 oz fresh tomatoes, chopped (or
half a 227 g/8 oz can tomatoes, drained)
4 tbsp low-fat plain yogurt
450 ml/3/4 pt water
1 tsp garam masala (see page 64)
1 tbsp fresh coriander leaves, finely chopped

Mix the onions, garlic, ginger and green chilli to a smooth paste in a blender. Heat the oil in a large, heavy-based saucepan. Add the cardamoms, cloves, peppercorns, cinnamon, bay leaves and cumin seeds; stir-fry for a few seconds, then add the onion paste. Stirring frequently, fry the mixture over medium heat for about 10 minutes, adding a spoonful of water from time to time to prevent the mixture sticking.

Once the oil begins to separate, add the remaining spices (except the garam masala) and the salt. Stir-fry for a few seconds, add the tomatoes and fry until they begin to soften and the oil starts to separate once more. Slowly blend in the yogurt, stirring all the time. Continue cooking until the sauce has thickened and is deep rust-coloured, and the oil has separated.

Add the chicken pieces to the sauce and fry them until they are thoroughly coated with the spices. At this stage the chicken will have become slightly tender and the oil will start to separate again. Stir in the water and cover the pan with a tight-fitting lid. Reduce the heat and simmer, stirring occasionally, for about 45 minutes.

About 5 minutes before serving, sprinkle the garam masala into the pan and cover. Serve the chicken in the sauce, sprinkled with coriander leaves.

KILOCALORIES	445	SUGARS	12g
TOTAL FAT	19g	SODIUM	480mg
SATURATED FAT	4g	FIBRE	2g

BENGALI KALI MACH
Spiced fish Bengali-style

Any chunky white fish such as cod or monkfish can be used in this recipe.

450 g/1 lb white fish fillets, skinned
1 tsp turmeric
1/2 tsp salt
2 medium-sized onions, chopped
2.5 cm/1 in piece fresh root ginger, peeled
and chopped
1 garlic clove, chopped
3 tbsp vegetable oil (or mustard oil)
225 g/8 oz small potatoes,
peeled and quartered lengthwise
1 bay leaf
2.5 cm/1 in piece cinnamon stick
2 whole cloves
2 green cardamoms
1 tsp white cumin seeds
1/2 tsp chilli powder
1 tsp brown sugar
2 tbsp low-fat plain yogurt

Wash, bone and dry the fish before cutting into 5 cm/2 in size pieces. Mix together half the turmeric and half the salt and rub this over the pieces; leave them to firm in the fridge. Reduce the onion, ginger and garlic to a smooth paste in a blender.

Heat the oil to smoking point in a large frying-pan. Add the fish pieces and fry them over medium heat for 2–3 minutes, turning them once. Lift them out and set aside. Add the potatoes to the pan and fry for 5 minutes, stirring frequently; lift them out and set aside.

Increase the heat, then add the bay leaf, cinnamon, cloves, cardamoms and cumin seeds to the oil in the pan. As soon as the cumin seeds pop and splutter, stir in the onion paste and fry for 5–10 minutes until it becomes a rich golden colour. Blend in the chilli powder, sugar and the rest of the turmeric and salt; stir-fry for another second, then add the yogurt and, stirring continuously, fry until the oil starts to separate out.

Stir the potatoes into the spice mixture; cover the pan, reduce the heat and cook for about 10 minutes, stirring frequently, until the potatoes are almost tender. Now add the fried fish, shaking the pan to mix all the ingredients without breaking up the fish pieces. Cover the pan tightly and cook for another 10 minutes over very low heat so that the fish can absorb the flavours. Remove the bay leaf and cinnamon stick and transfer the contents of the pan to a warm serving dish.

KILOCALORIES	252	SUGARS	6g
TOTAL FAT	11g	SODIUM	360mg
SATURATED FAT	–	FIBRE	1g

KHATE BHARVE BAINGAN
Tangy stuffed aubergines

The unique taste of aubergines blends happily with other vegetables and spices.

SERVES 4 (V)

8 long thin or 4 large aubergines
1 garlic clove, crushed
1 green chilli, deseeded and finely chopped
1½ tsp ground cumin
2 tsp ground coriander
¾ tsp garam masala (see page 64)
3 tsp dry mango powder
¼ tsp chilli powder
½ tsp salt
2 tbsp vegetable oil
3 medium-sized onions, thickly sliced
1 tbsp fresh coriander leaves, finely chopped

Wash and dry the aubergines; carefully slit each lengthwise into four segments, but do not cut through the stalk end.

Mix together the garlic, chilli, dry spices and salt and sprinkle this mixture into the slits in the aubergines. Close up the slits and wind lengths of thin cotton round each aubergine.

Heat the oil in a large, heavy-based pan over medium heat and add the aubergines; as soon as they start colouring on one side turn them carefully and continue cooking until they are evenly coloured. Lower the heat and add the onions and coriander leaves. Mix well, cover the pan and leave to cook for 15 minutes or until the aubergines are tender. Remove the lid and increase the heat so that any excess moisture can evaporate and allow the onions to brown slightly.

Remove the cotton before serving.

KILOCALORIES	125	SUGARS	9g
TOTAL FAT	8g	SODIUM	250mg
SATURATED FAT	–	FIBRE	6g

Clarified butter Melt 225 g/8 oz of salted butter over gentle heat; without stirring or browning, let the butter come to a foam. Continue to cook gently until the foam subsides; remove from the heat and leave until the butter deposit has sunk, leaving a clear liquid on top. Pour this carefully through muslin.

CHAPPATI

Wholemeal unleavened bread – chappati, roti or phulka, as it is known in different regions of India – forms a major part of the diet.

Chappatis are baked on a special cast-iron implement called a *tava*, but a heavy-based, shallow frying-pan (or griddle) is quite adequate. Chappatis must be baked fresh, though they can be frozen uncooked and reheated under a hot grill.

MAKES 10 (V)

275 g/10 oz wholemeal flour
150 ml/¼ pt water (approx)
vegetable oil (or ghee)

Place all but 50 g/2 oz of the flour in the bowl of a food processor. Add water a little at a time until the dough has a soft and pliable consistency similar to shortcrust pastry. Keep kneading until the dough leaves the sides of the bowl clean; cover it with a lid or damp cloth and set it aside for 15 minutes.

Put the *tava* or griddle over medium heat. When a few drops of water sprinkled over it splutter, spread a teaspoonful of oil or ghee over the whole surface.

Divide the dough into 10 equal parts and shape them into smooth balls. Coat each ball with the reserved flour and roll it out into a round 12.5 cm/5 in across. Lift the chappati on to the hot *tava*. Within a few seconds the underside will cook and the upper side become lightly coloured and show small bubbles. Carefully turn the chappati over and cook the other side for a few seconds; turn it over again, pressing down the edges with a tea towel to ensure even cooking. The top will now have small brown specks and the underside will be crisp.

Remove the chappati, spread a little oil or ghee on top and serve hot, or keep it covered in a cloth until required.

[Nutritional value is per chappati.]

KILOCALORIES	175	SUGARS	1g
TOTAL FAT	11g	SODIUM	–
SATURATED FAT	–	FIBRE	2.5g

Right Modern Indian cookery *(clockwise from top) Coriander rice, okra in yogurt, cumin chicken, lamb chops in tamarind sauce, roasted sweet peppers, black chickpea soup, spicy black chickpeas and spinach, and a basket of chappatis. In the centre are apple and fish fillets, and at the back (top right) oranges in jaggery sauce next to the yogurt drink lassi.*

SEVIAN
Vermicelli pudding
——— • ———

This is a favourite sweet dish best made with the thin vermicelli type known as sevian and available from most Indian grocery stores.

SERVES 4 Ⓥ

*75 g/3 oz sevian (or other vermicelli),
broken into small pieces
1 tbsp vegetable oil (or ghee)
1.5 l/2½ pt semi-skimmed milk
50 g/2 oz sugar
25 g/1 oz blanched almonds, cut into slivers
25 g/1 oz green raisins, washed
crushed seeds of 2 green cardamoms
10 unsalted pistachio nuts*

Melt the oil or ghee in a large, heavy-based saucepan, sprinkle over the sevian and, stirring continuously, fry for 1–2 minutes or until it is a pale golden colour. Add the milk and bring it slowly to the boil. Lower the heat and let the milk simmer gently, uncovered, for about 1 hour or until it has thickened and reduced to half its original quantity. Stir occasionally.

Add the sugar and stir until dissolved, then blend in the remaining ingredients. Serve warm or cold.

KILOCALORIES	385	SUGARS	36g
TOTAL FAT	14g	SODIUM	220mg
SATURATED FAT	4g	FIBRE	1g

GARAM MASALA
——— • ———

A highly aromatic mixture of six spices: black peppercorns, cloves, cinnamon, cardamoms, cumin and bay leaves. The spices should be ground in small quantities so the mixture can be used up quickly.

*2.5 cm/1 in cinnamon stick
1 tbsp black peppercorns
2 tsp white cumin seeds
4 black* or 10 green cardamoms
4 bay leaves*

Place the ingredients in a blender and grind to a fine powder. *(If black cardamoms are used, crush them thoroughly first as the skin is very hard.) Store in an airtight container.

MODERN MENU
———————————

MACHCHI SABE KE SAATH
Apple and fish fillets
——— • ———

Spices for fish should be mixed subtly so as not to ruin the delicate flavour of the fish.

SERVES 4

*1 large lemon sole (or plaice), skinned and filleted
1–2 tbsp vegetable oil
1½ tsp ajowan seeds
2 medium-sized cooking apples, peeled, cored and
coarsely grated
½ tsp chilli powder
pinch salt*

Cut each fillet in half lengthwise, to give four long, thin strips; pat them dry and set them aside.

Heat a tablespoonful of oil in a small frying-pan until it is very hot; sprinkle in the ajowan seeds – they should pop and splutter at once. Mix in the grated apple and stir-fry over high heat for a few minutes. Add the chilli powder and the salt and continue stirring and cooking until all moisture has evaporated. Remove the pan from the heat and allow the mixture to cool.

Preheat the oven to 180°C/350°F/gas 4. Spread the apple and spice mixture evenly over the fish fillets and roll them up from the widest end, tucking the narrow end securely underneath. Place the fish rolls in a lightly oiled ovenproof dish and brush them with a little oil. Bake for 15 minutes.

Serve hot, on a bed of finely shredded lettuce.

KILOCALORIES	195	SUGARS	4g
TOTAL FAT	14g	SODIUM	200mg
SATURATED FAT	4g	FIBRE	1g

BHINDI KA RAITA
Crisp okra in yogurt
——— • ———

Also known as ladies' fingers, this pale green, white-seeded oriental vegetable is available throughout the year from Indian stores and specialist greengrocers. Buy them firm and crisp.

SERVES 4 (V)

125 g/4 oz okra
450 ml/³/₄ pt low-fat plain yogurt
1 tsp white cumin seeds
1–2 tbsp vegetable oil
1 green chilli, deseeded and finely sliced
pinch salt

Wipe the okra thoroughly with a damp cloth; cut off the stalk ends and the tips, and thinly slice the okra crossways.

Sprinkle the cumin seeds into a small frying-pan, turn the heat to high, and as soon as the seeds start popping remove the pan from the heat. Place the seeds on a dry surface and grind them to a powder with a rolling-pin, or use a pestle and mortar.

Heat the oil to smoking point in a deep frying-pan; add the okra and fry them until crisp and golden, after a few seconds. Drain them on kitchen paper and leave to cool.

Lightly whip the yogurt in a serving bowl and blend in the chilli, roasted ground cumin and salt. Just before serving sprinkle the crisp okra on top.

KILOCALORIES	135	SUGARS	9g
TOTAL FAT	8g	SODIUM	195mg
SATURATED FAT	2g	FIBRE	1g

HARE DHANIA WALE CHAWAL
Fresh coriander rice

— • —

Highly aromatic coriander leaves lend a freshness to any dish: coriander is available from oriental grocery shops and some supermarkets.

SERVES 4 (V)

275 g/10 oz basmati rice
1 tbsp vegetable oil
1 garlic clove, crushed
2 tbsp coriander leaves, finely chopped
150 ml/¹/₄ pt semi-skimmed milk
pinch salt

Place the rice in a dry tea towel and rub the grains gently to remove any excess powder.

Heat the oil in a heavy-based saucepan, add the rice and stir-fry until it is pale golden in colour. Stir in the garlic, coriander and milk, mixing well.

Level the rice in the pan, then carefully pour in enough water to come about 2.5 cm/1 in above the top

of it. Add the salt, stir once, then cover the pan with a tight-fitting lid, reduce the heat to low and leave the rice to cook undisturbed for about 20 minutes. Turn off the heat and let the rice settle for a few minutes before removing the lid; gently fluff it up with a fork and serve it at once.

KILOCALORIES	140	SUGARS	2g
TOTAL FAT	5g	SODIUM	120mg
SATURATED FAT	–	FIBRE	–

MEETHI MIRCH KA BHARTHA
Roasted sweet peppers

— • —

This mildly spiced dish can be served with a meat or fish course or constitute a vegetarian meal, accompanied by chappatis.

SERVES 4 (V)

2 green peppers
2 red peppers
1 orange pepper (optional)
2 tbsp vegetable oil
1 tsp white cumin seeds
3 medium-sized onions, finely chopped
3 ripe medium-sized tomatoes, roughly chopped
1 garlic clove, finely chopped
¹/₂ tsp salt
¹/₂ tsp chilli powder

Place the peppers on a wire rack over a naked flame or under a hot grill; char the skins completely, turning the peppers over several times. Once cool, carefully peel off the charred skins, cut off the stalk ends, split open the peppers and remove the seeds. Chop the flesh.

Heat the oil in a heavy-based sauté pan, add the cumin seeds and when they pop, stir in the onions and fry to a pale golden colour. Add the tomatoes and garlic and fry, stirring frequently, until soft.

Add the peppers, salt and chilli powder to the pan, stirring well. Reduce the heat to low and continue frying the mixture until the little oil soaked up by the onions is released.

Serve the peppers hot.

KILOCALORIES	155	SUGARS	17g
TOTAL FAT	8g	SODIUM	260mg
SATURATED FAT	1g	FIBRE	6g

MURGH ZEERE KA
Cumin chicken

————— • —————

Here white cumin, whole and ground, is used to flavour a chicken dish which can be served either as a starter or as a main course.

SERVES 4

*2 large chicken breasts, skinned, boned and cut into
2.5 cm/1 in pieces
1¼ tbsp vegetable oil
1 tsp white cumin seeds
1 green and 1 red pepper, deseeded and cut into
6 mm/¼ in slices
2.5 cm/1 in piece fresh ginger, peeled and thinly sliced
1 garlic clove, crushed
1½–2 tsp ground white cumin
½ tsp chilli powder
½ tsp garam masala
½ tsp salt
1 tsp dried mint flakes
juice of 1½ lemons or limes*

Heat the oil in a heavy-based pan and add the cumin seeds; as soon as they pop, add the chicken pieces and stir-fry for a few minutes over high heat to seal in the juices. Reduce the heat and, stirring continuously, fry the chicken to a golden colour.

Mix in the peppers, ginger, garlic, the rest of the spices, salt and mint flakes; continue stir-frying until the peppers and the chicken are well coated with the spices and the peppers are beginning to soften.

Pour the lemon or lime juice into the pan, increase the heat to high and, stirring constantly, fry the mixture until most of the juice has been absorbed.

Serve at once.

KILOCALORIES	168	SUGARS	4g
TOTAL FAT	8g	SODIUM	310mg
SATURATED FAT	1g	FIBRE	1g

KALE CHANNE MASALE WALE
Spicy black chickpeas and spinach

————— • —————

Black chickpeas, which are really yellow-brown in colour, have a high protein and fibre content. They need to be soaked for at least 12 hours and can be cooked in a pan or a pressure cooker.

SERVES 4 Ⓥ

*225 g/8 oz black chickpeas
1 l/1¾ pt water
2 tbsp vegetable oil
1 tsp ajowan seeds
2 medium-sized onions, finely chopped
2.5 cm/1 in piece fresh ginger, peeled and
finely chopped
1 clove garlic, finely chopped
2 green chillies, deseeded and finely chopped
3 ripe medium-sized tomatoes, finely chopped
½ tsp salt
225 g/8 oz frozen leaf spinach, thawed and
roughly chopped
1 tbsp coriander leaves, finely chopped*

Wash the chickpeas in several changes of cold water; leave them to soak in plenty of cold water for at least 12 hours and preferably 24. Drain, discard any peas which have not doubled in size and rinse the rest in a sieve under cold, running water. Place the peas and the measured water in a large pan and boil for 10 minutes. Cover the pan and simmer until the chickpeas are tender but still retaining their shape (1–1½ hours).

Heat the oil in a large frying-pan. Add the ajowan seeds, which should pop and splutter at once, and the onions; stir-fry until they are a rich golden-brown. Mix in the ginger, garlic and chillies, stirring for a few minutes before adding the tomatoes and the salt. Continue stir-frying until the tomatoes have softened slightly.

Add the chickpeas and the chopped spinach; reduce the heat and thoroughly mix. Partially cover the pan and cook for about 15 minutes, stirring frequently.

Serve hot, garnished with coriander.

KILOCALORIES	220	SUGARS	7g
TOTAL FAT	13g	SODIUM	120mg
SATURATED FAT	2g	FIBRE	5g

KALE CHANNE KA SHORBA
Black chickpea soup

————— • —————

This delicate soup, flavoured with lime and a spicy garnish, can be served hot or chilled.

SERVES 4 Ⓥ

*225 g/8 oz black chickpeas
1 l/1¾ pt water*

½ tsp salt
juice of 2 fresh limes
1 tbsp vegetable oil (or ghee)
1 tsp white cumin seeds
1 cm/½ in piece fresh ginger, peeled and finely shredded
1 small garlic clove, crushed
1 green chilli, deseeded and finely chopped
2 tbsp coriander leaves, finely chopped

Wash the chickpeas in several lots of cold water, then leave them to soak for at least 24 hours. Drain the peas and place with the measured water in a large pan; bring to the boil and cook for 10 minutes. Cover the pan and leave the peas to simmer for about 1½ hours or until they are quite tender though still retaining their shape; add more water if necessary.

Strain the chickpeas, retaining the liquid (it should measure approx 600 ml/1 pt). Pour it into a saucepan and gently bring it to just below boiling point. Reduce the heat and allow to simmer. Mix in the salt and lime juice and let the soup barely simmer.

Heat the ghee in a small frying-pan, add the cumin seeds and as soon as they pop and splutter, mix in the ginger, garlic and green chilli. Stir-fry over medium heat for a few minutes until the ginger turns golden. Serve with the spicy garnish and coriander.

KILOCALORIES	90	SUGARS	1g
TOTAL FAT	3g	SODIUM	250mg
SATURATED FAT	–	FIBRE	2.5g

IMLI WALI CHOPS
Lamb chops in tamarind sauce

Concentrated tamarind pulp is readily available from most Indian supermarkets; the juice can also be extracted from a pressed slab of tamarind pods.

SERVES 4

8 lean lamb chops
100 g/4 oz tamarind pods (or 2 tbsp concentrated tamarind pulp)
300 ml/¼ pt warm water
1 medium-sized onion, grated
1 garlic clove, crushed
2 green chillies, finely chopped
1 cm/½ in piece fresh ginger, peeled and finely chopped

2 tbsp brown sugar
1 tsp garam masala (see page 64)
½ tsp salt
300 ml/½ pt water
1 tbsp coriander leaves, finely chopped

Soak the tamarind pods in the warm water for 25–30 minutes, then squeeze all the pulp from the pods; strain through a sieve and reserve the liquid, discarding fibre and seeds. Thoroughly blend the tamarind juice with the onion, garlic, chillies, ginger, sugar, garam masala, salt and water.

Trim the chops and arrange them in an ovenproof dish, pour the tamarind mixture over them and leave to marinate for 5–8 hours.

Bake the chops in the oven pre-heated to 165°C/325°F/gas 3 for about 50 minutes or until they are tender; baste them frequently and turn them once.

Serve with coriander leaves.

KILOCALORIES	295	SUGARS	22g
TOTAL FAT	11g	SODIUM	310mg
SATURATED FAT	5g	FIBRE	–

GUR KE MEETHE
Oranges in jaggery sauce

Unrefined brown sugar can be substituted for jaggery.

SERVES 6–8 Ⓥ

6–8 oranges
50 g/2 oz butter
100 g/4 oz brown sugar (or coarsely grated jaggery)

Peel the oranges, taking care to remove all the pith and stringy membranes; cut them crossways into 6 mm/¼ in thick slices and remove pips.

Melt the butter with the jaggery or sugar in a large heavy-based sauté pan over low heat, stirring constantly to prevent the sugar sticking to the pan and caramelising. Carefully spread the sliced oranges in the pan, preferably without overlapping them; spoon the sauce over them and simmer gently for no more than 5 minutes before serving.

KILOCALORIES	150	SUGARS	14g
TOTAL FAT	5g	SODIUM	70mg
SATURATED FAT	3g	FIBRE	2.5g

MEAT

In addition to high-quality protein, red meat is rich in minerals and vitamins, covering all the important vitamins in the B complex and (in the case of liver and to some extent kidney) providing more vitamin A than any other food source. But red meat also contains a high proportion of saturated fat and is high in cholesterol.

Proportions of lean and fat vary according to cut: the leanest meats – steaks and chops, fillets, topside and legs – are also the dearest, making them expensive forms of protein. Cuts with more fat, such as brisket and breast of lamb, may appear cheaper, but once they are trimmed of surplus fat they may, weight for weight, be equally expensive.

PREPARATION

Nowadays, large chunks or layers of fat on meat are largely absent, though all meat is marbled with fat to a lesser or greater degree. Beef should look moist and smooth, pinkish-blue in colour; lamb should have pink flesh and creamy-white fat; pork should have a similar appearance and be firm not flabby in texture. After purchase, remove all wrappings from the meat, cover it loosely and store in the fridge for a couple of days; let it 'come to' at room temperature before cooking.

COOKING

During cooking, the protein in the meat coagulates and becomes firm, resulting in some shrinkage and weight loss. At the same time, the juices run free with some loss of nutrients which escape into the cooking medium (fat or water). Don't add to the amount of saturated fat with such substances as lard.

Because ovens vary so greatly, it is a good idea to use a meat thermometer to ensure meat is cooked through. It should be stuck into the thickest part of the joint before it is placed into the oven (see page 73).
Roasting is the preferred method of cooking large joints of prime meat. The fat content of pork and lamb makes it unnecessary to add any further fat to the pan. Cook them at around 210°C/425°F/gas 7. Pot-roasting

is better for small tough joints like brisket of beef and boned, rolled breast of lamb. Brown the meat in fat and set it on a wire rack or a bed of chopped root vegetables in a heavy-based pan, cover it with a lid and cook over low heat on top of the stove, or in the oven at 160°C/325°F/gas 3, allowing 45 minutes per pound.
Grilling is suitable for small individual cuts, such as steaks, rashers or chops. Trim them of excess fat, brush lightly with oil and set the meat on a rack over a foil-lined pan under a pre-heated high grill. Give steaks 7–15 minutes depending on the thickness and whether the meat is preferred rare, medium or well-done, chops 15–20 minutes, cutlets 10 minutes, bacon rashers 5–10 minutes.
Gravies can be made from the juices of the cooked meat. Place the juices in the fridge or freezer to help the fat to solidify. This can then be scraped off and the juices used for gravy or a sauce.

PAPRIKA LAMB CASSEROLE

This dish is reminiscent of Hungarian goulash, but while goulash is *always* made with beef, lamb chops are used for this nourishing family-style casserole.

SERVES 4

1 kg/2 lb lean lamb chops
25 g/1 oz seasoned flour
2–3 tbsp vegetable oil
2 large onions, roughly chopped
1/2–1 tbsp Hungarian paprika
2 tbsp tomato purée
600ml/1 pt stock
2 large carrots, thinly sliced
150 ml/5 fl oz low-fat plain yogurt

Trim fat from the chops, wipe them clean and toss in seasoned flour. Heat the oil in a heavy-based pan and fry the chops to seal them. Remove, and add the onion and paprika to the pan. Fry over medium heat for about 8 minutes or until golden. Stir in the rest of the seasoned flour, cook for 1 minute, then stir in the tomato purée and the stock. Return the chops to the pan and season to taste.

Transfer the contents to an ovenproof casserole, cover with a lid and cook in an oven preheated to 165°C/325°F/gas 3 for 1½ hours. Add the carrots and cook for a further 30 minutes.

Spoon a little yogurt over each helping and serve with noodles or mashed potatoes.

KILOCALORIES	555	SUGARS	13g
TOTAL FAT	31g	SODIUM	560mg
SATURATED FAT	11g	FIBRE	3g

BEEF GOULASH

Goulash, a hot, spicy stew, was named after the Magyar *gulyas* (herdsmen) of Central Europe. It has become a classic of Hungarian cuisine.

SERVES 4

450 g/1 lb stewing steak, trimmed and cubed
2–3 tbsp vegetable oil
1 large green pepper, deseeded and finely chopped
450 g/1 lb onions, thinly sliced
600 ml/1 pt beef (or chicken) stock
2 tbsp Hungarian paprika
1 tbsp tomato purée
2 tbsp brown sugar
½ tsp caraway seeds
1 small can (225 g/8 oz) tomatoes, roughly chopped
pinch salt, pepper
150 ml/5 fl oz low-fat plain yogurt

Heat the oil in a heavy-based, deep pan and fry the meat briskly until sealed and brown all over (about 7 minutes). Lift it from the pan and set it aside.

Add the pepper and onions to the pan and fry them over low heat for 20–25 minutes or until soft but not browned. Return the meat to the pan and add the hot stock; bring gently to the boil, then stir in the paprika, tomato purée, sugar and caraway seeds, and the tomatoes with their juice.

Bring slowly to the boil, stirring frequently; season to taste. Cover the pan and leave it to simmer over the lowest possible heat for about 1½ hours.

Stir in the yogurt and heat through gently without bringing to the boil. The dish is traditionally served with noodles, but freshly cooked brown macaroni or small potatoes cooked in their skins would be equally suitable.

KILOCALORIES	390	SUGARS	18g
TOTAL FAT	22g	SODIUM	440mg
SATURATED FAT	7g	FIBRE	3g

BAKED LAMB LOAF

All edible remains of a joint can be used up in this lamb loaf. Add other cold meats for variety.

SERVES 4

350 g/12 oz cold roast lamb
50 g/2 oz brown breadcrumbs
25–50 g/1–2 oz shredded suet (optional)
1 large egg, beaten
1–2 tbsp vegetable oil
1 small onion, finely chopped
1 garlic clove, finely chopped
pinch salt, pepper
1 tsp ground cumin
4–6 sprigs of mint (or coriander), chopped
2 tbsp gravy (or meat stock or redcurrant jelly)

Mince the lamb, mix in the breadcrumbs and suet, if used, and bind the mixture with the egg.

Heat the oil in a small pan and fry the onion and garlic over gentle heat for about 8 minutes or until they are soft and golden. Add the onion to the meat, with salt and pepper to taste, cumin and coriander. Stir in the gravy, stock or jelly, or a mixture – just enough to moisten the ingredients.

Spoon the mixture into a greased loaf tin. Smooth the top, add a few more sprigs of herbs and cover the tin with foil. Stand the tin in a roasting tin with water coming halfway up the sides. Bake the loaf in an oven preheated to 180°C/350°F/gas 4 for 1–1½ hours. (When cooked, the juices should run clear.)

Serve the loaf hot with a puréed vegetable or cold with a green salad.

KILOCALORIES	410	SUGARS	2g
TOTAL FAT	27g	SODIUM	370mg
SATURATED FAT	11g	FIBRE	0.5g

or until soft but not coloured. Add the apricot purée, sugar and vinegar, and season to taste. Simmer the sauce gently for about 20 minutes.

Remove the bacon from the oven, cut off the rind and carve the meat into slices. Garnish with the reserved apricot halves. Serve with, for example, new potatoes and courgettes.

KILOCALORIES	550	SUGARS	16g
TOTAL FAT	21g	SODIUM	2850mg
SATURATED FAT	6g	FIBRE	1g

BAKED BACON WITH APRICOT SAUCE
— • —

Vacuum-packed bacon joints are inexpensive and unsmoked joints do not need soaking before cooking. The sour-sweet apricot sauce also goes well with lamb or pork.

SERVES 4

1 kg/2¼ lb slipper or *corner bacon, smoked*
or *unsmoked*
400 g/14 oz can apricot halves, in natural juice
1–2 tbsp vegetable oil
1 small onion, finely chopped
1 cm/½ in fresh root ginger, peeled and cut into slivers
1 tbsp brown sugar (optional)
2 tbsp vinegar
pinch salt, pepper

Soak a smoked joint for 6–7 hours in cold water, changing the water once; drain and pat dry with kitchen paper. Place the bacon in a square of foil large enough to make a loose parcel; seal the edges well. Set in a roasting tin in an oven, preheated to 220°C/425°F/gas 7, and bake, allowing 25–30 minutes for every 450 g/1 lb.

Set four or six apricot halves aside for the garnish and purée the rest with the juice. Heat the oil in a small pan and fry the onion and ginger for about 5 minutes

NECK OF LAMB HOT-POT
— • —

A most satisfying and inexpensive winter stew thickened with pearl barley.

SERVES 6

1 kg/2 lb scrag or *middle neck of lamb*
pinch salt, pepper
3 large onions, roughly chopped
3 large carrots, sliced
2 celery sticks, sliced
1 bay leaf and a few sprigs of thyme
75 g/3 oz pearl barley
150 g/5 oz frozen peas

Have the lamb cut into single ribs, remove any bone splinters and wipe it dry. Fry the meat in a large, heavy-based pan over gentle heat until the fat begins to run, then increase the heat slightly and continue frying until the lamb pieces are golden. Transfer them to a deep fireproof casserole, and season lightly.

Fry the onions, carrots and celery in the fat left in the pan until they just begin to colour; add them to the casserole with the bay leaf and thyme sprigs. Rinse the pearl barley in a sieve under cold running water and add it to the dish with 1 litre/1¾ pt cold water. Bring to the boil, cover with a lid and place the casserole near the bottom of the oven (preheated to 165°C/325°F/gas 3); cook for 1½–2 hours or until the meat is almost tender. Check the seasoning and stir in the peas. Continue cooking in the oven for another hour.

Serve with mashed potatoes.

KILOCALORIES	455	SUGARS	8g
TOTAL FAT	24g	SODIUM	470mg
SATURATED FAT	12g	FIBRE	3.5g

SHOULDER OF LAMB WITH PRUNE AND ROSEMARY STUFFING

— • —

Ask the butcher to bone the shoulder; after stuffing the meat, tie it neatly with some fine string. Leg of lamb can also be used in this recipe.

SERVES 4

1 shoulder or *leg of lamb*
(approx 1.5 kg/3½ lb), boned
225 g/8 oz stoned prunes
300 ml/½ pt cold tea (or dry cider)
1 medium-sized onion, coarsely chopped
2 tbsp vegetable oil
3 sprigs rosemary
75 g/3 oz fresh brown breadcrumbs
pinch salt, pepper
1 small egg, beaten
oil for glazing

Soak the prunes in the cold tea or cider for 8 hours or overnight. Wipe the meat and trim any excess fat. Roughly chop the prunes. Fry the onion in half the oil for about 5 minutes over medium heat, until soft but not brown; remove from the heat. Strip the needles from one rosemary sprig, chop them and add to the onion along with the prunes and breadcrumbs. Season to taste, then add sufficient beaten egg to bind the stuffing. Spoon as much of this as will fit into the bone cavity in the meat, roll it up and tie it firmly with string into a neat joint.

Place the remaining rosemary sprigs in an oiled

roasting tin, set the meat on top and brush it lightly with oil (any leftover stuffing can be placed round the joint for the last half-hour). Roast in the oven preheated to 200°C/400°F/gas 6 for 1 hour, then reduce the heat to 180°C/350°F/gas 4, and cook for another 1½ hours or until the meat is tender; test with a skewer.

Remove the string, carve the lamb into thick slices and serve it with gravy made from the pan juices and with new potatoes and, for example, purée of peas with herbs (page 154).

KILOCALORIES	885	SUGARS	23g
TOTAL FAT	36g	SODIUM	490mg
SATURATED FAT	15g	FIBRE	4.5g

LAMB WITH APRICOTS AND ALMONDS

— • —

This recipe from medieval times uses a mixture of fruit and meat.

SERVES 4

450 g/1 lb boned shoulder or *lean neck of lamb*
2 tbsp vegetable oil
1 large onion, chopped
50 g/2 oz ground almonds
300 ml/½ pt chicken stock (see page 17)
225 g/8 oz fresh apricots
(or 1 large can in natural juice)
pinch salt, pepper
parsley, finely chopped

Wipe the meat and cut it into 2.5 cm/1–2 in cubes. Heat the oil in a heavy-based pan over high heat and quickly seal the lamb cubes. Lift them out and fry the onion for about 5 minutes. Return the lamb to the pan, stir in the ground almonds and the chicken stock; reduce the heat, cover the pan and simmer for 1 hour or until the lamb is tender.

Add the stoned and halved fresh apricots, or the drained canned ones; simmer for another 10 minutes. Season to taste.

Spoon the lamb and sauce into a serving dish and sprinkle with the parsley. Serve with rice or potatoes.

KILOCALORIES	345	SUGARS	6g
TOTAL FAT	24g	SODIUM	380mg
SATURATED FAT	6g	FIBRE	2g

PIQUANT BEEF WITH CHEESE CRUMBLE

— • —

Lean stewing steak makes a warming dish for wintry days.

SERVES 4

450 g/1lb stewing beef, trimmed and cubed
2–3 tbsp vegetable oil
100 g/4 oz onions, sliced
2 carrots, diced
1 turnip (or parsnip), diced
450 ml/¾ pt stock (or water)
3 tsp French mustard
pinch salt, pepper
1 tbsp flour

CRUMBLE

175 g/6 oz wholemeal flour
75 g/3 oz margarine (or butter)
40 g/1½ oz Edam (or Cheddar), finely grated

Heat the oil in a large heavy-based pan and fry the beef over medium heat until sealed and brown, after about 7 minutes. Remove the beef from the pan.

Add the onions, carrots and turnip or parsnip to the pan and fry over medium heat for about 10 minutes or until golden, stirring frequently. Return the beef to the pan, with the stock (or water) and mustard. Bring to the boil, stirring continuously, then cover the pan tightly and lower the heat. Simmer for 1½ hours.

Mix the flour to a smooth paste with about 3 tablespoonfuls of cold water and stir it into the stew; continue to cook until the sauce has thickened. Correct the seasoning. Spoon the stew into a 1.25 litre/2 pt lightly greased ovenproof dish and leave to cool completely.

For the crumble topping, rub the margarine or butter with flour until the mixture resembles coarse breadcrumbs, then blend in the cheese. Sprinkle the crumble over the beef and bake for 30–35 minutes in the centre of an oven preheated to 190°C/375°F/gas 5.

Serve with crisply cooked cabbage or Brussels sprouts and mashed potatoes.

KILOCALORIES	655	SUGARS	7g
TOTAL FAT	41g	SODIUM	630mg
SATURATED FAT	10g	FIBRE	6.5g

EASTERN LAMB PILAFF

— • —

The national dish of Turkey is pilaff, based on rice – or occasionally bulghur wheat. Fruit is added as a sweetener, and herbs, especially fresh mint, are traditional.

SERVES 4

350 g/12 oz cold cooked lamb, diced
2–3 tbsp vegetable oil
1 medium-sized onion, chopped
225 g/8 oz long-grain rice (brown or white)
40 g/1½ oz currants
600 ml/1 pt boiling water
10 cm/4 in strip of orange peel, washed and dried
pinch salt
2 tbsp mint, finely chopped

Heat the oil in a large frying-pan. Add the onion and fry for about 5 minutes until pale gold. Stir in the washed, drained rice and the currants, and fry for a further 3 minutes, stirring continuously.

Gradually add the water, forking it through the rice. Add the lamb, orange peel and salt. Bring the mixture to the boil, stir once or twice with a fork, then lower the heat. Cover the pan and cook for 20 minutes until the rice grains are tender and have absorbed all the liquid (brown rice will take about 40 minutes).

Take the pan off the heat, remove the lid and cover the pan with a folded tea towel for 5 minutes. Fork through the rice, remove the strip of orange peel and spoon out the pilaff. Garnish with mint and serve immediately.

KILOCALORIES	395	SUGARS	8g
TOTAL FAT	21g	SODIUM	170mg
SATURATED FAT	5g	FIBRE	1g

POTATO PASTRY MEAT PIE

Potato pastry is quick to make, soft and easy to handle and should be spread thickly over the filling to seal it. It can be flavoured with a good pinch of dry mustard for fish pies.

SERVES 6

1 kg/2 lb lean stewing pork
1 large onion, roughly chopped
1 tbsp parsley, finely chopped
½ tsp sage, finely chopped
pinch salt, pepper
75 g/3 oz plain flour
600 ml/1 pt ham, pork or chicken stock
40 g/1½ oz margarine (or butter)
75 g/3 oz mashed potatoes
½ tsp baking powder

Trim the pork of fat, wipe it clean and cut it into large even-sized cubes; add the onion, parsley, sage, salt and pepper with 15 g/½ oz of the flour. Mix thoroughly and transfer to a 2 litre/3 pt pie dish; pour in stock (see page 17) to half-fill the dish, cover it with a lid or a double layer of foil and cook for 1 hour near the bottom of the oven preheated to 165°C/325°F/gas 3.

Cream the margarine or butter until soft and mix it lightly with the potatoes; sift in the remaining flour and the baking powder, mix, and knead the pastry lightly until smooth. Remove the pie dish from the oven and turn up the temperature to 220°C/425°F/gas 7.

Spread the potato pastry over the meat and return the dish, uncovered, to the oven for 10 minutes. Reduce the temperature to 180°C/350°F/gas 4 and cook for a further 40–45 minutes until the potato topping is golden.

Serve hot with crisp cabbage or beans.

KILOCALORIES	290	SUGARS	1g
TOTAL FAT	16g	SODIUM	360mg
SATURATED FAT	6g	FIBRE	0.5g

Please see the introduction for a full explanation of the nutritional factboxes.

PUMPES

These subtly spiced meatballs do not differ greatly from other kebabs though the recipe is medieval English. They can be made in bite-sized pieces to serve with drinks, or walnut- or apple-sized for a main course with boiled rice and a salad.

SERVES 4

450 g/1 lb minced meat (lean pork, lamb or beef)
good pinch each of salt, ground ginger, mace,
cinnamon and cloves
1 tbsp currants
1 small egg, beaten

Mix the minced meat with the salt, spices and currants, and bind the mixture with the egg. Shape it into small balls. If time permits, leave the meatballs to settle in the fridge for about 1 hour.

Bring a pan of water to the boil; lower the meatballs into the gently simmering water and poach them, 10 minutes for pork balls, 5 minutes for lamb or beef. Remove them and leave to drain.

Thread them on to skewers and grill under a medium-hot grill until browned.

As an appetiser, small meatballs can be half-grilled, placed on a baking tray and finished in the oven at 190°C/375°F/gas 5 for 10 minutes. Serve with tartare sauce or mayonnaise (see page 32).

KILOCALORIES	285	SUGARS	5g
TOTAL FAT	20g	SODIUM	360mg
SATURATED FAT	8g	FIBRE	–

Roasting meats

Because ovens vary considerably, use a meat thermometer to ensure that the meat has been thoroughly cooked inside. Place the meat thermometer into the thickest part of the cut. The following temperatures are guidelines.

Beef (on the bone)	60°C/140°F (rare)
	70°C/158°F (medium)
Beef (off the bone)	72°C/162°F (well-done)
Lamb (on the bone)	72°C/162°F (pink)
Lamb (off the bone)	75°C/168°F (well-done)
Pork	75°C/168°F

each side; turn the escalopes once, brushing them with marinade and sprinkling them with the remaining breadcrumbs.

Serve hot, accompanied, for example, with a tomato salad and a bowl of cold tartare sauce (see page 32).

KILOCALORIES	370	SUGARS	5g
TOTAL FAT	30g	SODIUM	340mg
SATURATED FAT	5g	FIBRE	1.5g

GRILLED LAMB ESCALOPES

Ask the butcher to cut each breast of lamb into two or three pieces and prepare them by shaving off as much fat as possible.

SERVES 4

2 breasts of lamb
2 medium-sized onions, coarsely chopped
1 medium-sized carrot, coarsely chopped
5 cm/2 in piece cinnamon stick
5 cm/2 in fresh root ginger, peeled
2 tbsp vinegar
4 tbsp fresh brown breadcrumbs

MARINADE
2 tbsp ground coriander
1 tbsp black pepper (or ½ tsp chilli powder)
½ tsp salt
4 garlic cloves, crushed
2 bay leaves, crumbled
2 tbsp vinegar
6 tbsp vegetable oil (approx)

Place the pieces of lamb in a large saucepan with the vegetables, spices and vinegar; add water to cover and bring slowly to the boil. Cover the pan and leave the contents to simmer for 1–1½ hours or until the bones come easily away from the meat. Remove from the heat and allow to cool. Lift the lamb from the stock, remove the bones from each piece, and pat the meat dry with kitchen paper.

Prepare the marinade by mixing together the ingredients; coat each piece of lamb thoroughly and set aside for 1 hour, turning occasionally. Lift the meat from the marinade and coat with about half the breadcrumbs, pressing them in firmly.

Set the lamb escalopes on a grill pan covered with foil and grill under fairly high heat for 3–5 minutes on

HUNTINGDON PIE

There is no immediate association between Huntingdonshire and ham with apricots, but the combination goes back to the seventeenth century when cured hams stuffed with fruit were popular at country fairs.

SERVES 4

1 thick gammon slice (approx 450 g/1 lb)
1–2 tbsp butter, melted
225 g/8 oz fresh apricots, halved and stoned (or
1 can apricots in natural juice)
1 medium-sized onion, thinly sliced
pepper
500–750 g/1–1½ lb potatoes, thinly sliced
300 ml/½ pt stock (approx)

Cut the rind and fat from the gammon and, if it is very thick, slice it through horizontally to give two thinner rashers. Lightly butter a shallow ovenproof dish just large enough to hold the gammon in a single layer. Lay the apricots over the gammon, the onion over the apricots, pepper well and place the potatoes on top.

Pour stock, or the juice from canned apricots mixed with water, into the dish – the liquid should just cover the apricots but not reach the potato layer. Cover the dish with a lid or foil and bake it near the top of an oven preheated to 190°C/375°F/gas 5 for about 1 hour. Remove the covering, brush the potatoes with a little melted butter and cook for a further 15 minutes.

Serve with, for example, green beans or Brussels sprouts sprinkled with toasted almond slivers.

KILOCALORIES	445	SUGARS	7g
TOTAL FAT	17g	SODIUM	1540mg
SATURATED FAT	9g	FIBRE	3g

Grill the kebabs under a hot grill for about 10–15 minutes, turning them at least once and brushing with the marinade.

Remove the bay leaves from the marinade and reheat it to serve as a sauce, with hot pitta bread or a crusty loaf.

KILOCALORIES	320	SUGARS	8g
TOTAL FAT	18g	SODIUM	200mg
SATURATED FAT	7g	FIBRE	1g

SOSATIES
Lamb kebabs

Sosaties (or sassaties) are a South African speciality resembling Middle Eastern kebabs, but the curry-flavoured marinade/sauce shows the strong influence of Indian and Malay cooking. The apricots are a South African contribution.

SERVES 6

1 kg/2 lb (approx) boned lean lamb (leg or shoulder)
200 g/7 oz canned apricot halves
in natural juice
2 medium-sized onions, finely chopped
2 garlic cloves, crushed
2–3 tbsp vegetable oil
1 tbsp curry powder
2–3 tbsp herb vinegar
1 tbsp brown sugar (optional)
pinch salt, black pepper
2 bay leaves

Cut the lamb into 2.5 cm/1 in cubes. Prepare the marinade by blending the apricots and juice to a purée; it should yield about 200 ml/7 fl oz.

Fry the onions and garlic in hot oil for 5 minutes until soft but not browned. Stir in the curry powder and cook for 1 minute; add the apricot purée, vinegar (sugar if used) and salt and pepper to taste. Remove from the heat and leave to cool.

Thread the meat on to wooden or bamboo skewers, place them in a shallow glass or glazed earthenware dish and pour over the marinade. Add the bay leaves and stand, covered, for about 8 hours, turning the kebabs occasionally.

MOUSSAKA

This version is made with minced beef and potatoes.

SERVES 4

350 g/12 oz lean minced beef (uncooked)
700–900 g/1½–2 lb potatoes
2 tbsp vegetable oil
1 medium-sized onion, finely chopped
1 garlic clove, crushed
1 tbsp plain flour
1 can (400 g/14 oz) tomatoes, chopped
2 tbsp tomato purée
1 tsp mixed herbs
pinch salt, pepper
300 ml/½ pt basic white sauce (see page 29)
1 small egg, beaten
50 g/2 oz Cheddar cheese, grated

Scrub the potatoes and boil them in their skins until just tender. Peel them when cool and cut into fairly thick slices. Fry the onion and garlic for about 5 minutes. Stir in the minced beef and fry until brown.

Stir the flour, tomatoes and their juices, tomato purée and herbs into the pan; bring the mixture to the boil while still stirring. Reduce the heat and simmer, uncovered, for 5 minutes; season.

Preheat the oven to 190°C/375°F/gas 5. Lightly grease a 1½ litre/2½ pt ovenproof dish and fill it with alternate layers of sliced potatoes and the minced beef mixture. Finish with a layer of potatoes. Stand the white sauce over low heat and blend in the egg and half the cheese. Pour over the moussaka and sprinkle the rest of the cheese on top. Bake for 45 minutes.

KILOCALORIES	680	SUGARS	12g
TOTAL FAT	33g	SODIUM	450mg
SATURATED FAT	13g	FIBRE	5g

STIR-FRIED LAMB'S LIVER

— • —

The Chinese are partial to pork, and pig's liver is a relatively expensive delicacy. To the British, lamb's liver, nutritious and economical, may be more palatable.

SERVES 4

450 g/1 lb lamb's liver
4 cm/1½ in fresh root ginger, peeled
4 tbsp vegetable (or groundnut) oil
8–10 spring onions, cut into 4 cm/1½ in pieces, white and green parts separated
1 tbsp medium-dry sherry (or Shao-hsing wine)

MARINADE
½ tsp salt
¼ tsp sugar
1 tbsp thick soya sauce
2 tsp medium-dry sherry (or Shao-hsing wine)
pepper
1½ tsp cornflour

SAUCE
1 tsp cornflour
2 tsp thick soya sauce
salt
4 tbsp water

Cut the liver into pieces about 5 cm/2 in wide and 6 mm/¼ in thick, discarding the membrane and any remaining gristle.

For the marinade, mix the salt, sugar, soya sauce and sherry or wine with a light seasoning of pepper. Coat the liver with the mixture and leave it to marinate for 45–60 minutes. Mix in the cornflour just prior to cooking.

Slice the ginger into narrow, thread-like strips. Prepare the sauce by mixing together flour, soya sauce, salt and water.

Set a wok over high heat until the smoke rises; add the oil and swirl it around, then throw in the ginger and let it sizzle for about 10 seconds before stirring in the white spring onion. Add the liver pieces and toss them for about 1 minute. Splash the sherry or wine in the wok, continuing to stir until the sizzling subsides. Lower the heat, push the liver to the sides of the wok, leaving a well in the centre, and pour in the sauce, stirring as it thickens. Stir the liver back in, tossing it until just cooked and still juicy.

Arrange the liver on a warm dish. Add the green spring onion to the wok and stir lightly to mop up the sauce. Spoon this on top of the liver and serve with plain boiled rice.

KILOCALORIES	350	SUGARS	2g
TOTAL FAT	25g	SODIUM	430mg
SATURATED FAT	4g	FIBRE	1g

BESENGEK DAGING
Boiled silverside in a spicy sauce

— • —

Silverside is a lean, economical joint, ideal for boiling and pot-roasting. For this spicy dish of Indonesian origin make sure that the meat has not been cured.

SERVES 4

450 g/1 lb silverside
1 slice terasi (optional) (see page 85)
½ tsp chilli powder
1 tsp ground coriander
½ tsp turmeric
1 tbsp vegetable oil
1 medium-sized onion, sliced
1 tsp brown sugar
2 tbsp tamarind water (optional) (see page 108)
pinch salt
600 ml/1 pt thick coconut milk (see page 111)

Wipe the meat, put it in a pan with water to cover, and bring slowly to the boil. Remove any scum, cover the pan with a lid and simmer gently for about 1 hour or until tender. Lift the beef from the cooking liquid; leave it to cool before slicing it into serving pieces. Strain the stock and set 300 ml/½ pt aside.

Crush the terasi (if used) with a spoon and mix it with the chilli, coriander and turmeric. Heat the oil in a large saucepan and sauté the onion for 2 minutes; add the spice mixture and stir-fry for another minute. Add the meat, the reserved stock, sugar, tamarind water (if used) and salt to taste. Bring slowly to the boil, cover the pan and let the meat simmer for 5 minutes, then add the coconut milk. Continue cooking, stirring occasionally, until the sauce has thickened (about 15 minutes).

Serve the meat in the spicy sauce, accompanied by boiled rice and a vegetable dish.

KILOCALORIES	270	SUGARS	10g
TOTAL FAT	9g	SODIUM	1290mg
SATURATED FAT	3g	FIBRE	0.5g

KIDNEYS SIMLA

Kidneys are an excellent source of iron and B vitamins. Serve as a light snack or breakfast dish; for a main course, increase the quantities by half.

SERVES 4

8 lambs' kidneys
2–3 tbsp vegetable oil
3–4 tsp English mustard
2–3 tsp Worcestershire sauce
3–4 tbsp low-fat plain yogurt
small bunch spring onions, finely chopped

Remove the suet from fresh kidneys. Peel the thin membrane from the kidneys, cut them in half horizontally and snip out the cores.

Heat the oil in a large frying-pan and cook the kidneys, turning them once, until lightly browned on the outside. Cover the pan with a lid, reduce the heat and cook for a further 5–8 minutes. Blend the mustard and Worcestershire sauce together; stir it into the pan to coat the kidneys evenly and cook for 2 minutes.

Stir in the yogurt and heat through without boiling. Serve the kidneys and the sauce at once, piled on to hot toast or with plain boiled rice; garnish with spring onions.

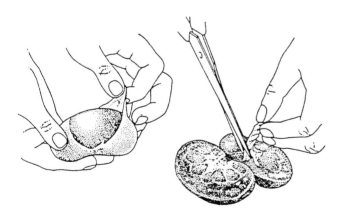

To prepare kidneys, peel away the outer thin membrane, cut them in half lengthwise and scissor out the white core

KILOCALORIES	300	SUGARS	5g
TOTAL FAT	16g	SODIUM	440mg
SATURATED FAT	3g	FIBRE	0.5g

COUSCOUS

This is the traditional dish of North Africa (see also page 130); it takes its name from the semolina grain which is the main ingredient.

SERVES 6–8

450 g/1 lb chicken portions
450 g/1 lb lean, boned lamb
2 tbsp vegetable oil
2 large onions, roughly chopped
cayenne pepper
pinch salt, pepper
450 g/1 lb couscous
100 g/4 oz canned chickpeas, drained and rinsed
75 g/3 oz sultanas (or raisins)
2 tbsp tomato purée
Tabasco sauce
50 g/2 oz butter (or margarine)
paprika (chilli powder or parsley)

Remove the skin and wipe the chicken pieces clean. Cut into serving portions. Cut the lamb into 2.5 cm/ 1 in cubes. Heat the oil in a large, heavy-based pan and brown the chicken and lamb in it. Add the onion and enough cold water to cover; season with cayenne, salt and pepper, cover the pan and bring to the boil. Reduce the heat and simmer the contents for about 45 minutes.

Meanwhile, sprinkle the couscous over a large flat dish and moisten it with water, working it through with the fingers a little at a time to keep the grains separate as they absorb the moisture; leave for about 15 minutes. Line a large steamer with muslin or cheesecloth and tip in the couscous.

Stir the chickpeas and sultanas or raisins into the meat with the tomato purée. Bring it back to the boil, then set the steamer on top and cover with a tight-fitting lid. Steam for about 30 minutes.

Stir Tabasco sauce to taste into the meat and correct the seasoning. Turn the meat into a serving dish. Tip the couscous into another dish, stir in the butter or margarine and sprinkle with paprika, chilli powder or chopped parsley. Alternatively, serve the couscous on a flat dish and top with the meat mixture; serve the cooking liquid as a sauce.

KILOCALORIES	470	SUGARS	9g
TOTAL FAT	19g	SODIUM	270mg
SATURATED FAT	8g	FIBRE	1g

VEAL STEW WITH MUSHROOMS AND TOMATOES

———— • ————

Because of its natural leanness, veal can be somewhat bland in flavour, though home-produced veal compares well with the more expensive imports.

SERVES 4

450 g/1lb stewing veal
1 tbsp vegetable oil
1 large onion, chopped
1 can tomatoes (400 g/14 oz), coarsely chopped
100 g/4 oz mushrooms, thinly sliced
pinch salt, pepper
1 tbsp parsley, finely chopped
grated lemon rind

Wipe the veal and cut it into 2 cm/³⁄₄ in cubes. Heat the oil and fry the veal for a few minutes to seal it. Lift it out with a slotted spoon; add the onion to the pan and fry it for 5–8 minutes until golden-brown. Stir in the tomatoes with their juice, bring to the boil and return the meat to the pan over a simmer.

Add the mushrooms, cover the pan and simmer for 1½ hours; season to taste with salt and pepper, add the parsley and a little lemon rind. Simmer for another 5 minutes.

Serve the veal stew with potatoes, and a green vegetable, or with noodles.

KILOCALORIES	180	SUGARS	4g
TOTAL FAT	7g	SODIUM	260mg
SATURATED FAT	2g	FIBRE	1.5g

LAMB AND MANGO CURRY

———— • ————

Curries are not exclusively from the East. South African versions typically include fruit, often apricots or raisins.

SERVES 4

1 kg/2½ lb (approx) neck end of lamb
50 g/2 oz dried apricots
1–2 tbsp vegetable oil
225 g/8 oz onions, thinly sliced
4 tsp curry powder
1 tbsp wholemeal flour
300 ml/½ pt hot water (approx)
1 bouquet garni (see page 17)
1 tsp powdered cinnamon
1 small cooking apple, peeled, cored and
coarsely grated
2 tbsp mango chutney
1 tbsp tomato purée
pinch salt

Have the lamb cut into single rib sections; trim away as much fat as possible, then wash and dry them thoroughly. Meanwhile, soak the apricots.

Heat the oil in a large, heavy-based pan, add the lamb, a few pieces at a time, and fry over fairly brisk heat until browned. Lift out the pieces as they are finished. Add the onions to the pan and fry for about 5 minutes or until golden. Stir in the curry powder, cooking it through for 2 minutes before adding the flour. Stir constantly for a couple of minutes, then gradually blend in the hot water.

Add the bouquet garni, cinnamon, the drained and chopped apricots, the apple, chutney, tomato purée and salt. Bring the sauce to the boil, stirring constantly. Put the lamb back into the pan and cover the pieces with the sauce. Cover the pan with a lid, reduce the heat and simmer for about 1½ hours, stirring occasionally. Remove the bouquet garni.

Cool the curry and refrigerate it, covered, until a layer of fat has solidified on top. Remove the fat and reheat the curry before serving.

Serve with side dishes of lightly toasted coconut, yogurt mixed with grated cucumber and a hint of garlic, tomato and onion salad, and bananas sprinkled with lemon juice.

KILOCALORIES	730	SUGARS	11g
TOTAL FAT	38g	SODIUM	590mg
SATURATED FAT	15g	FIBRE	3g

Cover the casserole and cook in an oven preheated to 150°C/300°F/gas 2 for 2¼–2½ hours or until the meat is tender. Cut the French loaf into thick slices, spread one side with mustard, and place them, mustard side down, over the meat. Alternatively, prepare horseradish dumplings (see below) and add them to the casserole after 2 hours.

Increase the oven temperature to 200°C/400°F/gas 6; return the casserole, without the lid, and cook for 20–25 minutes or until the bread is crisp and brown.

Serve straight from the dish with baked or mashed potatoes and a green salad.

KILOCALORIES	520	SUGARS	8g
TOTAL FAT	24g	SODIUM	500mg
SATURATED FAT	5g	FIBRE	1.5g

CARBONADE OF BEEF
— • —

Also known as Flemish stew, this is one of Belgium's national dishes. Brown or pale ale imparts the characteristic flavour and rich brown gravy. It is traditionally topped with mustard-spread bread but horseradish dumplings (see right) are just as good.

SERVES 4

750 g/1½ lb lean beef (chuck or shin),
trimmed and cubed
25 g/1 oz seasoned flour
4 tbsp vegetable oil
2 large onions, thinly sliced
2 garlic cloves, crushed
450 ml/¾ pt brown (or pale) ale
stock or water (if necessary)
1 tsp brown sugar
1 tsp wine vinegar
1 bouquet garni (see page 17)
pinch salt, pepper
½ French loaf
1–2 tbsp French mustard
parsley, finely chopped

Toss the beef in seasoned flour. Heat half the oil in a large, heavy-based fireproof casserole and fry the onions and garlic until soft and golden; remove and reserve them. Add the remaining oil and fry the meat until browned. Blend in any remaining flour, return the onions and garlic to the casserole and gradually stir in the ale; add a little water or stock if necessary to just cover the meat. Mix in the sugar, vinegar and the bouquet garni; season with salt and pepper.

HORSERADISH DUMPLINGS
— • —

MAKES 12

50 g/2 oz fine breadcrumbs
50 g/2 oz self-raising flour, sifted
½ tsp each paprika and salt
40 g/1½ oz shredded suet
2 tbsp grated horseradish
1 tbsp semi-skimmed milk
1 egg, beaten

Mix the breadcrumbs, flour and seasonings; then stir in the suet, and the horseradish blended with the milk. Bind with a little beaten egg to a soft but not sticky dough. Divide the mixture into 12 walnut-sized balls and add them to any kind of beef stew or casserole. The stew should be at boiling point when the dumplings are added. Cover the dish and reduce the heat to a simmer for 30-40 minutes or until the dumplings are light and fluffy. Serve them sprinkled with chopped parsley.

[Nutritional values are per dumpling.]

KILOCALORIES	65	SUGARS	–
TOTAL FAT	4g	SODIUM	140mg
SATURATED FAT	2g	FIBRE	0.5g

Please see the introduction for a full explanation of the nutritional factboxes.

PAPER-WRAPPED PORK

Although this is rather a fiddly dish to prepare, the delicious end justifies the means. The greaseproof paper-bags allow the marinated pork to be deep-fried yet remain juicy.

SERVES 4

550 g/1¼ lb pork (neck, blade or leg)
vegetable (or groundnut) oil for deep-frying
egg white

MARINADE
12 garlic cloves, roughly chopped
4 cm/1½ in piece fresh root ginger, peeled and roughly chopped
1 green (or red) chilli, deseeded and roughly chopped (optional)
¾ tsp salt
¾ tsp sugar
1 tbsp thin soya sauce
2 tbsp gin (or Mei-kuei-lu wine)
1½ tsp potato flour (or cornflour)

Pat the pork dry (the fat can be left on or trimmed; if left on it becomes succulent when deep-fried). Cut the meat into 2.5–4 cm/1–1½ in chunks.

For the marinade, half-fill a wok or deep-fryer with oil and heat to 180°C/350°F, or until a cube of stale bread browns in 60 seconds. Put the garlic and ginger in a small metal sieve, lower it into the oil and fry until the garlic takes colour; lift out the sieve. When the garlic and ginger are cool, add them to the pork in a bowl with the rest of the marinade ingredients, mixing thoroughly. Let the pork marinate in the fridge for 4–5 hours or overnight.

Brush the inside of two greaseproof bags, 20 cm/8 in square, with a little oil. Put half the pork mixture into each bag, horizontally in one layer. Fold down the opening and seal with a little egg white. Reheat the oil in the wok or deep-fryer to 190°C/375°F. Tip the bags gently into the oil and deep-fry them for 8–10 minutes, turning them over periodically and taking care not to pierce them as they puff up.

Remove the bags, slit them open and serve the pork at once, accompanied with plain rice.

KILOCALORIES	475	SUGARS	1g
TOTAL FAT	36g	SODIUM	360mg
SATURATED FAT	4g	FIBRE	0.5g

BRAISED LIVER WITH ORANGE AND RAISINS

Liver is one of the most nutritious meats, a rich source of iron, vitamin A and most of the B vitamins. Lamb's liver has a milder flavour than pig's liver.

SERVES 4

450 g/1 lb lamb's (or pig's) liver
milk or water, for soaking
flour
pinch salt, pepper
2–3 tbsp vegetable oil
1 medium-sized onion, chopped
1 carrot, thinly sliced
1 large celery stick, sliced
1 small aubergine, diced
25 g/1 oz seedless raisins
1 tsp orange peel, finely chopped
1 bouquet garni (see page 17)
5 tbsp water

Wash the liver, cut it into 6 mm/¼ in slices and snip out any gristle. Leave the slices to soak for 1 hour in enough milk or water to cover them. Coat the liver lightly with flour, seasoned with salt and pepper.

Heat the oil in a frying-pan over medium heat and fry the liver briefly to brown it, turning the slices once. Remove from the pan and set aside. Add the prepared vegetables to the pan and fry, covered, over gentle heat for 10–15 minutes or until they are soft.

Preheat the oven to 190°C/375°F/gas 5. Spread the vegetable mixture in a lightly greased ovenproof dish, measuring about 25 × 20 cm/10 × 8 in. Mix in the raisins and orange peel and add the bouquet garni.

Arrange the liver slices on top and spoon in the water. Cover the dish with a lid or a double thickness of baking foil. Bake for 45 minutes just above the centre of the oven.

Remove the bouquet garni and serve the liver and vegetables while still hot, with creamed potatoes and a green vegetable.

KILOCALORIES	390	SUGARS	7g
TOTAL FAT	22g	SODIUM	340mg
SATURATED FAT	4g	FIBRE	2g

Please see the introduction for a full explanation of the nutritional factboxes.

Pork in Jalousie Pastry

A pastry case makes a little meat go a long way and uses up the remains of a roast.

Serves 4–6

350 g/12 oz lean cooked pork, diced
2 tbsp vegetable oil
1 medium-sized onion, finely chopped
3 tbsp flour
300 ml/½ pt stock
2 tbsp apple chutney (or 1 large cooking apple,
peeled and coarsely grated)
pinch salt, pepper
375 g/13 oz packet frozen puff pastry, thawed
1 small egg, beaten or milk, to glaze

Heat the oil in a heavy-based pan over medium heat; fry the onion for 8–10 minutes until golden and soft. Stir in the flour, cook through for 2 minutes, then gradually blend in the stock to make a smooth sauce. Add the diced pork to the pan, with chutney or grated apple, salt and pepper. Simmer for 5 minutes, then remove it from the heat and leave it to cool completely, with a piece of wet greaseproof paper pressed against the surface to prevent a skin forming.

Roll out the pastry to an oblong that measures about 28 × 30 cm/11 × 12 in; divide it in two and put one half on a wet baking sheet. Spread the pork mixture to within 2.5cm/1 in of the edges. Fold the other pastry piece in half and snip with scissors along the fold like a comb, stopping short 2.5 cm/1 in of the edges. Open the pastry out and place it over the filling, moistening the edges and pressing them lightly to create a seal.

Brush the pastry with beaten egg or milk and bake towards the top of the oven preheated to 220°C/425°F/gas 7 for 15 minutes; lower the heat to 190°C/375°F/gas 5 and bake for another 20–25 minutes or until the pastry is golden and well puffed.

Serve hot, accompanied by carrots and a green vegetable.

KILOCALORIES	565	SUGARS	8g
TOTAL FAT	29g	SODIUM	550mg
SATURATED FAT	3g	FIBRE	1g

Kheema Curry

Kheema is the Indian term for minced meat, either lamb or beef, which is used in numerous combinations with vegetables and spices, mild or hot according to individual taste.

Serves 4

450 g/1 lb lean minced beef
75 g/3 oz split peas
2 tbsp vegetable oil
1 large onion, finely chopped
2 garlic cloves, crushed
2.5cm/1 in piece fresh root ginger, peeled
and finely chopped
½ tsp ground turmeric
2 tsp ground coriander
1 tsp ground cumin
½ tsp chilli powder (optional)
1 tbsp lemon juice
pinch salt
150 ml/¼ pint hot water
garam masala (optional)

Rinse the split peas in several changes of water; cover them with cold water and leave to soak overnight. Rinse and cover with fresh water; bring to the boil and cook for at least 10 minutes.

Heat the oil in a large, heavy-based pan and fry the onion, garlic and ginger for 5–8 minutes or until golden; stir in the turmeric, coriander, cumin and chilli powder if used. Stir-fry for 1 minute, then add the lemon juice; when it sizzles, stir in the meat and cook until browned. Add the salt.

Drain the split peas and add them to the pan with the hot water. Bring to boiling point, cover the pan and lower the heat to a simmer; cook until the meat is tender (about 30 minutes). Stir occasionally.

Spoon the curry into a warmed serving dish, sprinkle the top with a little garam masala if liked, and serve with plain boiled rice and chutney.

KILOCALORIES	340	SUGARS	2g
TOTAL FAT	25g	SODIUM	200mg
SATURATED FAT	9g	FIBRE	1g

off the heat. Return the pan to the heat and warm through. Serve sprinkled with parsley and grated cheese.

KILOCALORIES	540	SUGARS	15g
TOTAL FAT	34g	SODIUM	1620mg
SATURATED FAT	15g	FIBRE	2.5g

OXTAIL STEW

Oxtail, sold skinned and jointed, is inexpensive.

SERVES 4

1 oxtail (1 kg/2 lb approx), jointed
2–3 tbsp seasoned flour
2–3 tbsp vegetable oil
2 medium-sized onions, thinly sliced
3 medium-sized carrots, sliced
225 g/8 oz turnips, cubed
1 can (400 g/14 oz) tomatoes, chopped
900 ml/1½ pt (approx) brown stock (or water)
1 small onion
3–6 cloves
1 bouquet garni (see page 17)
pinch salt, pepper
parsley, finely chopped

Trim excess fat from the oxtail, wash it thoroughly and plunge the pieces into a large pan of boiling water; blanch for 3 minutes. Drain and rinse the oxtail and dry the pieces on kitchen paper. Toss them in seasoned flour and fry them briefly in heated oil in a large, heavy-based pan. Remove them from the pan.

Fry the sliced onions, carrots and turnips for about 8 minutes; stir in the remaining seasoned flour and return the oxtail to the pan. Add the tomatoes and their juice, and enough stock to cover the meat.

Stud the small onion with the cloves and add to the stew with the bouquet garni; season to taste. Cover the pan and simmer over gentle heat for 3½ hours or until the meat comes easily away from the bones.

Remove the clove-studded onion and bouquet garni and leave the stew to cool completely. Remove the excess fat from the surface before the stew is reheated. Serve sprinkled with parsley and accompanied by jacket potatoes.

MEXICAN SKILLET

Use well-flavoured and coarse-textured butcher's sausages for this fiery Mexican dish.

SERVES 4

8 pork sausages
2 tbsp butter (or vegetable oil)
1 medium-sized onion, thinly sliced
1 green pepper, deseeded and cut into strips
1–2 tsp chilli powder
175 g/6 oz macaroni, cooked and drained
1 can (400 g/14 oz) tomatoes, roughly chopped
2 tbsp tomato purée
1 tsp basil
50 ml/2 fl oz stock
1 tbsp brown sugar
pinch salt, pepper
150 ml/5 fl oz low-fat plain yogurt
chopped parsley, grated cheese

Prick the sausages with a fork and grill them until brown. Heat the butter or oil in a deep frying-pan and add the onion and green pepper; fry for a few minutes until just softened, then stir in the chilli powder, the macaroni, sausages, tomatoes with their juice, the tomato purée, basil, stock, sugar and seasoning.

Cover the pan and simmer for 10 minutes. Whisk the yogurt and the milk together and stir it into the pan

KILOCALORIES	765	SUGARS	11g
TOTAL FAT	39g	SODIUM	980mg
SATURATED FAT	13g	FIBRE	4.5g

STIR-FRIED BEEF ON RICE STICKS

— • —

Packets of dry rice sticks (also known as rice noodles) can be bought from Chinese stores.

SERVES 4

450 g/1 lb rump steak
3–4 tbsp vegetable (or groundnut) oil for deep-frying
40 g/1½ oz rice sticks, broken into short lengths
4 garlic cloves, finely chopped
3 spring onions, trimmed into 2.5 cm/1 in sections,
white and green parts separated
2–3 celery sticks, thinly sliced
1 tbsp medium-dry sherry (or Shao-hsing wine)
1–2 tsp sesame oil

MARINADE
pinch salt, pepper
½ tsp sugar
1 tbsp thick soya sauce
2 tsp medium-dry sherry (or Shao-hsing wine)
1½ tsp potato flour
2 tbsp water
2 tsp vegetable (or groundnut oil)

SAUCE
1 tsp potato flour (or cornflour)
5 tbsp water
1 tbsp thick soya sauce

Wipe the meat dry and cut it across the grain into strips about 6.5 cm/2½ in long and 1 cm/½ in thick. Mix the marinade ingredients (except the oil), add the beef, and leave to marinate in the fridge for 30 minutes. Blend in the oil.

Prepare the sauce by dissolving the potato flour or cornflour in the water and adding the soya sauce.

Half-fill a wok or deep-fryer with oil and heat it to 180°C/350°F or until a rice stick dropped into it rises to the surface immediately. Lower the rice sticks into the hot oil; they will sink to the bottom, then rise to the surface, expanding into a white woven mass. Press them gently down once with a slotted spoon; then remove them from the oil and drain on kitchen paper. Keep them warm.

Reheat the oil to the same temperature; add the beef, separating the pieces with a wooden spoon. Fry for about 20 seconds, then remove immediately. Pour off the oil, leaving about 4 tablespoonfuls.

Reheat the oil over high heat until smoking. Add the garlic and, as soon as it sizzles and takes on colour, stir in the white spring onions, followed by the celery; stir about 10 times. Return the beef to the wok and toss the mixture for about 20 seconds. Splash in the wine around the side of the wok, continuing to stir. When the sizzling dies down, lower the heat and pour in the sauce, continuing to stir as it thickens. Mix in the green spring onion.

Remove the beef mixture from the wok and spread it over the rice sticks; serve, sprinkled with sesame oil.

KILOCALORIES	420	SUGARS	2g
TOTAL FAT	24g	SODIUM	180mg
SATURATED FAT	6g	FIBRE	1g

CASSEROLED LAMB ON THE BONE

Knuckle of leg or of shoulder is especially good; other suitable cuts are middle neck or shoulder. Ask the butcher to cut it in slices across the bone and trim off any chunks of fat.

SERVES 4–6

1.5 kg/3 lb lamb on the bone
2 tsp dried oregano (or thyme)
pinch salt, pepper
4 tbsp vegetable oil
2 large onions, roughly chopped
5 cm/2 in piece cinnamon stick
2 tsp ground cumin
1 tbsp vinegar
1 can (400 g/14 oz) tomatoes, finely chopped

Heat the oven to 180°C/350°F/gas 4. Trim all excess fat from the lamb slices, wipe them clean and arrange them in a large casserole; sprinkle with oregano or thyme, a little salt and half the oil. Place the casserole, uncovered, in the oven and cook for 20 minutes or until the meat is sealed and slightly crisped on the outside.

Heat the remaining oil in a pan and fry the onions for 8–10 minutes until soft and transparent; break the cinnamon stick into a few splinters and add to the onions (or add ground cinnamon to taste). Lower the heat, add the cumin and stir-fry for 1–2 minutes. Stir in the vinegar and the tomatoes with their juice.

Remove the casserole from the oven, pour the sauce over the lamb pieces and mix well; cover the dish tightly with a lid and return it to the oven. Lower the oven temperature to 150°C/300°F/gas 2 and cook for 2 hours. The casserole lid can be removed for the last 20 minutes to brown the meat.

Serve with boiled rice or potatoes, and cabbage.

KILOCALORIES	650	SUGARS	4g
TOTAL FAT	41g	SODIUM	400mg
SATURATED FAT	15g	FIBRE	1g

Coconut milk Also known as santen, it consists of water and oils extracted from the grated flesh. Do not allow recipes containing coconut milk to boil as it will curdle. Use within 24 hours. Coconut milk can also be made from desiccated or creamed coconut. (See also page 111.)

SATÉ PENTUL
Minced pork saté

In Indonesian cooking, saté is the name for skewers of grilled meat or poultry. They are grilled on bamboo skewers over charcoal and are suitable for barbecue cooking.

SERVES 4

450 g/1 lb leg or fillet of pork
3 garlic cloves, crushed
½ tsp chilli powder
1 tsp ground ginger
1 tsp coriander seeds, roasted and crushed
1 tsp brown sugar
2 tsp soya sauce
1 tbsp lemon (or lime) juice
6 tbsp thick coconut milk (see page 111)
2 tbsp desiccated coconut
pinch salt
1 large egg, beaten

Mince the pork, including a little of the fat. Pound the garlic, chilli, ginger, coriander, sugar, soya sauce and lemon or lime juice to a paste. Put about half a teaspoonful of this mixture into a bowl with 3 tablespoonfuls of the coconut milk and leave, covered, in a cool place until the saté is ready for grilling.

Mix the remaining spice mixture and the rest of the coconut milk into the minced meat, add the coconut and season to taste with salt. Bind the mixture with the egg and shape it into walnut-sized balls. Thread four meatballs on to each skewer just before you are ready to grill. The saté mixture can be made several hours ahead, but should then not be threaded on to skewers or moulded – otherwise the balls will tend to fall off.

Place the skewers on the grill pan under medium heat, turning them carefully from time to time. After 4–5 minutes, when the meat balls should be half-cooked, brush them with the spiced coconut milk and continue grilling until they are golden-brown.

Serve the saté with peanut sauce (see next recipe) or simply by themselves, accompanied perhaps by a green salad.

KILOCALORIES	230	SUGARS	3g
TOTAL FAT	12g	SODIUM	240mg
SATURATED FAT	6g	FIBRE	0.5g

LAMB SATAY

Satay is the Malay equivalent of the Indonesian saté and can be barbecued or cooked under a gas or electric grill. Peanut sauce is the usual accompaniment, and both this and the spiced meat can be prepared in advance and stored for up to 1 month in the freezer. Allow at least 8 hours to thaw before threading the meat on skewers and grilling them.

SERVES 4

750 g/1½ lb lean leg of lamb
1 tsp each of cumin, fennel and coriander seeds
6 shallots or 3 small onions, finely chopped
2 garlic cloves, crushed
1 stem fresh (or ½ tsp powdered) lemon grass
3 almonds (or cashews), blanched
½ tsp each of turmeric and chilli powder
1 tbsp soya sauce
1 tsp brown sugar
pinch salt

PEANUT SAUCE

100 g/4 oz peanuts (or ⅓ of a 350 g/12 oz jar
of crunchy peanut butter)
4 shallots, finely chopped
2 garlic cloves
½ tsp terasi (see below)
6 cashews (or almonds), blanched
2 stems fresh (or 1 tsp powdered) lemon grass
3 tbsp coconut (or peanut) oil
1–2 tsp chilli powder
300 ml/½ pint thick coconut milk (see page 111)
4 tbsp tamarind water (see page 108)
1 tbsp brown sugar
pinch salt

Cut the meat into 1 cm/½ in cubes and place them in a bowl. Dry-fry the cumin, fennel and coriander seeds for a few minutes over medium heat until they begin to splutter; then grind or pound them to a powder. Put the shallots or onions, garlic, fresh lemon grass which has been bruised and roughly chopped (or powdered lemon grass), with the nuts in a liquidiser or food processor and reduce to a paste. Grind or pound the nuts until fine, and stir them, together with the turmeric, chilli powder and soya sauce into the shallot mixture. Sprinkle the lamb pieces with sugar and a little salt, then mix them thoroughly with the paste until they are well coated. Leave for at least 4 hours to marinate.

For the sauce, roast the peanuts in a hot oven (200°C/400°F/gas 6) for about 10 minutes. Rub off the skins in a tea towel and grind the peanuts for a few seconds in a liquidiser or food processor; do not reduce them to a powder as this would spoil the consistency of the sauce (or use the crunchy peanut butter). Grind or pound the shallots and garlic with the terasi, then grind or pound the cashews or almonds and lemon grass together.

Fry the onion mixture in hot oil for a few minutes, then add the nut and lemon grass paste. Reduce the heat, add chilli powder to taste, and stir-fry for 2 minutes. Stirring constantly, add the coconut milk and bring the mixture almost to the boil; reduce the heat, stir in the tamarind water, sugar and ground peanuts. Season to taste with salt. Cook the sauce for 2–3 minutes, stirring frequently until it thickens.

Thread five meat cubes on to each bamboo skewer – soak these first in water to prevent burning; place the satay on a foil-covered grill pan under a hot grill or over a barbecue; brush with a little coconut or peanut oil and grill for 8–10 minutes or until cooked. Turn the skewers once or twice, brushing with a little more oil. Arrange the lamb satay on a warm serving dish, with chunks of cucumber and onion, and pour the hot peanut sauce into a bowl. Serve as a starter, or with plain boiled rice for a main course.

KILOCALORIES	585	SUGARS	15g
TOTAL FAT	37g	SODIUM	450mg
SATURATED FAT	16g	FIBRE	3g

Terasi Also known as blachan and an important flavouring in Far Eastern cookery. Made from salted and dried shrimps or prawns and with a pungent aroma. Available as cakes, powders or pastes and fried with other spices; store blocks of terasi in the fridge and keep them closely wrapped in foil to prevent the strong aroma pervading other foods.

Lemon grass Also known as sereh and used in Indonesian cooking to impart a lemon-like flavour. Available as dried grass blades or as a powder and used in minute quantities for flavouring.

Set the wrapped steaks on a greased baking sheet, apricots on top, and give the parcels a final brush with butter. Bake in the centre of the oven preheated to 180°C/350°F/gas 4 for 30–35 minutes or until the pastry is golden and crisp and the meat tender and moist.

Serve at once, with tiny new potatoes and a purée of peas and herbs (see page 154) or a green salad.

KILOCALORIES	440	SUGARS	9g
TOTAL FAT	24g	SODIUM	820mg
SATURATED FAT	10g	FIBRE	2.5g

VALENTINE LAMB STEAKS IN FILO PASTRY

— • —

Valentine steaks are a cut of lamb taken from the loin. Two chops are cut in a single piece, the bones removed and the chops almost – but not quite – cut in two; when the meat is opened out the two halves form a heart-shaped steak, hence the name. A wrapping of filo pastry makes a delightful contrast to the meat.

SERVES 4

4 Valentine lamb steaks
pinch salt, pepper
75 g/3 oz dried apricot halves
1 tbsp fresh mint, finely chopped (or 2 tsp dried mint)
12 sheets filo pastry
75 g/3 oz melted butter

If necessary, remove excess fat and any skin from the lamb steaks, and season them with salt and pepper. Rinse and dry the apricots, and arrange them evenly over the steaks; sprinkle with the mint.

Keep the pastry wrapped in the fridge while each sheet is prepared. Lay one pastry sheet on a board, brush it with melted butter and cover it with a second, then a third sheet, brushing each, including the top sheet, with butter. Make three more piles in the same way. Place a lamb steak at one corner of a pastry pile and wrap it, folding in the sides and brushing with melted butter where the bottom, unbuttered pastry sheet touches and overlaps. Make parcels in this way with the other steaks.

LAMB AND DATE RISSOLES

— • —

This mildly spiced dish of Persian origin makes a little meat go a long way. Fresh dates impart an interesting piquant touch.

SERVES 4

450 g/1 lb lean minced lamb
1 large onion, grated or finely chopped
1 large potato, grated or finely chopped
1 garlic clove, crushed
5 fresh dates, skinned, stoned and finely chopped
1 tsp ground cinnamon
¼ tsp allspice
2 tbsp chickpea flour (or plain flour)
pinch salt, pepper
1 egg, beaten
3 tbsp vegetable oil

Mix the minced lamb with the onion, potato, garlic and chopped dates; stir in the spices and flour and season to taste. Bind the mixture with the lightly beaten egg, working it in with the hands.

Heat the oil over medium heat in a large frying-pan; shape the minced lamb mixture into 'burgers' and fry them for about 8 minutes, or until brown, turning them once.

Serve hot, accompanied by plain boiled rice and a vegetable dish.

KILOCALORIES	430	SUGARS	12g
TOTAL FAT	22g	SODIUM	220mg
SATURATED FAT	7g	FIBRE	2g

press the meat. Leave in the fridge until set.

To serve, dip the tin briefly in hot water, unmould it on to a dish, and serve with salads and mayonnaise.

KILOCALORIES	275	SUGARS	–
TOTAL FAT	10g	SODIUM	370mg
SATURATED FAT	3g	FIBRE	–

PORK SPARE RIBS NORMANDY-STYLE

Barbecued spare ribs are typical of American-Chinese cuisine, while Normandy is famous for apples, cider and cream.

SERVES 4

4 pork spare rib chops
40 g/1½ oz seasoned flour
2 tbsp vegetable oil
1 medium-sized onion, coarsely chopped
3–4 firm dessert apples, peeled and quartered
300 ml/½ pt dry cider
pinch salt, pepper and nutmeg
5 tbsp low-fat plain yogurt (or single cream)
spring onions or chives, chopped

Trim the rind and fat from the chops and coat them with seasoned flour; reserve the excess flour. Heat the oil in a frying-pan over medium heat and fry the chops on both sides until golden. Transfer them to an ovenproof casserole.

Preheat the oven to 165°C/325°F/gas 3. Fry the onion in the pan for 5 minutes, until golden, then add the apples. Stir in the reserved flour and the cider. Add salt, pepper and nutmeg to taste, bring the sauce to the boil and cook gently for 1 minute.

Pour the sauce over the chops, cover the dish and cook in the oven for 1–1¼ hours. Skim off the fat and pour the sauce into a small pan; boil it rapidly for 2–3 minutes to reduce it slightly, then stir in the yogurt or cream.

Serve the chops with the sauce poured ·over them and sprinkled with chopped spring onion or chives.

KILOCALORIES	540	SUGARS	17g
TOTAL FAT	25g	SODIUM	490mg
SATURATED FAT	6g	FIBRE	2.5g

POTTED VEAL AND CHICKEN

Forerunners to pâtés and terrines, potted meat, game and fish were formerly extremely popular.

SERVES 4–6

300 ml/½ pt strong chicken stock (see page 17)
2 tsp powdered gelatine
pinch salt, pepper
600 g/1½ lb boned and skinned chicken, preferably breast
225 g/8 oz veal, thinly sliced
3 sprigs fresh tarragon, chopped (or 2 tsp dried)

Bring the stock gently to the boil in a saucepan; remove from the heat. Sprinkle the gelatine on to the stock, stirring until it dissolves. Season to taste.

Cut the chicken into small pieces and beat the veal slices into thin escalopes. Line the bottom and sides of a 500 g/1 lb loaf tin or mould with the veal slices. Add the chicken pieces, packing them into the tin, with tarragon leaves between the layers. Cover the meat with the stock and set the tin in a roasting pan, with hot water coming halfway up the sides. Cover the top of the tin loosely with foil.

Bake in the oven (preheated to 190°C/375°F/gas 5) for 1 hour. Leave it to cool completely. Cover with fresh foil and set a weighted plate or loaf tin on top to

Sunday Brunches

Elisabeth Lambart Ortiz

Brunch is a felicitous American invention described in the dictionary as a meal eaten late in the morning as a combination of breakfast and lunch. The term has taken on a wider meaning, and it is quite feasible in New York to be invited for brunch at 1 pm – an hour which might alarm some purists.

Brunch is naturally associated with Sunday since few people have a full breakfast on a weekday. It has also to some extent replaced the earlier tradition which decreed a great midday dinner of roast beef and Yorkshire pudding. Brunch is the type of meal which busy, hard-working people like to indulge in on a Sunday morning: getting up late, browsing through the Sunday papers and telescoping breakfast and lunch into one meal. In one sense, brunch echoes breakfast as it used to be in great English country houses, served in butlered and housemaided dining-rooms where silver covers hid heaped-up kedgeree, delicately pink lambs' kidneys, soft piles of scrambled eggs flanked by thinly sliced smoked salmon, and whole hams on great platters inviting the carver's knife. Toast was always freshly made, as were the tea and coffee.

The spirit, if not the scale, can be achieved without butler and silver cover, and a brunch party can be an elegant yet inexpensive way to entertain friends on a Sunday. Because of their connotations, brunch dishes are generally eggy and light. The drinks, too, are undemanding: Bloody Mary is a great favourite, as is Buck's Fizz (also called California Sunshine), and there is no need to spend money on champagne: a good sparkling white wine is perfectly acceptable for mixing with orange juice. Screwdrivers or rum punch are other good choices, or lightly chilled wine, a wine cup or ice-cold beer. There must, of course, be plenty of hot, freshly made tea and coffee.

Though brunch can be served to as many as space permits, six or eight is about right – enough for lively conversation, and not too much work. The wise host or hostess will invite no more guests than can be seated comfortably at table. Avoid an elaborate menu, though it can include unusual dishes.

The season will usually dictate the menu, as out-of-season foods are expensive and often not at their best. Starters could be small melons or papayas with lemon juice, cooked dried apricots and prunes served lightly chilled, mixed dried fruit or fresh fruit compote, peeled, sliced and lightly sugared oranges drizzled with orange liqueur. (Any of these starters could instead be served as the conclusion to the meal.) Soup, hot in winter and chilled in summer, is also an excellent starter. The following recipes, to serve 6–8 people, are but a small selection to stimulate the imagination.

CARNE FIAMBRE

This beef, ham and prawn sausage from the Dominican Republic could be the centrepiece of the brunch buffet, served, perhaps, with a potato salad.

SERVES 6–8

450 g/1 lb lean minced beef
100 g/4 oz lean boiled ham, coarsely chopped
225 g/8 oz peeled prawns, coarsely chopped
1 medium-sized onion, coarsely chopped
1 garlic clove, chopped
1–2 red (or green) chillies, deseeded and chopped
pinch salt, pepper
3 eggs
175 g/6 oz cream crackers
stock (or water)

Combine the beef, ham, prawns, onion, garlic, chillies, salt, pepper and two lightly beaten eggs in a food processor. Process the mixture to a moderately fine texture.

Reduce the cream crackers to a fine crumb with a rolling pin and little by little beat a good half of them into the mixture until it is firm enough to hold its shape (add more crumbs if necessary). Shape the meat into a roll about 25 cm long and 7.5 cm in diameter (10 × 3 in); wrap it in greaseproof paper or foil and chill it for about 2 hours.

Cover a large piece of greaseproof paper with the remaining crumbs. Beat the third egg thoroughly. Roll the sausage in the crumbs, pressing them in, then dip it in the egg before coating it once more with cracker crumbs. Wrap the sausage in a double thickness of butter muslin or fine cheesecloth; tie the ends securely with string.

Put the sausage in a heavy-based casserole large enough to hold it comfortably. Pour in enough hot water or stock to cover it by 5 cm/2 in, cover the pan and cook over moderate heat for 1 hour, or until the sausage is firm. Carefully lift it out of the casserole.

Let it cool thoroughly before removing the muslin, and transfer to a serving platter. Cut into slices.

KILOCALORIES	340	SUGARS	1g
TOTAL FAT	18g	SODIUM	540mg
SATURATED FAT	5g	FIBRE	1g

(V) This symbol denotes a recipe suitable for vegetarians.

SPINACH ROULADE

This dish makes a good accompaniment to drinks, or in larger slices an unusual first course.

SERVES 6–8

700 g/1½ lb fresh spinach
100 g/4 oz butter (or margarine)
25 g/1 oz plain flour
350 ml/12 fl oz semi-skimmed milk
½ tsp each salt and white pepper
¼ tsp grated nutmeg
4 large eggs, separated
100 g/4 oz mushrooms, sliced
100 g/4 oz ham, finely chopped
75 g/3 oz cream cheese
75 ml/3 fl oz soured cream
pinch salt, pepper

Drop the washed spinach, with only the water that clings to it, into a large saucepan; cook briskly for 2 minutes. Drain and squeeze the spinach; chop it coarsely and set it aside.

Line a baking tin (35 × 5 × 23 cm/14 × 2 × 9 in) with parchment paper or greased greaseproof paper. Preheat the oven to 180°C/350°F/gas 4.

Melt half the butter, stir in the flour and cook over a low heat for 2 minutes, gradually stir in the milk until the sauce is smooth. Add the salt, white pepper and nutmeg and cook, stirring, for 5 minutes. Off the heat, stir in the egg yolks, one by one, then mix in the spinach. Beat the egg whites until they stand in firm peaks and fold them in with a metal spoon.

Spread this mixture over the prepared tin and bake it in the oven for 15 minutes or until set. Allow to cool for 10 minutes, then gently ease it out of the tin, still on the paper. Sauté the mushrooms in half the remaining butter until the moisture has evaporated (about 5 minutes). Mix them with the ham, cream cheese and soured cream. Season with salt and pepper and spread this filling over the spinach soufflé, leaving a 1 cm/½ in border all round. Roll it up while still slightly warm, from one of the long sides.

Wrap it in foil and leave it for about 2 hours. Dip a sharp knife in warm water and cut into slices. To serve hot, place in a lightly buttered gratin dish, drizzle a little melted butter over and heat through in the oven.

KILOCALORIES	310	SUGARS	4g
TOTAL FAT	27g	SODIUM	680mg
SATURATED FAT	16g	FIBRE	2.5g

HUEVOS EN RABO DE MESTIZA

This is an old colonial Mexican dish using ingredients traditional to the cooking of the Old and the New Worlds – eggs and cheese in Spain, peppers, chillis and tomatoes in Mexico.

SERVES 6–8 (V)

3 red (or green) peppers
2–3 tbsp vegetable oil
1 large onion, finely chopped
450 g/1 lb tomatoes, skinned and chopped
1 or more fresh chillies, deseeded and chopped
225 g/8 oz mild crumbly white
cheese (or cream cheese)
8 hardboiled eggs, halved lengthwise
pinch salt

Place the peppers on a grill pan under medium heat, turning them occasionally until the skins blacken. Alternatively, spear each pepper on a cooking fork and toast them over a gas flame or electric burner. As the peppers become charred, put them into a small plastic bag, or wrap them in a damp towel, and leave for 20 minutes. The skins will then peel off easily. Slit the peppers, remove and discard the seeds, veins and stems, and cut the flesh into strips.

Heat the oil in a large skillet and sauté the onion and peppers over moderate heat until soft but not brown. Add the tomatoes and chilli peppers and season to taste with salt; simmer until the sauce is well blended and fairly thick.

Cut the cheese into eight slices, and arrange them on top of the sauce; cook for 2–3 minutes longer. Arrange the eggs cut-side up on top of the cheese and simmer the mixture for another minute or so. Serve straight from the skillet, with tortillas or with rice.

If cream cheese is used, stir it evenly into the sauce and top it with the sliced or halved eggs.

KILOCALORIES	290	SUGARS	5g
TOTAL FAT	23g	SODIUM	300mg
SATURATED FAT	8g	FIBRE	2g

Left *(clockwise from bottom) Spinach roulade, carne fiambre, rice pudding with glacé fruits, next to melons with scoops of fresh papaya, baked potatoes topped with a lumpfish and Mexican huevos en rabo de mestiza. In the centre is a dish of refried beans.*

FRIED TROUT

Served with crisp bacon and corn pudding (see page 92), trout make an unusual and delicious dish that can be prepared in advance.

SERVES 6–8

8 small trout
16 rashers bacon (green)
75 g/3 oz cornmeal (maize)
pinch salt, pepper
125 ml/4 fl oz semi-skimmed milk
50 g/2 oz butter (or margarine)

Sauté the bacon in a large frying-pan without added fat until crisp, then drain it on kitchen paper. Season the cornmeal with salt and pepper. Dip the washed and dried trout in the milk, then coat them with the cornmeal. Heat the butter or margarine with the bacon fat still in the pan, add the trout and cook them over brisk heat, turning them once, until they are done (after about 8 minutes). Serve at once with the bacon, accompanied with corn pudding.

KILOCALORIES	410	SUGARS	1g
TOTAL FAT	19g	SODIUM	1070mg
SATURATED FAT	2g	FIBRE	–

CARROT, ORANGE AND TOMATO SOUP

This flavourful soup is equally good hot in winter and chilled in summer.

SERVES 6–8

450 g/1 lb carrots, sliced
50 g/2 oz butter (or margarine)
1 medium-sized onion, finely chopped
1 litre/1¾ pt chicken stock (see page 17)
450 g/1 lb tomatoes, skinned, deseeded and chopped
5 cm/2 in strip of orange peel
225 ml/8 fl oz orange juice
2.5 cm/1 in piece root ginger, peeled
pinch salt, black pepper
soured cream (optional)

Melt the butter in a heavy saucepan, add the onion and cook over a low heat until soft. Add the carrots and cook for another 5 minutes, stirring from time to time.

Add enough chicken stock to cover the vegetables, bring to a simmer, cover the pan and cook until the carrots are tender (about 30 minutes).

Strain the liquid into a bowl and set aside. Pureé the onion, carrots and tomatoes in a food processor or blender and return the mixture to the pan with the reserved liquid, the orange peel and juice, the lightly crushed root ginger and the rest of the chicken stock. Simmer, covered, for 15 minutes. Remove the orange peel and root ginger, and correct the seasoning.

Serve hot or chilled, with a spoonful of soured cream swirled on the top, and accompanied with hot toast or wholemeal crackers.

KILOCALORIES	140	SUGARS	9g
TOTAL FAT	10g	SODIUM	480mg
SATURATED FAT	7g	FIBRE	2.5g

CORN PUDDING

Traditional in the Deep South of America, where sweetcorn made up the staple diet, this favourite dish appears in numerous variations, often with diced ham.

SERVES 6–8 (V)

500 g/18 oz sweetcorn kernels (canned or frozen)
1 green (or red) pepper
50 g/2 oz butter (or margarine)
25 g/1 oz plain flour
1 l/1¾ pt semi-skimmed milk
225 ml/8 fl oz single cream
pinch salt, white pepper
½ tsp paprika
6 large eggs

Blanch the pepper in briskly boiling water, uncovered, for 5 minutes. Drain it; and when cooled remove the stem, seeds and veins. Chop the flesh coarsely and pureé it in a food processor. Preheat the oven to 180°C/350°C/gas 4.

Melt the butter or margarine in a medium-sized saucepan and stir in the flour; cook over a low heat, stirring, for about 2 minutes, without letting the flour colour. Remove from the heat and gradually stir in the milk mixed with the cream. Return to the heat, bring the sauce to a simmer and cook, stirring constantly, until it has thickened. Season to taste with salt, pepper and paprika.

Remove the pan from the heat again and whisk in the eggs, one by one. Fold the corn kernels and the pepper pureé into the sauce. Spoon the mixture into a buttered 1.25 litre/2 pt soufflé dish and place this in a roasting pan with hot water coming halfway up the sides. Bake in the oven for 1–1½ hours or until the pudding is firm.

KILOCALORIES	340	SUGARS	11g
TOTAL FAT	21g	SODIUM	280mg
SATURATED FAT	11g	FIBRE	1.5g

RICE PUDDING WITH GLACÉ FRUITS

Cheese and fruit make a fine ending to a brunch, but if the guests are known to have a taste for sweet things, this pudding is elegant, easy and inexpensive.

SERVES 6–8

225 g/8 oz glacé fruits
75 ml/3 fl oz Kirsch (or Cointreau or
other orange liqueur)
175 g/6 oz short-grain (pudding) rice
725 ml/1¼ pt semi-skimmed milk
100 g/4 oz sugar
1 tsp vanilla essence
1½ tbsp gelatine
75 ml/3 fl oz water
3 egg yolks, lightly beaten

Chop the glacé fruits and steep them in the liqueur. Cook the rice in a large saucepan full of briskly boiling water for 5 minutes; drain thoroughly. Transfer the rice to the top of a large double boiler set over boiling water on low heat. Alternatively, use a heavy-based saucepan and set it on a heat-diffusing mat over very low heat. Stir in the milk, sugar and vanilla essence and cook, covered, stirring from time to time until the rice is tender and the milk absorbed (¾–1 hour). Remove from the heat.

Dissolve the gelatine in the water and stir it into the rice. Add the egg yolks and mix well; fold in two-thirds of the chopped fruits. Spoon the rice into a decorative mould (750 ml–1 litre/1½–2 pints) rinsed out with cold water, and refrigerate for several hours. Unmould the pudding and decorate it with the remaining glacé fruits.

KILOCALORIES	280	SUGARS	44g
TOTAL FAT	4g	SODIUM	70mg
SATURATED FAT	2g	FIBRE	0.5g

POULTRY AND GAME

Poultry is a good buy both economically and nutritionally. Roast chicken, for example, has similar protein values to roast lamb, but the latter contains almost six times as much fat. Turkey has similar nutrient values to chicken, while duck and goose contain twice as much saturated fat. Game birds and furred game surpass poultry in both protein and fat values. The fat of any poultry or game dish can be reduced by removing the skin before serving.

Chickens are bred to a more or less standard size of 1.5–2.5 kg/3–5 lb, while smaller birds, known as poussins, are approximately 500 g/1 lb.

More than half the poultry sold is frozen: the rule for all frozen birds is to defrost them thoroughly, preferably in the fridge, and to cook them right through. *Never* refreeze a thawed bird.

GAME

Game birds are generally in the expensive price range and fresh supplies depend on the season. Ideally, they should be hung for several days to develop their flavour and to tenderise the flesh. Allow one small game bird per person. Pheasant may be sold as a brace or singly, the hen on average yielding three portions, the cock four.

Furred game – hare and rabbit – is sold skinned and usually jointed. Both are economical buys.

Venison is considerably more expensive, especially the saddle and leg cuts. However, the gamey flavour is incomparable and the meat is an excellent source of protein.

PREPARATION

Most poultry is sold ready for cooking – plucked, drawn and trussed. For a roasting bird, allow about 275 g/10 oz per person. Before cooking, wipe the bird thoroughly with damp kitchen towels and clean the inside of the neck flap of any blood and tendons. Chickens may be stuffed with a traditional forcemeat stuffing of breadcrumbs flavoured with herbs, mush-rooms or celery and bound with a beaten egg – a rice stuffing (see page 94) is an unusual alternative.

Make sure that all stuffings are fully cooked first and used to stuff only the neck end of the poultry. For added flavour, place an onion or orange inside the cavity of the bird and discard it after cooking.

COOKING

Whole chicken can be **boiled**, with a bouquet garni and root vegetables, in sufficient water to cover it, and simmered for a couple of hours or until tender. Alternatively, balloon the chicken loosely in foil and cook in the oven. The meat can then be carved and cut up and used in other recipes or served in a sauce.

Roasting is the usual method for whole chicken, turkey, duck and goose, and for young game birds. The breast of chicken and turkey can be barded with bacon rashers or brushed with oil or melted butter. Baste frequently during cooking. The more fatty duck and goose should be pricked all over and placed on a rack in a baking tin to collect the fat. Game birds are rarely stuffed, merely seasoned well and a knob of butter placed in the body cavity to keep the flesh moist during roasting. Bard the breast with bacon.

A covering of foil helps to prevent the bird from drying out; it should be removed for the last 20 minutes to allow the bird to brown and crisp. Alternatively, enclose the bird in a roasting bag or, better still, roast chicken, duck, game birds and mini turkeys in a chicken brick which requires no additional fat, preserves flavours and leaves the oven clean.

Poultry joints can be **braised** on a bed of chopped, sauté vegetables, in a tightly covered pan over gentle heat; they are also ideal for **grilling**, brushed with a little oil or barbecue sauce. Small game birds, split through the backbone and flattened out, also grill well, but need frequent basting to prevent them from drying out.

Stocks can be prepared from the carcases and meat of poultry, and are infinitely preferable to the commercial stock cube. See page 17 for recipe details.

Rice stuffing goes well with poultry of all kinds. It can also be used to stuff marrows, peppers, courgettes, and small aubergines. Fry 1 medium-sized, finely chopped onion in 1½ tablespoonfuls of vegetable oil until golden, then mix in and stir-fry 125 g/4 oz long-grain brown rice. Cover the rice with 300 ml/½ pt of boiling water, add a pinch of salt and cook the rice, covered, for 30–35 minutes or until the water has been absorbed. Stir in 2 tablespoonfuls of finely chopped parsley and leave the stuffing to cool before use. [Nutritional values below are for the full quantity.]

KILOCALORIES	390	SUGARS	6g
TOTAL FAT	22g	SODIUM	400mg
SATURATED FAT	–	FIBRE	2.5g

CHICKEN IMPERIAL

A crisp, cheese-and-herb flavoured crumb topping is a novel idea; it also helps to keep the meat moist. The dish is suitable for a buffet or picnic party: wrap the chicken pieces in foil as soon as they are removed from the oven.

SERVES 4

4 chicken quarters or 8 drumsticks, skinned
40–50 g/1½–2 oz softened butter (or margarine)
pinch salt, pepper
1 medium-sized onion, finely chopped
75 g/3 oz Cheddar cheese, finely grated
50–75 g/2–3 oz brown breadcrumbs
1 heaped tbsp parsley (or tarragon), finely chopped

Wipe the chicken pieces and make two or three slashes into the flesh; spread them with the softened butter or margarine and season with salt and pepper. Mix the onion and cheese with the breadcrumbs and herbs.

Arrange the chicken pieces in a lightly oiled roasting tin or an ovenproof dish and press the crumb mixture lightly over the top. Bake in the centre of an oven preheated to 190°C/375°F/gas 5 for just under 1 hour or until the topping is crisp and brown and the chicken tender.

Serve the chicken accompanied by various salads.

KILOCALORIES	525	SUGARS	2g
TOTAL FAT	27g	SODIUM	760mg
SATURATED FAT	14g	FIBRE	1g

DRUNKEN CHICKEN

This is a familiar dish, in many versions, along China's eastern coastal provinces of Kiangsu and Chekiang. It can be served as part of a cold spread or as an appetiser with small bowls of hoisin or soya sauce in which to dip the chicken.

SERVES 6–8

1 chicken (1.5 kg/3 lb approx), jointed into
6 or 8 pieces
8 cm/3 in pieces fresh root ginger, peeled
3 spring onions, trimmed and halved
pinch salt
250 ml/8 fl oz medium-dry sherry (or Shao-hsing
wine)

Wipe the chicken pieces clean and arrange them in a not-too-shallow heatproof dish. Cut four slices, each about 6 mm/¼ in, from the root ginger and bruise them lightly; tuck the ginger and spring onions between the chicken pieces. Place the dish on a metal trivet in the centre of a wok and fill the wok with boiling water until it comes about 2.5 cm/1 in below the dish holding the chicken. Put the wok cover in place and steam the chicken for 25–30 minutes over fairly high heat. Steaming can also be done in a bamboo or metal steamer.

Remove the cooked chicken, discard the ginger and spring onions, but set aside the liquid in the dish. While it is still hot, remove the skin. Chop the remaining ginger and squeeze through a garlic press, adding water and reserving the juice; squeeze the ginger juice all over the chicken and leave it to cool completely.

Place the chicken in an earthenware dish; pour over the sherry or wine and add the reserved liquid. (Ideally, the marinade should just cover the chicken.) Leave to marinate for 24 hours.

To serve drunken chicken the Chinese way, chop the pieces, through the bones, into 2.5 cm/1 in pieces and rearrange them on a dish in the shape of a chicken. Alternatively, remove the chicken flesh from the bones and serve it cut into narrow strips.

KILOCALORIES	400	SUGARS	1g
TOTAL FAT	14g	SODIUM	160mg
SATURATED FAT	5g	FIBRE	–

Please see the introduction for a full explanation of the nutritional factboxes.

CHICKEN IN CABBAGE LEAVES

The chicken breasts retain their flavour and cabbage leaves keep them moist during cooking.

SERVES 4

4 chicken breasts, skinned and boned
4 large green cabbage (or savoy) leaves
pinch salt, pepper
12 juniper berries, crushed
2 rashers streaky bacon
25 g/1 oz melted butter (or 1 tbsp vegetable oil)

Wash the cabbage leaves and snip out their tough bases and ribs; cook the leaves in a little water until just tender (about 4–6 minutes).

Season the chicken breasts with salt and pepper and sprinkle them with juniper berries. Derind the bacon, cut the rashers in half and place a piece on each chicken breast; wrap a cabbage leaf round each and place, seam downwards, in a lightly greased ovenproof dish. Brush with butter or oil. Bake them in the centre of the oven, preheated to 220°C/425°F/gas 7, for 20 minutes. To serve, cut the chicken parcels in half diagonally and arrange them on a bed of green noodles.

KILOCALORIES	255	SUGARS	2g
TOTAL FAT	14g	SODIUM	540mg
SATURATED FAT	4g	FIBRE	1.5g

PIGEON PAPRIKA

Pigeons or squabs have always been a great delicacy in much classic country cooking.

SERVES 4–6

6 young pigeons
40–50 g/1½–2 oz butter (or margarine)
1 medium-sized onion, roughly chopped
1 red pepper, deseeded and diced
150 g/6 oz button mushrooms, sliced
1 tbsp Hungarian paprika
300 ml/½ pt chicken stock (see page 17)
salt, pepper
1 tbsp tomato purée
150 ml/5 fl oz low-fat plain yogurt

MARINADE
150 ml/5 fl oz medium-sweet cider
pinch salt
1 tsp brown sugar
8 black peppercorns
2.5 cm/1 in piece fresh root ginger, peeled and thinly sliced
1 bay leaf
3 sprigs thyme
6 juniper berries, crushed

Use a sharp knife to peel away the skin and cut the breast meat into thin slices (use the remainder for stock or soup). Wash and pat dry on kitchen paper. Mix together all the marinade ingredients, pour over the meat and leave, covered, in the fridge for 8 hours or overnight.

Melt the butter or margarine in a large, heavy-based pan and fry the onion over gentle heat for 5 minutes; add the red pepper and, after a few minutes, stir in the mushrooms. Sauté for 2 minutes, then stir in the paprika and add the pigeon. Toss the meat in the butter until sealed on both sides, then add the strained marinade and enough stock to cover the meat. Season to taste, bring to the boil, cover the pan and simmer gently for about 45 minutes. After 30 minutes, stir in the tomato purée and a little more stock if necessary. Just before serving, correct the seasoning and stir in the yogurt off the heat.

Serve with boiled or mashed potatoes and crisp boiled cabbage.

KILOCALORIES	510	SUGARS	9g
TOTAL FAT	33g	SODIUM	560mg
SATURATED FAT	10g	FIBRE	1.5g

SPICED CHICKEN CHAUDFROID

The classic French chicken chaudfroid and Hindle
Wakes chicken of medieval England are similar to this
elegant cold party dish. The subtle spicing, however,
has an Eastern influence.

SERVES 4

1 chicken (1½ kg/3 lb approx)
1 lemon
pinch salt, pepper
10 cardamom pods
1 tsp coriander seeds
½ tsp ground turmeric
1 small onion, finely chopped
2.5 cm/1 in fresh root ginger, peeled and sliced
*1 litre/1½ pt semi-skimmed milk (or half milk and half
chicken stock – see page 17)*
2 eggs

Wipe the chicken clean, inside and out, and slash the
flesh two or three times; set the chicken in a shallow
glass or glazed earthenware dish. Cut strips of rind
from the lemon and set them aside; squeeze the lemon
juice and pour it over the chicken. Stuff the empty
lemon halves inside the body cavity, and sprinkle the
chicken with salt and pepper.

Split the cardamom pods open with a pestle and
mortar, remove the outer husks and pound or grind
the seeds to a powder, together with the coriander
seeds. Add the turmeric. Pound the onion and ginger
together, stir in the spices and rub this mixture all over
the chicken. (A liquidiser or food processor can be
used for grinding the spice, onion and ginger mixture.)
Cover the bird and leave it to stand in a cool place for
at least 8 hours.

Heat the milk (or the milk and chicken stock) in a
deep pan which will hold the chicken comfortably. Just
as the milk comes to the boil, remove the pan from the
heat and lift in the chicken. Return the pan to low heat
and bring it to a simmer; cover the pan and cook over
gentle heat for 1–1¼ hours.

Lift the chicken out and leave it to cool. Remove the
skin, carve the flesh into neat serving pieces and
arrange them in a single layer on a shallow dish.

For the lemon sauce, beat the eggs in a bowl and
pour 450 ml/¾ pt of the strained, warm cooking
liquid over them. Transfer the mixture to a double
boiler, or to a bowl set over hot water, and whisk
constantly until the sauce thickens; do not let it come
to the boil or it will curdle. Season to taste with salt
and pepper. Strain the sauce and spread it over the cold
chicken. Leave to cool.

Serve the chicken, garnished with the reserved lemon
rind and perhaps strips of red or green pepper,
accompanied with a cold rice salad.

KILOCALORIES	710	SUGARS	13g
TOTAL FAT	24g	SODIUM	500mg
SATURATED FAT	9g	FIBRE	0.5g

CHICKEN WITH SPICED SAUSAGE AND RICE

Every country has its own version of pilaff, basically
rice flavoured with spices, herbs or vegetables, to
which are added small amounts of meat, poultry or
fish. The Spanish create spicy chicken pilaff with
garlicky sausage and juicy tomatoes.

SERVES 4

1 large chicken joint (450 g/1 lb)
pinch salt, pepper
225 g/8 oz long-grain brown rice
600 ml/1 pt chicken stock (see page 17)
1 small onion, finely chopped
*13 cm/5 in piece spicy sausage (chorizo or gulya),
thinly sliced*
1 can tomatoes (225 g/8 oz), coarsely chopped
1 tbsp parsley, finely chopped

Wash or wipe the chicken clean, put it in a pan with
enough water to cover, and add a seasoning of salt and
pepper; cover the pan with a lid. Poach the chicken
gently for about 25 minutes. Lift the chicken out,
remove skin and bone and cut it into small bite-sized
pieces; strain the stock and make it up to 600 ml/1 pt
with water.

Put the rinsed rice, the onion and the stock in a
heavy-based pan; bring it to the boil, stir once and
simmer for 15 minutes, covered. Stir in the sausage, the
chicken and the tomatoes with their juice. Mix
thoroughly, cover the pan and simmer for another 15–
20 minutes, or until the rice is cooked.

Spoon the chicken and rice on to a warm serving
dish and sprinkle with parsley.

KILOCALORIES	530	SUGARS	2g
TOTAL FAT	29g	SODIUM	690mg
SATURATED FAT	11g	FIBRE	1g

THAI CHICKEN CURRY

Unlike the curries of India, Thai curries generally contain only a few but fiery spices which remain as separate flavours. The curry can be hot or mild, according to the amount of chilli used. Boned breast fillets of chicken look most attractive for a dinner party, but any type of chicken joint can be used, with skin and excess fat removed.

SERVES 6

6 chicken joints, skinned
3–4 tbsp vegetable oil
2 large onions, finely chopped
2–4 chillies, deseeded
2 garlic cloves, finely chopped
100 g/4 oz creamed coconut
450 ml/¾ pt chicken stock (see page 17)
2 tsp lemon rind, finely grated and juice of 1 lemon
2 tbsp coriander or parsley, finely chopped
5 cm/2 in piece fresh root ginger, peeled and thinly sliced
pinch salt, pepper

Wash and wipe the chicken joints dry. Heat the oil in a large, heavy-based pan; add the onions, half the chillies, cut into thin rounds, and the garlic. Stir-fry for about 8 minutes over medium heat until they just begin to colour. Add the chicken pieces and fry them until golden. Crumble or grate the coconut into the pan, and stir in the stock; bring the mixture to the boil. Lower the heat, cover the pan and simmer for 15 minutes. Stir in half the prepared quantities of lemon rind, lemon juice, chopped coriander or parsley and ginger.

Cover the pan and continue to cook over gentle heat for another 30–40 minutes or until the chicken is tender. Season to taste and add more lemon juice.

For the garnish, mix together the remaining lemon rind, chopped chillies, coriander and ginger. If the curry is too mild, add another 1 or 2 finely chopped chillies to the garnish and stir some of it into the sauce.

Serve the chicken curry sprinkled with the remaining garnish and accompanied by plain boiled rice.

KILOCALORIES	370	SUGARS	3g
TOTAL FAT	26g	SODIUM	300mg
SATURATED FAT	12g	FIBRE	0.5g

Ginger Root ginger is a pale-coloured, knobbly shaped rhizome, or root, which should be peeled before use.

CHICKEN AND FRUIT KEBABS

Breast fillets are perfect for kebabs, but as the meat is almost fat-free it needs marinating beforehand and frequent brushing during grilling to prevent it drying.

SERVES 4

4 chicken breasts, boned and skinned
(approx 125 g/5 oz each)
16 large prawns, peeled
2–3 pineapple rings, fresh or canned
1 large firm banana
2 firm pears, peeled and cored
1–2 avocado pears, peeled and stoned
8 knobs stem ginger
12–16 fresh bay leaves

MARINADE

1 tbsp olive (or vegetable) oil
1 tbsp sweet chilli sauce
1 tbsp ginger syrup
1 tbsp medium-dry sherry
1 tbsp lemon (or lime) juice
1 tsp peeled and grated fresh root ginger
1–2 garlic cloves, crushed
1 shallot, finely chopped
1 bay leaf, crumbled
pinch salt, pepper

Wipe the chicken breasts clean, trim them and cut each into eight even-sized pieces. Mix the marinade ingredients together, shaking them in a screwtop jar. Arrange the chicken pieces and the peeled prawns in a shallow dish, pour the marinade over them and set aside for at least 1 hour.

Cut the fruit into small, even pieces. Lift the chicken and prawns from the marinade and thread on to eight stainless-steel skewers, about 25 cm/10 in long, alternating with the prepared fruits, the stem ginger cut into halves or quarters, and the bay leaves.

Place the skewers on a grill pan lined with kitchen foil; strain the marinade and brush it liberally over the kebabs. Set the pan under a medium-to-high grill for 15–20 minutes, turning and basting the kebabs.

Serve the kebabs on a bed of boiled brown or white rice, accompanied by a salad.

KILOCALORIES	455	SUGARS	24g
TOTAL FAT	24g	SODIUM	290mg
SATURATED FAT	5g	FIBRE	5g

high heat to brown them all over (about 2 minutes).

Add to the pan the stock and mushrooms and simmer gently for 8 minutes, uncovered. Remove the pan from the heat, stir in the soya sauce, the cornflour mixed to a paste with a little water, and chilli sauce to taste. Return the pan to gentle heat until the mixture has thickened slightly. Stir in two-thirds of the spring onion and red pepper strips.

Heat the mixture for 1 minute, season to taste and spoon the chicken livers in their sauce on to a serving dish. Garnish with the remaining spring onion and pepper strips and the coriander leaves. Serve with plain boiled rice or noodles.

KILOCALORIES	315	SUGARS	3g
TOTAL FAT	19g	SODIUM	550mg
SATURATED FAT	4g	FIBRE	1.5g

CHICKEN LIVERS ORIENTAL

Like other offal, chicken livers are a good source of essential minerals and are quick and easy to cook.

SERVES 4

2 × 225 g/8 oz cartons frozen chicken livers, thawed
2–3 tbsp vegetable oil
300ml /1½ pt chicken stock (see page 17)
175 g/6 oz button mushrooms, trimmed
1 tbsp soya sauce
2–3 tsp cornflour
chilli sauce
1 bunch of spring onions, trimmed
and roughly chopped
1 small red pepper, deseeded and cut into strips
pinch salt, pepper
fresh coriander leaves

Use scissors to cut away any membrane and discoloured pieces from the livers. Rinse them carefully, pat them dry and snip into 5 cm/2 in pieces. Heat the oil in a large frying-pan and fry the chicken livers quickly over

RED CHICKEN PILAFF

This Baghdadi dish takes its name from the tomato purée in which the chicken and rice are cooked. Boiling fowl is best for this dish; failing that roasting chicken can be used.

SERVES 4–6

1 chicken (1.5 kg/3 lb approx), cut into 4–6 pieces
325 g/12 oz long-grain brown rice
2 tbsp vegetable oil
2.5 cm/1 in piece cinnamon stick
2 cloves
4 cardamom seeds
2 tbsp tomato purée
225 ml/8 fl oz water
pinch salt, pepper
50 g/2 oz blanched almonds (optional)
50 g/2 oz sultanas (optional)
1–2 tbsp oil (optional)
coriander or flat-leaved parsley

Wash the rice thoroughly in cold water and leave it to soak for 1 hour. Wash the chicken pieces and wipe them dry. Heat the oil in a large heavy-based pan and fry the cinnamon, cloves and cardamoms for about 2 minutes, stirring, then mix in the tomato purée. Add the chicken pieces, water and a little salt. Bring the contents of the pan slowly to the boil, cover, and lower the heat; leave to simmer for 35–40 minutes.

Remove the chicken pieces and keep them warm.

Drain the rice and add to the cooking juices in the pan, with enough water to cover the rice by not more than 12 mm/½ in; mix thoroughly. Raise the heat and bring the rice quickly to the boil, then lower the heat to moderate; stir occasionally to prevent sticking. When the liquid is almost completely absorbed (3 minutes), with a few bubbles still on the surface, reduce the heat to the lowest possible, cover the pan and steam for 10 minutes.

To serve, bury the chicken in the red, cooked rice and transfer to a serving dish. If liked, almonds and sultanas can be folded into the rice. Garnish with sprigs of coriander or parsley.

KILOCALORIES	615	SUGARS	8g
TOTAL FAT	26g	SODIUM	280mg
SATURATED FAT	6g	FIBRE	1.5g

Roasting chart for poultry

	Temperature	Time (*approx*)
Chicken, stuffed (*2 kg/3½–4 lb*)	200°C/400°F/gas 6	1½ hours
Turkey, stuffed		
up to 4 kg/8 lb	160°C/325°F/gas 3	3–3½ hours
	210°C/425°F/gas 7	2¼–2½ hours
up to 5 kg/10 lb	160°C/325°F/gas 3	3½–3¾ hours
	210°C/425°F/gas 7	2½–2¾ hours
up to 7 kg/14 lb	160°C/325°F/gas 3	3¾–4¼ hours
	210°C/425°F/gas 7	2¾–3 hours
up to 9 kg/18 lb	160°C/325°F/gas 3	4¼–4¾ hours
	210°C/425°F/gas 7	3–3½ hours

CHICKEN BONNE FEMME

——— • ———

There are several versions of this classic dish, which uses chicken and potatoes cooked in their own juices and flavoured with bacon or pork.

SERVES 4

1 chicken (1.5 kg/3 lb approx)
pinch salt, pepper
6 tarragon sprigs
4 rashers streaky bacon, derinded and diced
2 celery sticks (or 1 small onion, thinly sliced)
450 g/1 lb potatoes, thinly sliced

Wash and dry the chicken inside and out; sprinkle salt and pepper into the cavity and push in the tarragon sprigs. Fry the bacon in its own fat over gentle heat until just crisp. Put the bacon and its fat in the bottom of an ovenproof casserole deep enough to hold the chicken, or in a slow-cooker. Place the chicken on top of the bacon. Spread the celery or onion slices round it and top with a layer of potatoes.

Cover the casserole tightly and cook in the oven, preheated to 180°C/350°F/gas 4, for 2 hours or until the chicken is tender and the potatoes cooked. For a slow-cooker, follow the manufacturer's instructions.

Carve and serve the chicken straight from the casserole, with the cooking juices spooned over it, and accompanied by a green vegetable.

KILOCALORIES	630	SUGARS	1g
TOTAL FAT	18g	SODIUM	950mg
SATURATED FAT	6g	FIBRE	2g

AYAM PANGGANG KECAP

Roast grilled chicken with soya sauce

——— • ———

The Indonesian method of marinating roast chicken turns an ordinary chicken into a gastronomic delight.

SERVES 4

1 chicken (1.5 kg/3 lb approx)
2–3 tbsp vegetable oil
2 tbsp dark soya sauce
2 shallots, thinly sliced
2 garlic cloves, crushed
½ tsp chilli powder
2 tsp sesame (or peanut) oil
juice of ½ lemon (or lime)

Preheat the oven to 190°C/375°F/gas 5. Wipe the chicken clean, inside and out, and smear it lightly with oil. Cook for about 45 minutes until golden-brown. Let the chicken cool, then cut it into four even-sized pieces. Beat the flesh carefully with a meat-beater, enough to soften and loosen the fibres but without breaking the bones.

Mix the soya sauce with the shallots, garlic, chilli powder, sesame or peanut oil and lemon or lime juice; pour this over the chicken joints and leave them to marinate for at least 1 hour.

Heat the grill, line the pan with foil and arrange the chicken pieces on it; brush them with a little of the marinade and set beneath high heat for about 10 minutes or until golden-brown, turning the chicken once and brushing again with the marinade.

Serve the grilled chicken hot, with plain boiled rice or with jacket potatoes and a green vegetable.

KILOCALORIES	625	SUGARS	–
TOTAL FAT	31g	SODIUM	280mg
SATURATED FAT	6g	FIBRE	–

CREAMED CHICKEN SHORTCAKES

——— • ———

This Americn dish combines chicken and sweetcorn. The freshly baked scones, which are part of the dish, are often made from equal amounts of white and wholewheat flour.

SERVES 4

350 g/12 oz cooked chicken (or turkey), skinned, boned and diced
300 ml/½ pt basic white sauce (see page 29)
50 g/2 oz mushrooms, thinly sliced
4 tbsp cooked sweetcorn
pinch salt, pepper
225 g/8 oz self-raising flour
½ tsp salt
50 g/2 oz butter (or margarine)
150 ml/¼ pt semi-skimmed milk
extra milk

Put the white sauce in a pan over low heat, stir in the chicken or turkey, mushrooms and sweetcorn. Heat the mixture through gently, keeping the pan covered. Season to taste.

For the scones, sift the flour and salt into a bowl; add the fat, cut into small pieces, and rub it into the flour with the fingertips. Add the milk and stir to a softish dough with a fork.

Preheat the oven to 220°C/425°F/gas 7. Turn the dough out on to a lightly floured surface and knead it lightly until smooth. Roll it out to a thickness of 1 cm/½ in, and cut out four rounds with a 9 cm/3½ in biscuit cutter. Transfer these to a non-stick or greased baking tray and brush the tops with a little extra milk.

Bake the scones near the top of the oven for 10 minutes until golden-brown and well risen. Remove them from the oven and break them carefully apart; set the bases on four warm plates.

Cover the scone bases with the hot chicken mixture and top with the scone lids. Serve at once, accompanied by a green vegetable or salad.

KILOCALORIES	540	SUGARS	7g
TOTAL FAT	26g	SODIUM	1340mg
SATURATED FAT	9g	FIBRE	2.5g

CHICKEN CURRY KAPITAN

This dish comes from Penang where it is served in many restaurants as a local speciality. It is a very mild curry, possibly created for the many Europeans who used to live there.

SERVES 4

1 chicken (1¼ kg 2½ lb), jointed into 8 pieces
and skinned
1 tbsp sugar
3 garlic cloves, crushed
5 cm/2 in piece fresh root ginger, peeled and sliced
1 tsp turmeric
1 tsp black peppercorns, finely ground
600 ml/1 pt coconut milk (see page 111)
pinch salt

GARNISH
1 red chilli, deseeded
1 lemon

Wipe the chicken joints clean and rub them with sugar to help release the juices. Pound the garlic, ginger, turmeric and peppercorns to a paste and rub this into the chicken pieces. Set them aside for 30 minutes.

Prepare the coconut milk; place it in a wide pan over gentle heat and let it come to the boil. Add chicken pieces, a pinch of salt and cook, uncovered, for 40 minutes – until the chicken is tender and the liquid has

almost evaporated. Stir occasionally.

Pile the chicken into a shallow bowl, cut the chilli into rounds and the lemon into wedges and garnish; serve with boiled rice.

KILOCALORIES	590	SUGARS	15g
TOTAL FAT	21g	SODIUM	500mg
SATURATED FAT	7g	FIBRE	–

TURKEY OLIVES

In British cookery, olives have nothing to do with the olive tree but refer to thin slices of poultry or meat rolled up around a savoury stuffing of some kind.

SERVES 4

4 turkey escalopes (each 150 g/5 oz approx)
pinch salt, pepper
100 g/4 oz ricotta cheese
1 tbsp fresh sage, finely chopped
2 tbsp vegetable oil
300 ml/½ pt white wine
2 tbsp blanched almonds, toasted

Place the turkey escalopes between sheets of non-stick paper and beat them almost paper-thin with a rolling pin. Cut each escalope in half and season lightly.

Beat the ricotta cheese until smooth and blend in the sage; spread this mixture thinly over the escalopes, leaving the edges free, and roll them up from the short side. Tie each olive firmly with soft string or secure them with wooden cocktail sticks.

Heat the oil in a frying-pan large enough to take all eight olives, sauté them over medium heat until golden-brown (after 5–8 minutes). Lift out the olives and arrange them in an ovenproof dish. Preheat the oven to 180°C/350°F/gas 4. Pour the wine into the pan, bring it to the boil, then pour it over the meat. Cook in the oven for 20–25 minutes.

Take the turkey olives from the oven, remove the string and keep the meat warm while reducing the cooking liquid to a sauce or thickening it.

Pour the sauce over the turkey olives, sprinkle with golden-toasted almonds and serve.

KILOCALORIES	400	SUGARS	1g
TOTAL FAT	17g	SODIUM	490mg
SATURATED FAT	3g	FIBRE	0.5g

parsley into the sauce and set it aside until cold. Divide the pastry into 4 pieces and roll them out on a lightly floured surface into circles, about 17.5 cm/7 in diameter. Line two 16 cm/6¼ in foil plates with half the pastry and spoon the turkey filling over them. Preheat the oven to 190°C/375°F/gas 5.

Dampen the pastry edges with milk and place the remaining pastry circles over the filling. Press the edges together, trim away any excess pastry – use this for decoration – then knock up and flute the edges and decorate the tops.

Bake for 15 minutes; make a hole in the top of each pie, brush them with milk and return to the oven for another 30–40 minutes or until the pastry is golden.

Serve hot with a green vegetable.

KILOCALORIES	590	SUGARS	2g
TOTAL FAT	33g	SODIUM	1420mg
SATURATED FAT	15g	FIBRE	–

TURKEY AND SWEETCORN PIES

Sweetcorn can help to stretch a small amount of meat – for special occasions sweetcorn could be replaced with asparagus.

SERVES 4–6

350 g/12 oz roast turkey (or chicken), diced
350 g/12 oz wholemeal shortcrust pastry
(see page 199)
50 g/2 oz butter (or margarine)
50 g/2 oz plain flour
600 ml/1 pt chicken stock (see page 17)
pinch salt, pepper
1 can (329 g/11½ oz) sweetcorn
1 tbsp parsley, finely chopped
milk (optional)

Prepare the pastry and leave it to rest while preparing the filling. Melt the butter in a pan and add the flour; cook the roux for 2 minutes, then remove the pan from the heat and stir in the stock. Return the pan to gentle heat and bring the sauce to the boil, stirring continuously. Season with salt and pepper and remove the pan from the heat.

Fold the turkey, drained sweetcorn and chopped

CASSEROLE OF PIGEON

Small wood pigeons have a deliciously gamey flavour, but the meat tends to be tough and for this reason is best marinated and tenderised before cooking.

SERVES 6

6 pigeons
1 large onion, thinly sliced
2–3 tbsp vegetable oil
100 g/4 oz button mushrooms, trimmed and left whole
25 g/1 oz plain flour
2 tbsp tomato purée
450 ml/¾ pt brown stock
lemon juice

MARINADE
2 tbsp vegetable oil
4 tbsp beer (or cider or red wine)
pinch salt, pepper
1 bay leaf
4–6 parsley stalks

Singe any feathers from the pigeons over a flame; cut the birds in half through the backbone, using a sharp knife, and clean them thoroughly with kitchen paper. The skin may be left on or peeled carefully away. For the marinade, mix the oil with beer, cider or red wine and season with salt and pepper; add the bay leaf and parsley stalks and pour the mixture over the pigeon

halves. Leave them to marinate, covered, preferably overnight in the fridge.

Lift the pigeons from the marinade and pat them dry. Heat the oil in a large pan and brown the pigeons over medium heat, allowing about 5 minutes for each side. Transfer to a large casserole.

Fry the onion in the oil for 5 minutes, then add the mushrooms and fry for another 3 minutes. Transfer the onion and mushrooms to the casserole. Heat the oven to 180°C/350°F/gas 4. Stir the flour into the pan and cook it gently to a roux for 2 minutes, blend in the tomato purée, the stock and the strained marinade. Bring the mixture to the boil, stirring all the time; correct the seasoning and pour the sauce into the casserole. Cover, and cook for 45–60 minutes.

Lift the pigeons on to a heated serving dish, add lemon juice to taste to bring out the flavours. Pour a little of the sauce over the pigeons and the rest into a

sauceboat. Serve with mashed potatoes and a cooked green vegetable.

KILOCALORIES	340	SUGARS	3g
TOTAL FAT	20g	SODIUM	340mg
SATURATED FAT	1g	FIBRE	1g

Roasting chart for game birds

	Temperature	Time (*approx*)
Grouse	200°C/400°F/gas 6	30–45 min
Partridge	200°C/400°F/gas 6	30–45 min
Pheasant	210°C/425°F/gas 7	20 min per 450 g/1 lb
Quail	210°C/425°F/gas 7	20 min

TERRINE OF RABBIT

Wild rabbit is occasionally sold at specialist poulterers and has a true gamey flavour. Domesticated rabbit, sometimes labelled Chinese rabbit, is sold skinned, often boned, by weight.

SERVES 6–8

450 g/1 lb boned rabbit
225 g/8 oz pig's liver
2 tbsp vegetable oil
1 large onion, finely chopped
2 garlic cloves, crushed
1 tsp ground cumin
2 tsp ground coriander
1 large egg, lightly beaten
pinch salt, pepper
2 tbsp red wine (or sherry or stock)
325 g/12 oz streaky bacon rashers, derinded

Remove membrane and gristle from the liver, wash and dry it thoroughly, then mince the rabbit meat and liver coarsely. Heat the oil in a small pan and fry the onion over gentle heat for 5–8 minutes or until soft and golden. Add this to the rabbit and liver mixture, with the garlic, cumin and coriander.

Bind the mixture with the egg and season to taste. Stir in the wine, sherry or stock, enough to moisten the mixture. Test-fry a walnut-sized piece of the terrine mixture and adjust seasonings if necessary. Heat the oven to 165°C/325°F/gas 3.

Stretch the bacon rashers with a knife and use them to line a 750 g/1½ lb loaf tin. Spoon in the rabbit mixture and fold the ends of the rashers over the top. Cover the tin with foil and stand it in a roasting tin; pour hot water into the roasting tin until it comes halfway up the loaf tin. Bake near the bottom of the oven for about 1½ hours or until the juices run clear when tested with a skewer.

Take the terrine from the oven, remove the foil and replace it with a fresh piece. Place a weighted board over the terrine and leave it to firm and become cold.

Chill the terrine in the fridge. Turn it out of the tin and serve it, cut into thick slices, with crusty bread and a salad.

KILOCALORIES	375	SUGARS	1g
TOTAL FAT	28g	SODIUM	840mg
SATURATED FAT	9g	FIBRE	–

CHICKEN WITH LIME SAUCE

Butter sauce flavoured with lemon juice and parsley is a classic accompaniment to grilled or sautéed chicken; fresh limes have a sharper, more tangy flavour.

SERVES 4

4 chicken breasts, skinned and boned
pinch salt, pepper
2–3 tbsp vegetable oil
juice of 1 lime
2 tbsp butter (or margarine)
1 tsp chives, finely chopped
1 tsp fresh dill (or ½ tsp dill weed)

Season the chicken breasts with salt and pepper; heat the oil in a large frying-pan over medium heat and sauté the chicken for about 4 minutes; turn the chicken, cover the pan with a lid and reduce the heat. Cook slowly for another 10 minutes or until tender.

Lift the chicken breasts on to a serving dish and keep them warm. Drain the surplus oil from the pan and add the lime juice; bring it to the boil over gentle heat, then mix in the butter, stirring thoroughly until well blended. Add the herbs.

Pour the sauce over the chicken and serve with boiled rice or new potatoes, and leaf spinach.

KILOCALORIES	290	SUGARS	–
TOTAL FAT	17g	SODIUM	210mg
SATURATED FAT	3g	FIBRE	–

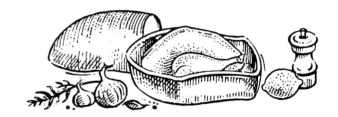

Tarragon chicken in a brick

Clay cookery is one of the oldest cooking methods. It has many advantages over modern cooking methods: it seals in the flavour, juices and aromas of the food being cooked and needs no fat or liquid. Before use, a brick should *always* be immersed in cold water for a couple of hours so as to be thoroughly soaked through; it should *never* be placed directly in a hot oven, nor be greased or oiled. And it should *never* be cleaned in washing-up detergents. After cooking, scrub the brick with a stiff brush; if necessary, clean it out in hot water to which a little coarse salt or vinegar has been added. Leave the cleaned brick to dry out thoroughly before putting it away, or mould spots may appear.

SERVES 4

1 chicken (approx 1.5 kg/3–3½ lb)
pinch salt, pepper
6–8 tarragon sprigs
1 tbsp melted butter (optional)

Wipe the chicken clean, inside and out; sprinkle a little salt and pepper through the neck opening. Work the skin away from breast and legs and insert small tarragon sprigs between flesh and skin. Retruss the chicken. Alternatively, lay the tarragon over the bird.

Brush the chicken lightly with butter; place it in the brick, and cover with the lid. Cook for about 1½ hours in the oven at 200°C/400°F/gas 6. Serve the chicken with jacket potatoes and a green salad.

KILOCALORIES	530	SUGARS	–
TOTAL FAT	19g	SODIUM	530mg
SATURATED FAT	8g	FIBRE	–

Chicken liver pâté

Pâtés and terrines are no novel invention: they have been part of the cook's repertoire for centuries – known as potted meat or fish. The pâtés were made airtight with a thick covering of melted suet or clarified butter, but today such covering is not really necessary. This pâté will keep for 3 days in the fridge and for up to 1 month in the freezer.

SERVES 4

225 g/8 oz chicken livers, fresh (or *frozen and thawed*)
50 g/2 oz butter
¼–½ tsp allspice
1 garlic clove, crushed (optional)
1 tbsp brandy (or *sherry*)
pinch salt, pepper
clarified butter

Rinse the chicken livers carefully, pat them dry on kitchen paper and snip out discoloured and stringy bits before chopping them into small pieces. Melt half the butter in a frying-pan large enough to hold the livers in one layer. Fry them over gentle heat for 5 minutes until they are sealed and pale brown on the outside, still pink inside.

Lift out the livers with a slotted spoon and put them in a liquidiser goblet. Add the allspice and the garlic, if used, to the butter in the pan, with several grindings of black pepper. Pour in the brandy or sherry, bring to the boil and, away from the heat, add the rest of the butter, stirring until it has melted. Add the liquid to the livers and blend them to a smooth paste. Add salt if necessary.

Spoon the pâté into a serving bowl and cover with clarified butter. Cover the dish with foil and chill in the fridge.

Serve the pâté as a first course with fingers of toast, or as a light lunch with a salad and chunks of wholemeal bread.

KILOCALORIES	220	SUGARS	–
TOTAL FAT	18g	SODIUM	280mg
SATURATED FAT	6g	FIBRE	–

Clarified butter is an expensive cooking fat as the yield is almost halved: to obtain 125 g/4 oz of clarified butter, melt 225 g/8 oz of salted butter in a small pan over gentle heat; without stirring or browning, let the butter come to a foam. Continue to cook gently until the foam subsides; remove from the heat and leave until the butter deposit has sunk to the bottom of the pan, leaving the clear liquid on top. Pour this carefully through muslin, taking care to leave the deposit behind. For a covering, pour the liquid butter over the pâté and chill until it has solidified.

The Dutch call it 'Rijsttafel'

When I was a little girl in West Sumatra, my parents spoke the local language to me, but Dutch to each other. They ate Dutch, with knives and forks at the dining-room table, while I sat cross-legged in the kitchen and ate with my fingers. Years later, I went with my husband to the Netherlands. We bought *krupuk* – thin, crisp savoury crackers – in little Indonesian shops in Amsterdam's side-streets and *saté* – meat kebabs – from stalls on the beach at Scheveningen. We ate Indonesian every night, expensively when we felt rich and modestly for the rest of the time. In the Netherlands, Indonesian food covers the whole price range, from cheap café to elegant restaurant.

After a while, however, I began to feel a little exasperated by the Dutch assumption, at least in some of the more expensive restaurants, that the only proper Indonesian meal must be a *rijsttafel*. The word is peculiarly Dutch. Would you enter a restaurant in London that advertised its rice-table? If you tried using a literal translation of the word when ordering a meal in Jakarta, the waiter would either laugh at you or bring you whatever the chef most wanted to get rid of.

Around 1900, a young Dutch girl, Augusta de Wit, newly arrived in the colonies, recorded her first encounter with a *rijsttafel* at a large hotel in what was then Batavia: 'Rice and chicken . . . fish, flesh and fricassées, all manner of curries, sauces, pickles, preserved fruit, salt eggs, fried bananas, sambals of fowls' liver, fish roe, young palm shoots . . . I sat me down, heaped up my plate with everything that came my way, and fell to.' She at once burnt her mouth on the chillies in a hot sambal, swallowed a glass of water which made her feel worse, and swore never to go near a *rijsttafel* again. 'I have broken that vow . . . and now I know how to eat rice, I love it.'

Augusta had made the mistake foreigners often make when they first see a lavish Indonesian dinner table. The right way to approach a *rijsttafel* is to put some rice on your plate and choose two or three dishes to sample first. Most Indonesians like their food spicy, but that does not mean that every dish on the table is chilli-hot. You are expected to go back for as many helpings as you can manage, rather than load your plate with food you cannot finish.

The recipes here will be sufficient for a dinner party of 12 which should, I think, satisfy any Indonesian (or Dutchman) without being too elaborate, or demanding an excessive amount of work. Any one of the recipes can, of course, be cooked on its own, in which case the quantities should be sufficient for fewer people. Conversely, if you want a more elaborate spread, you can add other dishes from other Indonesian recipes in this book. One good Dutch idea is to drink lager, though you may prefer lemon tea or water – as long as you remember the tale of Augusta and do not rely on it as an antidote to too much chilli.

GADO-GADO
Mixed vegetable salad with peanut sauce

———— • ————

Making the peanut sauce, known as *bumbu*, may appear a little laborious; if time is at a premium, a passable compromise can be made from satay powder (available from Chinese stores) boiled with water to the necessary consistency.

SERVES 12

175 g/6 oz cabbage (or spring greens), shredded
100 g/4 oz French beans, sliced
100 g/4 oz carrots, thinly sliced
1 small cauliflower, divided into florets
100 g/4 oz bean sprouts
1 large potato, unpeeled
lettuce
watercress
quarter of a cucumber, sliced

SAUCE (BUMBU)
vegetable oil
225 g/8 oz raw peanuts, skinned
thin slice of terasi (see glossary)
1 garlic clove, crushed
3 shallots, finely chopped
pinch salt
½ tsp chilli powder
1 tsp brown sugar
600 ml/1 pt water
juice of ½ lemon

GARNISH
2 eggs, hardboiled and sliced
fried onions (optional)
prawn crackers (optional)

First prepare the vegetables (the brownish roots on the bean sprouts should be discarded). Heat enough oil in a wok or a frying-pan to cover the skinned peanuts. Fry the peanuts for 4 or 5 minutes, then remove them and let them drain and cool on kitchen paper. Pour all but a teaspoonful of the oil out of the pan. Pound or grind the peanuts to a fine powder. Grill the terasi for a few minutes on each side.

Pound the garlic, shallots and terasi with the salt to a paste. Fry the paste in the remaining oil for 1 minute, then add the chilli powder, sugar, and stir in the water. Bring this mixture to the boil and add the ground peanuts. Simmer, stirring occasionally, until the sauce becomes thick (about 4–6 minutes). Set it aside.

Boil the vegetables (except the lettuce, watercress and cucumber) separately: the potato for 15 minutes, the green vegetables, carrots and cauliflower for 4 minutes and the bean sprouts for 2–3 minutes. When the potato has cooled a little, peel it and cut it into thin slices.

Arrange the vegetables on a large serving dish: cabbage, cauliflower, carrots and bean sprouts in the centre, lettuce, watercress and cucumber slices round the edge, and the sliced potato on top. Garnish with the egg slices.

Heat the sauce and stir in the lemon juice; pour it over the salad and garnish with fried onions and prawn crackers (if liked) broken into small pieces.

KILOCALORIES	175	SUGARS	3g
TOTAL FAT	13g	SODIUM	60mg
SATURATED FAT	2g	FIBRE	2.5g

SAMBAL IKAN
Fish relish

———— • ————

This easy tuna sambal (or side dish), which can also be made with anchovies, is not too hot; it can be made several days in advance and kept in the fridge.

SERVES 12

1 can tuna fish (about 200 g/7 oz) in brine or water
2 tbsp vegetable oil
4 shallots, finely chopped
4 red (or green) chillies, deseeded and finely chopped
2 garlic cloves, crushed
1 tsp ground ginger
5 tbsp desiccated coconut
2 tsp tomato purée
1 tsp brown sugar
scant 300 ml/½ pint water

Drain the tuna and flake it with a fork. Heat the oil in a wok or small, heavy-based saucepan and stir-fry the shallots and chillies together with the garlic over high heat for about 2 minutes, then add the ginger, coconut, tomato purée, sugar and water. Stir, bring to the boil, then reduce the heat and simmer for 2 minutes. Add the tuna and continue stirring for 1 or 2 minutes. Serve the sambal hot or cold.

KILOCALORIES	90	SUGARS	2g
TOTAL FAT	7g	SODIUM	110mg
SATURATED FAT	2g	FIBRE	0.5g

SAMBAL GORENG UDANG
Prawns in rich coconut sauce

Sambal goreng is a general term for any kind of compound dish of meat, poultry or fish cooked with an assortment of spices among which chillis play a dominant part.

SERVES 12

1.8 kg/4 lb prawns (or scampi), peeled
100 g/3–4 oz mange-tout (or sugar peas)
6 shallots, finely chopped
3 garlic cloves, crushed
5 almonds (or kemiri – see opposite)
1 slice (6 mm/¼ in) terasi (see glossary)
5 red chillies, deseeded (or
1 tsp chilli powder and 2 tsp paprika)
pinch of powdered lemon grass (see glossary)
pinch of ground laos (see opposite)
1 tsp ground ginger
2 tsp ground coriander
2 tbsp vegetable oil
300 ml/½ pt water
2 tbsp tamarind water (see below)
pinch salt
1 tsp brown sugar (optional)
1 bay leaf (or 2 kaffir lime leaves – see glossary)
3 ripe tomatoes, skinned and chopped
300 ml/½ pt thick coconut milk (see page 111)

Top and tail the mange-tout (or sugar peas) and set aside. Pound the shallots, garlic, kemiri, terasi and chillies in a mortar or blend in a food processor. Turn the paste into a bowl and mix in the ground spices.

Heat the oil in a wok or large, heavy-based pan. Add the paste and stir-fry for 2 minutes over medium heat. Pour in the water and the tamarind water, and bring to the boil. Add a pinch of salt, the sugar (if used), the kaffir lime or bay leaves, and the tomatoes; reduce the heat and simmer for 8 minutes. Stir in the coconut milk and continue to simmer until the sauce is quite thick. Add the prawns (or scampi) and the mange-tout (or sugar peas) and simmer for 5 minutes, stirring occasionally; do not let the mixture reach boiling point. Remove the kaffir lime or bay leaves and serve hot.

KILOCALORIES	310	SUGARS	4g
TOTAL FAT	6g	SODIUM	620mg
SATURATED FAT	–	FIBRE	0.5g

KAMBING BUMBU BACEM
Spicy boiled lamb

Laos (or galangal/galingale) is a popular spice in Indonesia. It is a member of the ginger family and its roots resemble ginger in appearance and flavour: it is available in powder form from specialist shops.

SERVES 12

1 leg or shoulder of lamb (about 2 kg/4 lb)
2 large onions, sliced or chopped
3 garlic cloves, crushed
1 tsp chilli powder
2 tsp ground ginger
2 tsp ground coriander
pinch of ground laos (see opposite)
2 bay leaves
1 tbsp brown sugar
15 g/½ oz tamarind (see below)
pinch salt

Trim any excess fat from the lamb and put the joint with all the other ingredients in a deep saucepan. Add enough water to cover. Bring to the boil, cover the pan and simmer for 1¼ hours. Remove the meat and let it cool, then carve it into large thin slices. Strain the stock into another pan and adjust the seasoning. Bring to the boil over high heat until the sauce has reduced by half (after about 25 minutes). Add the slices of lamb, heat through, and serve at once.

KILOCALORIES	305	SUGARS	3g
TOTAL FAT	12g	SODIUM	140mg
SATURATED FAT	6g	FIBRE	–

Tamarind Also known as asam or asem, the hard seed pods of the tamarind tree are much used in Indonesian cookery and impart a sour-fruity flavour. Tamarind pulp is sold in sticky blocks which must be softened to extract the juice. Break off a small knob and cover it with warm water (25 g/1 oz tamarind pulp will yield approximately 300 ml/½ pt tamarind water); when the water has cooled, squeeze and rub the pulp repeatedly to free fibres and the large seeds; rub the mixture through a sieve and reserve the water.

AYAM RICA
Grilled chicken in hot chilli sauce
———— • ————

This recipe comes from Menado in North Sulawesi, where chilli is called *rica*. It is said that the name 'ayam rica' indicates that the dish is moderately hot only. With twice as much chilli, it becomes 'rica-rica ayam'.

SERVES 12

2 chickens, each about 2 kg/4 lb
juice of a lime
3 tbsp vegetable oil
½ tsp salt
5 red chillies, deseeded
5 cm/2 in piece root ginger, peeled and finely chopped
2 large onions, chopped
5 garlic cloves, crushed
10 tomatoes, skinned and roughly chopped

Mix the lime juice with a tablespoonful of the oil and the salt. Clean and cut each chicken into two halves; beat them with a meat beater or the flat blade of a large knife so as to soften the flesh; remove the skin. Rub the chicken halves all over with the lime juice mixture and set them aside.

Pound the chillies, ginger, onions and garlic to a paste, either by hand or in a food processor. Heat the rest of the oil in a small, heavy-based saucepan or wok and stir-fry the chilli paste for 2 minutes over medium heat. Add the tomatoes and continue stirring for another 2 minutes or until they have pulped. Cool the mixture and reserve half of it for the sauce. Spoon the the other half over the chicken halves, rub it in well, and leave them to marinate for 30 minutes.

Line the grill pan with foil before grilling the chicken slowly for about 30 minutes until it is cooked, turning the joints at half-time and brushing them with more marinade. Heat the sauce and pour it over the chicken.

KILOCALORIES	480	SUGARS	4g
TOTAL FAT	16g	SODIUM	300mg
SATURATED FAT	4g	FIBRE	1g

Kemiri Also known as candlenuts, these are rich in an oil so volatile that it burns readily, hence the name. The flavour is somewhat tart; the nuts are available shelled, canned or vacuum-sealed.

NASI KUNING
Yellow savoury rice
———— • ————

For almost any kind of *selamatan* or celebration, Indonesians traditionally serve yellow rice.

SERVES 12

5 cups long-grain rice
2 tbsp vegetable oil
2 tsp turmeric
2 tsp ground coriander
1 tsp cumin
6 cups chicken stock (or 1 chicken stock cube dissolved in 6 cups water)
1 stick cinnamon
3 cloves
½ tsp salt
1 bay leaf (or salam leaf – see glossary)

Soak the rice in cold water for 1 hour, then wash and drain it. Heat the oil in a saucepan and sauté the rice for 2 minutes. Add the turmeric, coriander and cumin and sauté for another 2 minutes. Pour in the stock and add the cinnamon, cloves, salt and bay or salam leaf. Cook, uncovered, until the stock has been soaked up by the rice (about 7 minutes), then transfer to a steamer for 10 minutes. Alternatively, cover the saucepan tightly and leave the rice to cook undisturbed over low heat for 10 minutes. Remove the cloves, cinnamon and leaf before serving.

KILOCALORIES	135	SUGARS	–
TOTAL FAT	3g	SODIUM	140mg
SATURATED FAT	–	FIBRE	–

See **Glossary of food terms** at the back for explanations of some of the less well-known ingredients and cooking methods found in this book.

Laos Also known as galangal or galingale, this is a strongly flavoured spice obtained from the roots of a member of the ginger family. Its is used sparingly to flavour oriental stews and curries and is very popular in Thai cookery.

SERUNDENG
Roasted grated coconut

—— • ——

Serundeng is a popular side dish that can be made well in advance, so there will be one dish less to make on the day of the dinner party. It is usually served cold. Fried peanuts are optional, but give a crunchy texture.

SERVES 12

175 g/6 oz desiccated coconut
4–6 tbsp vegetable oil
75 g/3 oz unsalted peanuts
5 shallots, finely chopped
3 garlic cloves, crushed
1 slice terasi (see glossary)
½ tsp ground cumin
½ tsp ground laos (see page 109)
1 tsp ground coriander
2 tbsp tamarind water (see page 108)
1 tsp brown sugar
1 bay leaf
pinch salt
300 ml/½ pt water

Heat about half the oil in a wok or frying-pan, add the peanuts and stir-fry them over high heat for 4 minutes. Drain on absorbent paper and leave them to cool.

Pound or blend together the shallots, garlic and terasi. Heat 2 tablespoonfuls of oil in the wok and fry this mixture for 1 minute before adding the spices, tamarind water, sugar, bay leaf and salt. Stir-fry for another minute, then mix in the coconut. Add the water and continue cooking, stirring from time to time, until the coconut becomes dry. Continue until the coconut is golden-brown; add the fried peanuts, stir for 1 minute, then remove the pan from the heat. Leave the mixture to cool before serving.

KILOCALORIES	240	SUGARS	2g
TOTAL FAT	24g	SODIUM	40mg
SATURATED FAT	8g	FIBRE	2.5g

Left (from top left) Yellow savoury rice garnished with crisp onion rings next to spicy boiled lamb. Beneath is a tempting array of gado-gado with a separate bowl of peanut sauce. giant prawns nestle in rich coconut sauce above a dish of grilled chicken (ayam rica). Bowls of sambals and relishes provide extra spice.

NASI PUTIH
Boiled or steamed rice

—— • ——

Boiled rice is the most suitable variety for any combination of dishes, whether they are chilli-hot or sweet-and-sour, or with coconut or peanut sauce.

SERVES 12 Ⓥ

*5 cups long-grain rice
6 cups water*

Wash the rice in several changes of cold water. Boil it in a saucepan with the measured water, uncovered, until all the liquid has been absorbed; stir once or twice to prevent the rice from sticking to the pan. Cover the pan very tightly with the lid, lower the heat and continue cooking for 10 minutes. Alternatively, steam the rice, after the initial boiling, for 10 minutes.

KILOCALORIES	115	SUGARS	–
TOTAL FAT	1g	SODIUM	–
SATURATED FAT	–	FIBRE	–

Coconut milk Also known as santen, it is commonly used in Indonesian cookery. It consists of a mixture of water and oils extracted from the grated flesh. Do not allow recipes containing coconut milk to boil or they will curdle. Use within 24 hours.

Fresh coconut Punch a couple of holes in the nut, shake out the liquid and saw up the coconut. Grate the flesh into a bowl and add 300 ml/½ pt water; squeeze the flesh thoroughly until the liquid is milky-white and the coconut gratings are quite dry. Strain through a sieve, then add another 300 ml/½ pt water to the coconut and repeat the process.

Desiccated coconut Place 350 g/12 oz desiccated coconut in a pan with 150 ml/¼ pt of water and simmer. Pour the mixture into a liquidiser, with the same amount of water as specified for coconut milk in the particular recipe; blend for about 30 seconds. Squeeze the coconut through a sieve and into a bowl, as above, the first extract being thick coconut milk; repeat to make the required amount.

Creamed coconut Dissolve about 100 g/4 oz in 300 ml/½ pt of hot water for thick coconut milk, half the amount of coconut in the same amount of water for the thin version. Strain both before use.

Eggs and cheese

Gone are the days when we were exhorted to 'go to work on an egg'. Nowadays, recommendations are that on average the weekly personal consumption should not exceed three to four eggs, including those used in cooking. These figures reflect the high amount of saturated fat and cholesterol present in an egg.

Eggs are a useful source of protein, iron, vitamin D, retinol and riboflavin of the B complex and, to some extent, vitamin C; most of the nutrients – and all the cholesterol – are contained in the yolk, the white being chiefly protein.

A size-3 egg gives an energy value of approximately 85 calories. The colour of the egg shell depends upon the breed of hen – there is no nutritional difference between white and brown eggs.

Store eggs in a separate container because the porous shells absorb smells from other foods and place in a fridge or cool place away from direct heat. As an egg ages, the yolk rises; to prevent it from sticking to the shell, store it pointed end down so that the yolk rises towards the air pocket at the rounded end. Use eggs at room temperature, removing them from the fridge 30 minutes before cooking.

Boiling Timing depends upon personal taste, but generally allow 3–3½ minutes for medium-sized eggs and 4–5 minutes for firm whites and barely soft yolks. For hard-boiled eggs, place them in a pan of cold water and bring it to the boil; reduce the heat and simmer for 10 minutes. Remove the eggs and plunge them immediately into cold water; crack and peel them under running water.

Frying For each egg allow just 1 teaspoonful of oil for cooking. Even so, the calorific content is now almost 50 per cent higher than that of a boiled egg.

Scrambling For an average portion, allow 2 medium-sized eggs and beat them lightly with pepper (salt tends to toughen the whites during cooking). Cook with a little butter over gentle heat, stirring continuously. Alternatively, scrambled eggs can be cooked in a microwave.

BASIC SOUFFLÉ

These are based on eggs and a thick white sauce, with various savoury additions for a hot soufflé and cold flavourings for a cold dessert soufflé. All kinds of leftovers can be turned into an airy soufflé: cooked, diced chicken and ham, flaked fish, such as cod and haddock, cooked cauliflower florets, asparagus tips, cooked, chopped spinach, or grated cheese.

SERVES 4 Ⓥ
300 ml/½ pt thick white sauce (see page 29)
3 medium-sized eggs, separated
pinch salt, pepper

Preheat the oven to 180°C/350°F/gas 4 and set a shelf in the centre position.

Lightly butter a straight-sided 1½ pt soufflé dish; and add a collar around the outside.

Prepare the white sauce and set it aside to cool slightly before beating in the egg yolks, one at a time, incorporating each thoroughly before adding the next. Fold in the preferred filling and correct the seasoning.

Beat the egg whites until stiff, then fold them thoroughly into the mixture with a metal spoon, and transfer the soufflé to the prepared dish. Set this in a roasting tin and add hot water until it comes halfway up the sides. Bake the soufflé in the oven for about 45 minutes or until it is well risen and golden-brown. Do *not* open the oven door before the end of the cooking time or the soufflé will collapse.

KILOCALORIES	145	SUGARS	4g
TOTAL FAT	9g	SODIUM	330mg
SATURATED FAT	5g	FIBRE	0.5g

Please see the introduction for a full explanation of the nutritional factboxes.

FRESH HERB OMELETTE

For a light lunch or supper dish, little can rival an omelette. It is particularly delicious with fresh herbs – parsley, chives and mint. Soda water can be substituted for plain water to make the omelette even fluffier.

SERVES 4 (V)

8 eggs
3 tbsp water
1½ tbsp parsley, finely chopped
1 tbsp chives, finely chopped
½ tbsp mint, finely chopped
pinch salt, white pepper
25 g/1 oz butter (or margarine)

Beat the eggs thoroughly with the water. Stir in the parsley, chives and mint, reserving a little for garnishing; season lightly with salt and pepper and ladle the mixture equally into four cups.

Heat a quarter of the butter in a 15 cm/6 in omelette pan with curved sides, or in a non-stick frying-pan. When it is hot but not brown, pour one cup of the omelette mixture into the centre of the pan, and immediately tilt the pan all round until the base is completely covered. After about 15 seconds, push the edges of the omelette in towards the centre, simultaneously tilting the pan so that the uncooked egg flows out to the edges.

Cook for a further minute until the base of the omelette is lightly brown and the top just moist. Fold it in half with a spatula and slide it out on to a warm plate. Garnish with a few of the reserved herbs and serve at once. Repeat the process for the other three omelettes.

Serve accompanied by crusty bread and a crisp salad.

KILOCALORIES	195	SUGARS	–
TOTAL FAT	16g	SODIUM	430mg
SATURATED FAT	6g	FIBRE	–

Soufflés are simpler than the inexperienced cook might imagine; in fact the only real problem is resisting the temptation to open the oven door to check on the progress of the soufflé before the correct cooking time has elapsed. See the **Sweets and puddings** chapter for recipe ideas for sweet soufflés.

OVEN-BAKED OMELETTE WITH COURGETTES AND TOMATOES

Most cooking cheeses should be of the dry and hard type so that they can absorb moisture from other ingredients. It is a good idea to use half Parmesan and half Cheddar cheese for this omelette.

SERVES 4–6 (V)

4 eggs
450 g/1 lb small courgettes, diced
pinch salt, pepper
3–4 tbsp vegetable (or olive) oil
1 small onion, chopped
1–2 large garlic cloves, crushed
225 g/8 oz tomatoes, skinned and chopped
1 tsp sugar
1 can (400 g/14 oz) tomatoes, chopped
2 tbsp herbs (parsley, chives, basil), freshly chopped
50 g/2 oz cheese, finely chopped
100 g/4 oz boiled potatoes, diced
pinch nutmeg

Line the base of an ovenproof dish with non-stick paper and brush the sides lightly with a little oil; a round provençal *tian* about 23 cm/9 in across and 5 cm/2 in deep is particularly suitable.

Put the courgettes in a pan over low heat, add a little salt and cook, stirring, until the juices begin to run. Add half the oil, cover, and cook for 10–15 minutes until the courgettes are tender.

In another pan, heat the remaining oil and fry the onion and garlic for about 6 minutes, until soft but not brown. Add the fresh tomatoes, salt, pepper and sugar. Cook, uncovered, for 10–15 minutes until the tomato mixture thickens, then add the canned tomatoes with their juice and half of the herbs. Cook until most of the liquid has evaporated.

Heat the oven to 190°C/375°F/gas 5. Lift the courgettes from the pan with a slotted spoon and add to the tomato mixture. Remove the pan from the heat and let the mixture cool for a few minutes, then beat in the eggs, cheese, potato, nutmeg and herbs.

Turn the omelette mixture into the prepared dish and bake in the oven for 20–25 minutes until risen and firm to the touch. Serve the omelette hot or cold, with a green salad and crusty bread.

KILOCALORIES	255	SUGARS	7g
TOTAL FAT	19g	SODIUM	360mg
SATURATED FAT	4g	FIBRE	2.5g

BAGHDADI OMELETTES

These small, herb-flavoured omelettes make perfect snacks, light lunches, suppers and picnic food. They are easy to make and excellent cold with bread and salads or as pitta fillings.

MAKES 10–12

8 eggs
1 small onion
1 medium-sized potato
large bunch of parsley and/or *coriander leaves*
2 mushrooms (optional)
75 g/3 oz lean minced beef (or lamb)
1 tsp ground coriander seeds
pinch salt, pepper
2–3 tbsp vegetable oil

Chop the onion, potato, herbs and mushrooms (if used) very finely. Break the eggs into a large bowl, beat well, and mix in all the ingredients, except the oil, seasoning well. Make sure that the mince is thoroughly separated.

Heat the oil in a large, heavy-based frying-pan over medium heat for a couple of minutes. Drop table-spoonfuls of the mixture into the hot oil. Allow each omelette to cook for 1 minute, then turn it with a spatula and cook the other side for 1 minute. Lift the omelettes from the pan and drain on kitchen paper. Several omelettes can be cooked at the same time in a large frying-pan; otherwise, drop in more mixture as the cooked omelettes are removed.

Serve them hot, or wrap them in foil and keep them in the fridge to be eaten cold (do not re-heat).

[Nutritional values are per omelette.]

KILOCALORIES	165	SUGARS	–
TOTAL FAT	12g	SODIUM	190mg
SATURATED FAT	3g	FIBRE	0.5g

A wok is an essential piece of equipment for the Chinese – and Malaysian – cook. The basin-shaped pot distributes the heat evenly and is especially suitable for rapid stir-frying of mixed ingredients: as one type of food is cooked, it is pushed up the sloping sides, leaving the well in the centre clear for the next ingredient. Apart from stir-frying, a wok is also suitable for steamed and braised dishes, as well as for boiling and deep-frying; it uses less fat than a conventional fryer.

DADAR PADANG
Omelette with coconut

Duck eggs are extremely popular in the Far East. They are occasionally available from health and farm shops in the UK and appreciated for their distinctive taste.

SERVES 2 or 4 Ⓥ

3 duck or *large hen's eggs*
2 shallots, finely chopped
1 garlic clove, crushed
1 red chilli, deseeded and finely chopped (or ½ tsp chilli powder)
1–2 tbsp freshly grated (or desiccated) coconut
pinch salt
1 tbsp vegetable (or groundnut) oil

Mix together the shallots, garlic, chilli and coconut with a tablespoonful of water, or pound them to a paste. Add salt to taste. Beat in the eggs, mixing them thoroughly with a hand whisk; the mixture needs more beating than an ordinary omelette and should become quite fluffy.

Heat the oil in a wok or an omelette pan, tilting to make sure that the sides are well coated. If you are using an omelette pan, divide the mixture into two. Otherwise, pour all the omelette mixture into the hot wok, and swirl the liquid round so that the omelette will not be too thick in the centre. Let it cook for 2 or 3 minutes over medium heat. Turn it over carefully (it should be perfectly circular) and cook slowly for another 3 or 4 minutes or until the middle, the thickest part, is firm, the edges delicately crisp, and the whole omelette lightly browned.

Serve the omelette cut into slices like a cake, either hot with rice and vegetables or cold with salads.

KILOCALORIES	185	SUGARS	2g
TOTAL FAT	15g	SODIUM	220mg
SATURATED FAT	3g	FIBRE	0.5g

Hard cheeses and milk are the most important sources of calcium (eggs also, though to a lesser extent). This mineral is essential for the construction of bones, teeth and nails, and plays a vital part in blood clotting.

COUCOU SABZI

— • —

This popular Iranian omelette is strongly flavoured with aromatic herbs and served hot or cold as an appetiser, side dish or main course.

SERVES 6–8 Ⓥ

75 g/3 oz flat-leaved parsley, finely chopped
6 medium-sized spring onions, finely chopped
1 leek (or medium-sized onion), finely chopped
100 g/4 oz (approx) heart of a small Cos lettuce, finely chopped
50 g/2 oz fresh herbs (dill, basil, tarragon, chives, coriander), chopped
pinch salt, pepper
8 large eggs
2–3 tbsp olive oil

In a large bowl combine the parsley, spring onions, leek or onion, lettuce, herbs and salt and pepper. Beat the eggs with 1 tablespoonful of oil in another bowl and add to the herbs, mixing gently.

Heat the remaining oil in a large, heavy-based frying-pan; pour in the omelette mixture, cover the pan and cook over low heat for about 10 minutes or until the omelette has almost set.

Place the omelette in its pan under a medium-hot grill for a few minutes to brown the top, or ease it away from the edges with a knife, cover the pan with a flat plate or pan lid and quickly invert the omelette on to the plate. Slide it carefully back into the pan, browned side uppermost; cover the pan and cook the omelette for another 5 minutes to brown the other side. Slide the omelette on to a serving dish and cut it into wedges.

KILOCALORIES	185	SUGARS	2g
TOTAL FAT	15g	SODIUM	170mg
SATURATED FAT	3g	FIBRE	1.5g

FONDUE

— • —

Not the Swiss classic which is made with Gruyère cheese and white wine, but a less expensive, English version, and an equally welcoming and warming winter dish. Edam has less fat than Cheddar and has a good consistency when melted.

SERVES 4 Ⓥ

175 g/6 oz mature Cheddar cheese, grated
175 g/6 oz Edam cheese, grated
1 garlic clove, split in half
150 ml/¼ pt medium-dry cider
1 tsp lemon juice
1 tbsp cornflour
15 g/½ oz margarine (or butter)
cayenne (or black) pepper
1 tbsp warm semi-skimmed milk
brown bread cubes

Have ready for the table a fondue set or a flameproof dish and a spirit stove.

Rub the cut sides of the garlic round the inside of the fondue or flameproof dish. Pour in the cider and lemon juice, and heat on top of the cooker until the liquids are almost boiling.

Meanwhile, mix the cheese and cornflour together. Gradually add them to the hot cider and cook, stirring continuously until the cheese has melted and the fondue mixture bubbles.

Stir in the margarine or butter, a good pinch of cayenne or black pepper and the milk. Move the fondue pan to the spirit stove on the table.

To serve, offer bread cubes and fondue forks, and let each guest swirl the bread in the bubbling fondue.

KILOCALORIES	395	SUGARS	1g
TOTAL FAT	29g	SODIUM	780mg
SATURATED FAT	17g	FIBRE	–

CHEESE AND CHIVE SOUFFLÉ

———— • ————

Light and airy, rich in protein and suitable as a lunch or supper dish.

SERVES 4 (V)

175 g/6 oz stale mature Cheddar cheese, finely grated
50 g/2 oz butter (or margarine)
50 g/2 oz plain flour
300 ml/½ pt warm semi-skimmed milk
4 eggs, separated
2 tbsp chives, finely chopped
1 tsp prepared English mustard
pinch salt
2–3 drops malt vinegar

Brush a 1½ litre/2½ pt soufflé dish with a little melted butter or margarine. Tie a collar of greaseproof paper round the outside of the dish, making sure it comes at least 10 cm/4 in above the upper edge. Brush the inside of the paper with more butter or margarine. Set the oven to 190°C/375°F/gas 5 with a shelf and baking tray in centre position.

Melt the butter or margarine in a large pan, stir in the flour to form a roux and cook for 2 minutes without letting it brown. Gradually blend in the warm milk, stirring all the time until the mixture comes to the boil and thickens. Remove it from the heat, and allow it to cool.

Beat in the egg yolks, one at a time and add the cheese, chives and mustard; season to taste with salt. Add the vinegar to the egg whites and whisk to a very stiff snow. Beat a little of them into the cheese mixture to 'loosen' it, then fold in the rest of the egg whites with a metal spoon or spatula, flipping the mixture over and over until the egg whites have been thoroughly incorporated and all streaks have disappeared.

Spoon the soufflé mixture into the prepared dish and bake, undisturbed, for 45 minutes. (Do *not* open the oven door during cooking as the soufflé will collapse.) Remove it from the oven, carefully take away the paper collar, and serve the soufflé immediately, with a crisp side salad and brown bread rolls.

KILOCALORIES	415	SUGARS	4g
TOTAL FAT	31g	SODIUM	600mg
SATURATED FAT	18g	FIBRE	0.5g

———————

(V) This symbol denotes a recipe suitable for vegetarians.

SCRAMBLED EGGS WITH VEGETABLES

———— • ————

It is a mistake to cook scrambled eggs quickly over high heat. To prevent them becoming stringy and rubbery, they should be cooked slowly over low heat until set but still soft.

SERVES 4 (V)

6 eggs
225 g/8 oz waxy potatoes
2 leeks, trimmed
450 g/1 lb spinach (or chard or 225 g/8 oz frozen leaf spinach)
25 g/1 oz butter (or margarine)
1 tbsp semi-skimmed milk
50 g/2 oz Gruyère (or Cheddar) cheese, grated
½ tsp grated nutmeg
3 tbsp fresh tarragon, chopped (or coriander leaves or 1 tbsp dried tarragon)
pinch salt, pepper

Cut the potatoes and leeks into slices 6 mm/¼ in thick. Wash the spinach or chard and shred it (thaw frozen leaf spinach in a pan with very little water, drain and chop it coarsely). Boil the potatoes in a heavy-based pan large enough to take all the vegetables. When the potatoes are almost cooked, add the other vegetables and cook for another 2–3 minutes until they are cooked but still *al dente*. Drain thoroughly. Return the vegetables to the pan and allow them to cool to lukewarm.

Break the eggs into a bowl and beat them lightly. Add them and the butter, milk, cheese, nutmeg and herbs to the vegetables over low heat. The eggs should remain soft and liquid and coat the vegetables like a sauce. As soon as that stage is reached transfer the vegetables and eggs to a serving dish and season well with salt and pepper.

KILOCALORIES	280	SUGARS	3g
TOTAL FAT	18g	SODIUM	500mg
SATURATED FAT	8g	FIBRE	3g

Under EC regulations, eggs are graded in three classes of quality (A, B and C). Class A are sold as whole eggs while the less-than-perfect B and C are sold to food and non-food manufacturers. Eggs are also graded in seven sizes, with grades 3 and 4 being the most popular.

GOUGÈRE EN FROMAGE

This classic French appetiser is made with an airy, cheese-flavoured choux pastry. It can be served as a first course or as an accompaniment to drinks. Suitable for freezing, the pastry should be thawed at room temperature before baking.

SERVES 4–6 Ⓥ

40 g/1½ oz butter
150 ml/¼ pt water
65 g/2½ oz plain flour, sifted
2 eggs, lightly beaten
75 g/3 oz strong cheese, grated
pinch of salt

Line a baking tray with non-stick or oiled greaseproof paper and mark out a 20 cm/8 in circle using a plate as a guide. Preheat the oven to 220°C/425°F/gas 7.

Bring the butter and water to the boil in a medium-sized pan. Remove from the heat and stir in all the flour at once; beat thoroughly and quickly until the mixture forms a smooth ball. Allow it to cool. Add two-thirds of the beaten eggs to the pan and again beat well with an electric or hand whisk. Add most of the remaining egg if necessary to give the dough a piping consistency. Stir in 50 g/2 oz of the grated cheese and beat thoroughly; add a little salt if necessary.

Spoon the dough into a forcing bag fitted with a 1 cm/½ in plain nozzle, and pipe a ring along the outline on the paper. Pipe further rings inside, to fill the outer circle, until all the mixture has been used. Brush the pastry with the rest of the beaten eggs and sprinkle with the grated cheese.

Bake the gougère in the oven for 30 minutes. Serve it hot (or cold) cut into wedges or fingers.

KILOCALORIES	195	SUGARS	–
TOTAL FAT	14g	SODIUM	260mg
SATURATED FAT	8g	FIBRE	0.5g

Choux pastry, properly made, is smooth and shiny, firm enough to hold its shape when piped through a forcing bag.

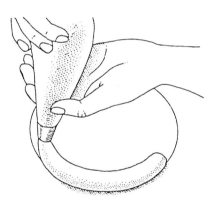

Choux pastry rings are easiest piped along a guideline drawn on paper; a second circle can be piped inside the first or on top of it.

EGG MAYONNAISE CHANTILLY

Chantilly is the French term for a savoury or sweet sauce beaten fluffy with cream. For this elegant hors d'oeuvre yogurt replaces the cream and reduced-calorie mayonnaise stands in for the full-fat variety. Stiffly whisked egg whites provide the classic airiness.

SERVES 4 Ⓥ

4–6 eggs, hard-boiled
12 round lettuce leaves
150 ml/5 fl oz reduced-calorie mayonnaise
3 tbsp low-fat plain yogurt
2 egg whites
3 drops lemon juice
1 small carrot, grated
2 tbsp parsley, chopped
40 g/1½ oz walnuts, finely chopped
2 medium-sized tomatoes, sliced (optional)

Arrange the washed and dried lettuce leaves on four plates. Shell the eggs and halve them lengthways; arrange three halves, cut sides down, over the lettuce.

Stir the mayonnaise and the yogurt together in a bowl. Whisk the egg whites and lemon juice to a stiff snow and fold them, using a metal spoon, into the mayonnaise until the mixture is smooth and evenly combined.

Spoon equal amounts of mayonnaise over the eggs, then sprinkle grated carrot, chopped parsley and chopped walnuts over them; garnish with tomato slices. Serve with brown bread or rolls.

KILOCALORIES	285	SUGARS	7g
TOTAL FAT	22g	SODIUM	440mg
SATURATED FAT	3g	FIBRE	1.5g

BREAD AND BUTTER CHEESE PUDDING WITH PEANUTS

A healthy twist on an old theme – savoury bread and butter pudding with cheese and nuts, suitable as a main course. Any quick-melting cheese will do, such as Lancashire, Leicester or Red Cheshire.

SERVES 4 Ⓥ

6 slices wholemeal bread
butter (or margarine) for spreading
175 g/6 oz hard cheese, crumbled or grated
1 tsp mustard powder
50 g/2 oz unsalted peanuts, finely chopped
3 eggs
600 ml/1 pt semi-skimmed milk
pinch salt

Lightly spread the bread with butter or margarine and cut each slice into four triangles. Mix together the cheese, mustard and peanuts. Arrange half the bread triangles in a 1.75 litre/3 pt greased ovenproof dish, buttered sides uppermost. Sprinkle them with half the cheese mixture. Arrange the remaining bread triangles on top, buttered side up, and cover with the rest of the cheese and peanut mixture.

Whisk together the eggs, milk and a pinch of salt; strain this batter mixture gently into the dish. Let the pudding stand for 30 minutes; then bake it for about 45 minutes in the centre of the oven set to 180°C/350°F/gas 4. When ready, the pudding should be golden-brown and puffy (see opposite).

Serve at once, on its own or with a green salad.

KILOCALORIES	585	SUGARS	9g
TOTAL FAT	39g	SODIUM	810mg
SATURATED FAT	20g	FIBRE	4g

COTTAGE CHEESE AND NUT LOAF

This vegetarian main course dish is packed with protein and essential minerals. Curd cheese, flavoured with herbs, can be used instead of cottage cheese.

SERVES 6 Ⓥ

350 g/12 oz cottage cheese
125 g/4 oz chopped nuts, preferably unsalted peanuts
250 g/9 oz cold cooked porridge
1 medium-sized onion, chopped
100 g/4 oz dry brown breadcrumbs
1 tbsp vegetable oil
1 tsp Worcestershire sauce (or 1 tbsp soya sauce)
pinch salt, pepper
2 tsp sage (or mixed herbs)

Heat the oven to 200°C/400°F/gas 6. Thoroughly mix the cottage cheese with the nuts, porridge, onion and breadcrumbs. Bind the mixture with the oil and Worcestershire or soya sauce, and season it to taste with salt, pepper and herbs. Press into a lightly greased 1 kg/2 lb loaf tin and bake in the centre of the oven for 25–30 minutes or until the top and sides are well browned.

Turn the loaf out on to a warm serving dish and serve it hot, cut into thick slices; offer a tomato or mushroom sauce and a green vegetable or side salad.

KILOCALORIES	305	SUGARS	6g
TOTAL FAT	17g	SODIUM	670mg
SATURATED FAT	3g	FIBRE	2g

CHEESE CROQUETTES

Leftover strong-flavoured cheese which has become hard is ideal for these croquettes, which can be served as a light lunch or supper snack or made into bite-sized shapes for offering with drinks.

SERVES 4–6 Ⓥ

225 g/8 oz strong cheese, grated
75 g/3 oz butter
50 g/2 oz plain flour
300 ml/½ pt semi-skimmed milk
pinch salt, pepper
ground nutmeg, allspice or mace (optional)

2 large egg yolks
1 tbsp single cream
100 g/4 oz fresh wholemeal breadcrumbs
1 small egg, beaten
butter and oil for frying

Melt the butter in a medium-sized saucepan, stir in the flour and cook the roux for a couple of minutes. Gradually add the milk, stirring all the time until the sauce thickens. Away from the heat, stir in the cheese, with salt, pepper and spices to taste. Beat in the egg yolks, the cream and half the breadcrumbs.

Cover the cheese mixture and allow it to cool completely. Divide the mixture into eight or twelve equal portions and shape them into cork-shaped croquettes. Dip them in the beaten egg and coat them with the rest of the breadcrumbs. Chill for 1 hour.

Heat the butter and oil in a large frying-pan and fry the croquettes for about 5 minutes or until they are crisp and golden. Drain on kitchen paper. Serve the croquettes hot, or lukewarm but still crisp, accompanied, perhaps, by a green salad.

[Nutritional values are per croquette.]

KILOCALORIES	280	SUGARS	2g
TOTAL FAT	21g	SODIUM	340mg
SATURATED FAT	11g	FIBRE	–

All hard cheeses made from cow's milk – Cheddar, Emmental and Parmesan – have comparable protein and fat values. Edam has the lowest fat content (about half that of other cheeses). Blue cheeses differ according to the cheese-making process: Roquefort, made from ewe's milk, and Danish Blue contain less fat (and less calcium) than Cheddar, but Stilton has more fat. Soft cheeses include cream, cottage and curd cheeses; they require refrigeration.

Soft-matured cheeses are halfway between the soft and hard types; examples include Brie and Camembert. Do not refrigerate these cheeses, as they do not improve at low temperatures – quite the contrary.

QUICHE LORRAINE

Commercial versions notwithstanding, the classic Quiche Lorraine *never* contains cheese. The traditional recipe uses thick cream but health-conscious cooks can substitute semi-skimmed milk for cream.

SERVES 4

175 g/6 oz shortcrust pastry (see page 199)
125 g/4 oz lean bacon
300 ml/½ pt semi-skimmed milk
3 medium-sized eggs
pinch salt (optional)
nutmeg

Prepare the pastry, roll it out fairly thinly on a floured surface and use to line a 20 cm/8 in flan ring set on a lightly greased baking tray, or a sandwich tin. Chill the pastry while the filling is prepared.

Grill the bacon and cut into narrow strips. Beat the milk with the eggs, and season with salt (optional). Preheat the oven to 200°C/400°F/gas 6.

Cover the pastry with bacon. Strain the egg mixture over the top and sprinkle with a little nutmeg. Bake for 15 minutes, then reduce the temperature to 165°C/325°F/gas 3 and continue baking for another 35–45 minutes, or until the filling has set and turned golden-brown.

Serve the quiche hot or warm with cooked vegetables, or cold with salads.

Variation Replace the bacon filling with one medium-sized chopped onion, fried soft and golden in 1 tablespoonful polyunsaturated fat and mixed with 90 g/3½ oz canned tuna fish, drained and flaked. Cool this mixture before spreading it over the pastry base; strain the egg and milk mixture on top and bake as before.

KILOCALORIES	410	SUGARS	4g
TOTAL FAT	25g	SODIUM	1100mg
SATURATED FAT	10g	FIBRE	1g

FILO, CHEESE AND TOMATO PIE

This Greek pie made with thin filo pastry is traditionally filled with equal amounts of feta and cottage cheese.

SERVES 6 Ⓥ

225 g/8 oz low-fat cream cheese (or half cream cheese and half cottage cheese)
7 sheets filo pastry
15 g/½ oz butter, melted
4 large tomatoes, skinned and thinly sliced
pinch salt, pepper
1 tbsp chopped fresh (or 2 tsp dried) marjoram

Heat the oven to 200°C/400°F/gas 6. Cut the cream cheese into slices as thin as possible. Brush a shallow, preferably rectangular, ovenproof dish, about 20 cm/8 in long, with butter; cover the base with two sheets of filo pastry, both brushed with butter. Top with a thin layer of cheese slices, turn over any overlapping pastry and cover with another sheet of buttered filo pastry. On top of this place a layer of sliced tomatoes, and sprinkle lightly with salt, pepper and marjoram. Lay the next sheet of buttered filo over the tomatoes, followed by more cheese slices, another layer of filo, the remaining tomatoes and finally two buttered sheets of filo pastry. Brush the top with butter.

Bake the pie in the centre of the oven for 20–30 minutes or until it is puffed up and golden-brown. Serve it hot or cold, accompanied with a green salad.

KILOCALORIES	220	SUGARS	2g
TOTAL FAT	16g	SODIUM	300mg
SATURATED FAT	9g	FIBRE	1g

Filo (or phyllo) pastry is a paper-thin pastry used in Greek cookery for both savoury and sweet dishes. It is a simple flour and water paste, worked so thin that it dries and breaks on exposure to air; it must be stored, wrapped in plastic, in the fridge.

RICES & CEREALS, PULSES & PASTA

T hese products are the most important sources of vegetable protein, with rice, wheat and maize being the mainstay of diets throughout the world; beans and pulses are an essential part of vegetarian diets.

RICE

This grain is a staple food for half the world's population. Hundreds of different rice varieties are grown in the East, but as far as the West is concerned, rice comes in either short- or long-grained types (short generally preferred for sweets and puddings, long-grain – Basmati and Patna – for savoury dishes). Rice is marketed as polished (white) and unpolished (brown). The latter has a higher nutrient and fibre content. It has a nutty flavour and is more easily digested than white rice.

Parboiled, ready-cooked and instant rice should be cooked according to the packet instructions. Other types, whether brown or white, should be washed to remove all traces of milling dust before cooking.

Absorption method The rice and water are measured out in cups.

Type	Uncooked	Water	Cooked yield	Servings
Brown	1 cup	2½ cups	4 cups	4–6
White	1 cup	2 cups	3 cups	4
White, parboiled	1 cup	2–2½ cups	4 cups	4–6

Bring the water and a pinch of salt to the boil and add the washed and drained rice. When the water boils again, cover the pan with a tight lid and reduce the heat to a simmer; cook until all the water has been absorbed. Do not remove the lid during cooking. White rice takes 10–15 minutes, brown rice 30 minutes. Fluff up the rice before serving. A little oil or butter can be added whilst cooking to help keep the grains separate.

Oven cooked Stir-fry the rice either dry or in a little oil or butter, then transfer it to a casserole dish with measured water (see above) and cook in an oven preheated to 200°C/400°F/gas 6 for 25 minutes for white rice, 45–50 minutes for brown rice.

CEREALS

This is the term for grains derived from various types of grass: barley, oats, rye, millet, maize.

Wheat is a staple grain throughout the world and is either soft or hard. Hard wheat has the higher protein content, especially the durum wheats used in pasta-making. Bulghur wheat has been cracked, steamed and toasted and has had some of the bran removed. Wheatgerm is a by-product from the milling process.

Barley Barley was once used to make unleavened bread; nowadays, it is chiefly used in beer-making and in the form of pearl barley for cooking. The husked grains come in coarse, medium and fine grades and are used as a thickening agent, most notably in soups.

Oats Most oats are husked and either steam-rolled for breakfast cereals or stone-ground to fine, medium or coarse meal.

Rye Rye is the staple bread cereal in Northern Europe and is also popular in America.

Millet It is used in the Western world as animal fodder, but is grown in poor regions of the world, where little else will grow.

Corn Better known as maize, corn is to the Mississippi Basin and Latin America what rice is to the East. Usually stone-ground to meal, corn is sold hulled when it is known as hominy or hominy grits.

PULSES

This is a general term for the dried edible seeds of beans, peas and lentils; they are the richest source of vegetable protein.

Peas These include dried varieties of garden pea, sold green or yellow, whole or split. The term is also applied to any dried seeds that are round in shape, such as chickpeas. Unlike split peas, chickpeas require pre-soaking and prolonged cooking (see opposite).

Lentils These small seeds from a Middle Eastern legume are round, brown or green when whole, yellow or orange-red when split.

Beans There is a bewildering choice of dried beans: the broad (or fava) bean, haricot bean, including the Mexican black bean, Italian cannellini and borlotti beans, the Spanish pinto bean and the red kidney bean used in chilli con carne. Among the small white beans are the navy and pea beans; butter beans are popularly known as lima beans in America, while the French prefer the flageolet bean.

Black-eyed beans are varieties of cowpeas; mung beans, popular for sprouting, are tiny, green, yellow or black with yellow flesh.

Soya beans comprise the richest, most complete natural vegetable food; from them are derived such protein-rich products as bean curd (tofu), soya milk and soya oil.

Pulses double in bulk during cooking; on average a 450 g/1 lb weight will provide 4 to 6 servings. Dried beans, whole dried peas and chickpeas require soaking, preferably overnight. Drain the soaked pulses and put them in a large pan with four times their weight in water (three times for lentils and split peas). Bring the contents slowly to the boil and, in the case of dried beans, keep the pan at a steady boil for ten minutes in order to destroy potentially dangerous toxins. Cover the pan and simmer: 30–40 minutes for split peas and lentils, 1 hour or more for most beans and up to 2 hours for chickpeas and soya beans. Cooking time can be greatly minimised by using a pressure cooker. For chickpeas use 1.25 litres/2 pt water for every 150 g/5 oz chickpeas, cook for 1 minute without pressure, set the cooker aside for 2 hours, then add a scant tablespoonful of oil and cook at 15 lb pressure for 45 minutes.

Alternatively, the time-consuming cooking processes can be avoided by using canned peas and beans, all of which have already undergone the cooking procedures. Discard the liquid from the can and rinse the beans thoroughly.

PASTA

More than 50 types of pasta exist, all made from water and durum wheat (white or wholemeal). Some are enriched with eggs, such as tagliatelle, lasagne and ravioli, and/or flavoured and coloured with spinach (*verde*) or tomato. The majority of pasta is mass-produced, but many Italian delicatessens offer fresh, home-made pasta of a superior quality. All pasta should be cooked in plenty of boiling, lightly salted water until *al dente* (just tender). Wholemeal types take about 15 minutes, dry pasta 10–12 minutes, fresh about 5 minutes.

The chart shows suggested cooking times. These will vary depending on how old the pulses are, and how soft you want them.

	Soaking [1]	Cooking time (mins)	Rapid boil? [1]
Aduki beans	yes	60	yes
Black-eyed beans	yes	40–50	
Broad beans	12 hrs	60	
Butter beans	yes	50–60	
Flageolet beans	yes	40–50	yes
Haricot beans	yes	50–60	yes
Mung beans	no	30–40	
Pinto beans	yes	50–60	
Kidney beans	yes	50–60	yes
Soya beans	12 hrs	120	yes
Chickpeas	yes	40–50	
Split peas	no [2]	35–40	no
Green lentils	no	30–40	no
Brown lentils	no	40	no
Red split lentils	no [3]	40	no

[1] the table shows where eight-hour soaking or 10 to 15 minutes rapid boiling is advisable, and when it is not necessary; where no entry is given, rapid boiling is optional
[2] alternatively, soak in boiling hot water for 30 minutes and reduce cooking time to 30 minutes
[3] alternatively, soak in boiling hot water for 30 minutes and reduce cooking time to 20 to 30 minutes

BROWN RICE RING

Unpolished or brown rice is considerably healthier than white rice, from which the fibrous outer husks have been removed.

SERVES 4 Ⓥ

250 g/9 oz brown rice
pinch salt
1 red pepper (or 2 canned pimientos), chopped
100 g/4 oz black olives, stoned and sliced
bunch of spring onions, thinly sliced
4 tbsp parsley, finely chopped
4 celery sticks, finely chopped
1–2 tsp vegetable oil

Rinse the rice thoroughly and drain it well. Cook the rice in just over 450 ml/³⁄₄ pt water with a pinch of salt added for about 45 minutes or until it is soft and tender and all the moisture has been absorbed. Meanwhile, blanch the red pepper for 2 minutes in boiling water; drain well, remove seeds and dice.

Fluff up the rice with a fork and fold in the olives, spring onions, red pepper or pimientos, parsley and celery; season to taste. Preheat the oven to 180°C/350°F/gas 4.

Lightly oil a ring mould and pack the rice mixture into it. Bake in the oven for 30 minutes or until heated through. Invert the mould on to a warmed serving dish and fill the centre with carrots or baby mushrooms in tomato sauce (see page 44).

KILOCALORIES	125	SUGARS	4g
TOTAL FAT	3g	SODIUM	120mg
SATURATED FAT	–	FIBRE	2g

BURAS
Steamed, stuffed rice

In Indonesia small dollops of stuffed rice are wrapped in banana leaves and cooked in the traditional rice steamer. Buras can also be steamed in a heatproof dish or pudding basin or rolled up in small squares of aluminium foil.

SERVES 4 Ⓥ

225 g/8 oz long-grain rice
700 ml/24 fl oz coconut milk (see page 111)
pinch salt

FILLING
1 tbsp vegetable oil
2 shallots, sliced
4 medium-sized carrots, diced
1 medium-sized potato, diced
pinch of chilli powder
1 tbsp soya sauce
1 tsp tomato purée

Wash and drain the rice. Put the coconut milk in a pan with the salt, add the rice and let it boil and bubble, uncovered and over gentle heat, until it has absorbed all the coconut milk and is soft and moist. Set the rice aside to cool.

Heat the oil in a wok or heavy-based pan, add the shallots and fry them for 1 minute, then stir in the carrot and potato cubes, and add chilli powder, soya sauce and tomato purée. Continue to stir-fry for another 3 minutes or until the vegetables are tender. Remove the wok from the heat and let the filling rest for a couple of minutes.

Put half the rice in a heatproof dish that will fit a double saucepan. Top with the filling and cover with the remaining rice. Tie foil or a pudding cloth over the dish and steam it for 10–15 minutes. Alternatively, fill a pudding basin with layers of rice and filling and steam it like a Christmas pudding.

Buras can be eaten hot, but is better cold when it can be cut into wedges and served on its own or with cold meat and salads.

KILOCALORIES	205	SUGARS	15g
TOTAL FAT	5g	SODIUM	320mg
SATURATED FAT	–	FIBRE	2.5g

MUSHROOM RISOTTO

Italian risottos, traditionally cooked with wine-flavoured stock and topped with Parmesan, accompany many classic dishes. In this version, stock replaces wine and Cheddar the Parmesan cheese.

SERVES 4

350 g/12 oz round-grain (or risotto) rice
2–3 tbsp vegetable oil
1 medium-sized onion, finely chopped
175 g/6 oz mushrooms, thinly sliced
1.25 litres/2 pt boiling chicken stock (see page 17)
125 g/4 oz mature Cheddar cheese, grated
pinch salt, pepper

Rinse and thoroughly drain the rice. Heat the oil in a large, heavy-based pan and gently fry the onion, covered, for about 10 minutes or until beginning to soften without browning. Remove the lid.

Mix the rice with the onion in the pan and stir-fry it for 2 minutes. Add the mushrooms and continue stir-frying for a further 3 minutes over medium heat. Gradually add the stock, letting the rice absorb the liquid before adding more. Keep the mixture bubbling and stir frequently until all the stock has been added, and the rice is tender but still nutty in texture. If the rice remains hard, cover the pan to prevent excess evaporation, and continue to simmer slowly for another 10–15 minutes.

Fork in the cheese. Remove the pan from the heat and continue forking until the cheese has melted. Season to taste and spoon the risotto on to a warmed serving dish.

KILOCALORIES	355	SUGARS	1g
TOTAL FAT	22g	SODIUM	490mg
SATURATED FAT	7g	FIBRE	1g

BROWN RICE APPETISER

— • —

This dish can be served as a first course or as a light lunch or supper with a green side salad.

SERVES 4 Ⓥ

225 g/8 oz brown rice
pinch salt, pepper
50 g/2 oz butter
1 garlic clove, crushed
1 small onion, finely chopped
100 g/4 oz button mushrooms, roughly chopped
1 tbsp tomato purée
pinch of brown sugar
lemon juice
1 small green (or red) pepper, deseeded and diced
25 g/1 oz sultanas
25 g/1 oz chopped walnuts

Wash and drain the rice thoroughly. Cook it in boiling, lightly salted water for about 35–40 minutes or until it is tender but still slightly nutty in texture. Melt the butter in a small pan over gentle heat and fry the garlic and onion until soft; add three-quarters of the chopped mushrooms and sauté for another 2 minutes.

Drain the rice, return it to the pan over low heat, and fold in the garlic, onion and mushroom mixture

and the tomato purée, with sugar and lemon juice to taste. Check the seasoning. Gently fold in the raw mushrooms, the diced pepper, sultanas and chopped nuts. Serve the rice hot or warm, accompanied by a salad of watercress, lettuce hearts or dandelion leaves.

KILOCALORIES	220	SUGARS	8g
TOTAL FAT	12g	SODIUM	120mg
SATURATED FAT	–	FIBRE	2g

FRIED RICE

— • —

This is a wonderful way of using up cold cooked rice and leftover meat, poultry, fish or vegetables.

SERVES 4

225 g/8 oz long-grain rice, cooked
3 shallots, thinly sliced
2 red chillies, deseeded and sliced (or ½ tsp chilli powder)
1 tbsp vegetable oil
1 tbsp butter (or margarine)
1 garlic clove, crushed (optional)
100–125 g/4 oz skinned chicken breast (or lean bacon or lean pork), diced
100–125 g/4 oz button mushrooms, sliced
1 tbsp clear soya sauce
2 tsp tomato purée
1 tsp paprika (optional)
cucumber and tomato slices

Cook the rice a couple of hours in advance. Pound the shallots and chillies to a paste in a mortar or grind them in a blender. Heat the oil and butter in a wok or large frying-pan over medium heat, add the shallot mixture and the garlic, if used, and stir-fry for 1 minute. Stir in the chicken (or bacon or pork) and the mushrooms and fry for 2 minutes. Add soya sauce, tomato purée, and paprika if used; stir-fry for another minute or so.

Mix the rice into the contents in the pan, stirring constantly until it is heated through. Adjust seasoning. Pile the fried rice on to a warmed serving dish and garnish with sliced cucumber and tomatoes.

KILOCALORIES	205	SUGARS	3g
TOTAL FAT	9g	SODIUM	90mg
SATURATED FAT	3g	FIBRE	1g

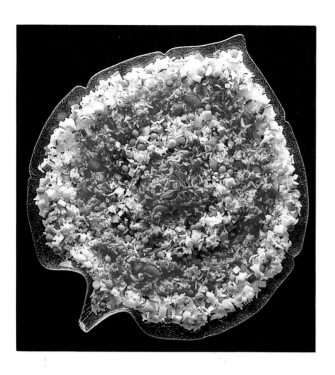

Soak the rice in plenty of water for at least 1 hour. Drain and rinse the rice and add to a large pan of fast boiling water with a pinch of salt. Boil for about 4 minutes, and when the rice is still a little hard and only partly cooked, drain it thoroughly, then return it to the pan with the olive oil, vinegar and plenty of freshly ground pepper. Stir well and steam over very low heat for about 10 minutes, with a folded tea towel stretched beneath the lid to absorb excess steam. Fluff up the rice with a fork.

Put half the rice in a bowl and mix in all the green ingredients. Adjust the seasoning if necessary. Mix the red ingredients into the rice in the pan. Arrange alternate bands of the red and green rice mixtures on a large serving dish.

KILOCALORIES	180	SUGARS	7g
TOTAL FAT	7g	SODIUM	140mg
SATURATED FAT	1g	FIBRE	3.5g

RED AND GREEN RICE SALAD

For this attractive salad, red and green vegetables are mixed separately with rice and arranged in alternating bands or circles.

SERVES 8–10 Ⓥ

450 g/1 lb long-grain rice
pinch salt, pepper
3–4 tbsp olive oil
2 tbsp white wine (or cider vinegar)

GREEN INGREDIENTS
4 young courgettes, grated or finely chopped
1 green pepper, deseeded and chopped
225 g/8 oz shelled peas (or broad beans), boiled
3 spring onions, finely chopped
2 sprigs fresh mint, finely chopped
bunch of parsley, finely chopped

RED INGREDIENTS
2 tbsp tomato purée (optional)
2 large tomatoes, skinned, deseeded and chopped
1 red pepper, deseeded and chopped
5 radishes, thinly sliced
2 medium-sized carrots, coarsely grated or chopped
1 red onion, finely chopped

KICHRI BAGHDAD-STYLE

Kichri is a mixture of rice and lentils cooked with various spices and other ingredients. It probably originated in Western India.

SERVES 4 Ⓥ

275 g/10 oz long-grain rice
175 g/6 oz lentils (small pink or large yellow)
1.25 litres/2 pt water
pinch salt
1 tbsp tomato purée
6 tbsp vegetable oil
4 garlic cloves, finely chopped
2 tsp ground cumin
75 g/3 oz Cheddar cheese, thinly sliced (or Haloumi or Gruyère, grated)

Wash the rice in several changes of cold water and leave it to soak for 1 hour. Wash and drain the lentils and place them, together with the measured water, in a large pan with a tight-fitting lid. Bring the lentils slowly to the boil and let them simmer, covered, for 10–20 minutes, depending on type, until nearly tender. Season lightly with salt. Stir in the tomato purée and 2 tablespoonfuls of oil. Drain the rice and add it to the lentils. The level of the water in the pan should now be about 12 mm/½ in above the rice and lentils; if not,

add or remove water as necessary. Raise the heat and bring the contents of the pan to the boil, then lower the heat to moderate so that the water will continue to bubble. Do not cover, but stir occasionally. When most of the water has been absorbed, but there are still a few bubbles (after about 3 minutes), reduce the heat to the lowest level possible and cover the pan tightly. Leave to steam for 10 minutes.

Meanwhile, heat the remaining oil in a small pan, add the garlic and fry it over moderate heat for 1 minute, lower the heat, add the cumin and stir-fry for a few seconds. Stir this mixture into the rice and lentils after they have steamed for 10 minutes; mix thoroughly with a wooden spoon. Steam the contents, covered, over low heat for another 5 minutes or until fluffy.

Fry the sliced Haloumi cheese, if used, for 2 minutes in the pan with the traces of oil and spices. Spoon the kichri on to a hot serving dish and top with the crisp cheese slices or sprinkle with grated Cheddar and/or Gruyère. Serve with a bowl of low-fat plain yogurt.

KILOCALORIES	400	SUGARS	1g
TOTAL FAT	27g	SODIUM	250mg
SATURATED FAT	4g	FIBRE	1g

SUNFLOWER SEED CASSEROLE
———— • ————

This vegetarian main-course dish contains a good balance of nutrients.

SERVES 6 Ⓥ

*725 g/1 lb 10 oz cooked brown rice
(350 g/12 oz uncooked rice)
300 g/11 oz sunflower seeds
100 g/4 oz cashew nuts, unsalted
175 ml/6 fl oz water
75 g/3 oz mushrooms, chopped
1 tbsp yeast extract (or 2 tbsp dried yeast flakes)
1 large onion, finely chopped
pinch salt
¼ tsp each onion powder, sage, thyme, marjoram,
garlic powder and sweet pepper flakes
3 tbsp soya sauce
1 tbsp parsley, finely chopped*

Preheat the oven to 165°C/325°F/gas 3. Put the sunflower seeds in a liquidiser and blend them to a powder; turn them into a mixing bowl. Liquidise the cashew nuts with the water to a smooth paste and stir it into the sunflower seeds, together with the cooked rice, the mushrooms, yeast extract (or flakes), onion, salt and flavourings. Add the soya sauce and chopped parsley and mix thoroughly.

Spoon the mixture into a large ovenproof dish, cover it with a lid and bake in the oven for 1½ hours. Remove the lid halfway through cooking time. Serve the casserole hot, accompanied by creamed spinach or kale.

KILOCALORIES	575	SUGARS	3g
TOTAL FAT	33g	SODIUM	300mg
SATURATED FAT	4g	FIBRE	5g

Yeast flakes Dried flakes, the result of a fermentation process of baker's yeast, yielding a high-protein product with a distinct cheese flavour; used commercially in cheese biscuit production.

MILLET LOAF
———— • ————

Millet consists of small edible grains from various grasses, which in inhospitable regions, drought-stricken or waterlogged, provide the staple food in many developing countries.

SERVES 4 Ⓥ

*175 g/6 oz millet
1–2 tbsp vegetable oil
1 medium-sized onion, finely chopped
4 celery sticks, diced
50 g/2 oz mushrooms, roughly chopped
75 g/3 oz cashew nuts, finely chopped
4 tbsp wholemeal flour
300 ml/½ pt water
475 ml/¾ pt soya milk
1 tsp soya sauce
pinch salt
pinch dried sage
75 g/3 oz stoned olives, sliced*

Put the millet in a liquidiser and blend it to a coarse meal. Heat the oil in a pan over medium heat and sauté the onion and celery, covered, for about 5 minutes or until soft. Add the mushrooms and cook for another 2 minutes. Remove the pan from the heat.

Thoroughly mix the millet, vegetables and cashew nuts in a large bowl. Blend the wholemeal flour with 4 tablespoonfuls of the measured cold water to a smooth paste. Add the remaining water to the soya milk and bring to just below boiling point. Add the flour paste to the hot milk, stirring the sauce constantly to prevent lumps forming. Preheat the oven to 180°C/350°F/gas 4.

Stir the soya into the sauce and season it to taste with salt and sage. Pour it over the dry ingredients, mix thoroughly, then add the sliced onions. Spoon the mixture into a lightly oiled loaf tin or ovenproof dish and bake for 1½ hours. Stir the mixture once or twice during baking to prevent the millet settling at the bottom of the dish and becoming too thick.

To serve, either turn the millet loaf out of the tin and cut it into thick slices, or serve it straight from the dish, accompanied by vegetables and perhaps a tomato sauce (see page 44).

KILOCALORIES	470	SUGARS	4g
TOTAL FAT	21g	SODIUM	590mg
SATURATED FAT	2g	FIBRE	4g

CRACKED WHEAT SALAD

The hard wheat grains are cracked and softened by boiling, then dried, ground and sieved before being sold variously as bulghur (or bulgar), burghul, pourgouri or bourgouri, as cracked wheat is variously called. It comes in different grades – fine, medium and coarse. For this Syrian dish, known as *tabbouleh*, use fine cracked wheat.

SERVES 4–6 (V)

175 g/6 oz fine cracked wheat
½ small cucumber
pinch salt, pepper
1 medium-sized onion (or 12 spring onions incl. green parts), finely chopped
large bunch parsley, finely chopped
fresh coriander (or mint leaves), chopped
rind and juice of 1 large lemon
approx 2 tbsp olive oil
50 g/2 oz pine nuts, roasted
tomato slices, black olives

Put the cracked wheat in a large bowl with plenty of cold water; as it soaks it will swell and more than double in size – in about 30 minutes. Meanwhile, peel and dice the cucumber and layer it in a colander with a sprinkling of salt to extract excess water; leave it for at least 30 minutes; rinse off the salt under running water and wring the cucumber dry in a cloth.

Drain the cracked wheat, squeezing out as much water as possible with the hands and drying it further in a tea towel. Lightly crush the onion or spring onions in a large bowl with the end of a rolling pin, mix in the cracked wheat, cucumber, parsley and coriander or mint, lemon rind and juice and enough olive oil to moisten the salad. Season to taste. Finally toss the freshly roasted, cooled pine nuts in the salad.

Pile the salad into a bowl and garnish with tomato slices and black olives.

KILOCALORIES	250	SUGARS	2g
TOTAL FAT	13g	SODIUM	80mg
SATURATED FAT	1g	FIBRE	0.5g

SPROUTED WHEATBURGERS

Sprouted seeds and grains give a particularly nutty texture to salads. Use hard Canadian whole wheat, obtainable from health-food shops.

SERVES 4 (V)

150 g/5 oz sprouted wheat
175 g/6 oz fine millet (or *barley*)
40 g/1½ oz sunflower seeds
40 g/1½ oz pumpkin seeds
1 tbsp unsweetened peanut butter
2 tbsp chopped onion (or *spring onions*)
½ tsp each dried thyme and sage (or 1 tsp each fresh thyme and sage, chopped)
1 tbsp soya sauce
pinch salt
2–3 tbsp soft brown breadcrumbs
2–3 tbsp vegetable oil

Steam the millet (or barley) in a double boiler by placing 350 ml/12 fl oz of water, with a pinch of salt, in the upper part and bringing it to a rapid boil. Set it over the steadily simmering water in the lower part of the boiler and gradually pour the millet into the upper part, stirring constantly until the mixture begins to thicken. Leave it to cook, uncovered, for about 20 minutes or until the millet is tender and all the water has been absorbed by the grains. Stir occasionally. Set aside to cool.

Grind the sunflower and pumpkin seeds in a liquidiser. Mix them into the millet, with the peanut butter, chopped onions and herbs. Fold in the sprouted wheat and mix thoroughly with the soya sauce; season to taste with salt. Bind the mixture with breadcrumbs; divide it into four equal portions and shape them into patties.

Heat the oil in a large pan and fry the burgers over medium heat for 10 minutes or until golden-brown on both sides, turning them once.

Serve the burgers as a snack, placed in split sesame buns, or as a main vegetarian course accompanied with vegetables and salads.

KILOCALORIES	330	SUGARS	3g
TOTAL FAT	24g	SODIUM	165mg
SATURATED FAT	3g	FIBRE	2.5g

(V) This symbol denotes a recipe suitable for vegetarians.

Please see the introduction for a full explanation of the nutritional factboxes.

For a vegetarian main course, fold into the cooked cracked wheat cooked aubergines, diced or thinly sliced, and/or skinned, roughly chopped fresh tomatoes, cooked diced pumpkin or cooked broad beans.

KILOCALORIES	255	SUGARS	–
TOTAL FAT	7g	SODIUM	100mg
SATURATED FAT	–	FIBRE	–

CRACKED WHEAT PILAFF

Cracked wheat (bulghur) is a staple ingredient of the Middle East, now available in British supermarkets.

SERVES 4 Ⓥ

225 g/8 oz coarse cracked wheat
300–450 ml/½–¾ pt white stock (see page 17)
or water
pinch salt, pepper
1–2 tbsp vegetable oil (or butter)

Put the cracked wheat in a sieve and rinse it quickly but thoroughly under cold running water. Place it in a large pan with the stock or water and a seasoning of salt and pepper. Cook, covered, over very low heat for 10–15 minutes or until the wheat is tender and all the liquid has been absorbed; if necessary, add a little more water if it dries out before it is cooked. Stir in the butter or oil and leave the pan, covered, off the heat, or over the lowest possible, for about 20 minutes, to allow the wheat to swell.

Serve cracked wheat instead of rice or potatoes, as an accompaniment to fish, poultry or meat, on its own or smothered with low-fat plain yogurt.

Variation Add 2–3 tablespoonfuls of roasted pine nuts, or blanched, slivered almonds, and 2 tablespoonfuls of raisins into the cracked wheat. Or add a handful of broken vermicelli dry-roasted in a frying-pan, or cooked and flaked smoked haddock, whiting or cod, or leftover diced lamb, chicken or turkey.

VEGETARIAN COUSCOUS

This classic North African dish is traditionally cooked in a *couscousière*, an earthenware open-topped pot. A stainless-steel steamer lined with a tea towel is a good modern substitute.

SERVES 4 Ⓥ

100 g/4 oz chickpeas or 200 g/8 oz cooked chickpeas
175 g/6 oz couscous
450 ml/¾ pt vegetable stock
8 button onions
2 medium-sized leeks, coarsely chopped
1 medium-sized carrot, coarsely chopped
1 celery stick, coarsely chopped
pinch salt, pepper
2 courgettes, coarsely chopped
4 tomatoes, skinned and roughly chopped
1 tsp fresh mint, chopped
2 tsp fresh parsley, chopped
pinch each of dried oregano and saffron or a few
shreds soaked in 1 tbsp warm water

SAUCE
4 tbsp hot stock
1 tsp each cumin and ground coriander
½ tsp chilli powder
2 tbsp tomato purée

Soak the chickpeas in cold water for at least 3 hours and preferably overnight. Drain them, add fresh cold water and bring to the boil. Boil for 10 minutes, then reduce the heat and simmer, covered until tender, after 1–2 hours. Add a little salt after 45 minutes. Drain the chickpeas when they are tender.

Put the couscous in a bowl and cover it with 225 ml/ 8 fl oz cold water; leave it for 10 minutes to absorb the liquid. Put the stock, onions, leeks, carrot and celery, with a seasoning of salt and black pepper, in the lower half of a large steamer. Line the steamer top with a piece of muslin or tea towel and tip the wet couscous

into it. Cover the pan tightly, bring to the boil over gentle heat, and steam for 30 minutes.

Add the courgettes to the other vegetables and fork the couscous through to remove any lumps; return the lid. Cook for another 10 minutes. Add the tomatoes, mint, parsley and oregano to the vegetable mixture and again cover and cook for a further 10 minutes. Spoon the couscous on to a flat dish and keep it warm.

Add the chickpeas and saffron (with its soaking water) to the vegetables and heat through. Drain off most of the stock. Mix 4 tablespoonfuls of the hot stock with the cumin, coriander, chilli powder and tomato purée.

Pile the vegetables, with a cupful of stock, on top of the couscous. Serve the spicy sauce separately.

KILOCALORIES	230	SUGARS	11g
TOTAL FAT	3g	SODIUM	460mg
SATURATED FAT	–	FIBRE	6.5g

CHICKPEA AND SESAME SPREAD

Sesame seeds give a deliciously nutty flavour to this nutritious sandwich filling.

SERVES 4 (V)

200 g/7 oz chickpeas
4 spring onions, chopped
2 garlic cloves, crushed
2–3 tbsp parsley, finely chopped
2 tbsp sesame seeds
pinch salt
1 tsp cumin
2 tbsp single cream
2–3 tbsp vegetable oil

Rinse the chickpeas thoroughly, then leave them to soak in plenty of cold water for 8 hours. Boil for 10 minutes, then drain them thoroughly. Grind the chickpeas, spring onions, garlic and parsley in a food processor. Mix in the sesame seeds and season to taste with salt and cumin; bind with cream.

Heat the oil in a large, heavy-based pan; lower the heat and fry the mixture for about 15 minutes until brown and heated through. Turn it frequently and moisten with a little water if necessary.

Serve hot, as a filling, in hot pitta bread or wholewheat pancakes or piled on hot toast.

KILOCALORIES	195	SUGARS	1g
TOTAL FAT	15g	SODIUM	110mg
SATURATED FAT	1g	FIBRE	3g

OATBURGERS

Nutritionally, oats contain more fat than wheat though they are a good source of vitamins of the B complex. Oats are stone-ground in grades of fine, medium or coarse (pinhead).

SERVES 4–6 Ⓥ

125 g/4 oz fine oatmeal
3–4 tbsp vegetable oil
1 small onion, diced
25 g/1 oz walnuts, chopped or coarsely ground
25 g/1 oz sunflower seeds, coarsely ground
½ tsp each sage and thyme
pinch marjoram
1 tsp yeast extract (or 2 tsp dried yeast flakes)
scant 3 tbsp soya sauce
350 ml/12 fl oz boiling water

Heat a little of the oil in a small frying-pan and sauté the onion over gentle heat for about 5 minutes or until soft but not coloured. Mix the onion with the ground walnuts, sunflower seeds, herbs and yeast extract (or flakes), stir in the soya sauce and the boiling water, mixing thoroughly. Carefully fold in the oatmeal and set the mixture aside to cool and firm.

Divide the mixture into six large or eight smaller portions and shape them into patties or burgers. Fry the oatburgers, ideally in a non-stick pan, otherwise in an ordinary, heavy-based pan with a little vegetable oil, over medium heat for about 6 minutes, turning them once. Serve hot, with spinach or carrots.

KILOCALORIES	270	SUGARS	1g
TOTAL FAT	18g	SODIUM	90mg
SATURATED FAT	1g	FIBRE	2.5g

CHILLI BEANS

Kidney beans – and most other dried beans – contain an enzyme which can be harmful in large amounts. The enzyme is destroyed at boiling temperature, and for this reason most dried beans, irrespective of their further treatment, should be brought to the boil and kept bubbling steadily for 10 minutes (see page 123).

SERVES 4 Ⓥ

200 g/7 oz red kidney beans or pinto beans
600 ml/1 pt water
½ tsp salt
175 g/6 oz cracked wheat
2 tbsp vegetable oil
2 medium-sized onions, chopped
1 small garlic clove, crushed
4 celery sticks, chopped
1 large green pepper, deseeded and chopped
250 g/9 oz canned tomatoes (or
125 g/4 oz tomato paste)
1 tsp each, ground cumin and chilli powder
1 tsp oregano or marjoram, freshly chopped or
½ tsp dried oregano (or marjoram)
1 tsp basil, freshly chopped (or ½ tsp dried basil)
1 tsp honey (optional)

Rinse the beans in several changes of water, put them in a pan with the measured amount of water and leave them to soak for 8 hours. Bring the beans in their soaking water to the boil; boil them over high heat for 10 minutes, then lower the heat, and simmer, covered, for 1–1½ hours or until the beans are almost tender; add salt for the last hour.

Meanwhile, rinse the cracked wheat thoroughly and put it in a pan with 500ml/17 fl oz of cold water. Bring to the boil and simmer gently for 20–25 minutes. Drain well.

Heat the oil in a wok or frying-pan and sauté the onions and garlic for about 5 minutes, add the celery and pepper and sauté for another 2–3 minutes. Stir the drained wheat, the sautéed vegetables and the tomatoes into the beans, add the spices and herbs and honey, if used. Mix all the ingredients thoroughly, cover the pan and simmer for about 30 minutes.

Serve the beans hot, with crusty bread and perhaps a green side salad.

KILOCALORIES	395	SUGARS	10g
TOTAL FAT	9g	SODIUM	150mg
SATURATED FAT	–	FIBRE	10g

CELLOPHANE NOODLES WITH DRIED SHRIMPS

— • —

Transparent and wiry, cellophane noodles are made from the highly nutritious mung bean. They are much used in Chinese cooking and chiefly served as a vegetable dish to accompany rice.

SERVES 4

75 g/3 oz cellophane noodles
25 g/1 oz dried shrimps, rinsed
3–4 spring onions
2–3 tbsp groundnut (or corn) oil
300 ml/¹⁄₂ pt chicken stock
2 tsp thin soya sauce
black pepper

Soak the cellophane noodles in about 1.5 litres/2¹⁄₂ pt of boiling water for 20 minutes or until they have expanded and become pliable. Drain the noodles and cut them up with scissors.

Meanwhile, rinse the shrimps, put them in a bowl with enough boiling water to cover them and leave them to soak for about 20 minutes. Drain them, reserving the soaking liquid. Trim the spring onions and cut them into 2.5 cm/1 in pieces, keeping white and green parts separate.

Set a wok or heavy-based pan over high heat until smoke rises. Add the oil and swirl it around, then stir in the white spring onion before adding the shrimps. Stir about a dozen times so that the fragrance of the shrimps is released. Add the cellophane noodles, the shrimp soaking liquid and the chicken stock. Bring to the boil, cover the wok and lower the heat to medium. Continue cooking for about 15 minutes or until most of the stock has been absorbed.

Add the green spring onion to the noodles, season to taste with soya sauce and pepper and serve at once.

KILOCALORIES	95	SUGARS	1g
TOTAL FAT	7g	SODIUM	450mg
SATURATED FAT	1g	FIBRE	0.5g

Soya sauce The best-known and most widely used by-product of the versatile soya bean. Numerous grades are available, from dark, dense and pungent to pale-coloured, thin soya sauces for delicate flavouring; the best are always those made by natural fermentation.

MASOOR DAL LAVANG WALI

Egyptian lentils with cloves

— • —

Split pink or red Egyptian lentils form the basis for numerous Middle Eastern dishes. Easy and quick to cook, they have a higher protein content than any other pulse, except soya beans.

SERVES 4 Ⓥ

175 g/6 oz split red lentils
600 ml/1 pt water
¹⁄₂ tsp salt
1 green chilli, deseeded and chopped
small pinch of asafoetida (see glossary)
¹⁄₄ tsp turmeric

GARNISH
1 tbsp vegetable oil (or ghee)
4–5 whole cloves
¹⁄₄ tsp mustard seeds
3–4 curry leaves, crumbled
¹⁄₄ tsp chilli powder

Thoroughly clean and wash the lentils in several changes of cold water, leave to soak for about 20 minutes; then drain.

Place the lentils in a large, heavy-based pan with the measured water, salt, green chilli, asafoetida and turmeric. Mix well; bring the contents of the pan to the boil, cover with a lid and cook over low heat 30–40 minutes until the lentils are tender. Remove the pan from the heat and keep the lentils warm.

Heat the vegetable oil or ghee in a small frying-pan, add the cloves and the mustard seeds and, as soon as they pop, blend in the crumbled curry leaves and the chilli powder. Shake the pan a couple of times to mix the ingredients thoroughly, but do not let them burn.

Spoon the lentils into a warmed serving dish, top with the spicy garnish, cover with a lid and let the flavours infuse for a couple of minutes before serving.

KILOCALORIES	80	SUGARS	–
TOTAL FAT	4g	SODIUM	250mg
SATURATED FAT	–	FIBRE	1g

Shape the mixture into 12 patties and set them on lightly oiled, foil-covered baking sheets. Bake for 30 minutes and serve hot with vegetables or a green salad.

[Nutritional value is per patty.]

KILOCALORIES	320	SUGARS	1g
TOTAL FAT	21g	SODIUM	100mg
SATURATED FAT	1g	FIBRE	1g

LENTIL PATTIES

Red or green lentils, which do not need soaking, can be used for these wholesome patties.

SERVES 6 Ⓥ

200 g/7 oz lentils, red or green
pinch salt
1 medium-sized onion, finely chopped
60 g/2½ oz walnuts, finely chopped
75 g/3 oz soft brown breadcrumbs (or 350 g/12 oz cooked brown rice)
1–2 tsp fresh sage, finely chopped (or ½ tsp dried sage)
1 tbsp soya sauce
tomato juice or soya milk (optional)

Wash the lentils thoroughly and put them in a large pan with a generous 1.25 litres/2 pt of cold water. Cover the pan and bring to the boil over high heat; reduce the heat and simmer the lentils for about 45 minutes or until tender and near-mushy. Stir occasionally and add a pinch of salt near the end of cooking time. Drain the lentils, let them cool slightly, then reduce them to a purée in a food processor.

Preheat the oven to 165°C/325°F/gas 3. Mix the lentil purée with the onion, walnuts and breadcrumbs (or brown rice); add the sage and soya sauce. The mixture should be firm, but not moist – if necessary, add enough tomato juice or soya milk.

Shape the mixture by hand into 6 patties, place them on a lightly greased baking tray and bake in the centre of the oven for 30 minutes. Serve the patties hot, with a cooked vegetable and a tomato sauce (see page 44). The patty mixture can also be baked as a roast, in an ovenproof casserole, at 180°C/350°F/gas 4 for 1 hour.

KILOCALORIES	155	SUGARS	2g
TOTAL FAT	7g	SODIUM	170mg
SATURATED FAT	1g	FIBRE	1.5g

WALNUT-TOFU PATTIES

Tofu is the Japanese name for soya bean curd. It is extremely rich in protein, bland in flavour but a good base for savoury or sweet ingredients.

SERVES 4 Ⓥ

250 g/9 oz walnut pieces
450 g/1 lb block tofu, grated
6 tbsp dried onion flakes (or 1 small onion, finely chopped and lightly sautéed)
8 tbsp fresh parsley, chopped (or 4 tbsp dried)
pinch each of sage and marjoram
pinch salt
100 g/4 oz soft brown breadcrumbs

Place the walnuts on a baking sheet and roast them in the oven at the lowest possible heat (110°C/225°F/gas ¼) for 15 minutes. Chop them coarsely.

Preheat the oven to 165°C/325°F/gas 3. Mix together the walnuts, tofu, onion and herb seasonings; work in the breadcrumbs, kneading the mixture by hand; if necessary, moisten with a little vegetable stock.

cover the pan and simmer for 45–60 minutes, adding ¼ tsp salt after 30 minutes. When the beans are tender, add the shredded green vegetables and cook for a few minutes until these are soft.

Serve the beans and vegetables, with the cooking liquid, like a soup, accompanied by chunks of bread for dipping. Alternatively, blend the oil with lemon juice and spices and mix this dressing into the beans and vegetables.

As an accompaniment to grilled meat, drain the beans and greens before dressing them with oil, lemon juice and spices.

KILOCALORIES	480	SUGARS	3g
TOTAL FAT	33g	SODIUM	120mg
SATURATED FAT	5g	FIBRE	7.5g

PEASE PUDDING

This British dish is traditionally served with boiled bacon. It can be served as an accompaniment to poached eggs, bacon, pork and ham.

SERVES 4 Ⓥ

275 g/10 oz split yellow peas
15 g/½ oz butter (or margarine), melted
1 egg, lightly beaten
pinch salt, pepper

Wash the peas in several changes of water, then leave them to soak overnight in a bowl of water. Drain the peas and put them in a large pan, with water to cover. Bring to the boil, lower the heat and cover the pan. Simmer the peas over gentle heat for about 1½–2 hours or until quite soft and tender. Top up with boiling water if necessary to prevent the peas from boiling dry.

Drain the peas and leave them to cool slightly before blending them to a coarse purée. Preheat the oven to 180°C/350°F/gas 4. Beat the melted butter or margarine and the egg into the purée, and season. Spoon the purée into a 600 ml/1 pt well-greased ovenproof dish and bake, uncovered, in the centre of the oven for 30 minutes.

KILOCALORIES	135	SUGARS	1g
TOTAL FAT	5g	SODIUM	150mg
SATURATED FAT	3g	FIBRE	2g

BLACK-EYED BEANS WITH GREENS

Simple, delicious and inexpensive, this nutritious dish originates from the Middle East. Use tender young turnip tops for preference, or spinach, Savoy cabbage, spring greens, Swiss chard or leeks.

SERVES 4 Ⓥ

225 g/8 oz black-eyed beans
450 g/1 lb green vegetables (trimmed weight)
1.25 litres/2 pt water
¼ tsp salt
125 ml/4 fl oz olive oil (optional)
juice of 1 lemon (optional)
1 tsp ground cumin (optional)
pinch of chilli powder (optional)

Soak the black-eyed beans for 8 hours. Rinse them thoroughly and put them in a pan with the measured water and bring to the boil; boil for 10 minutes, then

LENTIL LOAF

Lentils are bland in flavour, so they generally require the addition of flavouring and/or fats.

SERVES 4–6 Ⓥ

225 g/8 oz split lentils
25 g/1 oz butter (or margarine)
1 large onion, roughly chopped
3 tbsp tomato purée
75–100 g/3–4 oz fresh brown breadcrumbs
1 tbsp curry powder
pinch salt, pepper
2 large eggs, lightly beaten

Rinse the lentils thoroughly, drain and put them in a large pan with enough water to cover. Bring to the boil over medium heat and simmer for about 30 minutes or until quite tender. Drain the lentils thoroughly, then mash them to a smooth pulp. Melt the margarine or butter in a small pan and fry the onion until soft and golden, then stir the onion and fat into the lentils, together with the tomato purée.

Preheat the oven to 190°C/375°F/gas 5. Mix in the breadcrumbs and curry powder and season to taste. Bind the lentils with enough beaten eggs to give a moist but not sloppy mixture.

Spoon the mixture into a well-greased 1 kg/2 lb loaf tin and smooth the top. Bake in the centre of the oven for 45 minutes or until the loaf is set and lightly browned.

Serve hot or cold, cut into thick slices, as a main vegetable dish accompanied by a salad.

KILOCALORIES	210g	SUGARS	4g
TOTAL FAT	8g	SODIUM	350mg
SATURATED FAT	4g	FIBRE	2g

GADON TAHU
Steamed bean curd with coconut and chilli

Tahu is the Indonesian term for tofu or soya bean curd.

SERVES 4

4 squares fresh tofu (or 2 packets pasteurised tofu)
60 g/2½ oz shrimps (or cooked chicken), minced (optional)
2 tbsp spring onions, chopped

1 tbsp chives, chopped
2 green chillies, deseeded and chopped
150 ml/5 fl oz thick coconut milk (see page 111)
juice of ½ lime (or lemon)
1 egg, beaten
½ tsp ground coriander
pinch salt
2 bay leaves

Mash the tofu with a fork and blend in the chicken or shrimps, spring onions, chives and chillies; beat in the coconut milk, lime or lemon juice and the egg to give the mixture a custard-like consistency. Season to taste with coriander and salt.

Divide the mixture between four ramekins or heat-proof dishes; top each dish with half a bay leaf. Steam the custards for 15 minutes in a large steamer or set the dishes in a roasting tin, with hot water coming halfway up the sides of the ramekins, and bake in the oven, preheated to 200°C/400°F/gas 6, for 20–25 minutes or until set.

Serve hot or cold as a side dish with rice.

KILOCALORIES	440	SUGARS	3g
TOTAL FAT	18g	SODIUM	740mg
SATURATED FAT	1g	FIBRE	0.5g

CHICKPEA ROAST

Rich in nutrients, a vegetarian main course such as this chickpea roast is a good substitute for a meat dish even for non-vegetarians.

SERVES 6–8 Ⓥ

400 g/14 oz chickpeas
pinch salt
350 g/12 oz fine cracked wheat
1 tsp dried sage
1 tsp oregano
1 small onion, diced
1 small green pepper, chopped
1 small red pepper, chopped
3 celery sticks, chopped
50 g/2 oz mushrooms, chopped
50 g/2 oz stoned olives, chopped

Rinse the chickpeas thoroughly, then leave them to soak in a large bowl of water overnight. Drain them and put them in a large pan, with cold water to cover; bring to the boil, boil for 10 minutes, then cover the pan and reduce the heat. Simmer the chickpeas for 1–2 hours or until tender, adding more boiling water if required; towards the end of cooking time, add a little salt.

Drain the chickpeas and put half of them in a liquidiser with 225 ml/8 fl oz of cold water; blend until smooth. Put the cracked wheat with 450 ml/¾ pt of water, the sage, oregano and a pinch salt in a pan; bring to the boil and simmer for 5–10 minutes. Preheat the oven to 180°C/350°F/gas 4.

In another pan simmer the onion, peppers, celery, mushrooms and olives in a little water for about 10 minutes; drain well. Mix together the chickpea purée, whole chickpeas, cracked wheat and vegetables; adjust seasoning if required and spoon the mixture into a lightly greased ovenproof dish or large foil-lined loaf tin. Bake in the centre of the oven for 1 hour, covering the top for the first 45 minutes.

Serve hot, cut into slices, as a vegetarian main course accompanied by jacket potatoes and a salad.

KILOCALORIES	320	SUGARS	2g
TOTAL FAT	9g	SODIUM	70mg
SATURATED FAT	1g	FIBRE	3g

SOYA BEAN ROAST

The bland soya bean is flavoured with peppers, olives and herbs in this dish.

SERVES 4–6 Ⓥ

75 g/3 oz soya beans
350 ml/12 fl oz water
3–4 celery sticks, diced
1 onion, diced
2 red peppers, diced
3–4 tbsp stoned green olives, sliced
4 sprigs parsley, finely chopped
1–2 tsp fresh sage, finely chopped or 1 tsp dried sage
1 tbsp dried yeast flakes or yeast extract
1 tbsp soya sauce
pinch salt, paprika
3 tbsp soft brown breadcrumbs or oatmeal

Rinse the soya beans in several changes of water; leave them to soak overnight. Put the beans in a pan with 1.5 l/2½ pt of cold water, bring to the boil, boil for 10 minutes, then lower the heat and simmer the beans for about 2 hours until tender; add ½ tsp salt after 1½ hours. Drain the cooked beans and set them aside until quite cold.

Preheat the oven to 150°C/300°F/gas 2. Put the soya beans and measured water in the liquidiser and blend until smooth. Mix the beans with the celery, onion, peppers, olives, parsley, sage and yeast flakes. Blend in the soya sauce and season the mixture with salt and paprika; bind it to a manageable dough with the breadcrumbs or oatmeal.

Transfer the mixture to a lightly oiled ovenproof dish, cover and bake in the oven for 2 hours; remove the lid for the last 20 minutes. Serve straight from the dish with baked potatoes and a green vegetable.

KILOCALORIES	145	SUGARS	6g
TOTAL FAT	4g	SODIUM	590mg
SATURATED FAT	1g	FIBRE	4.5g

CHICKPEAS WITH CHILLI SAUCE

Chickpeas need overnight soaking before cooking.

SERVES 4 Ⓥ

225 g/8 oz chickpeas
2 tbsp vegetable oil
1 large onion, roughly chopped
2 garlic cloves, crushed
450 g/1 lb tomatoes, skinned and roughly chopped
pinch of brown sugar
2–4 fresh chillies, deseeded and finely sliced
pinch salt, pepper

Rinse the chickpeas thoroughly and leave them to soak in plenty of cold water overnight. Bring to the boil, boil for 10 minutes, then drain. Heat the oil in a large, heavy-based pan and gently fry the onion for 5 minutes, then add the garlic and continue to stir-fry for a few minutes. Stir the tomatoes and sugar into the fried onion; bring to the boil, then simmer over low heat for 15 minutes.

Add the chillies. Stir the well-drained chickpeas into the sauce with plenty of pepper, and salt to taste. Cover the pan and simmer for 45–60 minutes or until the chickpeas are tender. Remove the lid towards the end of cooking time if the sauce is too liquid and needs reducing.

Serve hot, accompanied by wholemeal bread rolls or pitta.

KILOCALORIES	145	SUGARS	2g
TOTAL FAT	9g	SODIUM	230mg
SATURATED FAT	–	FIBRE	2.5g

PASTA SALAD NEAPOLITAN

—— • ——

Freshly made pasta is available from supermarkets and Italian delicatessens. Tagliatelle can be plain or flavoured and coloured green with spinach or red with tomato.

SERVES 4

*150 g/5 oz each, fresh plain and green tagliatelle (or
300 g/10 oz pasta shapes)
pinch salt, pepper
150 g/5 oz (approx) cooked flaked fish (haddock or
cod) or smoked mackerel or trout
6–8 tbsp French dressing
2 tbsp tarragon, parsley (or dill), freshly chopped
red pepper strips*

Bring a large pan of lightly salted water to a rapid boil and tip in the tagliatelle (fresh pasta needs 3 minutes, dry pasta about 10). Boil pasta shapes according to the packet instructions. Drain the pasta through a colander, rinse it under plenty of cold water and leave it to drain thoroughly.

Put the pasta in a serving bowl, add the flaked fish, French dressing and the herbs. Toss well and taste for seasoning.

Serve the salad garnished with strips of grilled red pepper as a first course or light lunch accompanied with crusty bread, or as a buffet dish.

KILOCALORIES	265	SUGARS	2g
TOTAL FAT	23g	SODIUM	570mg
SATURATED FAT	3g	FIBRE	–

VEGETARIAN LASAGNE

This version of the classic Italian pasta dish has a high nutritious content. Tomato sauce replaces the Bolognese *ragù*, and a cashew nut and tofu mixture the béchamel sauce.

SERVES 6 (V)

25 g/8 oz wholewheat lasagne

TOMATO SAUCE
1 can (400 g/14 oz) tomatoes, roughly chopped
75 g/3 oz lentils
2 tbsp vegetable oil
1 large onion, finely chopped
2–3 celery sticks, diced
1 large carrot, grated
1 medium-sized green pepper, finely chopped
1 tsp each of oregano and basil, freshly chopped

TOPPING
150 g/5 oz unsalted cashew nuts
225 ml/8 fl oz water
1 tsp salt
4 tbsp vegetable oil
5 tbsp lemon juice
2 red peppers, blanched and diced or
½ can (400 g/14 oz) pimientos, drained
pinch each of onion salt and garlic salt
2 tsp yeast extract (or 3 tbsp dried yeast flakes)
450 g/1 lb tofu

Cook the lasagne strips in a large pan of boiling, lightly salted water for 10 minutes or until barely tender. Drain them thoroughly and rinse with cold water to prevent them sticking together. (Alternatively, use the pre-cooked variety.)

Cook the rinsed lentils in plenty of water for 20–30 minutes or until tender; drain the lentils and reduce them to a purée in a liquidiser. Heat the oil in a large, heavy-based pan and sauté the onion, celery, carrot and green pepper for 5 minutes or until soft; add the lentil purée, herbs, the tomatoes and their juice; simmer over gentle heat for 30 minutes, stirring from time to time.

Prepare the topping by placing the cashew nuts, measured water and salt in a liquidiser; then gradually add the oil, with the motor running, until the mixture thickens. Add the lemon juice, red peppers, seasonings and yeast flakes, blending thoroughly. Mash the tofu in a mixing bowl, add the cashew mixture and stir thoroughly until well blended. Preheat the oven to 180°C/350°F/gas 4.

Line a large oiled ovenproof dish with a layer of lasagne, followed by a layer of tomato sauce, then a layer of the cashew-tofu mixture. Continue with these layers, topping finally with the cashew nuts.

Bake in the centre of the oven for 45–60 minutes. Serve at once, perhaps with a green side salad.

KILOCALORIES	665	SUGARS	12g
TOTAL FAT	38g	SODIUM	280mg
SATURATED FAT	2g	FIBRE	4.5g

SICILIAN PASTA

The pasta can be wholewheat or white spaghetti or tagliatelle, rigatoni or penne. The Italian caciocavallo and mozzarella are curd cheeses which could be replaced by feta cheese and low-fat Edam.

SERVES 4–6

450 g/1 lb spaghetti
1 garlic clove, finely chopped
3 anchovy fillets, drained and finely chopped
125 g/4 oz tuna in brine, drained
1 yellow pepper, deseeded and finely chopped
2 large tomatoes, skinned, deseeded and chopped
1 tbsp capers
125 g/4 oz caciocavallo cheese, cut into thin strips
125 g/4 oz mozzarella cheese, diced
2 tbsp pine nuts or flaked almonds, dry-roasted
4 tbsp olive oil
pinch salt, pepper

Mix together the garlic, anchovy fillets, flaked tuna, pepper, tomatoes and capers in a large serving bowl. Add the cheeses and dry-roasted pine nuts or almonds and toss the mixture thoroughly with the oil.

Put the pasta in a large pan of lightly salted, boiling water and cook for about 10 minutes or until *al dente*. Drain the pasta, add it to the serving bowl, with freshly ground black pepper, mix thoroughly and serve at once.

KILOCALORIES	400	SUGARS	4g
TOTAL FAT	27g	SODIUM	720mg
SATURATED FAT	8g	FIBRE	2g

(V) This symbol denotes a recipe suitable for vegetarians.

LASAGNE VERDE

——— • ———

In this lightweight lasagne fresh tomatoes replace the customary Bolognese sauce. Spinach-flavoured (green) lasagne is especially good.

SERVES 4 Ⓥ

175 g/6 oz (8 sheets) lasagne verde
450 ml/15 fl oz white sauce (see page 29)
200 g/7 oz Edam (or Cheddar cheese), grated
pinch salt, pepper
350 g/12 oz tomatoes, skinned and chopped

Preheat the oven to 200°C/400°F/gas 6. Cook the lasagne, two strips at a time, in a shallow pan (a large frying-pan is suitable) with enough boiling, lightly salted water to allow the lasagne to float. Cover the pan and cook for about 12 minutes. Lift out with a slotted spoon, rinse in cold water and transfer the pasta to a tea towel to drain. (Alternatively, use the pre-cooked variety.)

Place the white sauce over low heat, mix in 125 g/ 4 oz of the cheese and heat through until the cheese has melted. Season to taste with salt and pepper.

Grease a shallow ovenproof dish (25 × 20 cm/10 × 8in), and fill it with alternate layers of lasagne, sauce and tomatoes, starting and finishing with lasagne. Sprinkle the rest of the cheese on top and bake near the top of the oven for 20–30 minutes. Serve the lasagne at once, straight from the dish, with creamed spinach or a green side salad.

KILOCALORIES	345	SUGARS	9g
TOTAL FAT	20g	SODIUM	920mg
SATURATED FAT	13g	FIBRE	1.5g

TAGLIATELLE CARBONARA

——— • ———

Many of the most delicious Italian pasta dishes are cooked quite simply. 'Alla carbonara' describes pasta with bacon, eggs and cheese.

SERVES 4

350 g/12 oz brown or green tagliatelle (or
mixture of the two)
225 g/8 oz streaky bacon rashers, derinded
2–3 eggs
4 tbsp low-fat plain yogurt
pinch salt, pepper
4 tbsp Parmesan cheese, grated

Put the tagliatelle in a large pan of rapidly boiling, lightly salted water and cook for 7–10 minutes or until *al dente*. Drain in a colander and return to the pan.

Meanwhile, grill the bacon rashers until crisp, then break them into small pieces and add them to the tagliatelle. Beat together the eggs, yogurt and 3 tablespoonfuls of the cheese; add salt and pepper to taste. Pour this mixture over the tagliatelle, set the pan over low heat and toss the pasta and egg mixture.

As soon as the egg mixture has thickened (without scrambling), transfer it to individual plates. Sprinkle with the rest of the cheese and serve at once, as a first course or light lunch, perhaps with a crisp side salad.

KILOCALORIES	335	SUGARS	4g
TOTAL FAT	18g	SODIUM	1640mg
SATURATED FAT	7g	FIBRE	0.5g

TOSSED NOODLES SHANGHAI-STYLE

——— • ———

People in Shanghai love to eat cold noodles dressed with vegetables and often topped with meat; the sauce is vinegary or even spicy hot.

SERVES 4

350 g/12 oz dried Chinese egg noodles
4 tbsp white sesame seeds
1 cucumber, thinly sliced
225 g/8 oz lean sliced ham

SAUCE
2–3 tbsp thin soya sauce
2–3 tbsp white wine vinegar (or rice vinegar)
1½ tsp caster sugar
3–4 tbsp groundnut or corn oil
hot chilli oil (optional)

Plunge the noodles into a large pan of lightly salted, boiling water, let it come back to the boil and cook the noodles, uncovered, for 3–4 minutes or until *al dente*, separating them with chopsticks or a fork. Drain the noodles in a colander, rinse with cold water and leave them to drain.

Heat a wok or frying-pan until hot but not smoking. Add the sesame seeds and dry-fry them over moderate heat for about 2 minutes or until they are golden and have released their aroma. Remove from the heat and leave them to cool.

Cut the cucumber and ham slices into strips about 6mm/¼ in wide. Set them aside. For the sauce, mix together the soya sauce, vinegar and sugar; stir in the oil, and hot chilli oil to taste, adding it drop by drop.

Transfer the noodles to a serving dish or bowl. Top with the cucumber strips, add the sauce and toss the noodles thoroughly. Add the ham strips and the sesame seeds and toss again. Serve cold.

KILOCALORIES	320	SUGARS	4g
TOTAL FAT	22g	SODIUM	710mg
SATURATED FAT	4g	FIBRE	2g

DRESSED PASTA AND CABBAGE
——— • ———

Most types of thin pasta can be used for this dish – spaghetti, spaghettini or tagliatelle – which has contrasting textures: *al dente* pasta and crisp and crunchy cabbage.

SERVES 4 Ⓥ

225 g/8 oz thin pasta
pinch salt
450 g/1 lb Savoy cabbage (trimmed weight),
thinly shredded

DRESSING
75 g/3 oz Cheddar (or Gruyère) cheese, grated
2 tbsp soured cream
3 tbsp chopped fresh mint, chives, basil or tarragon
pepper

Bring a large pan of lightly salted water to the boil and add the pasta. If the pasta is fresh, add the cabbage at the same time and allow to cook for 3 minutes. Dry pasta will need 8 minutes in total; put the pasta in the boiling water and after 5 minutes add the cabbage. The best way to guard against overcooking is to test strands of both ingredients after 7 minutes.

Drain the cooked pasta and cabbage well and place them in a warm serving bowl and mix together. Dress the pasta and cabbage with the soured cream dressing, tossing the ingredients thoroughly and seasoning with freshly ground pepper.

KILOCALORIES	185	SUGARS	3g
TOTAL FAT	10g	SODIUM	460mg
SATURATED FAT	6g	FIBRE	3g

LENTILS AND PASTA WITH TOMATOES AND GARLIC
——— • ———

This Arab dish can be served on its own as a light lunch or as a first course.

SERVES 4–6 Ⓥ

225 g/8 oz green lentils
225 g/8 oz tagliatelle
pinch salt, pepper
1–2 tbsp vegetable oil
2–3 garlic cloves, crushed
4 large ripe tomatoes, skinned and chopped

Rinse the lentils in several changes of water, put them in a pan with enough water to cover and bring them slowly to the boil. Cover the pan and simmer the lentils for about 25–30 minutes or until tender; add the salt after 20 minutes.

Meanwhile, heat the oil in a frying-pan and sauté the garlic over gentle heat for a few minutes; add the tomatoes and cook for 4–5 minutes.

Bring a large pan of lightly salted water to a rapid boil, tip in the tagliatelle and cook for 10–12 minutes or until *al dente*; fresh tagliatelle needs only 3 minutes.

To serve, drain the lentils and the tagliatelle, place them in a large serving bowl, add the garlic and tomato mixture and toss all the ingredients until thoroughly mixed.

KILOCALORIES	135	SUGARS	2g
TOTAL FAT	6g	SODIUM	90mg
SATURATED FAT	–	FIBRE	2.5g

Italian Dinners

A una Del Conte

An Italian dinner party is more a dinner than a party – above all else it is the food and wine that matter. The dishes will be unmistakably Italian, which does not mean tomatoes and garlic with everything, but the best and freshest ingredients, cooked simply and with great care.

An Italian dinner, usually of three courses, is conceived as a whole, rather than as a succession of different and sometimes unrelated tastes. For instance, it might be based on a fish theme, with seafood salad as a starter, followed by sea bass roasted with herbs, daurade (a kind of sea bream) with fennel, or grey mullet with courgettes. The sweet would be a 'semi-freddo' (soft ice-cream) or fresh fruit salad. For less formal occasions, a meal could consist of minestrone or bean and pasta soup, followed by braised beef or veal stew with tomato sauce, either one accompanied by a vegetable; at the end cheese and fresh seasonal fruit.

The following two menus are built on these two prototypes: an informal dinner for four people, composed of spaghetti with mussels, squid stewed with spinach, followed by a bowl of crisp raw fennel dressed with olive oil and lemon juice, and finally cheese and fruit.

For a more elegant dinner serving six people, I would present French bean moulds or ricotta and spinach roll, then pork cooked in milk with creamed potatoes to mop up the delicious sauce. After that I would pass round a bowl of crisp green salad to cleanse the palate in preparation for a light and delicate, fresh-tasting ricotta cake.

The food will, of course, be accompanied by Italian wines. A Pinot Grigio from the Veneto or a Frascati would be ideal with fish. A meat main course could be accompanied by Chianti Classico or a Barbera from Piedmont, but the delicate pudding deserves a sweet wine, such as the sparkling Moscato d'Asti Spumante from the vineyards in Piedmont.

SPAGHETTINI IN BIANCO CON LE COZZE
Thin spaghetti with mussels

This Neapolitan sauce is made without tomatoes, and is a delicious change. The mussels should be cooked and eaten on the day of purchase.

SERVES 4

1 kg/2 quarts mussels
½ tbsp salt
400 g/14 oz thin spaghetti
2–3 tbsp olive oil
3 garlic cloves, finely sliced
2 tbsp chopped parsley (preferably flat-leaved)
1 red chilli
black pepper

Scrub the mussels thoroughly in cold water, pulling away the beards and scraping off any barnacles. Wash them in several changes of cold water. Discard any which are cracked or which remain open after tapping them hard.

Place the mussels in a large pan with only the water which clings to them; cook, covered, over high heat, shaking the pan frequently for about 3–4 minutes, until all the mussels have opened (discard any which remain closed). Remove the flesh from the shells, reserving the liquid and discarding the shells. Line a sieve with kitchen paper and strain the mussel liquid through it into a saucepan; if necessary, reduce it by fast boiling until there is 200 ml/7 fl oz.

Bring a large saucepan of water (about 3.5 litres/ 6¼ pt) with the salt to a fast boil. Add the spaghetti, stirring briefly; replace the lid and bring the pan back to a fast boil. Adjust the heat so that the pasta cooks fast and steadily.

Heat the oil and sauté the garlic in a frying-pan. As soon as the garlic begins to sizzle, add the parsley and the whole chilli; cook, stirring constantly, for 1 minute. Mix in the mussels liquid and bring the sauce slowly to the boil. Remove the chilli and add the mussels; reduce the heat and cook for 2 minutes until they are hot (prolonged cooking makes them tough). Season to taste with pepper.

As soon as the spaghetti is *al dente* (about 8 minutes), drain it quickly (do not overdrain) and transfer it to the frying-pan. Heat through for a minute or so, tossing the spaghetti until it is coated with the sauce. Serve at once.

KILOCALORIES	395	SUGARS	1g
TOTAL FAT	15g	SODIUM	720mg
SATURATED FAT	2g	FIBRE	1.5g

CALAMARI IN ZIMINO
Squid stewed with spinach

———— • ————

This traditional recipe from Liguria brings together two unlikely ingredients, squid and spinach, to produce a novel and tasty dish. In Genoa, calamari in zimino are served on their own, but they would also go well with boiled rice dressed with a little olive oil.

SERVES 4

900 g/2 lb squid
1 kg/generous 2 lb fresh spinach (or 450 g/1 lb frozen spinach – thawed)
1 small onion, finely chopped
1 celery stick, finely chopped
2–3 tbsp olive oil
3 fresh tomatoes, skinned or 3 canned plum tomatoes, roughly chopped
1 tsp tomato purée
pinch salt, black pepper

Clean the squid: holding the tubular pocket with one hand, pull off the tentacles and all the contents of the

pocket. Cut off the head just beyond the tentacles and set these aside. Discard the head and the internal organs, and remove the bone from inside the pocket. Rinse out the inside of the body and peel off the purple membrane; cut the body into thin strips. Rinse the tentacles thoroughly and cut them into small pieces.

Remove the stalks and wash the leaves of fresh spinach in plenty of cold water; cut them roughly into large strips. Cut frozen, thawed spinach into chunks.

Put the onion, celery and the olive oil in a sauté pan over medium heat and cook for about 5 minutes or until the vegetables are soft. Mix in the spinach and cook, covered, for about 5 minutes if fresh, 2 minutes if frozen, stirring occasionally. Add the squid, mix well, then add the tomatoes, tomato purée, salt and a generous grinding of pepper. Cook for 2–3 minutes, turning the mixture.

Cover the pan and cook for about 30 minutes or until the squid is cooked through – prod the flesh with a darning needle to gauge its progress. Adjust seasoning and serve.

KILOCALORIES	320	SUGARS	5g
TOTAL FAT	14g	SODIUM	780mg
SATURATED FAT	2g	FIBRE	6g

ARROSTO DI MAIALE AL LATTE
Loin of pork braised in milk

———— • ————

This combination of pork and milk produces a delicate and tasty dish. By the end of the cooking, the sauce has thickened and clotted and is beautifully golden in colour.

SERVES 6

1 kg/2¼ lb loin of pork, boned and derinded
100 ml/4 fl oz vegetable oil
5 juniper berries, lightly crushed
sprig of rosemary
2 garlic cloves, crushed
pinch salt, black pepper
25 g/1 oz butter (or margarine)
600 ml/1 pt semi-skimmed milk

Tie the pork with string in several places to keep its shape. Put half the oil, the juniper berries, rosemary, garlic, salt and pepper in a dish, lay the pork on top and marinate it for 4–5 hours, turning the meat.

Lift the pork from the marinade and dry it thoroughly with kitchen paper. Heat the butter or margarine and the rest of the oil in a flame-proof casserole in which the meat will fit snugly. When the butter foam begins to subside, add the meat and brown it well on all sides, over gentle heat, taking care not to burn and brown the butter.

Add the milk, salt and pepper to the pan, bring gently to the boil and cook slowly, covered, for 1½–2 hours. Turn the meat over occasionally during the cooking, and add a little more milk if the sauce begins to dry out. At the end of cooking, the milk should have turned into golden-brown clusters.

Lift the meat on to a wooden board and leave it to cool for a few minutes; remove the string. Carve it into 1 cm/⅜ in slices, and arrange them, slightly overlapping, on a heated dish and keep them warm. Skim as much fat as possible from the sauce, add 2–3 tablespoonfuls of hot water and boil briskly and reduce until rich and syrupy. Spoon the sauce over the meat and serve.

KILOCALORIES	715	SUGARS	5g
TOTAL FAT	65g	SODIUM	300mg
SATURATED FAT	20g	FIBRE	–

ROTOLO DI RICOTTA E SPINACI
Ricotta and spinach roll

—— • ——

This attractive and delicious dish can be made success-fully only with good-quality floury potatoes, such as mature King Edwards, and fresh spinach is preferable to frozen.

SERVES 6

300 g/11 oz floury potatoes
1 small onion, finely chopped
25 g/1 oz unsmoked streaky bacon (derinded), diced (or mortadella)
75 g/3 oz butter (or margarine)
500 g/1 lb 2 oz fresh spinach, cooked and chopped (or 225 g/8 oz frozen leaf spinach, thawed and chopped)
100 g/4 oz ricotta cheese
¼ tsp grated nutmeg
75 g/3 oz Parmesan cheese, freshly grated
1 egg yolk
salt, black pepper
1 egg
100 g/4 oz plain flour, sifted

Scrub the potatoes and cook them in their skins in a pan of unsalted water until they are tender.

Meanwhile, sauté the onion and the bacon or mortadella in 15 g/½ oz of the butter or margarine, for about 5 minutes. Squeeze all the water from the spinach, then mix it into the onion and bacon or mortadella mixture. Cook for a further 2 minutes, stirring frequently. Transfer to a bowl and add the ricotta, nutmeg, 25 g/1 oz of the Parmesan, the egg yolk, and salt and pepper to taste. Mix thoroughly.

Drain the cooked potatoes and peel them while still hot. Purée them in a food mill or rub them through a sieve directly on to the work surface. Make a well in the centre of the purée and drop in the whole egg, a teaspoonful of salt and most of the flour. Knead the mixture, adding more flour if necessary, until the dough is softly smooth and slightly sticky.

Moisten a piece of muslin, wring it until just damp and lay it out flat on the worktop. Place the potato dough in the centre of the cloth and roll it out to a rectangle, about 1 cm/⅜ in thick, and 30 × 15 cm/ 12 × 6 in long and wide.

Spread the spinach filling evenly over the dough, leaving a border of 2 cm/¾ in all around. With the help of the cloth, roll the potato dough into a sausage shape from the long side. Wrap it tightly into the muslin and tie at both ends.

Bring a large oval casserole or fish kettle of lightly salted water to the boil and lower the roll into it. When the water comes back to the boil, adjust the heat to keep the water at a gentle simmer. Cook for 30 minutes, then gently lift the spinach roll out of the water. Place it on a wooden board and unwrap it as soon as it can be handled.

Leave the spinach roll to cool completely. Cut into 2 cm/¾ in slices and arrange them, slightly overlapping, in a greased ovenproof dish. Preheat the oven to 200°C/400°F/gas 6. Melt the remaining butter and pour it over the spinach slices. Sprinkle over the rest of the Parmesan and bake near the top of the oven for 15 minutes. Allow to stand for 5 minutes before serving.

KILOCALORIES	250	SUGARS	2g
TOTAL FAT	13g	SODIUM	680mg
SATURATED FAT	7g	FIBRE	3g

Please see the introduction for a full explanation of the nutritional factboxes.

SFORMATI DI FAGIOLINI
French bean moulds
—— • ——

Sformato is an elegant dish popular as a first course in Northern Italy. The bean mixture, cooked in a single ring mould or in individual ramekins, may be served with a tomato sauce.

SERVES 6 Ⓥ

450 g/1 lb French beans
40 g/1½ oz butter (or margarine)
1 tbsp shallot, finely chopped
4 tbsp low-fat plain yogurt (or double cream)
25 g/1 oz flour
250 ml/scant ½ pt hot semi-skimmed milk
salt, pepper
½ tsp grated nutmeg
2 eggs, lightly beaten
25 g/1 oz Parmesan cheese, freshly grated
2 tbsp dry breadcrumbs

Top and tail the beans, cut them into even-sized pieces, wash them thoroughly and cook in boiling, lightly salted water for about 5 minutes, or until they are just tender. Drain the beans well and purée them in a food processor or push them through the coarsest disc of a food mill. The purée should remain fairly chunky.

Heat 15 g/½ oz of the butter or margarine in a small frying-pan, add the shallot and cook gently until golden; mix in the bean purée and sauté for about 3 minutes, tossing and turning it frequently. Spoon the bean mixture into a bowl and add the yogurt or cream.

Melt the rest of the butter in a small saucepan, add the flour and cook over a low heat, stirring, for 1 minute; draw off the heat and gradually add the hot milk, beating constantly. Return the pan to the heat and cook for another 10–15 minutes after the sauce has begun to simmer again. Season with salt, pepper and nutmeg. Add the eggs, Parmesan and sauce to the bean mixture and blend thoroughly; adjust the seasoning.

Preheat the oven to 190°C/375°F/gas 5. Butter six ramekins and cover the bases with discs of greaseproof paper buttered on both sides. Sprinkle each ramekin with a few breadcrumbs, fill them with the bean mixture and place them in a roasting tin. Pour in boiling water to come two-thirds up the sides of the ramekins. Bake for about 20 minutes or until a wooden tooth-pick inserted in the middle of the mixture comes out clean. Leave to cool for 5 minutes.

To unmould the ramekins, run a palette knife around the inside of each, invert it on to a warmed serving plate, remove the paper and serve at once.

KILOCALORIES	170	SUGARS	6g
TOTAL FAT	10g	SODIUM	250mg
SATURATED FAT	6g	FIBRE	2g

SALSA DI POMODORO
Tomato sauce
—— • ——

Serve this tomato sauce as an accompaniment to the French bean moulds (see left).

SERVES 6 Ⓥ

400 g/14 oz canned plum tomatoes (including juice)
1 small onion, coarsely chopped
1 small celery stick, coarsely chopped
1 bay leaf
1 garlic clove, crushed
1 sprig parsley
1 tsp sugar
salt, pepper
15 g/½ oz butter (or margarine)

Put all the sauce ingredients except the butter into a small saucepan, bring to the boil and simmer, uncovered, fo 40 minutes. Stir occasionally and add a little hot water if it gets too dry. Discard the bay leaf. Purée the sauce through a food mill or a sieve, then beat in the butter or margarine, cut into small knobs. Stir well and adjust the seasoning.

KILOCALORIES	140	SUGARS	3g
TOTAL FAT	2g	SODIUM	115mg
SATURATED FAT	1g	FIBRE	0.5g

Ricotta is a soft, ewe's-milk cheese that is used widely in Italian cookery for both savoury and sweet dishes.

TORTA DI RICOTTA
Ricotta cake
—— • ——

Ricotta is a highly perishable soft cheese, made from the whey of other cheeses. This delicate cake is best eaten soon after it has been baked.

SERVES 6 Ⓥ

300 g/11 oz ricotta cheese
100 g/4 oz caster sugar
100 g/4 oz ground almonds
2–3 drops pure almond essence
5 eggs, separated
grated zest of 1 orange
50 g/2 oz candied orange peel
2 tbsp Grand Marnier
1½ tbsp potato flour, sifted
icing sugar (optional)

Line a 20 cm/8 in spring-form tin with non-stick paper. Heat the oven to 180°C/350°F/gas 4.

Purée the ricotta through a food mill or a sieve into a bowl, add the sugar and beat until the mixture is creamy and smooth. Mix in the almonds and the almond essence, followed by the egg yolks, one by one, beating hard after each addition. Mix in the orange zest, candied peel and liqueur.

Whisk the egg whites until stiff. Fold them into the ricotta mixture a little at a time, alternately with the potato flour, blending thoroughly and carefully with a metal spoon. Pour the mixture into the prepared tin, level the top and bake for about 30–40 minutes or until set.

Let the cake cool in the tin before removing it; serve it on its own, lightly sprinkled with icing sugar, or accompanied by orange sauce.

KILOCALORIES	325	SUGARS	19g
TOTAL FAT	19g	SODIUM	110mg
SATURATED FAT	6g	FIBRE	1.5g

SALSA DI ARANCIA
Orange sauce
—— • ——

Serve this orange sauce as an accompaniment to the ricotta cake (see left).

SERVES 6 Ⓥ

2 oranges
175 g/6 oz granulated sugar
juice of ½ lemon

Remove the rind from the oranges, stripping it of all the white pith. Cut the rind into julienne strips and put them in a small saucepan; cover with cold water, bring to the boil and cook until the rind is soft and slightly transparent; drain.

Bring the sugar and 3 tablespoonfuls of water slowly to the boil. When the sugar has dissolved, add the orange rind and the juice from the oranges and the lemon. Simmer for 1–2 minutes, then leave the sauce to cool.

KILOCALORIES	135	SUGARS	35g
TOTAL FAT	–	SODIUM	–
SATURATED FAT	–	FIBRE	1g

Right *(from top) French bean moulds with tomato sauce, milk-braised tender pork, and ricotta cake with orange sauce.*

VEGETABLES

Vegetables play an important part in the diet because they are rich in vitamins, minerals and fibre. No one vegetable contains all the vitamins and minerals needed, which is why a wide selection should be eaten. Most vegetables are virtually fat-free, have a low calorific value and contain a high percentage of fibre. Vegetarians may lack certain elements unless they supplement their diets with dairy produce or yeast extracts and vegetable protein products fortified with iron and vitamins.

The nutritional content of each vegetable depends on its grouping (i.e. root, stalk, legume, leaf, etc.), and the amount will vary according to the method of cultivation, storage, preparation and cooking.

Legumes These are rich in vegetable protein and B-group vitamins. Examples include chickpeas, soya beans, kidney beans and butter-beans (see also pages 122–37).

Roots and tubers These are rich in carbohydrates, calcium and vitamin C. Examples include parsnips, swedes and carrots – carrots are also rich in vitamin A. Potatoes have a significant protein content.

Green and leafy All are rich in vitamin C and some in vitamin A, but this group are the most vulnerable to loss of nutrients through storage and abuse during preparation. There is a greater concentration of nutrients in the outer leaves. Examples include cabbage, cauliflower, spinach, Brussels sprouts and broccoli.

Fruits and squashes All contain a high percentage of water but are rich in vitamins A and C, as well as minerals. Many require little or no cooking. Examples include tomatoes, peppers, marrows and courgettes.

BUYING

The fresher the vegetable the higher the nutritional value. Don't buy more vegetables than you can use within two or three days. Choose crisp and firm leafy and root vegetables and avoid any limp or bruised ones. Cleaned and packaged vegetables are not necessarily fresher and are always more expensive.

STORING

Exposure to light and warmth destroys valuable vitamins, so remove the vegetables from plastic bags and store them in a cool airy place. Prepared vegetables can be stored in the salad compartment of the fridge and eaten as soon as possible.

PREPARATION

There is a greater concentration of nutrients just under the skin of most vegetables, so peel thinly or avoid peeling whenever possible. Root vegetables and potatoes should be scrubbed to remove dirt or traces of pesticides. Cut, chop or slice them just before cooking.

Discard outer leaves of leafy vegetables if they are yellow, coarse or have been eaten by insects. Wash the leaves in several changes of cold water and leave to drain in a colander. Do not soak as the nutrients will be lost. Tear large leaves immediately prior to cooking.

COOKING

Always use vegetables raw, if possible, otherwise cook for as short a time as necessary in the minimum amount of boiling water. Never add bicarbonate of soda – it destroys vitamins – and try to avoid salt, too. Serve cooked vegetables as soon as possible as keeping them warm increases vitamin loss.

Microwaving This method retains more of the vitamin content. Cut the vegetables into even-sized pieces, add sufficient boiling water to half cover them, cover the dish and cook according to the manufacturer's instructions. Leafy vegetables can be cooked in a 'cooking' bag or covered dish with no added water except that which clings to the leaves after rinsing.

If time is short baked potatoes can be cooked in a microwave. If a crisper skin is preferred, semi-cook in the microwave and finish them off in the oven.

STUFFED MARROW

Marrows are the larger relations of courgettes; they have a high water content. Do not overcook or the flavour will be lost. The centre can be stuffed with a variety of fillings.

SERVES 4

1 medium-sized marrow (900 g/2 lb)
2–3 tbsp vegetable oil
450 g/1 lb lean minced beef
1 onion, sliced
1 garlic clove, crushed
1 tbsp tomato purée
300 ml/½ pt white stock (see page 17)
½ tsp mixed spice
2 tsp marjoram, chopped
175 g/6 oz cooked long-grain rice (brown)
pinch salt, pepper
300 ml/½ pt mustard sauce (see page 30)

Prepare the stuffing: heat the oil in a heavy-based pan and fry the minced beef over high heat for a few minutes until brown. Remove the meat with a slotted spoon and fry the onion in the pan for 5 minutes until soft but not browned. Return the meat, together with the garlic, tomato purée, stock, mixed spiced and marjoram. Mix thoroughly, and simmer, uncovered, over gentle heat for 30 minutes until the meat is tender and the liquid has reduced to almost nothing. Stir in the cooked rice.

Set the oven to 200°C/400°F/gas 6. Wash the marrow, but do not peel it unless the skin is very coarse; cut it across into four 5 cm/2 in thick slices; scoop out the seeds from the middle. Set the marrow slices in a shallow ovenproof dish, sprinkle lightly with salt and pepper and cover with foil. Bake for 20 minutes.

Remove the dish from the oven, strain off all the juices and pat the rings dry with kitchen paper. Return the marrow rings to the dish, pack the stuffing into the centres, pour the mustard sauce over the marrow and return the dish to the oven for 20 minutes or until the top is golden-brown and the marrow tender but not mushy.

Serve the stuffed marrow straight from the dish, with crusty bread or floury boiled potatoes.

KILOCALORIES	450	SUGARS	7g
TOTAL FAT	29g	SODIUM	300mg
SATURATED FAT	8g	FIBRE	2g

GRATIN OF CAULIFLOWER IN MUSHROOM SAUCE

Gratin describes the upper crust, usually of bread-crumbs and/or cheese, sprinkled over a savoury mixture and finished off in the oven or under the grill. Cooked vegetables, fish, poultry and meat can be folded into a sauce and served in this way. Individual portions can be cooked in deep scallop shells.

SERVES 4 Ⓥ

1 medium-sized cauliflower, broken into florets
2 tbsp vegetable oil
1 medium-sized onion, coarsely chopped
1 garlic clove, crushed
100 g/4 oz mushrooms, sliced
300 ml/½ pt vegetable (or mushroom) stock
1 tsp cornflour
1 tbsp tomato purée
1 tbsp parsley, finely chopped
pinch salt, pepper
25 g/1 oz grated cheese (optional)
2–3 tbsp wholemeal breadcrumbs

Heat the oil in a heavy-based pan and fry the onion and garlic gently for 5 minutes over medium heat. Add the mushrooms, lower the heat and sauté them for 5 minutes. Meanwhile, warm the stock. Mix the corn-flour to a smooth paste with 2 tablespoonfuls of water and blend into the stock with the tomato purée and parsley. Add salt and pepper to taste.

Set the oven to 190°C/375°F/gas 5. Remove the mushrooms and onions from the heat, stir in the sauce, mixing it thoroughly. Return the pan to the heat, bring the sauce to the boil and simmer, stirring continuously, for 5 minutes.

Arrange the cauliflower in a lightly greased oven-proof soufflé or gratin dish, pour the mushroom sauce over the florets and sprinkle with the breadcrumbs mixed with the cheese (if used). Bake the gratin near the top of the oven for 35 minutes until the topping is crisp and the cauliflower just cooked.

Serve at once as a light lunch dish.

KILOCALORIES	175	SUGARS	5g
TOTAL FAT	11g	SODIUM	460mg
SATURATED FAT	2g	FIBRE	4g

Ⓥ This symbol denotes a recipe suitable for vegetarians.

tray, turning them once, until they are tender. Alternatively, heat the oil in a deep-fryer to 190°C/375°F and fry the aubergine fritters for 3–5 minutes or until crisp on the outside, soft and tender inside.

Serve at once.

KILOCALORIES	565	SUGARS	4g
TOTAL FAT	58g	SODIUM	230mg
SATURATED FAT	4g	FIBRE	3.5g

AUBERGINE AND SESAME FRITTERS

Aubergine is the chief ingredient in such classic dishes as French ratatouille, Italian melanzane ripieni, Greek moussaka and Turkish imam bayaldi.

SERVES 4 Ⓥ

2 medium-sized aubergines
2 tbsp brown breadcrumbs
2 tbsp sesame seeds
2 tbsp finely chopped herbs: chives, parsley, coriander, chervil (or 1 tbsp dried mixed herbs)
2 tsp yeast extract (or 2 tbsp yeast flakes)
125 ml/4 fl oz soya milk
4 tbsp vegetable oil for frying

Dry-roast the breadcrumbs in a small pan over gentle heat for a few minutes until crisp and dry. Remove from the heat. Mix the sesame seeds and herbs into the breadcrumbs and add the yeast flakes. Alternatively, blend the yeast extract with a little of the soya milk in a liquidiser.

Wash and dry the aubergines and cut into 1 cm/⅜ in slices. Dip the slices in the soya milk, then coat with the breadcrumb mixture.

Heat the oven to 200°C/400°F/gas 6 and bake them for about 35 minutes on a flat oiled dish or baking

AUBERGINE CASSEROLE

Aubergines come in all shapes, sizes and colours: squat and egg-shaped, club-like or thin and narrow, and white, pale or dark green, yellow, purple and near black.

SERVES 4 Ⓥ

1 medium-sized aubergine, diced
1 medium-sized onion, thinly sliced
1 small green pepper, deseeded and diced
1 stick celery, finely chopped
100 g/4 oz button mushrooms
½ tsp oregano
1 tsp dill weed
2½ tbsp tomato purée
pinch salt, pepper

Mix the aubergine cubes with the onion, green pepper and celery. Trim the mushrooms, wipe them clean, and leave whole if small, otherwise cut them into halves. Put them in a small pan with 4 tablespoonfuls of boiling water, cover the pan with a lid and poach the mushrooms over gentle heat for 2 minutes. Add the mushrooms to the other vegetables and retain the poaching liquid. Preheat the oven to 180°C/350°F/gas 4.

Mix the herbs and seasoning into the vegetables; blend the tomato purée with the mushroom liquid and 4 tablespoons of cold water and stir this into the vegetables. Correct seasoning. Spoon the aubergine mixture into an ovenproof 1 litre/1½ pt casserole dish, cover and bake in the centre of the oven for 1 hour.

Serve the aubergine casserole hot, with jacket potatoes or plain boiled rice.

KILOCALORIES	40	SUGARS	6g
TOTAL FAT	–	SODIUM	180mg
SATURATED FAT	–	FIBRE	3g

BROCCOLI WITH BEAN SPROUTS

Broccoli has a high vitamin A and C content and blends well with contrasting flavours, textures and colours.

SERVES 6 Ⓥ

450 g/1 lb fresh broccoli (or calabrese)
275 g/10 oz bean sprouts
2 cm/¾ in piece root ginger, peeled and sliced
2 garlic cloves, halved
1½ tbsp vegetable oil
2 tbsp soya sauce
1 tsp sesame oil

Break off the broccoli florets and discard all coarse stalks. Rinse the florets and dry them on kitchen paper. Discard any bean sprouts that are wilted; rinse and drain the remainder thoroughly. Heat the oil in a large frying-pan over gentle heat; add the ginger and garlic and sauté for 2 or 3 minutes until the oil is flavoured. Discard the ginger and garlic; add the broccoli to the oil and toss it over high heat for 3 minutes, taking care not to brown it.

Add the bean sprouts and soya sauce to the pan and continue to toss for about 2 minutes until the sprouts begin to wilt. Sprinkle the sesame oil over the contents, heat through for a few minutes and serve at once.

KILOCALORIES	100	SUGARS	2g
TOTAL FAT	8g	SODIUM	10mg
SATURATED FAT	–	FIBRE	2.5g

STUFFED PEPPERS

Sweet peppers are rich in vitamin C. They make marvellous containers for all kinds of wholesome stuffings; the following can also be used for marrow rings (see page 149).

SERVES 6 Ⓥ

6 peppers (green, orange or red)
250 g/9 oz canned tomatoes, roughly chopped
100 g/4 oz tomato purée
3 sticks celery, diced
3 medium-sized onions, finely chopped
100 g/4 oz walnuts, coarsely chopped (or
75 g/3 oz mushrooms, chopped)
450 g/1 lb cooked brown rice (100 g/4 oz uncooked)
1 tsp basil, chopped
2 tsp sage, chopped
1 tsp thyme, chopped
pinch salt
pinch garlic powder (optional)
2–3 tbsp soft brown breadcrumbs (optional)

Slice the base and stalk end from the peppers, carefully scoop out the seeds, taking care not to break the skins. Blanch the peppers and stalk ends, which will serve as lids, in rapidly boiling water for 2 minutes; plunge them into cold water and leave them to drain.

Simmer the tomatoes with their juice, the tomato purée, celery and onions in a large, heavy-based pan for 15–20 minutes or until most of the liquid has evaporated and the onions are soft. Mix in the walnuts or mushrooms, and the rice, and add herbs and seasoning to taste; fold in enough of the breadcrumbs to absorb any surplus liquid.

Heat the oven to 200°C/400°F/gas 6. Arrange the peppers upright in a deep casserole dish; pack them loosely with the stuffing and set the stem lids in place. Add 1–2 tablespoonfuls of water to the dish, cover it with a lid or a double layer of foil and bake in the centre of the oven for 1 hour. Remove the casserole lid for the last 10 minutes.

Serve hot as a lunch or supper dish.

KILOCALORIES	290	SUGARS	11g
TOTAL FAT	13g	SODIUM	160mg
SATURATED FAT	1g	FIBRE	5.5g

Please see the introduction for a full explanation of the nutritional factboxes.

SPINACH ROMAN-STYLE

Spinach is rich in iron and calcium, though not in a form that is easily absorbed by the body. It is also rich in vitamins and makes a colourful addition to a meal.
See illustration page 102.

SERVES 4 Ⓥ

900 g/2 lb fresh spinach
¾ tsp salt
3 tbsp olive oil
1–2 garlic cloves, crushed
2 tbsp flaked almonds (or pine kernels)
3 tbsp green olives, sliced
3 tbsp black olives, sliced
1 tbsp capers, drained and coarsely chopped
1 large lemon

Wash the spinach in several changes of water; drain it thoroughly and put it in a large pan. Sprinkle with the salt, cover the pan and cook the spinach for 5 minutes. Drain and chop it.

Heat the oil in a heavy-based pan and sauté the garlic and pine kernels or almonds until pale golden. Stir in the olives and capers, and add the spinach. Correct the seasoning and heat the spinach through.

Serve the spinach, garnished with lemon wedges, as a side dish with fish or poultry.

KILOCALORIES	215	SUGARS	2g
TOTAL FAT	20g	SODIUM	1520mg
SATURATED FAT	3g	FIBRE	6.5g

ARTICHOKES À LA FRANÇAISE

Jerusalem artichokes have a creamy-white firm flesh and a characteristic sweet taste. The tubers are also rich in iron and phosphorus.

SERVES 4 Ⓥ

450 g/1 lb Jerusalem artichokes
1 tbsp lemon juice
350 g/12 oz young carrots
2 tbsp margarine (or butter or vegetable oil)
2 tbsp grated cheese (Lancashire)
2 tbsp brown breadcrumbs
2 tbsp parsley, finely chopped

Scrub the artichokes in cold water, peel and drop them into a bowl of cold water with added lemon juice to prevent discoloration. Cut the artichokes into walnut-sized pieces and put them in a pan of boiling water. Bring back to the boil before adding the carrots, scraped and cut into 2.5cm /1 in lengths. Cover the pan and simmer the vegetables for about 15 minutes or until just tender. Drain thoroughly.

Heat the margarine, butter or oil in a large, heavy-based pan and stir in the cheese, letting it melt over gentle heat; mix in the breadcrumbs. Add the artichokes and carrots, stirring all the time until they are heated through and coated with the cheese and breadcrumbs mixture.

Transfer the vegetables to a serving dish, sprinkle them with the finely chopped parsley and serve with grilled fish or lamb chops.

KILOCALORIES	140	SUGARS	6g
TOTAL FAT	7g	SODIUM	220mg
SATURATED FAT	2g	FIBRE	6g

ASPARAGUS CASSEROLE

The flavour of asparagus is unique; the vegetable also contains good quantities of vitamins A and C.

SERVES 4 Ⓥ

450 g/1 lb fresh asparagus (or 450 g/1 lb canned asparagus pieces, drained)
1 small green pepper, deseeded and finely chopped
3 eggs, beaten
125 g/4 oz Cheddar cheese, grated
100 g/4 oz water biscuit crumbs
pinch salt (optional)
225 ml/8 fl oz semi-skimmed milk
50 g/2 oz margarine (or butter), melted
4 tbsp wheatgerm

Trim the woody parts from the base of the asparagus stems and lightly scrape the stems. Rinse the asparagus carefully and tie them in bundles, tips together. Choose a deep saucepan in which the bundles can stand upright, and bring lightly salted water to the boil. Lower the asparagus so that the tips are above the water level (they will cook in the steam) and fix a domed cover of kitchen foil above them. Cook for 10–15 minutes.

Lift the asparagus from the pan, leave to cool and drain, then cut into 4–5 cm/1½–2 in pieces. Preheat the oven to 180°C/350°F/gas 4.

Mix together the asparagus pieces and green pepper, fold in the beaten eggs and the cheese mixed with the biscuit crumbs. Season to taste and stir in the milk. Spoon the mixture into a lightly greased ovenproof dish, pour the melted margarine or butter over the top and sprinkle with wheatgerm.

Bake in the centre of the oven for 20–30 minutes or until golden. Serve on its own or with cold ham.

KILOCALORIES	505	SUGARS	8g
TOTAL FAT	32g	SODIUM	690mg
SATURATED FAT	11g	FIBRE	5.5g

STIR-FRY VEGETABLES

Stir-frying is a classic Chinese cooking method. Most of the vitamins are retained as the vegetables are cooked at high heat for only a short time.

SERVES 4 (V)

1 onion, finely chopped
2½ cm/1 in piece root ginger, peeled and cut into slivers
2 garlic cloves, crushed
2 carrots, finely sliced
¼ medium-sized cauliflower, broken into florets
2 sticks celery, finely chopped
100 g/4 oz French beans, cut into 5 cm/2 in pieces
100 g/4 oz bean sprouts
few strips of red pepper
3–4 tbsp vegetable oil
1 tbsp soya sauce
1 tsp cornflour
pinch salt, pepper

Prepare all the vegetables and arrange them in separate piles on a large dish. Heat the oil in a wok or a large, heavy-based pan and stir-fry the onion, ginger and garlic over medium heat until soft but not brown.

Add the carrots, cauliflower florets, celery and beans and continue to stir-fry until they are coated with oil and just tender. Increase the heat, add the bean sprouts, red pepper, soya sauce and the cornflour stirred to a paste with 4 tablespoonfuls of cold water. Toss again for a few seconds until all the vegetables are glossy. Season to taste and serve immediately.

KILOCALORIES	205	SUGARS	6g
TOTAL FAT	17g	SODIUM	120mg
SATURATED FAT	2g	FIBRE	3.5g

TURNIP SOUFFLÉ

Young turnips in May have a more delicate flavour and texture than main-crop varieties. Best cooked plainly, after initial blanching, and finished off with yogurt or herbs. Main-crop types are more suitable for flavouring soups and casseroles and for vegetable purées – on their own or mixed with an equal amount of carrot purée.

SERVES 4 (V)

450 g/1 lb turnips (or 375 g/12 oz turnips plus 75–100 g/4 oz carrots)
40 g/1½ oz margarine (or butter)
40 g/1½ oz plain flour
150 ml/¼ pt semi-skimmed milk
2 large eggs, separated
1 egg white
pinch salt, pepper
ground cloves

Trim tops and bases from the turnips and peel them to remove all woody pith. Cut into quarters and boil in lightly salted water until tender – timing depends upon age. Drain the turnips through a colander and reserve the cooking liquid.

Reduce the turnips (and carrots) to a purée in a liquidiser or food processor. Make up a thick white sauce from the margarine, flour and milk, with 150 ml/¼ pt of the reserved turnip liquid. Blend in the purée and remove the pan from the heat.

Butter a 1.5 litre/2½ pt soufflé dish, and preheat the oven to 200°C/400°F/gas 6.

Beat the egg yolks, one by one, into the soufflé mixture and season it to taste with salt, pepper and ground cloves. Beat the egg whites until stiff and fold them into the mixture with a metal spoon. Spoon the soufflé into the prepared dish, smooth the top and bake in the centre of the oven for 30–35 minutes or until it has risen and is golden.

Serve at once, on its own as a light lunch or as an accompaniment to boiled ham or bacon.

Variation Fold 100 g/4 oz thinly sliced and sautéed mushrooms into the white sauce before adding the turnip purée; or sprinkle the top of the soufflé with fine brown breadcrumbs and/or grated Parmesan cheese before baking it.

KILOCALORIES	190	SUGARS	4g
TOTAL FAT	13g	SODIUM	290mg
SATURATED FAT	3g	FIBRE	2.5g

pulling out and discarding the small inner leaves until the cluster of hairy filaments near the base, known as the choke, is exposed. Use a stainless-steel teaspoon to scrape them away from the heart or *fond*, the most delectable part of the artichoke.

Meanwhile, drain the tuna fish and flake the flesh into a bowl; clean the lettuce, reserving the best outer leaves for later, and finely shred the heart. Add this to the tuna fish, with the tarragon or chervil and the chopped olives, if used. Mix the oil, vinegar and shallot to make a dressing, season to taste and pour over the tuna. Chill for 1 hour.

To serve, arrange the artichokes on a bed of the reserved lettuce leaves and fill the centres with the tuna fish mixture. Garnish with wedges of tomatoes and eggs, and top with lumpfish if desired.

KILOCALORIES	310	SUGARS	4g
TOTAL FAT	29g	SODIUM	520mg
SATURATED FAT	5g	FIBRE	1.5g

STUFFED GLOBE ARTICHOKES
— • —

In this recipe, artichokes are stuffed with tuna. Serve as a light lunch dish.

SERVES 4

4 medium-sized globe artichokes
juice of a lemon
1 can (200 g/7 oz) tuna fish in brine
1 lettuce
2 tbsp tarragon (or chervil), finely chopped
50 g/2 oz green olives, stoned (optional)
6 tbsp olive (or vegetable) oil
2–3 tbsp white wine vinegar
1 shallot, finely chopped
pinch salt, pepper
2 small tomatoes
1 egg, hard-boiled
4 tsp red lumpfish (optional)

Slice the stems off the artichokes, level with and close to the base of the leaves. Cut about 2.5 cm/1 in off the tops, remove any brownish outer leaves and trim the prickly points with scissors. Brush all cut edges with lemon juice to prevent discoloration. Soak the artichokes in a large bowl of cold water with added lemon juice.

Bring a large pan of lightly salted water to the boil, add the artichokes with any remaining lemon juice and bring back to the boil. Cover and simmer gently for 30–45 minutes, depending on their size; the artichokes are cooked when a leaf can be pulled out easily.

Drain them thoroughly, upside down. When cool enough to handle, open them carefully at the top,

PURÉE OF PEAS WITH HERBS
— • —

The herbs are a matter of personal taste, but freshness is important and dried herbs are no substitute.

SERVES 4 Ⓥ

450 g/1 lb fresh peas (shelled weight)
salt, pepper, sugar (to taste)
fresh mint, thyme or marjoram

Cook the peas gently in boiling, lightly salted water for 10–15 minutes, adding a sprig of herb. Undercook the peas slightly, drain them and tip them into a liquidiser or food processor. Reduce them to a purée with a little of the cooking liquid, adding salt, pepper and sugar to taste.

Reheat the purée over gentle heat, stirring constantly and adding chopped herbs to taste. Serve the purée as an accompanying vegetable or, slightly thinned, as a sauce.

KILOCALORIES	90	SUGARS	1g
TOTAL FAT	2g	SODIUM	200mg
SATURATED FAT	–	FIBRE	5g

Please see the introduction for a full explanation of the nutritional factboxes.

remaining margarine until golden, add the mushrooms and fry over gentle heat for a couple of minutes. Stir the cucumber into the pan with the remaining flour and cook it through for 2 minutes. Gradually stir in the rest of the milk, bring the sauce to boiling point and let it simmer gently for 5 minutes. Season to taste.

Spoon the filling into the flan case, garnish with chopped parsley, and serve at once with a salad or a cooked vegetable.

KILOCALORIES	510	SUGARS	7g
TOTAL FAT	38g	SODIUM	370mg
SATURATED FAT	6g	FIBRE	4g

MUSHROOM FLAN

Hazelnuts are the main ingredient in this wholesome flan. The filling of mushrooms and onions may be replaced with other vegetables.

SERVES 6 Ⓥ

225 g/8 oz button mushrooms, roughly chopped
75 g/3 oz margarine (or butter)
1 large onion, finely chopped
pinch of celery seeds
65 g/2½ oz plain flour
450 ml/¾ pt semi-skimmed milk
100 g/4 oz wholewheat breadcrumbs
225 g/8 oz ground hazelnuts
2 large eggs, lightly beaten
pinch salt, pepper
¼ small cucumber, peeled and diced
1 tbsp parsley, chopped

Melt 50 g/2 oz of the margarine in a small heavy-based pan and fry half the onion with the celery seeds for 10 minutes or until soft and golden. Stir in 25 g/1 oz of the flour, cook for a minute or two, then add 150 ml/¼ pint of the milk. Stir the sauce as it thickens. Remove from the heat, fold in the breadcrumbs and nuts, followed by the beaten eggs; season to taste.

Set the oven to 180°C/350°F/gas 4. Allow the mixture to cool before spreading it over the base and sides of a 23 cm/9 in flan dish (about 5 cm/2 in deep). Bake it in the centre of the oven for 25–30 minutes until it is golden-brown and cooked.

Meanwhile, fry the rest of the onion in the

POTATO AND LEEK SALAD

The first leeks of the season, in late summer/early autumn, are tender enough to be eaten raw. They can often replace spring onions and have a natural affinity with potatoes.

See illustration page 163.

SERVES 4 Ⓥ

750 g/1½ lb new potatoes
2 medium-sized leeks
1 tsp made mustard
4 tbsp vegetable oil
2 tbsp red wine vinegar
pinch salt, pepper
2 tsp capers, chopped
red pepper, chervil

Scrub the potatoes and cook them in their skins, in lightly salted water, until tender but still firm. Peel the potatoes (if desired) while still warm, then leave to cool slightly before cutting into thin slices. Trim the leeks, leaving as much of the green on as possible; wash them thoroughly and pat them dry. Slice the leeks finely and mix them with the potatoes.

Make a dressing from the mustard, oil and vinegar, seasoning to taste; stir in the capers and pour the dressing over the potatoes and leeks. Mix carefully and chill in the fridge for 1 hour.

Serve the salad garnished with strips of red pepper and with chopped chervil.

KILOCALORIES	155	SUGARS	5g
TOTAL FAT	1g	SODIUM	140mg
SATURATED FAT	–	FIBRE	3.5g

BROCCOLI WITH SESAME SAUCE

Purple and green broccoli (calabrese) and cauliflower are closely related and either can be used for this dish.

SERVES 4 (V)

900 g/2 lb broccoli
pinch salt (optional)
2 tbsp vegetable oil
4 tbsp sesame seeds
2 tbsp lemon juice

Discard the tough stalks and outer leaves from the broccoli and wash the heads well. Steam the broccoli over boiling, lightly salted water for 20–25 minutes or boil the heads gently for about 15 minutes until just tender. Drain the broccoli carefully and cover with a tea towel to keep warm.

Heat the oil in a small pan, add the sesame seeds and stir-fry over medium heat until they are golden-brown and the aroma rises. Add the lemon juice to the pan, stir quickly and pour the sauce over the hot broccoli in a serving dish. Serve as an accompaniment to fish or chicken.

KILOCALORIES	175	SUGARS	2g
TOTAL FAT	14g	SODIUM	130mg
SATURATED FAT	1g	FIBRE	6g

CABBAGE AND SOURED CREAM BAKE

Soured cream has a fat content of approximately 20 per cent, the same as single cream, but with a more refreshing taste.

SERVES 4–6 (V)

700 g/1½ lb white cabbage
300 ml/½ pt soured cream
pinch salt, pepper
1 large egg
½ tsp nutmeg

Remove the outer leaves from the cabbage, cut it into quarters, remove the tough core and shred the cabbage coarsely. Cook it in the minimum amount of lightly salted water for 5 minutes. Drain the cabbage and dry it by tossing it in a pan over low heat. Chop the cabbage finely, ideally in a food processor, but do not reduce it to a purée.

Preheat the oven to 180°C/350°F/gas 4. Whisk the soured cream with salt and pepper, add the egg and nutmeg. Fold in the cabbage and spoon the mixture into a 20 cm/8 in greased soufflé dish. Cover with foil and bake just below the centre of the oven for about 30 minutes. It should be just set; check by piercing the centre with a fine skewer. Serve the cabbage from the dish or turn it out and cut into wedges.

KILOCALORIES	165	SUGARS	5g
TOTAL FAT	14g	SODIUM	290mg
SATURATED FAT	8g	FIBRE	2.5g

COURGETTES WITH CHEESE

Choose quite small and dewy-fresh courgettes, trim off the stalk ends, but do not peel them.

SERVES 4 (V)

450 g/1 lb courgettes, thickly sliced
1 large onion, chopped
1 garlic clove, chopped (optional)
2 tbsp vegetable oil
pinch salt, pepper
3 tomatoes, skinned and roughly chopped
4 eggs, lightly beaten
150 g/5 oz mature Cheddar cheese, grated
grated nutmeg

Fry the onion (and garlic, if used) in the oil until golden. Boil the courgettes in a little salted water until just tender; drain and put them in a shallow, medium-sized ovenproof dish. Preheat the oven to 150°C/300°F/gas 2.

Add the tomatoes and the fried onions to the courgettes. Beat together the eggs and cheese, season to taste with nutmeg and freshly ground pepper and pour this mixture over the vegetables. Bake, uncovered, in the centre of the oven for about 20 minutes or until well risen and golden.

Serve hot, accompanied by a salad and a bowl of plain yogurt.

KILOCALORIES	355	SUGARS	6g
TOTAL FAT	28g	SODIUM	430mg
SATURATED FAT	11g	FIBRE	2.5g

GRATIN OF LEEKS AND HAM

Leeks are at their best during the winter months and have a natural affinity with ham and cheese. At the end of the season large leeks often have a tough woody centre – and little flavour.

SERVES 4

1 large leek (including green part), thinly sliced
pinch salt, pepper
600 ml/1 pt white sauce (see page 29)
125 g/4 oz lean cooked ham, diced
2 tbsp wholemeal breadcrumbs
2 tbsp grated cheese

Preheat the oven to 190°C/375°F/gas 5. Steam the leeks or boil them in a small amount of lightly salted water for 2 minutes. Drain thoroughly, then stir them into the warm white sauce, together with the ham and plenty of freshly ground black pepper.

Spoon the mixture into a 20 cm/8 in lightly greased gratin dish, sprinkle the breadcrumbs and cheese on top and bake near the top of the oven for 35–40 minutes or until the top is brown and bubbly.

Serve at once, as a light lunch or supper dish, accompanied by mashed or jacket potatoes.

KILOCALORIES	175	SUGARS	5g
TOTAL FAT	9g	SODIUM	820mg
SATURATED FAT	5g	FIBRE	1g

ANNA POTATOES

This adaptation of the butter-rich French pommes Anna is particularly suitable at the end of the season, when main-crop potatoes begin to lose their flavour.

SERVES 4 Ⓥ

900 g/2 lb firm, waxy potatoes
2 tbsp vegetable (or olive) oil
pinch garlic salt (optional), pepper
1 tbsp parsley, chopped

Scrub the potatoes thoroughly, wipe them dry and cut them into very thin slices. Heat the oven to 190°C/375°F/gas 5.

Lightly grease a shallow ovenproof dish; arrange the potato slices in overlapping layers, brushing each with a little oil and seasoning lightly with garlic salt (if desired) and plenty of black pepper. Cover the dish tightly with a lid or foil and bake in the centre of the oven for about 1 hour or until the potatoes are cooked. The lid can be removed for the last 15 minutes to crisp and lightly brown the top layer.

Sprinkle parsley on top and serve the potatoes straight from the dish, with fish, poultry or meat.

Variation Small sprigs of rosemary or shivers of garlic can be arranged between the potatoes for extra flavour; in this case the parsley garnish can then be omitted.

KILOCALORIES	230	SUGARS	1g
TOTAL FAT	7g	SODIUM	110mg
SATURATED FAT	1g	FIBRE	3g

GLAZED RED CABBAGE AND BEETROOT

A festive-looking winter vegetable accompaniment for roast pork and lamb, Christmas turkey, goose or duck. It is at its best when cooked in advance and reheated just before serving.

SERVES 4–6 Ⓥ

450 g/1 lb red cabbage, finely shredded
450 g/1 lb cooked beetroot, coarsely chopped
100 ml/4 fl oz vinegar
150 ml/¼ pt water
2 tbsp brown sugar
pinch salt, pepper
1 tbsp cornflour
50 g/2 oz margarine (or butter)

Bring the vinegar, water, brown sugar and a seasoning of salt and pepper to the boil in a large stainless steel pan. Add the shredded cabbage and cook for 3 minutes, then mix in the beetroot and heat through with the cabbage. Stir the cornflour to a smooth paste with a little water, add this to the pan, stirring continuously until the mixture thickens.

Remove the pan from the heat and leave it, covered, for at least 15 minutes and preferably longer, before reheating it with the margarine prior to serving.

KILOCALORIES	170	SUGARS	17g
TOTAL FAT	9g	SODIUM	260mg
SATURATED FAT	2g	FIBRE	3.5g

POTATO NESTS

These little nests are a variation of the duchesse potatoes which garnish so many classic French dishes.
See illustration page 163.

SERVES 4 (V)

750 g/1½ lb potatoes
1 tbsp margarine (or butter)
5 tbsp semi-skimmed milk
pinch salt, pepper

Scrub the potatoes well and cook in boiling water until quite tender. Drain, peel off the skins and mash the potatoes to a smooth purée.

Stir the margarine (or butter) and the milk into the potatoes and season to taste. Set the oven to 225°C/425°F/gas 7.

Cover one or two baking sheets with non-stick paper; drop 8 tablespoonfuls of creamed potatoes on to the paper and smooth and pat them into rounds about 6 cm/2¼ in across and 12 mm/½ in deep. Spoon the remaining mixture into a piping bag fitted with a large nozzle. Pipe two rings, one on top of the other, round the edge of each potato circle. Bake near the top of the oven for 15 minutes or until golden.

Fill the potato nests with hot, cooked vegetables such as tiny peas and diced carrots, shelled broad beans, creamed mushrooms or sweetcorn.

KILOCALORIES	190	SUGARS	3g
TOTAL FAT	6g	SODIUM	170mg
SATURATED FAT	1g	FIBRE	2g

SCANDINAVIAN RED CABBAGE

This is the traditional Danish vegetable dish to accompany the Christmas Eve roast pork, goose or duck and is reminiscent of German sauerkraut.

SERVES 4 (V)

900 g/2 lb red cabbage, finely shredded
40 g/1½ oz margarine (or butter)
1 medium-sized onion, chopped
225 g/8 oz cooking apples, peeled and coarsely grated
½ tsp caraway seeds (optional)
300 ml/½ pt water
3 tbsp vinegar
50 g/2 oz brown sugar
pinch salt

Melt the margarine or butter in a large, heavy-based pan over gentle heat. Add the onion and sauté for about 5 minutes or until soft; mix in the cabbage, tossing it in the butter until thoroughly coated. Stir in the apples, and caraway seeds if used, and add the water and the vinegar. Bring to the boil, stirring constantly. Lower the heat to the minimum, cover the pan and simmer for about 1¾ hours or until the cabbage is almost soft.

Season to taste with sugar, salt and more vinegar if necessary. Cover the pan and continue simmering the cabbage for another 15–30 minutes or until quite soft.

KILOCALORIES	180	SUGARS	16g
TOTAL FAT	9g	SODIUM	480mg
SATURATED FAT	2g	FIBRE	6g

RUNNER BEANS KASSANDRA

This recipe comes from Greece, from the Kassandra peninsula. It is usually made with runner beans, but French beans can be given the same treatment.

SERVES 4 (V)

700 g/1½ lb young runner beans, cut in chunks
salt, pepper
3 tbsp olive oil
1 large onion, roughly chopped
450 g/1 lb ripe tomatoes, skinned and chopped
2 tbsp oregano, finely chopped
1 tbsp parsley, finely chopped
pinch of brown sugar

Top and tail the beans, and cut them into 5 cm/2 in pieces. Arrange them in layers in a colander, sprinkling each layer with coarse sea salt. Leave them for about an hour to soften, then rinse the beans thoroughly under cold running water and leave them to soak in fresh cold water for 10 minutes; drain them.

Heat the oil in a large, heavy-based pan and fry the onion over gentle heat for 5 minutes or until soft. Add the beans, tomatoes, oregano and plenty of pepper. Cover the pan with a lid and simmer for about 40 minutes or until the beans are soft and the sauce fairly thick. Stir in the parsley, and sugar to taste.

Serve the beans accompanied by crusty bread.

KILOCALORIES	180	SUGARS	10g
TOTAL FAT	14g	SODIUM	500mg
SATURATED FAT	2g	FIBRE	5g

PARSNIP AND CARROT FLAN

—— • ——

The nutty flavour of wholemeal pastry complements parsnips and carrots. Choose young vegetables without woody cores.

SERVES 4 Ⓥ

450 g/1 lb parsnips, thinly sliced
175 g/6 oz carrots, thinly sliced
75 g/2½ oz white vegetable fat
150 g/5 oz wholemeal flour
pinch salt
300 ml/½ pt semi-skimmed milk
3 eggs
150 ml/5 fl oz fromage frais (or single
or whipping cream)
3 tbsp low-fat plain yogurt
pinch salt, pepper
25 g/1 oz chopped walnuts

Prepare the pastry by rubbing the fat into the flour, with a pinch of salt, until it resembles fine breadcrumbs. Add enough water to bind the dough. Heat the oven to 200°C/400°F/gas 6. Roll out the pastry and use it to line a 23 cm/9 in flan ring or flan dish; prick the base lightly and cover it with greaseproof paper weighted down with rice, baking beans or crumpled foil. Bake the flan case blind in the oven for 10 minutes. Remove the paper and weights, return the flan to the oven and bake for a further 10 minutes.

Meanwhile, put the prepared parsnips and carrots in a pan; add the milk and bring slowly to the boil; simmer the vegetables, uncovered, for 10–15 minutes or until tender. Liquidise the pan contents, add the eggs, cream and yogurt and liquidise again.

Spoon the vegetable mixture into the flan case and scatter the walnuts over the top. Bake at the same temperature for 20–25 minutes or until the flan has risen and the centre is just cooked through. Serve hot or cold with a green salad.

KILOCALORIES	500	SUGARS	17g
TOTAL FAT	28g	SODIUM	380mg
SATURATED FAT	7g	FIBRE	10g

Most main-crop potatoes are all-rounders, suitable for all cooking methods. Floury types, such as Desirée and King Edward, mash well, while the firm-textured Majestic and Red King are better for baking.

CELERIAC ALLA PARMIGIANA

Sometimes known as turnip-rooted celery, celeriac is a neglected winter vegetable in spite of having a good fibre and low calorie content. Buy smaller celeriacs in preference to large ones which can be coarse-textured, and avoid those with very knobbly skins.

SERVES 4

750 g/1½ lb celeriac
1 tbsp lemon juice
pinch salt, cayenne pepper
1½ tbsp margarine (or butter)
2 tbsp plain flour
300 ml/½ pt semi-skimmed milk
½ tsp dry mustard (optional)
50 g/2 oz lean mild-cured ham, diced
2 tbsp Parmesan cheese, grated

Cut root and stalk ends off the celeriac, peel the tough skin thickly and cut the flesh into 1 cm/½ in round slices; drop these into a bowl of water with lemon juice to prevent discoloration. Bring a pan of lightly salted water to the boil, add the celeriac slices, cover and simmer gently for 8–10 minutes or until just tender. Drain on kitchen paper and reserve the cooking liquid. Set the oven to 200°C/400°F/gas 6.

Make the basic white sauce (see page 29) from the margarine, flour and milk mixed with an equal amount of celeriac liquid. Season to taste with salt, cayenne and mustard and fold in the ham.

Arrange the celeriac slices in a lightly greased ovenproof dish, pour the sauce over them and sprinkle with the cheese. Bake in the centre of the oven for 20–25 minutes or until the cheese has browned.

Serve on its own as a light lunch dish or as a more substantial meal with poached eggs.

KILOCALORIES	270	SUGARS	7g
TOTAL FAT	16g	SODIUM	840mg
SATURATED FAT	6g	FIBRE	6.5g

POTATO AND SPINACH SOUFFLÉS

Plain baked potatoes can easily become a light main course if the flesh is scooped out and mixed with other ingredients, such as cheese, diced vegetables, flaked fish or chicken.

See illustration page 163.

SERVES 4 Ⓥ

4 large baking potatoes
450 g/1 lb fresh (or 225 g/8 oz frozen leaf) spinach
25 g/1 oz margarine (or butter)
3 tbsp low-fat plain yogurt
(or single cream)
1 tsp grated nutmeg
pinch salt, pepper
50 g/2 oz grated Gruyère cheese

Scrub the potatoes, cut a cross in the rounded top of each and bake them in the oven at 225°C/425°F/gas 7 for about 1 hour or until cooked through; test whether ready with a skewer.

Meanwhile, put the spinach, fresh or frozen, in a pan with only the liquid which clings to it, and cook over gentle heat for 8–10 minutes. Drain thoroughly, squeezing out all water, then chop the spinach finely.

Remove the baked potatoes from the oven, cut a lid off the top of each and scoop out the flesh, taking care not to break the skins. Mash the potato flesh in a bowl, beat in the margarine and yogurt and fold in the chopped spinach. Season to taste with nutmeg, salt and pepper and pile the mixture back into the potato skins; smooth the domed tops and sprinkle them with the cheese. Return the potatoes to the oven for 15 minutes or until the cheese has melted and browned.

KILOCALORIES	430	SUGARS	6g
TOTAL FAT	11g	SODIUM	300mg
SATURATED FAT	4g	FIBRE	7g

CABBAGE CASSEROLE

Cabbage should be boiled in very little water and for a very short time. This savoury custard transforms it from the plain to the interesting.

SERVES 4–6 Ⓥ

275 g/10 oz white cabbage, finely shredded
225 ml/8 fl oz water
3 eggs, lightly beaten
225 ml/8 fl oz semi-skimmed milk
2 tbsp plain flour
large pinch salt
1 tsp brown sugar (or 1 tbsp sultanas)
1 medium-sized onion, chopped
50 g/2 oz wholemeal breadcrumbs
3 tbsp margarine (or butter), melted

Bring the cabbage and water to the boil. Cook, covered, for 5 minutes, then drain thoroughly. Set the oven to 200°C/400°F/gas 6. Blend the eggs with the milk; mix the flour, salt and sugar or sultanas together and fold them into the egg custard mixture.

Fold the cabbage, onion, breadcrumbs and melted margarine into the custard mixture; mix thoroughly and spoon it into a lightly greased 900 g/2 lb loaf tin or soufflé dish. Set this in a roasting tin and add boiling water to come halfway up the sides of the tin or dish. Bake in the centre of the oven for about 30 minutes or until cooked.

Serve hot, as a main-course dish on its own or perhaps with plain boiled rice.

KILOCALORIES	400	SUGARS	6g
TOTAL FAT	31g	SODIUM	560mg
SATURATED FAT	14g	FIBRE	2g

BRAISED CELERY

Serve individual heads of celery for a special occasion, or buy one large head and cut it into manageable-sized pieces for a less expensive accompaniment.

SERVES 4 Ⓥ

4 heads of celery
25 g/1 oz margarine (or butter)
1 large onion, chopped
1 large carrot, chopped
450 ml/³⁄₄ pt white stock (see page 17)
1 bouquet garni (see page 17)
pinch salt, pepper
2 tbsp parsley, finely chopped

Cut the root ends off the celery and remove any damaged outer stems; trim each celery head to a length of 15–18 cm/6–7 in. Rinse well under cold running water, then drop the celery into a large pan of boiling water; simmer, covered, for 10 minutes. Plunge the celery at once into cold water before tying the heads into shape with string.

Set the oven to 180°C/350°F/gas 4. Melt half the margarine in a pan and fry the onion and carrot over gentle heat for 5 minutes; transfer them to an ovenproof dish, arrange the celery on top and pour over the stock. Add the bouquet garni and a sprinkling of salt and pepper. Cover the dish tightly and cook in the centre of the oven for about 1½ hours, removing the lid for the last 30 minutes to brown the celery slightly.

Remove the string from the celery hearts and keep them warm; strain the braising liquid and if necessary reduce it to a few tablespoonfuls by fast boiling. Stir in the remaining margarine and the parsley and pour over the celery just before serving.

KILOCALORIES	110	SUGARS	8g
TOTAL FAT	7g	SODIUM	640mg
SATURATED FAT	1g	FIBRE	8g

CURRIED CAULIFLOWER

Cauliflower is available throughout the year and should be cooked for the minimum amount of time so as to retain its crisp texture.

SERVES 4 Ⓥ

1 medium-sized cauliflower, broken into florets
pinch salt, pepper
1 small onion, finely chopped
1 small cooking apple, peeled, cored and chopped
25 g/1 oz margarine (or butter)
½–1 tbsp curry powder
1 tbsp plain flour
1 tsp brown sugar
25 g/1 oz chopped walnuts (or sultanas)

Cook the cauliflower florets in boiling, lightly salted water for 3 minutes. Drain them, reserving the cooking liquid. Sauté the onion and apple in the margarine or butter for about 5 minutes until soft and mushy. Stir in the curry powder and continue cooking over gentle heat for 1–2 minutes, stirring all the time. Add the flour and cook for 2 minutes, then pour in 350 ml/ 12 fl oz of the reserved cauliflower stock, stirring until the sauce thickens.

Add the cauliflower, salt, pepper and sugar. Cook for 5 minutes or until the cauliflower is just tender, stirring occasionally. Stir in half the walnuts or all the sultanas and leave the pan, covered, for 5 minutes to let the flavours permeate the cauliflower. Spoon into a warm serving dish and garnish with the remaining chopped walnuts.

Serve as an accompaniment to baked fish with plain boiled rice and a mild relish.

KILOCALORIES	200	SUGARS	8g
TOTAL FAT	12g	SODIUM	190mg
SATURATED FAT	2g	FIBRE	6g

Form the potato mixture into small balls. Heat oil in a deep-fryer to 190°C/375°F (or to a fairly hot temperature in a deep pan) and fry the croquettes for 3–5 minutes until crisp and golden.

Drain on kitchen paper and serve while hot.

KILOCALORIES	250	SUGARS	1g
TOTAL FAT	18g	SODIUM	150mg
SATURATED FAT	2g	FIBRE	1.5g

CARROT ROAST

Carrots are transformed by peanut butter into this interesting dish.

SERVES 4 Ⓥ

125 g/4 oz raw carrots, grated
175 ml/6 fl oz semi-skimmed milk
6 tbsp unsweetened peanut butter
1 medium-sized onion, chopped
1–2 tbsp vegetable oil
125 g/4 oz cooked brown rice
1 tsp chopped fresh sage (or ½ tsp dried sage)
½ tsp powdered mace
1 tsp ground ginger (or curry powder)
1 egg, lightly beaten

Preheat the oven to 180°C/350°F/gas 4. Blend the milk with the peanut butter until smooth. Fry the onion in hot oil until transparent. Mix the carrots, cooked rice and onion, stir in the peanut-milk mixture and season with sage, mace and ginger or curry power. Bind the mixture with the egg.

Transfer the mixture to a foil-lined greased loaf tin or ovenproof dish. Bake for about 30 minutes. Serve hot, cut into slices, as a main course.

KILOCALORIES	310	SUGARS	8g
TOTAL FAT	22g	SODIUM	200mg
SATURATED FAT	4g	FIBRE	2.5g

SESAME-SEED POTATOES

Ensure the oil is at the correct temperature, otherwise the croquettes will absorb oil. Cook in small batches and drain well.

SERVES 6 Ⓥ

700 g/1½ lb mashed potatoes
3 tbsp sesame seeds
pinch salt, pepper
1 large egg, lightly beaten
1 egg white
4 tbsp oil for deep-frying

Dry-roast the sesame seeds in a heavy-based pan until they are golden and start to splutter. Stir them into the mashed potatoes and season to taste. Mix the beaten egg into the potatoes, beat the egg white until stiff and fold it carefully into the mixture.

BAKED GARLIC POTATOES

An elegant concertina version of the baked potato.

SERVES 4 Ⓥ

8 medium-sized potatoes (each approx 150 g/5 oz)
6 tbsp olive (or vegetable) oil
juice of a lemon
2 garlic cloves, crushed
2 tsp fresh marjoram, chopped
pinch salt, pepper

Scrub and thoroughly dry the potatoes. Cut them downwards into thin slices without cutting them right through. Heat the oven to 200°C/400°F/gas 6.

Make a dressing from the other ingredients. Place the potatoes in a greased ovenproof dish and pour on the dressing. Bake for 50–60 minutes, basting frequently.

Garnish with marjoram, and serve with baked fish or chicken.

KILOCALORIES	405	SUGARS	2g
TOTAL FAT	20g	SODIUM	220mg
SATURATED FAT	3g	FIBRE	4g

ONION WHOLEMEAL TART

This is a more healthy version of the classic onion flan from Alsace. Wholemeal flour gives the pastry a slightly nutty flavour.

SERVES 6 Ⓥ

3 large onions, roughly chopped
175 g/6 oz wholemeal flour
1½ tsp baking powder
pinch salt, pepper
40 g/1½ oz margarine
40 g/1½ oz white vegetable fat
1 tbsp vegetable oil
2 large eggs
150 ml/¼ pt semi-skimmed milk
4 tbsp single cream
1 tbsp made mustard

Mix the flour with the baking powder and a pinch of salt; rub in the fats and if necessary add a little water to bind the pastry. Line a 20 cm/8 in tart tin with the pastry, prick the base and chill it. Fry the onions for about 10 minutes in the oil until they turn golden. Remove from the heat and leave them to cool slightly.

Heat the oven to 200°C/400°F/gas 6. Spread the onions over the pastry base. Whisk the eggs with the milk, cream, mustard and a seasoning of salt and pepper. Pour this mixture over the onions and bake the wholemeal tart on the middle shelf of the oven for 25–35 minutes, until the pastry is cooked and the filling is golden and risen.

Cut the onion tart into wedges, and serve hot with a puréed vegetable or rice, or cold with a salad.

KILOCALORIES	355	SUGARS	7g
TOTAL FAT	24g	SODIUM	230mg
SATURATED FAT	6g	FIBRE	4g

MIXED VEGETABLE PIE

A combination of pulses and crisp root vegetables provides a nutritious vegetarian main course. Yeast extract adds B vitamins but also salt, so there is no need to add extra to the sauce.

SERVES 4 Ⓥ

100 g/4 oz lentils
1 large onion, chopped
4 sticks celery, chopped
25 g/1 oz margarine (or butter)
225 g/8 oz carrots, diced
450 g/1 lb potatoes, diced
225 g/8 oz tomatoes, skinned and sliced
pepper
90 g/3½ oz margarine (or vegetable fat)
15 g/½ oz plain flour
175 g/6 oz wholemeal flour
1 tsp yeast extract

Rinse the lentils and cook them for 20–30 minutes until they are almost tender; drain them and reserve the cooking liquid. Fry the onion and celery in the margarine or butter for 8–10 minutes or until they are soft. Add the carrots and potatoes, frying them gently for 5 minutes and stirring occasionally. Layer the vegetables with the lentils and tomatoes in a pie dish and pepper lightly.

Melt 15 g/½ oz of the margarine or vegetable fat in a small pan, add the plain flour and cook for a few minutes before stirring in 300 ml/½ pt of the lentil liquid. Add a grinding of black pepper to the sauce and pour a little over the vegetables.

Preheat the oven to 200°C/400°F/gas 6. Make the pastry by rubbing the rest of the margarine or vegetable fat into the flour, add the yeast extract and mix to a dough with cold water. Roll out the pastry and cover the vegetables with it. Bake in the centre of the oven for 40 minutes, until the pastry is crisp.

Serve hot, with the remaining sauce gently reheated.

KILOCALORIES	515	SUGARS	9g
TOTAL FAT	25g	SODIUM	480mg
SATURATED FAT	6g	FIBRE	8.5g

Ⓥ This symbol denotes a recipe suitable for vegetarians.

Outdoor Eating

Claudia Roden

It is well worth taking picnics seriously and making them an occasion for good food, even if the weather takes a turn for the worse and you have to resort to eating indoors.

Until fairly recently most picnic food – sandwiches, cold meats and pies – has been of the same type as that packed into hampers in the nineteenth century. Sandwiches were allegedly invented by the 4th Earl of Sandwich during a 24-hour gambling session in 1762 as a way of eating without soiling the cards.

It is only since the Second World War that we have begun to look to other cultures for new inspiration. Eating in the open has a different importance in many countries, and each has its own traditional outdoor favourites.

In Egypt there are official occasions for picnics such as *mulids* (religious festivals), when people flock to public gardens, shrines and burial grounds, and *Shem el Nessim* which celebrates the arrival of spring, when everyone ventures into the country or on to the river.

When we lived in Egypt, we used to go picnicking in large groups of relatives and friends. We played canasta and backgammon, told stories and jokes, and we sang and danced the conga and the samba. Sometimes *gala-galas* (magicians) came to entertain us with baby chicks emerging from under silver cups and eggs pulled from our noses. We brought with us a large variety of foods: thick omelettes, vegetables, either cooked in olive oil or stuffed, tiny and large pies made with layers of paper-thin dough, pastries filled with spinach, cheese or minced meat. There were meatballs and fish balls, salads and rice dishes, and all kinds of sweets and pastries to follow.

It is different with the Japanese. They go on picnics to celebrate their deep and ancient love for the hills and waters and the progress of the year from spring to winter. They celebrate the blooming of chrysanthemums and cherry blossom with 'moon viewing' and 'flower viewing' picnic foods packed in stacks of vermilion and green lacquered boxes. *Sushi*, the delicate combinations of raw and marinated fish and seafood on a bed of fragrant rice, are their favourite take-away foods.

In India it is considered improper to eat in the open except when travelling and on hunting expeditions. Picnics are a relic of the Raj and as such are a British tradition exported to India. In China there are many traditional occasions for bringing out the food, such as the outing to watch the full harvest moon and the Dragon Boat Festival; graveside feasting is the happiest part of ancestor worship. For such events villagers bring cooked pigs, chickens and ducks, squid and eggs as well as all kinds of vegetables.

PICNIC FARE

Food for an alfresco party, for six to eight people, can be as simple and as elaborate as the inclination dictates. An impromptu wayside meal can be quickly rustled up and modelled on the French hors d'oeuvre or crudités and what the Italians term antipasti. The ingredients can be bought from good delicatessens and assembled on the spot. All you will need is crusty bread, one or two platters, a sharp knife and oil, vinegar, salt and pepper for a vinaigrette dressing.

Buy a selection of pâtés and cold meats, such as sliced salami, smoked and cooked ham, mortadella and sausages and arrange them on a bed of lettuce, together with sardines, tuna fish or anchovy fillets, cooked prawns, artichoke hearts, tomato wedges and lemon quarters.

A colourful and appetising vegetarian feast can be made up of radishes, cucumbers and young carrots, fat tomato slices, quartered fennel, cauliflower florets, boiled baby beetroots, green and red peppers cut into ribbons, and celery sticks. Very young mange-tout, courgettes and runner beans are delicious raw. Among the vegetables place one or two fruits, such as orange or grapefruit segments and thin slices of firm pears. Make up a vinaigrette dressing and pour it over the collection, then sprinkle it with chopped red onion or salad onions, or with sprigs of watercress, parsley, mint or coriander. Prepare in advance and pack into plastic boxes in the hamper or cool box.

MULTI-COLOURED PEPPER SALAD
—— • ——

A colourful vegetable salad that is simple to prepare.

SERVES 10–12 (V)

3 peppers, green, red and yellow
3 tbsp olive oil
1 tbsp wine vinegar
pinch salt, pepper
1 small red onion (or 5 spring onions), finely chopped
small bunch of parsley, finely chopped

Cut the peppers in half, remove seeds and cores, then cut the flesh into wide ribbons. Place them, skin side up, on a grill pan under medium heat, and leave them until the skins blister and blacken; do not let them burn. Drop the hot pepper strips into a polythene bag and close it tight – this makes peeling of the cooled peppers easier. Dress with oil and vinegar, and season to taste; sprinkle with the onion and parsley.

KILOCALORIES	45	SUGARS	2g
TOTAL FAT	4g	SODIUM	40mg
SATURATED FAT	1g	FIBRE	1g

ORIENTAL NOODLES
—— • ——

In China and Japan cold noodles are served as a summer appetiser. This recipe is inspired by both countries and is finished off with a dressing of delicate flavourings – sour and hot, sweet and spicy.

SERVES 10–12

350 g/12 oz yellow (or white) noodles
2 tbsp peanut (or sesame) oil
225 g/8 oz mange-tout peas, topped and tailed
225 g/8 oz bean sprouts
225 g/8 oz shelled prawns (fresh or frozen)
100 g/4 oz ham, diced
1 pepper (green, yellow or red), diced
6 spring onions, finely chopped

DRESSING
½ tsp ground chilli
1–1½ tbsp sesame sauce (tahini)
2½ tsp sugar
3–4 tbsp rice vinegar (or white wine vinegar)
3–4 tbsp dry sherry
3 tbsp peanut (or sesame) oil
pinch salt
4–5 tbsp soya sauce
2 garlic cloves, crushed
juice of 5–8 cm/2–3 in piece fresh root ginger

Right *Platters of crudités and cold meats, boxes with seafood and pepper salads, oriental noodles and sliced oranges. At the back is a mixed vegetable and fruit salad and in the foreground small green omelettes.*

Cook the noodles in plenty of boiling, lightly salted water until *al dente* (about 3–4 minutes), drain and rinse quickly under cold running water and toss them in the peanut or sesame oil to prevent them sticking.

Bring a large saucepan of lightly salted water to the boil. Add the mange-tout and boil rapidly for 1–2 minutes or until the peas are done but still crisp. Add the bean sprouts, boil for another minute and remove the pan from the heat as soon as the sprouts are slightly limp. Drain the mange-tout and bean sprouts thoroughly, put them in a large bowl with the prawns, ham, pepper and spring onions and fold in the noodles.

Carefully mix the dressing, blending the sesame sauce with the other ingredients and, starting with the lesser quantities, tasting frequently. The ginger juice can be extracted by cutting the root into several small pieces and squeezing them in a garlic press. Pour the dressing over the salad and toss well.

KILOCALORIES	150	SUGARS	4g
TOTAL FAT	7g	SODIUM	200mg
SATURATED FAT	1g	FIBRE	2g

SMALL GREEN OMELETTES

This Arab picnic favourite is usually made as one thick cake, but small individual ones look more elegant. The green colour can come from leaf vegetables such as spinach, lettuce and watercress or from fresh herbs like coriander, parsley, chives, mint and basil.

SERVES 10–12 Ⓥ

450 g/1 lb spinach
8 tbsp olive oil
6 eggs
½ small lettuce, shredded
½ bunch watercress, coarsely chopped
6 spring onions, finely chopped
large bunch of fresh herbs, finely chopped
1 tsp ground cinnamon
¼ tsp ground ginger
grating of nutmeg
pinch salt, pepper
2 tbsp raisins
2 tbsp walnuts, chopped

Wash the spinach thoroughly, remove the thick stalks and shred the leaves; put them in a pan with 2 tablespoonfuls of oil and let the spinach crumple to a soft mass over low heat. Beat the eggs lightly in a bowl, then add the lettuce, watercress and onions, herbs and

spices, and seasoning to taste; fold in the raisins and walnuts. Mix thoroughly, then spoon a ladleful on hot oil in a 20 cm/8 in frying-pan. Cook over gentle heat until the bottom sets, then turn the omelette carefully to cook the other side. Continue like this until all the mixture is used up.

KILOCALORIES	160	SUGARS	2g
TOTAL FAT	14g	SODIUM	130mg
SATURATED FAT	1g	FIBRE	1.5g

SEAFOOD AND RICE SALAD

If preferred, either all white or all shellfish can be used.

SERVES 10–12

450 lb/1 lb rice, white (or brown)
pinch salt, pepper
4 tbsp olive oil
700 g/1½ lb cod (or haddock, halibut, sea bream, sea bass, monkfish, turbot)
juice of 2 lemons (or to taste)
450 g/1 lb mussels in their shells (optional)
bunch of spring onions, finely chopped
large bunch of flat-leaved parsley (or a mixture of coriander, chives, tarragon and mint), finely chopped
225 g/8 oz cooked crab (or prawns)

Soak the rice in water for 1 hour; drain and rinse it in a colander. Throw it into rapidly boiling, salted water and cook white rice for 3 minutes, brown rice for 15 minutes; drain at once. The rice should still be slightly nutty; return it to the pan with 4 tablespoonfuls of olive oil, cover with the lid and steam for 15 minutes.

Poach the fish gently in water, with pepper and a squeeze of lemon, until it just begins to flake; remove the fish from the poaching liquid. Meanwhile, wash the mussels in several lots of water, discarding any which are broken or open, scrape off the beards, then add the mussels to the pan and cook until they open, after about 5 minutes (discard any that remain closed).

Stir the spring onions and herbs into the rice, fold in the flaked fish and toss in a dressing of, perhaps, olive oil, lemon juice, salt and pepper. Arrange the mussels on top of the salad, together with the crab or prawns.

KILOCALORIES	225	SUGARS	1g
TOTAL FAT	7g	SODIUM	520mg
SATURATED FAT	1g	FIBRE	0.5g

Cooking over the embers of a wood or charcoal fire imparts a unique smoky flavour to food which no other method can capture. It also gives out a tantalising smell. Barbecue cooking is popular because it is fun and not much effort for the cook; everyone wants to take part and the only accompaniments needed for grilled meals are salads, and fruit to follow. Although it is perfectly simple, and despite an Italian saying that 'even an old shoe tastes good if it is cooked over charcoal', many a good piece of meat ends up as a dried, blackened offering on the barbecue. Good grilling and roasting is an art – acquired by practice only.

First, you must learn how to make a good fire and how to control the heat and distribute it evenly. Secondly, you must discover, often through trial and error, the proper treatment for the food: the distance it should be from the fire, the grilling time and whether the food needs marinating, searing, protection in leaves or fat, or basting during cooking.

The simplest barbecue can be a home-made affair, made from a biscuit tin or metal tray, with holes punched around the sides, or simply a grill pan placed between two bricks. A few tools are indispensable: a grill with close-set bars, skewers and a sturdy spit for roasting.

The fire can be made with wood or charcoal. Slow-burning woods produce long-lasting coals; aromatic fruit woods give out a delicious perfume but you should avoid resinous woods. Charcoal is more manageable than wood and burns more easily and quickly to a bed of embers; charcoal briquettes give a more uniform heat, are longer-lasting and do not spark. Build the fire gradually, beginning with crumpled paper, dry leaves or bark; cover these with dry twigs, then sticks and thrust a match in the centre. When the fire is lit add larger pieces of wood, crossing them so as to let the air circulate, or cover with a pile of charcoal. Once the wood or charcoal has ignited and started to burn evenly, rake it and spread it out to cover the area needed for cooking. The fire will be ready for cooking only when it has reduced to glowing ash-covered embers and there are no more flames or smoke. Wood generally takes 30–45 minutes and charcoal briquettes about 20 minutes to reach this stage.

The cooking time depends upon the thickness and type of food, its distance from the fire and other foods, the quality of the charcoal, the size of the fire bed and the weather conditions. The heat can be regulated by raising or lowering the grill. For very slow cooking, such as a large roast, use gentle indirect heat, place the food a little to the side, with a tray underneath to collect the juices. For grilling, you can test the heat by putting a hand over the coals at the distance the food will be placed. If you can leave it for almost four seconds the fire is medium-hot.

BARBECUE FOOD

All types of meats, fish, shellfish, vegetables and fruit can be cooked on a barbecue with excellent results. Because barbecuing is a harsh form of cooking, all foods except fatty meat need moistening with fat or the result will be dry and hard. It is customary to bard lean meats with a covering of thin strips of bacon or pork fat. Other foods can be basted or brushed with melted butter, oil or a marinade; wrappings of vine, lettuce, papaya, palm and banana leaves are a traditional way of protecting and flavouring delicate foods.

A marinade of oil and wine, vinegar or lemon juice, or cider, beer or yogurt, mixed with herbs and spices, flavours and tenderises the food and prevents it from drying out. Another refinement is to throw branches or sprigs of herbs into the fire so that the food can catch and retain their aroma. Dried herbs, which burn too readily and lose their perfume quickly, should be added to the embers just before the food is ready to eat. Fresh herbs give out a more powerful and longer-lasting scent. Experiment using vine twigs and prunings, orange peel and garlic, dried fennel stalks and damp hickory chips.

BARBECUE MEAL FOR SIX

While the fire is burning down to embers or a joint of meat or chicken is roasting on the spit, quickly grilled appetisers – shellfish, mushrooms or cheese – are delicious to nibble at.

The main course in a barbecue dinner can, of course, be the usual hamburgers, sausages, chops or steaks or you can try spicy chicken drumsticks or Arab-inspired meat patties known as *kibbeh*. The main course need not be meat; fish is delicious grilled. It can be cooked whole, cubed or cut into thick slices and steaks. Plain everyday types of fish become rich and exotic when marinated and basted with a herb-flavoured dressing.

BARBECUED VEGETABLES

Many vegetables can be cooked over the fire, which gives them a particularly rich flavour. Sweetcorn is especially good and courgettes, tomatoes and long white radishes (moolis) can all be put on the grill. Red and green peppers can be peeled after roasting, cut into strips and dressed into a salad. Grilled aubergines become blackened and blistered on the outside, soft inside; the soft flesh can be scooped out and mixed with olive oil, lemon juice, salt and pepper.

Wrap well-scrubbed potatoes and sweet potatoes in foil and bury them in the ashes. Depending on size, they will take ½–1½ hours to cook through.

Cut peeled turnips into thick slices, brush them with olive oil; sprinkle with salt and pepper and cook over a gentle fire on an oiled grill under tender (after 10–15 minutes) and lightly browned, turning them over once and brushing with more oil.

SPICY FISH

Fish steaks make a good alternative to burgers and cuts of meat.

SERVES 6

6 fish steaks (cod, halibut, monkfish)
flour (optional)

MARINADE
large bunch of fresh coriander
(or parsley), finely chopped
4 tbsp olive oil
1 small onion, grated
2–3 garlic cloves, crushed
juice of a lemon (or 4 tbsp wine vinegar)
1–2 tsp ground cumin
½ tsp ground coriander
½ tsp ground cinnamon
¼ tsp ground ginger
1 tsp paprika
good pinch of cayenne pepper

Set a few sprigs of coriander or parsley aside for garnish, and mix the remainder with all the other marinade ingredients in a bowl – a food processor will chop and blend everything smoothly. Marinate the fish steaks in this mixture for 1 hour in a cool place, turning them over occasionally.

Lift the fish steaks from the marinade, dredge them in flour if a crust is wanted, then sprinkle again with the marinade. Cook on a well-oiled grill over a gentle fire for about 6–10 minutes or until the flesh begins to flake, turning them once. Brush with the marinade when the steaks are turned. Serve with lemon wedges and a sprinkling of chopped coriander or parsley.

KILOCALORIES	130	SUGARS	1g
TOTAL FAT	9g	SODIUM	50mg
SATURATED FAT	1g	FIBRE	–

Right *Spicy halibut steaks, cheese in vine leaves, and mussels grill over glowing embers, and stuffed meat patties and mushrooms with garlic butter (foreground) await guests.*

GRILLED CLAMS AND MUSSELS

Allow 6–8 mussels or clams per person. Scrub them thoroughly and remove beards and barnacles with a knife or scissors. Discard any which are broken or open, and wash the remainder well in several changes of water (see pages 52–3). Place the shells over a hot grill and serve them as soon as they open, with a bowl of oil and lemon juice, seasoned with salt and pepper.

MUSHROOMS WITH GARLIC BUTTER

Use large, flat-cap mushrooms and allow three per person.

SERVES 6 Ⓥ

18 large mushrooms
vegetable oil
pinch salt, pepper
50 g/2 oz unsalted butter
1 large garlic clove, crushed
large bunch of parsley, finely chopped

Wipe the mushrooms clean and trim the stalks level with the caps. Brush them with oil and sprinkle lightly with salt and pepper. Place them on an oiled grill over a gentle fire for around 15 minutes, turning them over once and brushing with oil to prevent them shrivelling.

Beat the butter to a smooth cream; season with salt and pepper and stir in the garlic and parsley. Remove the grilled mushrooms and spread a little of the garlic and parsley butter on each upturned mushroom before serving them.

[Nutritional value is per mushroom.]

KILOCALORIES	90	SUGARS	–
TOTAL FAT	9g	SODIUM	70mg
SATURATED FAT	5g	FIBRE	0.5g

CHICKEN DRUMSTICKS

A whole chicken can be spit-roasted or skinned and boned, cut into cubes and grilled on skewers. Chicken joints and drumsticks are other alternatives.

SERVES 6

12 chicken drumsticks
juice of a lemon
2–3 tbsp olive oil
2 garlic cloves, crushed
2.5 cm/1 in piece root ginger, peeled and grated
pinch salt, black pepper

Make a marinade from the lemon juice, oil, garlic and ginger and season well with salt and black pepper. Marinate the drumsticks in this mixture for at least 1 hour. Place them on an oiled grill over a medium fire for 25–35 minutes, turning them over occasionally and brushing frequently with the marinade.

KILOCALORIES	145	SUGARS	–
TOTAL FAT	10g	SODIUM	180mg
SATURATED FAT	2g	FIBRE	–

CHEESE IN VINE LEAVES

This recipe requires cheese that melts easily.

SERVES 6 Ⓥ

1 small can (or packet) vine leaves
450 g/1 lb cheese (Gruyère, Emmental, Cheddar, Bel Paese or Fontina)
black pepper
2 tbsp mint (or chives or rosemary), finely chopped (optional)

Drain canned vine leaves from the brine and steep them in cold water for at least 1 hour to remove the saltiness; change the water several times. Packaged vine leaves merely need soaking until they can be separated. Pat the vine leaves dry with kitchen paper. Cut the cheese into 1 cm/½ in thick slices and lay each slice on four overlapping vine leaves; sprinkle with a generous grating of pepper and a few chopped herbs. Wrap the leaves round the cheese, folding in the edges to form neat little parcels. Put these over the fire, turning them over once, until the cheese has melted and the vine leaves are crispy-brown.

KILOCALORIES	310	SUGARS	1g
TOTAL FAT	25g	SODIUM	500mg
SATURATED FAT	16g	FIBRE	–

STUFFED MEAT AND WHEAT PATTIES

— • —

In this Arab dish the crunchy shells consist of cracked wheat and minced savoury lamb and enclose a spicy and fruity meat filling.

SERVES 6

225 g/8 oz medium cracked wheat (see glossary)
1 kg/2 lb lamb shoulder, finely minced
1 onion, finely grated
1 tsp ground cumin
½ tsp ground coriander
pinch salt, pepper
bunch of parsley, finely chopped
2 tbsp vegetable oil for frying

FILLING
450 g/1 lb minced beef (or veal)
1 large onion, coarsely chopped
pinch salt, pepper
½ tsp ground cinnamon
¼ tsp ground allspice
2 tbsp pine kernels
2 tbsp raisins (or chopped apricots)

Wash the cracked wheat, and soak it in fresh cold water for 20 minutes. Drain through a fine sieve and squeeze out any excess water. Place in a large bowl with the minced lamb, onion, spices, salt, pepper and parsley. Work the mixture into a paste with the hands.

For the filling, fry the onion in a little oil over medium heat until golden (about 5 minutes). Add the meat and fry, stirring, until it changes colour and separates into grains. Mix in the seasoning, spices, pine kernels and raisins or apricots. Remove the mixture from the heat.

Shape the lamb and wheat mixture to egg-sized lumps and flatten them to round patties, about 8 cm/ 3 in across and 2.5 cm/1 in deep. Put a tablespoonful of the filling in the centre of half the patties, top with the remainder and press the edges well together. Grill the patties over a medium fire for about 15 minutes or until they are crisp and brown, turning them once. They do not require basting.

KILOCALORIES	645	SUGARS	9g
TOTAL FAT	33g	SODIUM	340mg
SATURATED FAT	12g	FIBRE	1g

SLICED ORANGES

— • —

The best finish to an outdoor meal is fruit; oranges are popular with most people, especially if they have already been peeled and cut into segments or slices.

SERVES 10–12 Ⓥ

6 oranges
3 tbsp Cointreau or brandy
cinnamon
caster sugar (optional)
100 g/4 oz blanched almonds, toasted

Peel the oranges with a sharp knife, taking care to remove all the pith. Cut them into thin slices and arrange in overlapping layers, sprinkled with liqueur, a light dusting of cinnamon and, if the oranges are on the sharp side, a little sugar. A few toasted almonds can also be trickled between the orange slices. They are most delicious served chilled.

KILOCALORIES	90	SUGARS	9g
TOTAL FAT	5g	SODIUM	10mg
SATURATED FAT	–	FIBRE	2g

SNACKS AND SAVOURIES

The term snack covers a multitude of sins, from illicit bags of crisps and chocolate bars between meals to a hurried burger. Correctly, it implies a quickly assembled or cooked substitute for a proper meal, from a sandwich to an omelette or a Welsh rarebit. The latter was known by the Victorians as a savoury and was served after the dessert course to cleanse the palate of the sweet taste. Savouries were usually spicy and included such favourites as devilled herring roes and kidneys. Today, the term snack and savoury have become synonymous and often constitute a quick but satisfying meal from leftovers.

There is no reason why a snack meal should be any less nutritious than one on which much time has been expended. Wholemeal sandwiches, baps and pitta bread filled with canned fish, cottage cheese and chopped nuts, cooked chicken and salad vegetables are both sustaining and healthy; wholemeal pizzas take no longer to prepare than the classic Italian versions; herb-flavoured potato sticks are better than salty crisps, and sesame bars preferable to chocolate.

SANDWICH FILLERS

The following three recipes are quick and versatile. They can be used as spreads or toppings for wholemeal sandwiches, plain or toasted, rolls, baps and pitta bread. They can be served as a light lunch with salads, and the mushroom and bacon filler is also suitable for omelettes and, folded into a white sauce, for vol-au-vent. The nutritional values are for the full quantities.

TUNA FISH

1 can (200 g/7 oz) tuna fish in brine, drained
1 celery stick, finely chopped
1 small onion, finely chopped
1 garlic clove, crushed

2–3 tbsp reduced-calorie mayonnaise (or Thousand Island dressing or low-fat plain yogurt)
pinch salt, pepper

Flake the drained tuna and mix it thoroughly with the celery, onion and garlic. Fold in the mayonnaise, dressing or yogurt and season to taste with salt and pepper. If you serve this as a salad, garnish it with sprigs of parsley or a little chopped red pepper.

KILOCALORIES	895	SUGARS	9g
TOTAL FAT	72g	SODIUM	2180mg
SATURATED FAT	8g	FIBRE	1.5g

MUSHROOMS AND BACON

4 rashers lean bacon, derinded and cut into
5 mm/¼ in pieces
1 small onion, finely chopped
1 garlic clove, finely chopped
225 g/8 oz mushrooms, sliced
pepper
2 tbsp parsley, finely chopped

Fry the bacon in its own fat until crisp; remove it from the pan and add the onion. Fry this for 1 minute, then add the garlic and the mushrooms and stir-fry for 3–4 minutes. Return the bacon to the pan, season to taste with pepper, add the parsley and use at once.

KILOCALORIES	350	SUGARS	5g
TOTAL FAT	20g	SODIUM	2250mg
SATURATED FAT	8g	FIBRE	3.5g

Right *(clockwise from top left) Spring rolls, potato sticks, prawn toasties and pizza with everything. Sesame bars (top left), popcorn (top right), carob sweets (bottom left) and halva (bottom right).*

EGG AND GREEN PEPPER

3 hard-boiled eggs
2–3 strips green pepper
2–3 tbsp reduced-calorie mayonnaise (or
low-fat plain yogurt)
pinch salt, pepper
garlic powder (optional)

Chop the eggs and pepper strips finely and fold them
into the mayonnaise or yogurt; season to taste with
salt and pepper, and garlic powder if liked.

KILOCALORIES	510	SUGARS	5g
TOTAL FAT	44g	SODIUM	1530mg
SATURATED FAT	5g	FIBRE	0.5g

HALVA

This Greek and Turkish sweetmeat is traditionally
made from semolina, sugar syrup and fried almonds. A
similarly delicious sweetmeat can be made from more
nutritious ingredients.
See illustration page 175.

75 g/3 oz sunflower seeds
65 g/2½ oz desiccated coconut
50 g/2 oz wheatgerm
4 tbsp sesame seeds
4 tbsp skimmed milk powder
4 tbsp honey (approx)
4 tbsp unsweetened peanut butter (approx)

Grind the sunflower seeds coarsely in a liquidiser or
food processor. Mix them with the coconut, wheatgerm, sesame seeds, milk powder and enough honey
and peanut butter to form a slightly sticky dough.

Shape the halva into a block to fit a shallow plastic
container lined with foil. Cover the halva, and store in
the fridge, compressed with a light weight. It will keep
for 4–6 weeks.

[Nutritional values are for the whole recipe.]

KILOCALORIES	2340	SUGARS	128g
TOTAL FAT	158g	SODIUM	720mg
SATURATED FAT	53g	FIBRE	30g

POTATO STICKS

Potato crisps, with their high salt and fat content, are
best avoided. These potato sticks make a better drinks
accompaniment for a special occasion, and caraway
seeds give them a distinctive flavour.
See illustration page 175.

MAKES 50 Ⓥ

275 g/10 oz potatoes
225 g/8 oz margarine, softened
225 g/8 oz plain flour (or a mixture of plain
and wholewheat flour)
pinch salt, pepper
1 egg, beaten
caraway (poppy or dill) seeds

Scrub or peel the potatoes and boil them until tender;
mash the potato flesh while still warm and work in the
margarine. Add the sifted flour and a seasoning of salt
and pepper; mix thoroughly to a smooth dough, then
leave to chill in the fridge for 2 hours.

Preheat the oven to 220°C/425°F/gas 7. Roll the
dough out, 6 mm/¼ in thick, and trim it to a square.
Brush the surface with beaten egg and scatter liberally
with caraway, dill or poppy seeds. Cut the dough into
fingers about 7.5 × 1 cm/3 × ½ in), lift them carefully
on to lightly oiled baking trays and bake them just
above the centre of the oven for 15–20 minutes.

[Nutritional values are per stick.]

KILOCALORIES	55	SUGARS	–
TOTAL FAT	4g	SODIUM	50mg
SATURATED FAT	1g	FIBRE	0.5g

PRAWN TOASTIES

For storing, open-freeze the prawn fingers before
packing them in rigid containers, separating the layers
with non-stick paper.
See illustration page 175.

MAKES 32

125 g/4 oz prawns, peeled
50 g/2 oz lean bacon, diced
1 garlic clove (optional)
2–3 water chestnuts, chopped
4–5 cm/1½-2 in piece root ginger, peeled
1 egg

pinch salt, pepper
dash oyster sauce
1 tbsp cornflour
8 slices wholemeal bread, crusts removed
oil for greasing
chopped chives (or *spring onions*)

Put the prawns, bacon, garlic, water chestnuts and ginger in a food processor and chop them finely. Add the egg, seasoning, oyster sauce and cornflour and process for about 1 minute until all the ingredients have been reduced to a smooth paste.

Spread the mixture over the bread slices and cut each into four fingers. Lay on an oiled baking sheet and bake in a pre-heated oven 190°C/375°F/gas 5 for 15–20 minutes until golden-brown.

Serve warm, sprinkled with chopped chives or spring onions.

[Nutritional values are per toastie.]

KILOCALORIES	35	SUGARS	–
TOTAL FAT	1g	SODIUM	90mg
SATURATED FAT	–	FIBRE	0.5g

SESAME BARS

These biscuits are packed with nutrients and suitable as snacks and for afternoon tea.

See illustration page 175.

MAKES 30 Ⓥ

175 g/6 oz stoned dates
125 ml/4 fl oz water
50 g/2 oz shredded coconut
75 g/3 oz sunflower seeds
75 g/3 oz whole sesame seeds
75 g/3 oz ground sesame seeds
75 g/3 oz cashew nuts, ground
3 tbsp water

Simmer the dates in the measured water until soft, then mash them with a fork and set them aside to cool. Thoroughly mix the dates with the coconut, sunflower and sesame seeds and the cashew nuts, binding the mixture to a dough with a few tablespoonfuls of water.

Preheat the oven to 180°C/350°F/gas 4. Place the dough on a foil-covered or non-stick baking tray, cover it with a sheet of greaseproof paper and roll the dough out thinly directly on the baking tray. Remove the paper.

Mark the dough into bars about 4 × 6 cm (1½ × 2½ in) with a knife and bake in the centre of the oven for 15–20 minutes or until lightly browned. Remove from the oven and leave the sesame bars to cool on a wire rack. Break them apart when cool enough to handle.

[Nutritional values are per bar.]

KILOCALORIES	75	SUGARS	2g
TOTAL FAT	6g	SODIUM	–
SATURATED FAT	2g	FIBRE	1g

CARROT HALVA

Commercial halva is pale gold in colour; when carrots replace semolina the sweetmeat becomes attractively orange-yellow. The authentic almond flavour is provided by ground almonds, and pistachio nuts give a crunchy texture.

SERVES 4–6 Ⓥ

25 g/1 oz clarified butter (or vegetable ghee)
150–175 g/5–6 oz carrots (peeled weight), grated
450 ml/¾ pt hot semi-skimmed milk
75 g/3 oz dark brown sugar
50 g/2 oz ground almonds
2 tbsp shelled pistachio nuts (unsalted)
½ tsp ground cardamom
few drops of almond (or vanilla) essence (optional)

Melt the butter or ghee in a wok or heavy-based pan over medium heat. Add the grated carrots and stir-fry them gently. In another pan, heat the milk and sugar, stirring until the sugar has dissolved. Gradually add the sweetened milk to the carrots, bring to the boil and cook for 10–15 minutes.

Add the almonds and simmer the halva mixture very gently for about 1 hour, stirring frequently to prevent scorching. Fold in the pistachio nuts, cardamom, and almond or vanilla essence if used. Stir thoroughly before pouring the mixture into a flat dish rinsed in cold water. Set the halva aside to cool, then cover it with a weight to compress it. Serve the carrot halva, cut into cubes, as a sweetmeat with after-dinner coffee.

KILOCALORIES	225	SUGARS	23g
TOTAL FAT	13g	SODIUM	80mg
SATURATED FAT	1g	FIBRE	2g

CARROT STICKS

These are the vegetarian's answer to fish fingers and can also be served as a light snack, main course or vegetable accompaniment to poultry or fish.

SERVES 4–6 Ⓥ

225 g/8 oz cooked carrots, mashed
1 medium-sized onion, finely chopped
½ small red pepper, blanched and finely chopped
3 tbsp margarine, melted
scant 150 g/5 oz soft breadcrumbs
1 egg, beaten
½ tsp celery salt (optional)
¼ tsp salt
breadcrumbs (or cornflake crumbs)

Preheat the oven to 190°C/375°F/gas 5. Mix the mashed carrots with the onion and red pepper, stir in the melted margarine and the breadcrumbs and bind the mixture with the beaten egg. Season to taste.

Shape the mixture into 8–12 small sausages or drumsticks and coat them with breadcrumbs or cornflake crumbs. Place the carrot sticks in a lightly buttered, shallow ovenproof dish and bake them in the centre of the oven for 25 minutes.

Serve the carrot sticks accompanied by boiled potatoes or rice and with parsley and lemon sauce (see page 29).

KILOCALORIES	225	SUGARS	6g
TOTAL FAT	7g	SODIUM	500mg
SATURATED FAT	2g	FIBRE	2.5g

PERGEDEL JAGUNG
Sweetcorn fritters

Corn fritters are considered typically American. Their flavour is most pronounced when made from fresh cobs, but canned sweetcorn is also suitable. These Indonesian-style fritters are a spicy Eastern version.

MAKES 10–12

6 fresh corn cobs (or 340 g/12 oz canned sweetcorn)
4 shallots
2 garlic cloves
1 red chilli, deseeded and finely chopped (or
½ tsp chilli powder)

75 g/3 oz prawns (fresh or frozen), peeled
2 tbsp spring onions (or chives), finely chopped
1 tsp ground coriander
pinch salt
1 large egg, lightly beaten
vegetable oil for frying

Strip the outer husks from fresh cobs and grate the kernels into a bowl. (Drain canned sweetcorn and roughly mash the kernels with a wooden spoon.)

Pound the shallots, garlic, chilli and prawns to a smooth paste or mince them in a food processor; mix them into the corn, with the coriander and salt. Add the egg and whisk the mixture quickly but thoroughly.

Heat 5 tablespoonfuls of oil in a large pan over medium heat and drop heaped tablespoonfuls of the sweetcorn mixture into the pan. Flatten the fritters with a fork and fry them for about 2 minutes on each side. Remove when golden-brown and leave to drain on crumpled kitchen paper.

Serve the fritters hot as an accompaniment to chicken and boiled rice, or as a snack, hot or cold. The batter can also be cooked in smaller fritters to be served with drinks.

[Nutritional values are per fritter.]

KILOCALORIES	90	SUGARS	4g
TOTAL FAT	5g	SODIUM	140mg
SATURATED FAT	–	FIBRE	0.5g

POPCORN

Commercially prepared popcorn is generally coated with sugar, whereas home-made popcorn is easy and quick, delicious and a great deal more nutritious than packaged types.

See illustration page 175.

SERVES 2 Ⓥ

100 g/4 oz popcorn
vegetable oil (optional)

Use a deep, heavy-based, preferably iron, pan with a well-fitting lid. Add enough oil to barely cover the base of the pan, heat it to almost smoking point and add a single layer of popcorn (repeat the process if the pan is too small to make popcorn in a single batch). Cover the pan and shake it over high heat, slightly lifting the lid from time to time to allow the steam to escape. The starchy grains swell as they are heated, and as the pressure builds up, they burst or pop.

Variation Corn may be popped without oil for a low-calorie snack with various flavourings; add curry powder, ginger, dried yeast flakes or paprika while still hot.

KILOCALORIES	295	SUGARS	1g
TOTAL FAT	21g	SODIUM	–
SATURATED FAT	–	FIBRE	–

VEGETABLE OMELETTE

This is reminiscent of Spanish omelettes, which contain a variety of diced vegetables and spicy sausage.

SERVES 4–6

4–6 eggs
25 g/1 oz margarine (or 2 tbsp vegetable oil)
1 small onion (or leek or
3 spring onions), finely chopped
1 small green (or red) pepper, deseeded and diced
1–2 courgettes, diced
50 g/2 oz button mushrooms, thinly sliced
2 tbsp peas (fresh or frozen)
1 cold boiled potato, diced
50 g/2 oz ham (salami, chorizo or
other continental sausage), diced
2 tbsp semi-skimmed milk
pinch salt, pepper
25 g/1 oz grated cheese

Melt the margarine or heat the oil in a large, heavy-based pan, add the onion, pepper, courgettes, mushrooms and peas and cook, covered, for about 5 minutes, until soft. Add the potato and meat and stir-fry for 2–3 minutes.

Beat the eggs thoroughly, mix in the milk, salt and pepper. Stir the cheese into the eggs and pour over the vegetables and meat. Loosen the edges gently as the omelette begins to set.

When it has almost set, place it (still in the pan) under a hot grill until golden. Alternatively, invert it on to a plate, slide it back into the pan to cook the other side for a minute or two. Serve the omelette hot or cold.

KILOCALORIES	255	SUGARS	2g
TOTAL FAT	18g	SODIUM	370mg
SATURATED FAT	6g	FIBRE	1.5g

PIZZA

The Italian pizza resembles the French pissaladière (see page 180) and consists of a yeast-risen dough base topped with various savoury mixtures.

SERVES 4 Ⓥ

275–325 g/10–12 oz wholemeal flour
½ tsp salt
1 tbsp dried yeast
300 ml/½ pt warm water

TOPPING
100 g/4 oz mushrooms, sliced
1 large garlic clove, crushed
1 large onion, finely chopped
½ medium-sized red (or green) pepper, finely chopped
175 g/6 oz tomato paste
1 can (400 g/14 oz) tomatoes, drained and chopped
75 g/3 oz black olives, stoned and sliced
½ tsp each oregano, basil and salt
125 g/4 oz Cheddar cheese, grated (or 50 g/2 oz
Parmesan cheese, grated or cashew mixture – see
vegetarian lasagne, page 139)

Put 225 g/8 oz of the flour with the salt in a warm mixing bowl. Sprinkle the yeast over the warm water, stirring to dissolve it, and add this to the flour. Beat thoroughly, then add the rest of the flour, or enough to form a soft, pliable dough. Cover the bowl with a lightly oiled polythene sheet and set it aside in a warm place for 30 minutes or until well risen.

Knead the dough and roll it out, on a lightly floured surface, to a 6 mm/¼ in thickness. Divide the dough into two large or four smaller pizza rounds and set these on greased baking trays to prove.

Meanwhile, place the mushrooms, garlic, onion and pepper, with 3–4 tablespoonfuls of water, in a heavy-based pan. Cover with a lid and simmer for 10 minutes. Add the tomato paste, canned tomatoes, olives, herbs and salt. Bring the contents slowly back to the boil, then simmer, uncovered, for a further 5 minutes. Preheat the oven to 230°C/450°F/gas 8.

Spread the mushroom and tomato mixture over the pizza bases and top with grated cheese or cashew nuts. Bake the pizzas for 20–25 minutes and serve them warm or cooled, on their own or as a snack, or with a green salad.

KILOCALORIES	470	SUGARS	12g
TOTAL FAT	15g	SODIUM	1220mg
SATURATED FAT	7g	FIBRE	11g

PIZZA WITH EVERYTHING

———— • ————

There are numerous variations on the theme of the Italian pizza, and combinations can be made up from available ingredients. Those listed below are suggestions only and can be used in amounts to suit the cook. The only essentials are cheese, preferably mozzarella, and tomatoes.

See illustration page 175.

SERVES 4

25 g/1 oz fresh yeast (or 15 g/½ oz dried yeast)
150 ml/¼ pt lukewarm semi-skimmed milk and water, mixed
2 tsp caster sugar
1 tbsp olive oil
225 g/8 oz plain flour
¼ tsp salt
2 tbsp tomato purée

TOPPING
50 g/2 oz lean ham, cut into narrow strips
50 g/2 oz salami, thinly sliced
75 g/3 oz continental sausage, sliced
100 g/4 oz mushrooms, sliced
4 small ripe tomatoes, thinly sliced
50 g/2 oz anchovy fillets, drained (optional)
50 g/2 oz black olives
2 tbsp fresh marjoram, chopped (or 2 tsp dried oregano)
4–5 spring onions, chopped
100 g/4 oz mozzarella cheese, thinly sliced (or 100 g/4 oz Cheddar cheese, grated)

Blend the fresh yeast with 1–2 tablespoonfuls of the warm liquid, add the sugar and stir until smooth. Add the yeast mixture to the rest of the liquid and blend in the oil. Alternatively, sprinkle dried yeast over 3 tablespoonfuls of the warm liquid, add a pinch of sugar and leave the mixture in a warm place for about 10 minutes until frothy. Blend the yeast mixture with the warm liquid, remaining sugar and oil as already described.

Sift the flour with the salt into a warmed bowl. Make a well in the centre and add the yeast liquid and tomato purée. Mix to a firm, soft dough and knead it vigorously for 10 minutes. Roll it into a ball and brush it lightly with oil all over. Place the dough in a bowl, cover with an oiled piece of polythene, and leave the dough to rise in a warm place until doubled in bulk (about 2 hours).

Knock the dough down and roll it out into two circles, each about 30 cm/12 in across, or into one large oblong. Draw the edges up slightly with the fingers to make a narrow rim. Leave to prove for 10 minutes.

Preheat the oven to 220°C/425°F/gas 7. Arrange the sliced meats over the pizza base, patterned with overlapping rows of mushrooms and tomatoes and interspersed with anchovy fillets and olives. Sprinkle with marjoram and spring onions and finally cover the pizza with the sliced or grated cheese.

Bake the pizza for 25 minutes or until it looks cooked on top.

KILOCALORIES	540	SUGARS	10g
TOTAL FAT	25g	SODIUM	1960mg
SATURATED FAT	9g	FIBRE	3.5g

PISSALADIÈRE

———— • ————

The traditional pizza from Nice is a far cry from commercial versions. A yeast dough is topped with soft fried onions, liberally flavoured with fresh summery herbs, red ripe tomatoes, black olives and anchovy fillets.

SERVES 6–8

350 g/12 oz strong plain flour (or a mixture of plain and wholewheat flour)
½ tsp salt
1 tsp caster sugar
150 ml/¼ pt warm water
2 tsp dried yeast
1 egg, beaten

TOPPING
3–4 tbsp vegetable oil
4 large onions, thinly sliced
2 garlic cloves, crushed
1 tbsp chopped mixed herbs, (basil, marjoram, thyme)
1 small can (50 g/1¾ oz) anchovy fillets, drained
3–4 tbsp semi-skimmed milk
4 tomatoes, skinned and thickly sliced
12 black olives

Sift the flour and salt into a bowl and prepare the yeast mixture: stir the sugar into the warm water until dissolved, sprinkle the yeast over the top and leave it in a warm place for 10 minutes or until the mixture is frothy. Mix the yeast mixture into the flour, with enough beaten egg to form a firm dough; knead it thoroughly for about 10 minutes or until the dough is smooth and pliable (1 minute in a food processor).

Place the dough in an oiled polythene bag; seal the

top, but leave plenty of room for the dough to rise. Set it in a warm place until it has doubled in size. Remove the dough from the bag and knock out the air bubbles on a lightly floured board. Knead the dough for 1 minute. Shape it into a round to fit a 28 cm/11 in flan dish or a 30 × 20 cm/12 × 8 in Swiss-roll tin.

Slit open the oiled plastic bag and use it to cover the dough, oiled side down. Leave it to prove in a warm place.

Sauté the onions in the oil over low heat for 15 minutes. Add the garlic and cook for a further 5 minutes. Draw the pan off the heat and stir in the herbs. Preheat the oven to 220°C/425°F/gas 7.

Lift the onions from the pan with a slotted spoon and spread them over the risen dough, leaving a narrow border all round. Arrange the drained anchovy fillets in a lattice pattern over the onion (excess salt can be removed by soaking the anchovy fillets in milk for 10 minutes). Place the tomato slices and olives between the anchovies and drizzle a little of the oil used for cooking the onions over the surface.

Bake the pissaladière for 10 minutes, then reduce the heat to 190°C/375°F/gas 5 for 15–20 minutes. Serve it hot or warm, cut into wedges, and accompanied with a green salad.

KILOCALORIES	320	SUGARS	6g
TOTAL FAT	13g	SODIUM	540mg
SATURATED FAT	1g	FIBRE	4g

Proving is another term for the second rising in breadmaking. The dough is kneaded a second time after the initial rising to knock out any air bubbles and to ensure an even texture. The dough is then shaped and placed on a baking tray or in a baking tin and left to prove in a warm place until it has doubled in size.

CHILLI MINCE PIZZA

A packet of pizza base or bread mix is a justifiable shortcut for a quick lunch or supper snack. This Mexican-style pizza has minced beef flavoured with fresh chillis.

SERVES 4

325 g/12 oz minced beef
1 large onion, finely chopped
2–3 tbsp vegetable oil
2–4 chillis, deseeded and finely chopped
150 ml/¼ pt beef stock
2 tbsp tomato purée
2 tsp fresh marjoram chopped, (or 1 tsp oregano)
pinch salt, pepper
275 g/10 oz packet pizza base mix
2 large tomatoes, skinned and sliced
1 tbsp olive oil

Sauté the onion in vegetable oil for 5 minutes over medium heat, until soft, add the mince and stir-fry it for another 5 minutes, until it has browned and broken into separate grains. Stir in half the chillis, the stock, tomato purée and herbs. Bring the contents of the pan to the boil, cover with a lid and simmer for 40–50 minutes or until the liquid has reduced and the mixture has the consistency of a thick sauce. Season to taste.

Prepare the pizza base mixture according to packet instructions (or follow other pizza dough recipes on pages 179–181). Roll out the dough as thinly as possible into two large circles or rectangles, keeping the edges slightly raised. Transfer the pizza bases to greased baking trays or Swiss-roll tins.

Preheat the oven to 230°C/450°F/gas 8. Spread the base with the mince mixture and sprinkle on the remaining chillis. Garnish with the tomato slices and brush with olive oil.

Bake for 15–20 minutes. Serve cut into large wedges.

KILOCALORIES	325	SUGARS	6g
TOTAL FAT	24g	SODIUM	400mg
SATURATED FAT	5g	FIBRE	1g

Please see the introduction for a full explanation of the nutritional factboxes.

CHEESE BALLS

—— • ——

These quick and easily made titbits can be served with pre-dinner drinks, as the conclusion to a meal or as part of a buffet.

SERVES 4 Ⓥ

125 g/4 oz soft blue cheese
100 ml/4 fl oz soured cream
2 tbsp spring onions (or chives), finely chopped
1 tbsp celery, finely chopped
herbs (or chopped nuts) (optional)

Mash the cheese to a smooth paste with the cream in a bowl, liquidiser or food processor. Fold in the spring onions, or chives, and the celery; leave the mixture to firm and chill in the fridge. Shape it into small balls before serving, coating them with finely chopped nuts or herbs if liked.

Variation Cream 125 g/4 oz grated Cheddar, Leicester or Double Gloucester cheese with 40 g/1½ oz low-fat cream cheese, season with a few drops of Worcestershire sauce, fold in spring onions and celery as above and bind the mixture with a little dry sherry. Chill and shape into small balls as already described.

KILOCALORIES	315	SUGARS	3g
TOTAL FAT	28g	SODIUM	250mg
SATURATED FAT	13g	FIBRE	1.5g

SPRING ROLLS

—— • ——

Chinese spring roll skins or wrappers can be bought frozen at Chinese delicatessens. They are usually made from wheat flour-and-water pastry, filled with various savoury stuffings and deep-fried.

See illustration page 175.

SERVES 4

1 packet frozen spring roll skins
3–4 tbsp vegetable oil
1 medium-sized onion, finely chopped
1 garlic clove, crushed
175–225 g/6–8 oz prawns, peeled and chopped
2 medium-sized carrots, grated
350 /12 oz celeriac, grated
225 g/8 oz bean sprouts
2 lettuce leaves (or Chinese leaves), shredded
1 spring onion, finely chopped

1 tbsp fresh coriander (or parsley), chopped
pinch salt, pepper
1 tbsp plain flour
oil for deep frying
tomato (or chilli or hoisin) sauce

Thaw the spring roll skins, cover them with a damp cloth and set them aside. Heat a little oil in a heavy-based pan or wok and fry the onion and garlic, followed by the prawns, carrots and celeriac. Stir-fry for about 2 minutes over high heat until all the vegetables are soft. Add the bean sprouts, stir-fry for 1 minute, then add the shredded lettuce, spring onion and coriander or parsley. Remove the pan from the heat at once, season to taste and allow to cool. Mix the flour to a paste with 1 tablespoonful of water.

To assemble the spring rolls, peel the skins off one by one; set them in a separate pile and keep them covered with the damp cloth to prevent them drying out. Arrange one skin on a working surface, one point facing towards you; place a spoonful of the filling near the point, fold the skin over the filling, then turn the two points from the sides to the centre, sealing with flour paste. Continue to roll up and seal the last point.

If a skin tears during the rolling up, set it aside and use it to repair any other tears, sealing them with the flour paste. Fill the remaining skins in the same manner.

Heat oil to 190°C/375°F in a deep fryer or wok and fry the spring rolls for 3–4 minutes, turning them once, until the skins are crisp and golden. Serve at once, with bowls of tomato, chilli or hoisin sauce.

KILOCALORIES	390	SUGARS	10g
TOTAL FAT	23g	SODIUM	420mg
SATURATED FAT	3g	FIBRE	7g

CAROB SWEETS

Carob powder is obtained from the seed pods of the carob or locust bean tree, also known as St John's Bread after John the Baptist. High in carbohydrates, carob products are nutritious, whereas refined sugar provides only 'empty' calories.

See illustration page 175.

MAKES ABOUT 20 (V)

175 g/6 oz honey
4 tbsp carob powder
100 g/4 oz skimmed milk powder
100 g/4 oz unsweetened peanut butter
few drops vanilla essence
65 g/2½ oz sunflower seeds
4 tbsp wheatgerm
desiccated coconut

Thoroughly mix the honey with the carob powder, milk, peanut butter and vanilla essence. Add the sunflower seeds and wheatgerm and shape the mixture into small balls about 2.5 cm/1 in wide. (If the mixture does not bind easily, heat it gently in a pan.) Roll the balls in desiccated coconut.

[Nutritional value is per sweet.]

KILOCALORIES	115	SUGARS	10g
TOTAL FAT	6g	SODIUM	80mg
SATURATED FAT	2g	FIBRE	1g

SALADS

Salads, as well as being attractive in appearance, can comprise a variety of ingredients and should not necessarily be thought of a summer dish. Fresh summer ingredients, lettuce, endive, cucumber, celery and spring onions, can be supplemented with cauliflower, beans, carrots and pulses to provide variety all year round. Yogurt, oil, herb and spice dressings add yet more variety, though remember that a healthy salad can all too quickly become an unhealthy one if drowned in a fatty dressing. Salads can be served as side dishes or as light meals in their own right.

FENNEL SALAD

Pale green fennel, distinguished by its sweet anise flavour, is imported from France and Italy. The roots, which are really swollen stem bases, have a crisp, crunchy texture, ideal for salads.

SERVES 4 Ⓥ

3 fennel roots
2–3 tbsp olive oil
2 tbsp lemon juice
1 garlic clove, crushed
pinch salt, pepper
2 tomatoes

Trim off top stems and any tough outer leaves near base. Trim root end. Slice the fennel thinly across, no more than 1 cm/½ in wide, rinse and dry thoroughly and arrange in a shallow dish. Blend the oil with the lemon juice and garlic and season to taste with salt and pepper. Pour the dressing over the fennel and leave it to chill and marinate for a couple of hours.

Serve, garnished with tomato wedges, as a side dish with grilled fish or chicken.

Variation Cook a couple of fennel roots, trimmed but left whole, in lightly salted water for 10 minutes or until just tender. Refresh in cold water. Cut the fennel,

crossways, into thin slices, mix them with strips of chicory and toss in the above dressing; garnish the salad with anchovies and roughly chopped walnuts and sprinkle with a few drops of sesame seed oil.

KILOCALORIES	100	SUGARS	4g
TOTAL FAT	9g	SODIUM	120mg
SATURATED FAT	1g	FIBRE	4g

BEAN SPROUT SALAD

Peanut oil, polyunsaturated and rich in protein, and soya sauce bring a new flavour to this Chinese-style crunchy salad.

SERVES 4 Ⓥ

225 g/8 oz bean sprouts
1 large carrot
¼ cucumber
10 spring onions
3 tbsp peanut oil
1 tbsp soya sauce
pinch salt, pepper
50 g/2 oz peanuts (unsalted)

Discard any bean sprouts that are wilted, and rinse and drain the remainder well. Cut the carrot, cucumber and spring onions into fine strips. Whisk the oil with the soya sauce and pour this dressing over the vegetables; toss them until well coated. Season with plenty of pepper and a pinch of salt.

Sprinkle the peanuts over the salad and serve with cold poultry or as a main-course vegetarian dish.

KILOCALORIES	210	SUGARS	7g
TOTAL FAT	16g	SODIUM	20mg
SATURATED FAT	3g	FIBRE	3.5g

WINTER SALAD

—— • ——

Winter salad is a variation on the coleslaw theme and consists chiefly of cabbage, which may be white or red or a combination of both. All types of raw vegetables and fresh fruits can be added.

SERVES 6 Ⓥ

350 g/12 oz cabbage, finely shredded
1 red pepper, deseeded and diced
3 celery sticks, diced
2 medium-sized carrots, coarsely grated
1 medium-sized red onion, grated
2 dessert apples, diced
1 tbsp lemon juice
50 g/2 oz seedless raisins
40 g/1½ oz walnuts, roughly chopped
300 ml/½ pt low-fat plain yogurt
pinch celery salt (optional)

Prepare all the vegetables and place them in a large bowl; sprinkle the diced apple with lemon juice to prevent discoloration and add them to the vegetables, together with the raisins and walnuts.

Mix the yogurt with the celery salt (if used). Pour into the salad bowl and toss the ingredients well. Chill in the fridge, and serve the salad on its own as a light lunch, accompanied with crusty bread rolls.

KILOCALORIES	160	SUGARS	22g
TOTAL FAT	6g	SODIUM	70mg
SATURATED FAT	1g	FIBRE	4g

EMPEROR SALAD

—— • ——

Sometimes known as Cardinal salad because of the rich purple colour which is 'set' with boiling vinegar, this makes a colourful and attractive accompaniment to cold cooked ham.

See illustration page 187.

SERVES 4 Ⓥ

¼ red cabbage (approx 275 g/10 oz)
50 ml/2 fl oz wine vinegar
1 can (425 g/15 oz) red kidney beans, drained
3 slices wholemeal bread, crusts removed
6 tbsp French dressing (see page 31)
chopped chives

Remove any damaged outer leaves and the hard central core from the cabbage; shred the remainder, and rinse and drain it well.

Bring the vinegar to the bowl over gentle heat. Put the cabbage in a salad bowl, pour over the boiling vinegar and toss thoroughly before adding the kidney beans. Toast the bread and cube it.

To serve, add the bread croûtons to the cabbage, pour the dressing into the bowl and toss again. Garnish with chopped chives.

KILOCALORIES	320	SUGARS	7g
TOTAL FAT	18g	SODIUM	750mg
SATURATED FAT	3g	FIBRE	9.5g

CAESAR SALAD

—— • ——

This classic salad from the United States is made with Webb's or cos lettuce and crunchy bread croûtons. It is customary to mix the ingredients at the table, tossing them in a dressing of a lightly boiled egg, oil and lemon juice. In some versions, French dressing with mustard replaces oil and lemon juice.

SERVES 4

4 large slices wholemeal bread, crusts removed
1 small Webb's (or cos) lettuce
125 g/4 oz Cheddar cheese, finely grated
8–10 canned anchovy fillets, drained and chopped
1 garlic clove, crushed
juice of ½ large lemon
1 large egg
1 tbsp salad oil
pinch salt, pepper

Toast the bread until crisp and deep gold, then cut it into small cubes. Wash the lettuce, dry it thoroughly and tear it into largish pieces. Put the lettuce in a salad bowl, add the cheese, anchovy fillets, garlic and lemon juice and toss all the ingredients well. Fold in the croûtons.

Boil the egg for 1 minute only. Break it over the salad, then add the oil and a seasoning of salt and pepper; toss the salad again and serve at once, as a side salad or on its own.

KILOCALORIES	290	SUGARS	2g
TOTAL FAT	18g	SODIUM	720mg
SATURATED FAT	8g	FIBRE	2.5g

Ratatouille can be served at once, but the flavours develop and mature if it is left for 24 hours before being served cold as a salad or reheated as a vegetable accompaniment.

KILOCALORIES	175	SUGARS	9g
TOTAL FAT	14g	SODIUM	30mg
SATURATED FAT	2g	FIBRE	4g

RATATOUILLE

Full of Mediterranean zest, ratatouille is a vegetable pot-pourri gently simmered in olive oil. It tastes equally good hot or cold, with meat, poultry, freshwater fish, eggs, brown rice or pearl barley.

SERVES 4 Ⓥ

4 tbsp olive oil
225 g/8 oz onions, chopped
1 garlic clove, crushed
225 g/8 oz aubergine, diced
225 g/8 oz courgettes (or marrow), thinly sliced
1 small green pepper, deseeded and coarsely chopped
225 g/8 oz tomatoes, skinned and coarsely chopped
2 tbsp tomato purée
pinch salt, pepper

Heat the oil in a large, heavy-based pan, add the onions and garlic and sauté over gentle heat for about 10 minutes.

Meanwhile, prepare the vegetables, leaving the skins on the aubergines and courgettes, but peeling and deseeding the marrow if used. Add them, with the pepper and tomatoes, to the onions in the pan, stir in the tomato purée; add salt and pepper to taste.

Bring the contents of the pan to the boil, stirring continuously. Reduce the heat, cover the pan and leave the vegetables to simmer for about 1 hour, stirring occasionally.

CUCUMBER MOULD

This is a pretty, refreshing and lightweight salad for a summer lunch or a buffet. It is best set in a shallow mould or cake tin or in small individual jelly moulds.

SERVES 4

1 large cucumber
2 large lemons
2 tsp powdered gelatine
300 ml/½ pt low-fat plain yogurt
1 tsp fresh dill, finely chopped
1 tsp fresh mint, finely chopped
pinch salt, pepper
watercress

Cut five or six thin slices from the middle of the unpeeled cucumber, then peel and dice the remainder. Finely grate the rind from the lemons and squeeze out the juice. Dissolve the gelatine in 150 ml/¼ pt of cold water, stir in the strained lemon juice, and pour a little of the mixture over the base of a 1 litre/1¾ pt soufflé dish or a 15 cm/6 in-deep cake tin. Leave it to set in the fridge.

Dip the cucumber slices lightly in the gelatine mixture, arrange them in a pattern over the set jelly and spoon a little more mixture over them, enough to hold and set the slices; return the dish to the fridge. Whisk the yogurt into the remaining gelatine mixture, stir in the diced cucumber, the chopped dill and mint and the lemon rind; season to taste. Spoon this mixture into the mould and leave it in the fridge until set.

To serve, carefully unmould the cucumber jelly on to a serving dish and garnish with watercress.

KILOCALORIES	65	SUGARS	8g
TOTAL FAT	1g	SODIUM	170mg
SATURATED FAT	–	FIBRE	0.5g

CARROT AND ORANGE SALAD

—— • ——

The combination of carrots and orange fulfils practically all the daily vitamin A and C requirements.

SERVES 4 Ⓥ

350–475 g/12–16 oz carrots
2 large oranges
3 tbsp sultanas
2 tbsp chopped nuts
pepper
lettuce leaves

Grate the carrots and orange rind into a bowl. Squeeze the juice from the oranges and leave the sultanas to steep in it for at least 30 minutes. Fold the sultanas and orange juice into the carrots, together with the mint and freshly ground pepper to taste.

Line a bowl with lettuce leaves and pile on the salad.

KILOCALORIES	140	SUGARS	33g
TOTAL FAT	1g	SODIUM	40mg
SATURATED FAT	–	FIBRE	5g

CAULIFLOWER SALAD

Crisp raw cauliflower has a deliciously nutty flavour, invariably lost in cooking.

SERVES 4–6 Ⓥ

1 large cauliflower
4 tbsp vegetable oil
150 ml/¼ pt lemon juice
½ tsp salt
½ tsp oregano
½ tsp basil
1 small garlic clove, crushed
12 black olives, stoned and sliced
1 medium-sized green pepper, deseeded and chopped
crisp lettuce leaves

Break the cauliflower into bite-sized florets, rinse them thoroughly under cold running water, drain well and put in a bowl. Blend together the oil, lemon juice, salt, herbs and garlic and pour this dressing over the cauliflower florets; add the olives and green pepper and toss all the ingredients in the dressing until completely coated. Chill the salad for 1–2 hours in the fridge.

Serve on a bed of crisp lettuce leaves, as a first course or as a light lunch dish.

KILOCALORIES	120	SUGARS	2g
TOTAL FAT	12g	SODIUM	360mg
SATURATED FAT	–	FIBRE	1g

BULGHUR SALAD

Bulghur, burghul, bulgar and bourgouri are all alternative names for cracked wheat. The coarse grade is deliciously nutty in flavour and texture and forms a good basis for other salad ingredients. Canned chick-peas can be used, rinsed of the brine and thoroughly drained.

SERVES 6 Ⓥ

175 g/6 oz cracked wheat
1 tsp salt
700 ml/24 fl oz cold water
large bunch spring onions, finely chopped
1 small green (or red) pepper, deseeded and diced
1 small head celery, diced
200 g/7 oz cooked chickpeas
3–4 tomatoes, skinned and chopped
6 tbsp parsley, finely chopped
2 tbsp mint, finely chopped (or 1 tbsp dried mint)
6 tbsp vegetable oil
4 tbsp lemon juice
pinch salt, pepper

Rinse the cracked wheat thoroughly, then put it in a bowl with the salt and the measured cold water and leave it to steep for 10 minutes. Drain the wheat through a fine sieve, put it in a serving bowl and mix with the spring onions, green or red pepper, celery, chickpeas and tomatoes; blend in the parsley and mint.

Whisk the oil with the lemon juice; season to taste with salt and pepper and pour over the salad.

Chill the salad for at least 2 hours in the fridge before serving as a main course, accompanied by wholemeal bread or rolls.

KILOCALORIES	235	SUGARS	3g
TOTAL FAT	10g	SODIUM	420mg
SATURATED FAT	–	FIBRE	2.5g

Please see the introduction for a full explanation of the nutritional factboxes.

Ⓥ This symbol denotes a recipe suitable for vegetarians.

ALFALFA SALAD
——— • ———

This salad is a veritable storehouse of raw ingredients which have retained the essential nutrients usually lost through cooking.

SERVES 6 Ⓥ

225 g/8 oz alfalfa sprouts
225 g/8 oz bean sprouts
75 g/3 oz button mushrooms
75 g/3 oz peas, freshly shelled
8 fresh (or dried) dates, stoned and chopped

DRESSING
1 large avocado pear
200 ml/7 fl oz low-fat plain yogurt
juice of a lemon
pinch salt
¼ garlic clove, crushed

Cut the avocado in half, remove the stone and scoop out the flesh; put it in a liquidiser with the yogurt, lemon juice, salt and garlic. Blend until smooth and leave the dressing to chill in the fridge.

Rinse the bean sprouts, drain and place them with the alfalfa sprouts in a large bowl, add the cleaned, thinly sliced mushrooms, the peas and roughly chopped dates. Pour the dressing over the vegetables, toss them thoroughly and serve the salad at once.

KILOCALORIES	155	SUGARS	13g
TOTAL FAT	8g	SODIUM	40mg
SATURATED FAT	2g	FIBRE	3.5g

MUSHROOM AND CELERY SALAD
——— • ———

It is essential that the mushrooms are perfectly fresh and unblemished; a wad of kitchen paper dipped in milk removes all traces of dirt.

SERVES 4 Ⓥ

225 g/8 oz button mushrooms
3 tbsp lemon juice
1 hard-boiled egg
¼ tsp dry mustard
2–3 tbsp olive (or salad) oil
pinch salt, pepper
3 celery sticks, diced
cress

Trim the base of the mushrooms, wipe them clean, slice them thinly and arrange in a shallow serving dish; sprinkle with a little of the lemon juice to prevent discoloration.

Separate the hard-boiled egg; mash the yolk and gradually blend in the rest of the lemon juice, the mustard and the oil to a consistency of thin mayonnaise; season with salt and pepper. Fold the celery into the dressing and spoon this over the mushrooms.

Garnish with finely chopped egg white and scissor-snipped cress for colour contrast and serve immediately.

KILOCALORIES	100	SUGARS	1g
TOTAL FAT	10g	SODIUM	40mg
SATURATED FAT	2g	FIBRE	1g

RADICCHIO SALAD
——— • ———

The Italian radicchio lettuce is increasingly available in Britain during the winter months. Some varieties are crimson with prominent white veins, others are pale pink, and shaped either like a cos or a lamb's lettuce. Mix with green lettuce for a cheaper alternative.

SERVES 4 Ⓥ

2–3 radicchio
2 kiwi fruit
3 tbsp olive (or walnut oil)
juice of a large lime (or small lemon)
1 tbsp honey
pinch salt

Trim the roots from the radicchio, separate the outer leaves and wash them in cold water; dry them thoroughly, and leave the small inner hearts whole. Arrange the large leaves round the edges of a shallow serving dish, hearts in the centre.

Peel the kiwi fruit, cut them across into thin slices and set them on top of the radicchio. Whisk a dressing from the oil, lime juice and honey and season it lightly with salt. Sprinkle the dressing over the salad and chill it in the fridge for 30 minutes before serving as a first course.

KILOCALORIES	140	SUGARS	10g
TOTAL FAT	10g	SODIUM	10mg
SATURATED FAT	1g	FIBRE	3g

Season the green dressing to taste with herbs and pepper; pour it over the salad ingredients and toss thoroughly. Serve the salad as a first course, arranged on crisp lettuce leaves.

KILOCALORIES	150	SUGARS	4g
TOTAL FAT	4g	SODIUM	260mg
SATURATED FAT	–	FIBRE	6g

ASINAN CAMPUR
Fruit and vegetable salad

Firm, just-ripe mangoes can replace the apples in this quick and refreshing salad. Use radishes instead of bean sprouts, and for a spicier dressing use chilli vinegar instead of white vinegar.

SERVES 4 Ⓥ

125 g/4 oz white cabbage
125 g/4 oz carrots
1 small cucumber, peeled
125 g/4 oz bean sprouts
2 large hard dessert apples
lemon juice

DRESSING
2 tsp caster sugar
pinch salt
3 tbsp white vinegar
pinch chilli powder

Prepare the vegetables and fruit: shred the cabbage finely and cut the carrots into thin strips, slice the cucumber in half lengthways, scoop out the seeds and cut the flesh into thin slices. Rinse and drain the bean sprouts. Mix all the vegetables thoroughly in a large serving bowl. Peel, core and thinly slice the apples and brush them with a little lemon juice to prevent discoloration. Add them to the vegetables.

Dissolve the sugar and salt in the vinegar, add chilli powder to taste and pour the dressing over the salad. Toss well and leave to chill in the fridge for about 1 hour before serving as a first course, as a side dish with cold poultry or meat, or as a separate last course.

KILOCALORIES	155	SUGARS	33g
TOTAL FAT	1g	SODIUM	620mg
SATURATED FAT	–	FIBRE	7g

CHICKPEA SALAD

Dried peas and beans are ideal for healthy salads and are high in protein. Use either 450 g/1 lb canned chickpeas or soak, cook and cool half that amount of dry peas (see page 123).

SERVES 4 Ⓥ

450 g/1 lb canned chickpeas
2 sticks celery, finely chopped
1 small red pepper, deseeded and chopped (or canned pimiento, chopped)
½ medium onion, finely chopped
2–3 tbsp parsley, finely chopped
150 ml/¼ pt green dressing (see page 34)
1 tsp summer savory (or oregano)
pepper
lettuce leaves

Mix the drained and rinsed chickpeas with the celery, red pepper, onion and parsley and leave them to chill in the fridge for at least 1 hour.

done but still retaining their crispness; drain thoroughly.

Meanwhile, make a dressing from the lemon juice, olive oil, orange blossom water (if used) and mint, with salt and pepper to taste. Pour the dressing over the hot vegetables, toss well and chill the salad before serving.

KILOCALORIES	240	SUGARS	8g
TOTAL FAT	16g	SODIUM	230mg
SATURATED FAT	2g	FIBRE	10g

WALDORF SALAD

The Waldorf salad, from the Waldorf-Astoria Hotel in New York, has become world-famous. The combination of tart, ideally red, apples, crisp celery and crunchy nuts goes well with poultry and egg dishes. Sometimes, bananas or dessert pears are used instead of apples.

SERVES 4 Ⓥ
*½ head celery
3 tart dessert apples
2 tbsp lemon juice
50 g/2 oz walnuts, coarsely chopped
50 g/2 oz seedless grapes (optional)
4–5 tbsp reduced-calorie mayonnaise
4 large lettuce leaves*

Trim the celery and cut it into thin slices. Wash the apples, core but do not peel them and cut them into small cubes. Put them in a bowl with the lemon juice, tossing them well to prevent discoloration, then add the celery, walnuts and grapes.

Fold in the mayonnaise, mixing all the ingredients thoroughly. To serve, place a crisp lettuce leaf on each plate and mound the salad on top. Serve at once.

KILOCALORIES	240	SUGARS	11g
TOTAL FAT	20g	SODIUM	410mg
SATURATED FAT	1g	FIBRE	2g

Please see the introduction for a full explanation of the nutritional factboxes.

GREEN VEGETABLE SALAD

A variety of flavours and textures makes this an elegant summer dish to be served as a first course or as an accompaniment.

SERVES 4 Ⓥ
*2 leeks
1 fennel
1 small cauliflower
225 g/½ lb broad beans (shelled weight)
4 small courgettes
125 g/4 oz mange-tout, (French or runner beans)
juice of a lemon
4 tbsp olive oil
1 tbsp orange blossom water (optional)
2 tbsp mint, chopped
pinch salt, pepper*

Prepare the vegetables: trim the root and top ends off the leeks and fennel, wash them thoroughly and cut each into four equal chunks. Break the cauliflower into florets and rinse them. Shell the broad beans, wash and thickly slice the courgettes, and top, tail and string the mange-tout or beans.

Bring a large pan of lightly salted water to the boil, add the leeks and cook for about 5 minutes, covered, then add the fennel, cauliflower and broad beans and boil for a further 6–8 minutes. Lastly, add the courgettes and mange-tout (or beans) and cook for only a few more minutes, until all the vegetables are

BEETROOT AND SPRING ONION SALAD

———— • ————

The small globe-shaped beetroots sold ready-cooked from early summer onwards are ideal for this prettily coloured side dish.

SERVES 4–6 Ⓥ

450 g/1 lb cooked beetroot, peeled
150 ml/5 fl oz low-fat plain yogurt
1 tbsp olive oil
juice of ½ small lemon
1 small garlic clove, crushed
pinch salt, pepper
1 bunch spring onions, finely chopped

For the dressing, lightly beat the yogurt with oil and lemon juice, stir in the garlic, and salt and freshly ground black pepper to taste.

Slice or dice the beetroot into a shallow glass dish, pour over the yogurt dressing and chill in the fridge. Just before serving, sprinkle on the spring onions. The salad goes well with cold ham, bacon and poultry.

KILOCALORIES	85	SUGARS	11g
TOTAL FAT	3g	SODIUM	130mg
SATURATED FAT	1g	FIBRE	2g

DRINKS

Water is vital, more essential for survival than food. Our daily fluid intake should equal 1 litre (approx 2 pt), and more in hot weather and when doing strenuous work. Theoretically, we could satisfy our bodily needs with plain tap water, but more often we derive our fluid intake from hot comforters (tea, coffee), from thirst-quenchers (non-alcoholic beverages) and from stimulants (beers, wines, spirits). Most of the following drinks contain no alcohol.

ICED LEMON AND MINT TEA

Basically, iced teas are made like hot teas but from a stronger brew which is diluted with ice cubes, and with additional refreshing flavours. For best results, make the tea in a china or pottery pot or jug – aluminium teapots give an unpleasant metallic taste. In hard-water areas a slight cloudiness is almost inevitable in iced teas, but this does not affect the taste. Whichever brand of tea is used it should be steeped, covered, in boiling water for about 3 minutes, maximum 5 minutes, then strained, ideally through a coffee filter, and left to cool completely before chilling in the fridge – the tea becomes cloudy if it is placed in the fridge while still warm.

SERVES 4 (tumblers) Ⓥ

750 ml/1¼ pt boiling water
6 level tsp tea leaves
6 sprigs mint
peel of a lemon
crushed ice
sugar (optional)
extra mint (or lemon)

Make the tea in the usual way, leave it to infuse for 3 minutes, then strain it into a jug, over the bruised sprigs of mint and the thin peel of a lemon. When it is quite cold, put the covered jug in the fridge to chill.

Remove the mint and lemon peel before pouring the chilled tea into tall tumblers half-filled with crushed ice. Sweeten to taste if necessary and decorate, if liked, with fresh sprigs of mint and/or lemon slices. Without the addition of sugar this drink has no nutritional factbox values.

EARL GREY'S APPLE PUNCH

SERVES 16 (wine glasses) Ⓥ

6 tsp Earl Grey tea leaves
750 ml/1¼ pt boiling water
10 whole cloves
3 tbsp granulated sugar
600 ml/1 pt unsweetened apple juice
6 sprigs mint (or lovage leaves)
1 tray ice cubes
600 ml/1 pt dry ginger ale, chilled
1 firm dessert apple

Pour the boiling water over the tea leaves, leave to infuse for 1 minute, then strain the tea and pour over the cloves and sugar. Stir until the sugar has dissolved, cool, then chill in the fridge. Add the apple juice and bruised mint or lovage leaves. Return to the fridge to chill again.

To serve, add the ice cubes and ginger ale to the tea punch and garnish with curls of apple peel and thin apple slices. (See page 195.)

KILOCALORIES	110	SUGARS	26g
TOTAL FAT	–	SODIUM	10mg
SATURATED FAT	–	FIBRE	–

Please see the introduction for a full explanation of the nutritional factboxes.

ICED ORANGE AND LIME TEA

SERVES 4 (tumblers) Ⓥ

750 ml/1¼ pt boiling water
6 level tsp Orange Pekoe tea leaves
1 lime
ice cubes
orange (or lime slices)

Make the tea in the usual way, leave it to infuse for 3 minutes, then strain it into a jug over thin slices of lime. Cool and chill in the fridge. Remove the lime slices before serving the tea in four tall glasses over ice cubes. Float half a slice of orange or lime in each glass. This drink has no nutritional factbox values.

SWEDISH NEW YEAR PUNCH

SERVES 12 (wine glasses) Ⓥ

juice and peel of a lemon
5 cm/2 in piece cinnamon stick
½ vanilla pod
6 whole cloves
1 nutmeg (optional)
2 sugar lumps
350 ml/12 fl oz each, red and dry white wine
350 ml/12 fl oz medium-dry sherry (amontillado)
100 ml/4 fl oz rum (or brandy)
350 ml/12 fl oz lemonade (or to taste)

Bring the juice and thin peel of the lemon, the cinnamon, vanilla, cloves, nutmeg and sugar lumps to the boil, simmer for 5 minutes, cover and leave to infuse for 30 minutes. Strain the liquid into a pan, add the wines, sherry and rum and bring slowly to just below boiling point. Pour the punch into a bowl and stir in the lemonade. Serve at once.

KILOCALORIES	100	SUGARS	4g
TOTAL FAT	–	SODIUM	10mg
SATURATED FAT	–	FIBRE	–

Please see the introduction for a full explanation of the nutritional factboxes.

Ⓥ This symbol denotes a recipe suitable for vegetarians.

ANN'S BANANA COCKTAIL

SERVES 4 (tumblers) Ⓥ

2–3 ripe bananas
1 litre/1¼ pt pineapple juice, chilled
4 tbsp parsley, roughly chopped

Place the peeled and sliced bananas in a liquidiser with the pineapple juice and the parsley. Blend until smooth, then pour the lime-green drink into four chilled tumblers and serve.

KILOCALORIES	375	SUGARS	95g
TOTAL FAT	–	SODIUM	30mg
SATURATED FAT	–	FIBRE	0.5g

SUMMER WINE CUP

SERVES 4 (tumblers) Ⓥ

225 g/8 oz strawberries (or 2–3 peaches), sliced
1–2 tbsp sugar
juice of a lemon
1 litre/1½ pt dry white wine, chilled
1 litre/1½ pt soda water, chilled

Place the strawberries (or peaches) in a bowl with the sugar, strained lemon juice and a third of the wine. Steep in the fridge for at least 1 hour, then pour into a large bowl, stir in the remaining wine and the soda water, with a tray of ice cubes if liked. Serve at once.

KILOCALORIES	185	SUGARS	11g
TOTAL FAT	–	SODIUM	10mg
SATURATED FAT	–	FIBRE	0.5g

Right *(top row) Mango frappé, Earl Grey's apple punch and avocado and cucumber cooler. (Bottom row) Raspberry and yogurt shake, melon buttermilk, iced coffee and tomato health drink.*

MELON BUTTERMILK

SERVES 4 (tumblers) Ⓥ

300 g/11 oz honeydew (or ogen) melon
1–2 tsp clear honey (optional)
juice and grated rind of ¹/₂ lime
600 ml/1 pt buttermilk, chilled
melon for garnishing

Peel the melon, remove the seeds and cut the flesh into cubes. Place them in a liquidiser with the honey, if used, the juice and rind of lime and the buttermilk. Blend until smooth and pour into four chilled glasses (do not add ice cubes as these may separate and dilute the buttermilk).

Garnish each glass with scooped out small balls of melon threaded on to cocktail sticks. (See page 195.)

KILOCALORIES	90	SUGARS	16g
TOTAL FAT	1g	SODIUM	110mg
SATURATED FAT	–	FIBRE	0.5g

AVOCADO AND CUCUMBER COOLER

SERVES 4 (tumblers) Ⓥ

2 ripe avocado pears
2 tbsp lemon juice
¹/₄ cucumber, peeled and finely chopped
1 tbsp mint, finely chopped
600 ml/1 pt low-fat plain yogurt
Tabasco sauce

Peel the avocado pears, remove the stones and dice the flesh with a stainless steel knife; put in a liquidiser with the lemon juice, cucumber and mint. Blend to a smooth purée, then gradually add the yogurt, liquidising until it is thoroughly incorporated. Sharpen to taste with Tabasco sauce. Chill in the fridge for about 1 hour before serving. (See page 195.)

KILOCALORIES	225	SUGARS	12g
TOTAL FAT	15g	SODIUM	130mg
SATURATED FAT	4g	FIBRE	2.5g

TOMATO HEALTH DRINK

SERVES 4 (tumblers) Ⓥ

475 ml/16 fl oz tomato juice, chilled
475 ml/16 fl oz low-fat plain yogurt, chilled
juice of ¹/₂ lemon
¹/₄–¹/₂ tsp Worcestershire sauce
Tabasco sauce
pinch celery salt
black pepper
celery sticks

Place the tomato juice, yogurt, lemon juice and Worcestershire sauce in a liquidiser, with a few drops of Tabasco, the celery salt and a good grinding of pepper.

Blend until thoroughly smooth and pour at once into four tall glasses; place a trimmed celery stick in each as a swizzle stick. (See page 195.)

KILOCALORIES	85	SUGARS	13g
TOTAL FAT	1g	SODIUM	470mg
SATURATED FAT	1g	FIBRE	0.5g

RASPBERRY AND YOGURT SHAKE

SERVES 4 (wine glasses) Ⓥ

175 g/6 oz raspberries, fresh or frozen
300 ml/¹/₂ pt skimmed milk
2 tsp honey or sugar (optional)
300 ml/¹/₂ pt low-fat plain yogurt

Rinse and thoroughly drain the raspberries (or thaw frozen ones); put them in a liquidiser with the skimmed milk and blend until smooth, or rub them through a fine sieve. Strain the raspberry purée to get rid of the pips and sweeten to taste with sugar or honey. Return the mixture to the liquidiser with the yogurt and four ice cubes; blend well.

Serve at once, in four chilled glasses. (See page 195.)

KILOCALORIES	90	SUGARS	15g
TOTAL FAT	1g	SODIUM	110mg
SATURATED FAT	–	FIBRE	1g

MANGO FRAPPÉ

SERVES 4 (tumblers) Ⓥ

1 large ripe mango
juice and grated rind of a lime
6 tbsp semi-skimmed milk
2 tsp clear honey
500 ml/17 fl oz unsweetened pineapple juice
crushed ice

Prepare the mango by scooping out the flesh and catching all the juices. Place in a liquidiser, add the lime juice and rind, the milk, honey and pineapple juice. Blend until smooth, then chill thoroughly in the fridge.

To serve, pour the frappé into four glasses with crushed ice and garnish, if liked, with thin slices of fresh lime. (See page 195.)

KILOCALORIES	345	SUGARS	86g
TOTAL FAT	1g	SODIUM	40mg
SATURATED FAT	–	FIBRE	4g

ICED COFFEE

SERVES 4 (tumblers) Ⓥ

4 tbsp instant coffee powder or *granules*
750 ml/1¼ pt boiling water
sugar (optional)

Dissolve the coffee in the boiling water, cool, then chill in the fridge. Pour part of the chilled coffee in two ice-cube trays and freeze solid.

To serve, half-fill tall tumblers with coffee ice cubes and top up with chilled coffee. Sweeten if necessary and serve. Without the addition of sugar this drink has no nutritional factbox values. (See illustration page 195.)

Variation 1 Make iced coffee as above, but fill glasses only halfway with coffee, then top up with chilled skimmed milk. Stir well and serve with drinking straws.

KILOCALORIES	65	SUGARS	12g
TOTAL FAT	–	SODIUM	60mg
SATURATED FAT	–	FIBRE	–

Variation 2 Prepare and chill coffee made from 4 tablespoonfuls of instant coffee powder or granules and 600 ml/1 pt boiling water. Place a scoop of vanilla ice-cream in each of four tall, chilled glasses. Top up with coffee and serve with drinking straws.

KILOCALORIES	150	SUGARS	20g
TOTAL FAT	6g	SODIUM	50mg
SATURATED FAT	4g	FIBRE	–

SWEETS AND PUDDINGS

From a nutritional standpoint, fresh fruit is the best pudding of all. Puddings as such contribute little to a healthy diet save to satisfy a craving for sugary foods. Sugar produces energy, but it already occurs naturally in foods in sufficient quantities for our daily needs. When sugar is extracted from its natural source it becomes pure refined sugar that is easier to eat and use in beverages, baking and confectionery. Up to 50 per cent of our daily sugar consumption is from hidden sugar used in manufactured and processed foods. Brown sugar is no better than white; it is less refined and therefore retains some essential minerals but the carbohydrate content is the same. The best sweetening product is fructose, the sugar found naturally in fresh fruit.

CEREAL PUDDINGS

Most of these are based on rice pudding and semolina derived from grains, and tapioca extracted from the cassava root. Use semi-skimmed or skimmed milk and reduce the amount of sugar used by substituting dried, fresh or puréed fruit.

PIES AND PUDDINGS

Calorie-laden steamed suet puddings served with syrup and jam are declining in popularity. Modern preference is for lighter fruit pies, tarts and crumbles, although these too can be highly calorific if served with cream (see table, opposite).

Shortcrust pastry (see recipe, opposite) This contains less than half the fat of flaky and puff pastry. To increase the fibre content, replace some or all of the flour with wholewheat flour (extra liquid will be needed) and use oats or other unrefined cereals in crumble toppings. Polyunsaturated vegetable and white fats can replace butter. Serve with low-fat plain yogurt or fromage frais instead of cream.

Fruit pies Pies are usually made by placing fruit in a deep pie dish with a wide rim upon which sits the pastry lid. Tarts are baked in shallow dishes or deep oven-proof plates and have a pastry base as well as a lid. Sweet pies and tarts usually have sugar sprinkled on them prior to baking (savoury pies are glazed with egg or milk). Flans are pastry cases moulded into flan dishes and baked blind.

Baking blind Cook the pastry case in the oven at 200°C/400°F/gas 6 for 15 minutes with greaseproof paper or foil weighted down with dried beans; remove the paper and beans and cook for a further 10 minutes. The pastry case can then be filled with various mixtures.

CREAM AND YOGURT

The main difference between milk and cream is the fat content; the amounts shown opposite are the minima and there is often more fat in individual products. **Half** and **single creams** are useful for pouring; they will not whip but can be poured on to hot desserts. **Whipping cream** is similar to double cream but with a thinner consistency; it can double in size when whipped but quickly loses its volume, so should be used to decorate cakes at the last minute.

Soured cream is single cream with an added bacterial culture and is refreshing in soups, salad dressings, meat and fish dishes as well as desserts. **Sterilised cream** comes in cans, has a slightly cooked flavour and a shelf-life of up to two years.

Evaporated milk is whole milk with a large percentage of the water removed, while **condensed milk** has had half the water removed and a large amount of sugar added. **Aerosol** and **artificial creams** contain a high percentage of sugar.

Yogurt This is whole or skimmed milk treated with bacteria. The curdled result is slightly tart but is refreshing on its own or with various flavourings. Yogurt makes a good substitute for many of the creams. Low-fat ones can be poured over desserts and stirred into savoury cooked dishes. Set yogurts or wholemilk thicker varieties (for example, Greek yogurt) can be used like double cream for serving, but will not whip.

per 100 g/4 oz	Calories	Total fat (grams)	Saturated fat (grams)
Clotted cream	586	64	40
Double cream	449	48	30
Whipping cream	373	39	25
Sterilised cream	239	24	15
Soured cream	205	20	13
Single cream	198	19	12
Half cream	148	13	8
Low-fat yogurt	56	1	1

ICE-CREAMS AND SORBETS

A freezer is essential for making home-made ices. It is also essential for the texture that ice crystals are broken down as they form by whisking the mixture at intervals during the freezing process.

Nutritionally, plain vanilla ice-cream, although high in calories, contains fewer than cream or custards but considerably more than low-fat plain yogurt.

CUSTARD

Custard made with skimmed or semi-skimmed milk is preferable to using cream on dessert dishes. For a traditional recipe for custard see page 200.

FRUIT

Fruit is the healthiest dessert as long as sugar and syrups are not added. For a fresh fruit salad, simply layer a bowl with the prepared fruit, add a little fruit juice, then cover and leave for at least one hour (stirring once) before serving.

SHORTCRUST PASTRY

MAKES 225 g/8 oz Ⓥ

225 g/8 oz plain white flour
pinch salt
50 g/2 oz margarine (or butter)
50 g/2 oz white vegetable fat (or lard)
2–3 tbsp cold water

Sift the flour and salt into a bowl; cut the margarine (or butter) and vegetable fat (or lard) into small pieces and add to the flour. Work the ingredients together with the fingers until they resemble fine breadcrumbs. Sprinkle the water evenly around the mixture and mix it in with the fingertips or a round-bladed knife.

Transfer the dough to a lightly floured surface and knead it gently until smooth and firm. Avoid over-handling. Allow to chill in the fridge before using the pastry. Roll it out on a lightly floured board, using light strokes and working from the centre outwards.

Wholemeal shortcrust pastry is made in much the same way except it is more difficult to roll out and you may need to add a little extra water to make the dough more pliable.

KILOCALORIES	1495	SUGARS	3g
TOTAL FAT	84g	SODIUM	1590mg
SATURATED FAT	19g	FIBRE	7g

OATMEAL-ALMOND PIE PASTRY

Most pastry cases are usually made with shortcrust. Oatmeal imparts a distinctive nutty flavour to the crust, which becomes a suitable case for otherwise bland custard fillings. The pastry is perhaps less well behaved than conventional shortcrust as it tends to tear when being rolled out.

SERVES 6 Ⓥ

100 g/4 oz fine or medium oatmeal
100 g/4 oz ground almonds
3 tbsp ground sesame seeds
pinch salt
6 tbsp water
fine oatmeal for dusting

Preheat the oven to 190°C/375°F/gas 5. Stir together the oatmeal, ground almonds, sesame seeds and salt and mix to a soft dough with the water. Dust it lightly with oatmeal and roll it out to a 30 cm/12 in circle for lining a 25 cm/10 in flat tin or dish.

Bake the flan case in the centre of the oven for about 12 minutes or until it is cooked through and lightly browned. Leave the flan to cool before filling it.

KILOCALORIES	200	SUGARS	1g
TOTAL FAT	14g	SODIUM	70mg
SATURATED FAT	1g	FIBRE	3g

Please see the introduction for a full explanation of the nutritional factboxes.

CUSTARD

— • —

Custard is traditionally made with whole milk, egg yolks and sugar; this version is a little healthier.

MAKES 300 ml/½ pt (V)

300 ml/½ pt semi-skimmed milk
vanilla pod
caster sugar (to taste)
2 large eggs yolks

Bring the milk and a piece of vanilla to the boil over a gentle heat; allow the mixture to infuse. Sweeten the milk to taste and gradually stir in the beaten egg yolks. Strain the mixture, return to the pan and continue stirring until the custard has thickened.

KILOCALORIES	390	SUGARS	41g
TOTAL FAT	19g	SODIUM	190mg
SATURATED FAT	7g	FIBRE	–

FRESH FRUIT YOGURT MOUSSE

— • —

Almost any kind of fresh fruit can be added to plain yogurt for a quick and refreshing dessert. A mousse is only slightly more time-consuming. Whichever fruit you choose it should first be reduced to a purée, and berry fruits should ideally be strained to remove all the pips.

SERVES 4

1 guava
2 nectarines (or peaches)
juice and rind of an orange
1–2 tsp honey (optional)
3 tsp powdered gelatine
450 ml/¾ pt low-fat plain yogurt
1 tbsp Curaçao or Cointreau (optional)
black grapes

Peel the guava and nectarines or peaches – easiest done if covered with boiling water for 1 minute, then with cold; remove seeds and stones and dice the flesh. Peel the orange thinly and extract the juice. Reduce the fruit pulp to a smooth purée in a blender or sieve, with half the orange juice. If necessary, sweeten with honey.

Dissolve the gelatine in the remaining orange juice mixed with 4 tablespoonfuls of boiling water. Stir this into the yogurt, together with the liqueur if used. Chill the mixture in the fridge until just beginning to set, then fold in the fruit purée, mixing thoroughly. Spoon the mousse into four serving dishes, and return to the fridge to set and chill.

Just before serving, decorate the mousse with orange peel and small clusters of halved, pipped grapes.

KILOCALORIES	125	SUGARS	18g
TOTAL FAT	1g	SODIUM	100mg
SATURATED FAT	1g	FIBRE	2g

CHOCOLATE PEPPERMINT SOUFFLÉ

— • —

This could be thought of as the hot version of chocolate peppermint ice-cream.

SERVES 4 (V)

50 g/2 oz margarine (or butter)
40 g/1½ oz plain flour
15 g/½ oz cocoa
300 ml/½ pt hot semi-skimmed milk
4 eggs, separated
65 g/2½ oz brown sugar
½ tsp peppermint essence
2–3 drops malt vinegar

Prepare a 1.5 litre/2½ pt soufflé dish, buttering it lightly and tying a paper collar round the outside. Set the oven to 190°C/375°F/gas 5 and place a shelf in the centre position.

Melt the margarine or butter in a pan, stir in the flour and cocoa to form a roux and cook for 1 minute. Gradually stir in the milk, whisking to prevent lumps, and cook until the mixture comes to the boil and thickens. Remove the pan from the heat. Beat in the egg yolks, one at a time, the sugar and peppermint essence.

Add the vinegar to the egg whites and whisk them to stiff peaks. Beat a quarter of the whites into the chocolate mixture, then gently fold in the rest with a metal spoon or spatula. Spoon into the prepared dish and bake for 45 minutes. Remove the soufflé from the oven, remove the collar and serve immediately.

KILOCALORIES	240	SUGARS	17g
TOTAL FAT	13g	SODIUM	200mg
SATURATED FAT	2g	FIBRE	0.5g

VANILLA AND BLACKCURRANT SOUFFLÉ

——— • ———

Light-as-air soufflés make impressive party desserts and present no real problems apart from resisting the temptation to open the oven door during cooking.

SERVES 4 Ⓥ

100 g/4 oz blackcurrant purée
50 g/2 oz margarine (or butter)
50 g/2 oz plain flour
300 ml/½ pt hot semi-skimmed milk
4 eggs, separated
soft light brown sugar
1 tsp vanilla essence
2–3 drops of malt vinegar

Prepare a 1.5 litre/2½ pt soufflé dish. Follow the method for chocolate peppermint soufflé (see opposite), adding the blackcurrant purée and sugar to taste at the same time as the egg yolks.

KILOCALORIES	175	SUGARS	8g
TOTAL FAT	10g	SODIUM	140mg
SATURATED FAT	–	FIBRE	1g

CUSTARDE LUMBARDE

——— • ———

This English pudding has been known for more than 500 years and was originally made with only the yolks of the eggs (egg whites were thought to be dangerous in medieval days) and thick cream; this modern version of the custard tart is prepared with whole eggs and semi-skimmed milk.

SERVES 4 Ⓥ

20–23 cm/8–9 in pastry case (baked blind)
4 large prunes, stoned
1 tbsp stoned dates, chopped
3 small eggs
450 ml/¾ pt semi-skimmed milk
small pinch cinnamon

Prepare the pastry case from wholemeal or ordinary shortcrust pastry (see page 199) and bake it blind for 10 minutes. Leave it to cool completely. Preheat the oven to 190°C/375°F/gas 5. Halve the prunes and cut them into thin slices. Sprinkle the prunes and chopped dates over the base of the pastry case. Beat the eggs

with the milk, pour this custard over the fruit and sprinkle a small pinch of cinnamon over the top.

Bake on the middle shelf of the oven for 20–25 minutes or until the custard is set. Serve hot or cold.

KILOCALORIES	460	SUGARS	16g
TOTAL FAT	27g	SODIUM	370mg
SATURATED FAT	2g	FIBRE	5.5g

LEMON PIE WITH GRANOLA CRUST

——— • ———

Made with pure, wholesome ingredients, this recipe is the nutritionist's version of the traditional lemon pie. The filling is a smooth, eggless lemon custard, fresh in flavour with the addition of unsweetened pineapple and orange juices.

SERVES 4 Ⓥ

200 g/7 oz granola (see page 14)
4–5 tbsp unsweetened fruit juice

FILLING
225 ml/8 fl oz unsweetened pineapple juice
225 ml/8 fl oz unsweetened orange juice
grated rind and juice of 2 lemons
10 dates (fresh or dried), stoned
1 tbsp unsalted cashew nuts
4 tbsp water
5 tbsp arrowroot (or cornflour)
¼ tsp salt
Greek yogurt, whipped cream or ice-cream (optional)

Preheat the oven to 200°C/400°F/gas 6. Put the granola in a food processor and reduce it to fine crumbs. Beat in the fruit juice with a wire whisk until the mixture is crumbly. Press it into a 20–23 cm/8–9 in flan case and bake in the oven for about 8 minutes.

Place all the filling ingredients in a liquidiser (in two batches if necessary) and blend until smooth. Transfer the mixture to a pan and cook over low heat, stirring constantly, until it thickens. Leave the filling to cool, then pour it into the granola case.

Chill the pie in the fridge until the filling has set. Serve with Greek yogurt, whipped cream or ice-cream.

KILOCALORIES	515	SUGARS	60g
TOTAL FAT	6g	SODIUM	370mg
SATURATED FAT	–	FIBRE	5.5g

MINCEMEAT AND APPLE CRUMBLE

The addition of muesli gives an interesting texture to a crumble topping. Granola or wheat flakes mixed with raisins are equally nutritious and crunchy.

SERVES 4

2 large cooking apples, peeled, cored and thickly sliced
1 tbsp lemon juice
3 tbsp water
4 tbsp mincemeat

TOPPING
75 g/3 oz margarine (or butter)
150 g/5 oz wholemeal flour
50 g/2 oz unsweetened muesli
50 g/2 oz dark brown sugar

Preheat the oven to 190°C/375°F/gas 5. Arrange the apple slices in a buttered shallow, ovenproof dish. Pour the lemon juice and the water over them, and spread the mincemeat on top.

Prepare the topping by rubbing the butter or margarine into the flour. Mix in the muesli and sugar, and spread it on top of the mincemeat. Bake for 20 minutes, then reduce the heat to 180°C/350°F/gas 4, and bake for a further 30 minutes.

Serve warm, with chilled plain yogurt, cream, ice-cream, fromage frais or custard.

KILOCALORIES	455	SUGARS	28g
TOTAL FAT	18g	SODIUM	210mg
SATURATED FAT	4g	FIBRE	5.5g

COFFEE SEMOLINA WHIP

Semolina imparts a lighter texture than flour, and the brown, fibre-rich types of semolina give extra flavour and crunchiness.

SERVES 4 Ⓥ

600 ml/1 pt semi-skimmed milk
1 tbsp instant coffee powder or granules
50 g/2 oz brown semolina
40 g/1½ oz brown (or molasses) sugar
2 medium eggs, separated

Bring the semi-skimmed milk, coffee and semolina to the boil over gentle heat, stirring constantly until the mixture thickens. Add in the sugar until it has melted.

Reduce the heat to the minimum and beat in the egg yolks, one at a time. Whisk the whites to stiff peaks and fold a third of them into the semolina mixture. Fold in the remaining whites with a large metal spoon until well combined. If the mixture should curdle it can be resuscitated by liquidising it briefly. Spoon the semolina into individual dishes and serve hot.

KILOCALORIES	165	SUGARS	8g
TOTAL FAT	3g	SODIUM	130mg
SATURATED FAT	1g	FIBRE	0.5g

FROZEN ORANGE YOGURT

Frozen yogurt is the slimmer's alternative to dairy ice-cream, and flavoured with orange and lemon juice it gives a good proportion of the daily vitamin C requirement.

SERVES 4–6

125 ml/4 fl oz unsweetened orange juice
4 tbsp lemon juice
2 tsp powdered gelatine
1 tbsp grated orange rind
225 ml/8 oz low-fat plain yogurt
3 egg whites
2–3 tbsp fructose (fruit sugar)

Combine the fruit juices, and measure 4 tablespoonfuls into a small pan. Sprinkle the gelatine on top and leave it for 10 minutes before dissolving it over low heat. Whisk together the rest of the juice, the orange rind and the yogurt until the mixture is creamy and smooth; stir the dissolved gelatine into it.

Whisk the egg whites in a separate bowl, gradually adding fructose to taste, until the mixture is a light, glossy foam. Fold one-third into the mixture, blending well, then fold in the rest of the egg whites.

Spoon the mixture into a 2 litre/3¼ pt lidded freezing container and freeze until firm. About half an hour before serving, scoop the orange yogurt into individual glasses or bowls and leave it to thaw slightly in the fridge.

KILOCALORIES	65	SUGARS	11g
TOTAL FAT	–	SODIUM	80mg
SATURATED FAT	–	FIBRE	–

CHOCOLATE CRUMB PUDDING

—— • ——

Steamed puddings are part of the English cookery tradition. Some are of the stodgy type, others, like the following, light and airy.

SERVES 4–6 Ⓥ

75 g/3 oz plain chocolate
100 g/4 oz margarine (or butter)
100 g/4 oz caster sugar
1 large egg, separated
150 g/5 oz fresh wholemeal breadcrumbs
50 g/2 oz self-raising flour
3 tbsp semi-skimmed milk

Melt the chocolate in a small bowl set over a pan of simmering water; allow it to cool slightly. Cream the margarine with the sugar, then beat in the chocolate and the egg yolk. Mix together the breadcrumbs and the flour and fold half into the creamed mixture with 2 tablespoonfuls of milk. Fold in the remaining dry ingredients with enough milk to give a fairly soft, dropping consistency.

Whisk the egg white until stiff, fold it into the pudding mixture and spoon this into a lightly buttered 1 litre/1½ pt basin. Cover the basin with buttered greaseproof paper, and foil; tie this firmly in place and steam or boil the pudding for 2 hours. Turn it out and serve with Greek yogurt or cream.

KILOCALORIES	460	SUGARS	31g
TOTAL FAT	22g	SODIUM	450mg
SATURATED FAT	7g	FIBRE	1g

COTTAGE CHEESECAKE

Most continental cheesecakes differ from the American versions in being baked. For this recipe, use a shortcrust pastry base, plain or wholemeal, baked blind; or a crumb base.

SERVES 6 Ⓥ

250 g/9 oz cottage cheese
15 g/½ oz margarine (or butter)
¼ tsp vanilla essence
150 ml/¼ pt semi-skimmed milk
1 tbsp cornflour
2 eggs, lightly beaten
50 g/3 oz sugar
pastry case (18 cm/7 in)

Preheat the oven to 180°C/350°F/gas 4. Blend the cottage cheese, margarine or butter and vanilla essence in a liquidiser until smooth. Mix the milk and cornflour and bring to the boil, stirring all the time until the mixture has thickened. Pour the hot milk over the eggs beaten with the sugar, stirring thoroughly; return the mixture to the pan over low heat until it acquires the consistency of custard.

Combine the cottage cheese mixture with the custard, and pour into a part-baked pastry case or a crumb-lined baking dish. Bake the cheesecake for about 30 minutes. Leave the cheesecake to cool before serving it.

KILOCALORIES	360	SUGARS	16g
TOTAL FAT	18g	SODIUM	400mg
SATURATED FAT	7g	FIBRE	1g

ELDERBERRY AND APPLE PLATE PIE

The tart flavours of apples and elderberries complement each other well and are particularly suited to a spicy pastry. Plums or blackberries go equally well with tart apples.

SERVES 6 Ⓥ

175 g/6 oz plain flour
1 tsp ground mixed spice
40 g/1½ oz margarine (or butter)
40 g/1½ oz white vegetable fat
450 g/1 lb apples (prepared weight)
225 g/8 oz elderberries (prepared weight)
100 g/4 oz granulated sugar

Sift the flour and spice into a bowl and rub in the margarine and white vegetable fat until the mixture resembles fine breadcrumbs. Mix in enough cold water to bind the dough. Roll out half the pastry to fit a greased 20 cm/8 in enamel or foil pie plate.

Peel, core and thinly slice the apples. Strip the elderberries from their stalks by dragging a fork through the clusters, rinse them and mix with the apple slices. Pile the fruit in layers over the pastry, sprinkling each layer with sugar. Reserve 1 tablespoonful of the sugar for the top crust.

Preheat the oven to 200°C/400°F/gas 6 and put a baking sheet to warm on the middle shelf. Roll out the remaining pastry for the lid: trim, seal and decorate the edges. Make a slit in the centre, brush the pastry with a little water and sprinkle it with the remaining sugar.

Bake the pie for 30–35 minutes or until golden-brown. Serve it warm with custard, low-fat plain yogurt or ice-cream.

KILOCALORIES	295	SUGARS	25g
TOTAL FAT	11g	SODIUM	110mg
SATURATED FAT	3g	FIBRE	2g

LEMON CHERRY MERINGUE PIE

Lemon meringue pie is a popular family pudding. The classic concoction can be given a touch of sophistication with a layer of cherries underneath the lemon mixture.

SERVES 4 Ⓥ

250 g/9 oz shortcrust pastry (see page 199)
100 g/4 oz can cherries, drained (optional)
2 tbsp cornflour
finely grated peel and juice of 2 large lemons
150 ml/¼ pt water
50 g/2 oz clover (or heather) honey
2 eggs, separated
50 g/2 oz caster sugar

Preheat the oven to 200°C/400°F/gas 6. Roll out the pastry on a lightly floured surface and use it to line a 20 cm/8 in flan dish set on a greased baking tray. Line the pastry with foil; weight it down with baking beans and bake it blind for 15 minutes near the top of the oven. Remove foil and beans and return the pastry to the oven for 5–10 minutes or until golden-brown. Leave to cool.

Thinly slice two-thirds of the cherries, if used, with a floured knife and spread them over the base of the flan case. Tip the cornflour into a small pan, blend in the lemon peel and gradually stir in the lemon juice, followed by the water and honey. Cook over gentle heat, stirring until it thickens; simmer for 2 minutes. Remove the pan from the heat and let the custard cool before stirring in the egg yolks. Pour the mixture into the pastry case.

Whisk the egg whites until stiff, add the sugar and continue to whisk until the whites are stiff. Pile the meringue over the lemon filling, bringing it right to the edges of the pastry. Bake in the centre of the oven set to 110°C/225°F/gas ¼ for 1½ hours. Stud the top with the rest of the halved cherries.

Serve the pie chilled.

KILOCALORIES	520	SUGARS	28g
TOTAL FAT	23g	SODIUM	320mg
SATURATED FAT	9g	FIBRE	1.5g

CHEESECAKE WITH PEACH AND PASSION-FRUIT TOPPING

Baked cheesecake tends to crack on the top, but this can be masked with a fruit topping.

SERVES 8 Ⓥ
75 g/3 oz digestive biscuits
50 g/2 oz margarine (or butter), melted
700 g/1½ lb curd cheese
100 g/4 oz caster sugar
3 large eggs
1 large lemon

TOPPING
2 peaches
175 g/6 oz passion-fruit pulp (or 8 tbsp fruit juice)
arrowroot

Crush the biscuits to fine crumbs and mix them with the melted margarine. Line an 18 cm/7 in loose-bottomed cake or deep flan tin with greaseproof paper and press the crumb mixture over the base. Preheat the oven to 165°C/325°F/gas 3.

Beat the curd cheese until smooth, and mix in the sugar and eggs. Finely grate the rind from the lemon and squeeze out the juice; add both to the curd mixture and spoon it gently into the prepared tin, smoothing the top.

Bake the cheesecake near the bottom of the oven for about 1 hour. When cooked, the top should be golden-brown and the centre should be just firm. Remove the cake from the oven and leave to cool completely.

For the topping, skin the peaches, remove the stones and cut the flesh into even-sized segments. Sieve the passion-fruit pulp to remove the black pips. Arrange the peach slices on top of the cheesecake and glaze them with the passion-fruit juice. For a slightly thicker sauce coating, thicken pulp or juice with a little arrowroot over gentle heat and leave to cool before glazing.

KILOCALORIES	315	SUGARS	20g
TOTAL FAT	20g	SODIUM	230mg
SATURATED FAT	8g	FIBRE	0.5g

CITRUS BREAD PUDDING

The traditional bread-and-butter pudding is given a citrus boost.

SERVES 4–6 Ⓥ
12 slices French bread, 6 mm/¼ in thick
40 g/1½ oz margarine (or butter)
2 tsp grated rind and 2 tbsp juice of lemon, (or orange, lime or tangerine)
600 ml/1 pt semi-skimmed milk
2–3 tbsp honey
2 large eggs
1 egg yolk

Grease a 1.5 litre/2½ pt ovenproof dish with a little of the margarine. Lightly spread the bread with the rest of the margarine and arrange it in layers in the dish, sprinkling each layer with citrus rind and juice. Preheat the oven to 180°C/350°F/gas 4.

Bring the milk to the boil over gentle heat and stir in the honey until dissolved. Beat the eggs and egg yolk in a bowl, then gradually add the milk and honey, beating constantly. Pour the mixture over the bread.

Set the dish in a roasting tin, pour in enough hot water to come halfway up the sides of the dish and bake the pudding for 1–1¼ hours, until the custard has set. Serve at once.

KILOCALORIES	320	SUGARS	18g
TOTAL FAT	12g	SODIUM	440mg
SATURATED FAT	3g	FIBRE	0.5g

4 tbsp arrowroot (or cornflour)
grated rind of ½ orange (optional)
3 medium-sized bananas, sliced

Preheat the oven to 190°C/375°F/gas 5. Mix the coconut and flour together, with enough soya milk to form a manageable dough. Press it over the base and sides of a 20–23 cm/8–9 in flan dish. Bake for about 15–20 minutes or until the pastry is light brown. Remove from the oven and leave to cool.

Put the cashew nuts, half the water, the dates, vanilla essence, salt and arrowroot in the liquidiser, with the orange rind if used. Blend until smooth, then add the rest of the water and liquidise again. Pour the mixture into a pan and cook over gentle heat, stirring until it thickens. Remove from the heat and allow the mixture to cool.

Cover the base of the flan case with half the banana slices; spoon over them half the cashew custard and lay the remaining bananas on top. Spread the rest of the filling over the bananas and smooth the top. Decorate with a little desiccated coconut and leave the tart to set and chill before serving.

KILOCALORIES	385	SUGARS	16g
TOTAL FAT	24g	SODIUM	80mg
SATURATED FAT	15g	FIBRE	5.5g

Cashew nuts are imported from India and Brazil. They are an important food source, with a high content of polyunsaturated oil, protein and carbohydrate, and rich in minerals and vitamins. Sold roasted and shelled, the white, sweet nuts are brittle and 'short' in texture and do not store well.

CASHEW-BANANA COCONUT TART

— • —

This tart has no added fat or sugar and hardly any flour, and a filling of wholesome cashew nuts, dates and bananas.

SERVES 6 Ⓥ

150 g/6 oz desiccated coconut
2 tbsp wholewheat flour
soya milk

FILLING
100 g/4 oz cashew nuts
600 ml/1 pt water
150 g/5 oz stoned dates
1½ tsp vanilla essence
pinch salt

TOFU CHEESECAKE

— • —

Rich in flavour and crunchy in texture, this cheesecake makes a welcome change of theme from the usual dairy-based mixtures.

SERVES 4 Ⓥ

75 g/3 oz rolled oats
100 g/4 oz rolled barley
2½ tbsp ground sunflower seeds
pinch salt
40 g/1½ oz walnuts, chopped

2 tbsp ground almonds
5–8 tbsp water

TOPPING
350 g/12 oz tofu
1 tbsp lemon (or lime) juice
1 tsp vanilla essence
550 g/20 oz canned crushed unsweetened pineapple
2 tbsp arrowroot (or cornflour)
1 banana

For the base, mix together the oats, barley, sunflower seeds, salt, walnuts and almonds with enough cold water to bind the mixture. Press over the base of a 20 cm/8 in flan dish and allow to stand for 15 minutes.

Preheat the oven to 180°C/350°F/gas 4. Blend the topping ingredients in a liquidiser and spread them evenly over the base. Bake the cheesecake near the bottom of the oven for 25–35 minutes or until it is beginning to brown at the sides.

Leave the cheesecake to cool before serving it, on its own or decorated with strawberries or mandarin orange segments.

KILOCALORIES	780	SUGARS	23g
TOTAL FAT	30g	SODIUM	120mg
SATURATED FAT	2g	FIBRE	7g

RASPBERRY VANILLA SUNDAES

Derived from the traditional summer dessert of Scandinavia, these sundaes can be made with any, or a mixture of, berry fruits in season.

SERVES 4 Ⓥ

175 g/6 oz fresh raspberries (or blackberries)
2 tbsp cornflour
300 ml/½ pt semi-skimmed milk
2 tbsp caster sugar
½ tsp vanilla essence
3 tsp heather honey

Tip the cornflour into a small pan and mix it to a smooth paste with a little of the milk. Blend in the rest of the milk and cook over medium heat, stirring all the time until the mixture comes to the boil and thickens. Off the heat, add the sugar and vanilla essence and continue stirring until the sugar has melted.

Spoon the custard into four sundae glasses. Crush the berries coarsely with a wooden spoon, push them

through a sieve and sweeten the purée to taste with honey.

Spoon the berry purée over the custard and chill for several hours in the fridge before serving.

KILOCALORIES	140	SUGARS	17g
TOTAL FAT	1g	SODIUM	50mg
SATURATED FAT	1g	FIBRE	1g

HUNGARIAN RICE PUDDING

Short-grain rice is sold especially for making puddings. The grains swell to absorb the liquid, clinging together and giving the creamy-rich consistency characteristic of our favourite milk puddings.

SERVES 4 Ⓥ

40 g/1½ oz pudding rice
butter for greasing
600 ml/1 pt semi-skimmed milk
100 g/4 oz caster sugar
2 eggs, separated
2 medium-sized cooking apples, peeled, cored and sliced
2–3 tbsp raspberry jam (optional)

Wash and drain the rice thoroughly and put it in a buttered 1.5 litre/2½ pt pie dish with the milk and 25 g/1 oz of the sugar. Set it aside for about 30 minutes to allow the rice to soften. Cook the rice in the oven at 150°C/300°F/gas 2 for about 1½ hours or until it starts to look set and creamy.

Remove the rice pudding from the oven, allow it to cool slightly, then stir in the egg yolks and return the dish to the oven for a further 30 minutes. Remove the rice pudding and let it cool; do not turn the oven off.

Meanwhile, cook the apples with 4 tablespoonfuls of water and 50 g/2 oz of the sugar until they pulp; allow them to cool. Warm the jam, if used, and spread it over the surface of the rice, then top with the apple purée. Whisk the egg whites until stiff, fold in the rest of the sugar and pile the meringue mixture on top of the pudding. Return it to the oven until the meringue is set and pale golden. Serve at once.

KILOCALORIES	290	SUGARS	51g
TOTAL FAT	6g	SODIUM	130mg
SATURATED FAT	3g	FIBRE	1g

GERMAN APPLE CAKE

This apple cake is equally delicious as a pudding and as a cake. It is popular with morning or afternoon coffee in Germany, where it is served dredged with icing sugar and generous helpings of cream.

SERVES 10 Ⓥ

300 g/12 oz plain flour
2 tsp baking powder
100 g/4 oz margarine (or butter)
75 g/3 oz white vegetable fat
100 g/4 oz caster sugar
1 large egg, beaten
semi-skimmed milk
1.3 kg/3 lb cooking apples
100 g/4 oz granulated (or light brown) sugar
1½–2 tsp ground allspice

Sift the flour and baking powder together and rub in the fats. Stir in the caster sugar and mix to a stiff dough with the egg and a little milk if necessary. Chill the dough for at least an hour.

Preheat the oven to 190°C/375°F/gas 5. Use two-thirds of the pastry to line a greased, loose-bottomed, deep, 20 cm/8 in cake tin. Prick the pastry thoroughly before lining it with foil and baking beans to prevent it rising during the initial blind baking. Bake on the middle shelf of the oven for 15 minutes.

Meanwhile, peel, core and slice the apples, and mix them with the granulated sugar and allspice. Remove the foil and beans and fill the pastry case with the apple slices. Roll out the rest of the pastry as a lid over the apples. Seal the edges, brush the top with milk and return the cake to the oven for another 40 minutes or until it is golden and cooked through.

Let the cake cool in the tin for 30 minutes before removing it. Serve cut into wedges and accompanied, perhaps, with ice-cream, fromage frais or Greek yogurt.

KILOCALORIES	355	SUGARS	31g
TOTAL FAT	15g	SODIUM	155mg
SATURATED FAT	4g	FIBRE	3g

KINGSTON PUDDING

This is an economical, less rich version of the old English trifle. The traditional decoration of whipped cream could be replaced by fromage frais or a crunchy topping.

SERVES 4 Ⓥ

225 g/8 oz gingernut biscuits
4 bananas, sliced
50 g/2 oz raisins
2½ tbsp custard powder
600 ml/1 pt semi-skimmed milk
50 g/2 oz caster sugar

Arrange whole ginger biscuits round the sides of a straight-sided 1 litre/1½ pt soufflé dish; crush the remainder of the biscuits and spread them over the base of the dish. Arrange layers of banana slices and raisins in the dish and set it aside.

Make up 600 ml/1 pt custard, using a proprietary custard powder. Alternatively, prepare a traditional custard sauce (see page 200).

Pour the custard into the soufflé dish and leave it to cool before chilling it in the fridge. The pudding can be decorated at the last minute with banana slices and crushed gingernut biscuits or chopped hazelnuts.

KILOCALORIES	550	SUGARS	70g
TOTAL FAT	9g	SODIUM	340mg
SATURATED FAT	4g	FIBRE	2g

KOLAK LABU
Pumpkin in coconut syrup

Pumpkin is available in late summer, the huge orange-red fruits being sold in wedges cut to weight. The Indonesians use coconut sugar for the thick coconut syrup; dark soft brown sugar can also be used.

SERVES 4 Ⓥ

450 g/1 lb pumpkin
225 g/8 oz desiccated coconut
2 pinches salt
75 g/3 oz brown sugar
1 cinnamon stick

Peel the pumpkin, remove the seeds and cut the flesh into bite-size chunks.

For the coconut milk, put the desiccated coconut in a liquidiser with 450 ml/¾ pt of warm water. Blend for a few seconds, then strain the milk into a pan, squeezing the coconut until quite dry. Put the coconut back in the liquidiser, add another 450 ml/¾ pt of warm water and repeat the process. Do not mix this thinner extraction of coconut milk with the first one, but squeeze it into a second pan. Discard the coconut.

Add the pumpkin pieces to the thin coconut milk, with a pinch of salt, and bring to the boil over gentle heat, simmering for about 8 minutes. Strain the contents, discard the thin coconut milk and return the pumpkin to the pan.

Bring the thick coconut milk slowly to the boil, with the sugar, cinnamon stick and a pinch of salt. When it reaches boiling point, stir continuously for about 3 minutes, until it has thickened to a syrup; taste for sweetness and discard the cinnamon. Pour the syrup over the pumpkin and simmer for another couple of minutes.

Serve the pumpkin in the syrup, hot or cold.

KILOCALORIES	430	SUGARS	25g
TOTAL FAT	35g	SODIUM	110mg
SATURATED FAT	30g	FIBRE	9g

BAKED BANANAS WITH RHUBARB

This is simplicity itself, ideal for cooking in the oven with the Sunday joint, and an attractive blend of flavours, the rhubarb sharpening the sweetness of bananas.

SERVES 4 Ⓥ

225 g/8 oz young rhubarb
4 medium-sized bananas
100 g/4 oz brown sugar
2 tbsp rum (dark or white)
juice of ½ orange
butter

Heat the oven to 200°C/400°F/gas 6. Butter a shallow, ovenproof dish. Split the bananas in half lengthwise; trim, wash and dry the rhubarb and cut the sticks to the same size as the bananas. Arrange the bananas and rhubarb side by side in the dish, preferably in a single layer.

Sprinkle the sugar, rum and orange juice over the bananas and rhubarb and bake, uncovered, for 20 minutes or until the fruit is tender and the juices become a glaze.

Serve hot or warm.

KILOCALORIES	225	SUGARS	48g
TOTAL FAT	1g	SODIUM	10mg
SATURATED FAT	–	FIBRE	2g

DADAR GULUNG
Pancakes with coconut filling

In Indonesia, these sweet coconut pancakes are flavoured with young aromatic leaves from the Pandanus or screw-pine.

SERVES 6–8 Ⓥ

125 g/4 oz plain flour
pinch salt
1 egg
150 ml/¼ pt semi-skimmed milk, mixed with
an equal quantity of water
1 tbsp margarine (or butter), melted
vegetable oil for frying

FILLING
300 ml/½ pt water
60 g/2½ oz brown sugar
125 g/4 oz desiccated coconut
1 cinnamon stick
2 tsp rice (or plain flour)
pinch salt
1 tsp lemon juice

Sift the flour and salt into a bowl, break the egg into a well in the centre and gradually mix in half the milk and water. Beat the batter thoroughly until smooth, then whisk in the melted butter followed by the rest of the liquid. Set the batter aside to rest while the filling is prepared.

For the filling, put the water and sugar in a pan; bring to the boil over gentle heat, stirring until the sugar has dissolved. Add the desiccated coconut, the cinnamon stick, flour and salt, and simmer until the coconut has soaked up the water. Add the lemon juice, stir for one minute, then discard the cinnamon stick. Keep the filling warm while frying the pancakes.

Heat a little vegetable oil in a small frying-pan over high heat. Ladle enough of the batter into the pan to just cover the base. Turn the pancake when the underside is dappled, and cook the other side. Keep the pancakes warm until all the batter is used up.

Divide the coconut filling between the pancakes, roll them up and serve hot or cold.

KILOCALORIES	345	SUGARS	11g
TOTAL FAT	19g	SODIUM	160mg
SATURATED FAT	10g	FIBRE	3.5g

PUMPKIN PIE

This classic American pudding has its origins in England, the recipe having been taken across the Atlantic by the Pilgrim Fathers. Pumpkin pie was served as a thanksgiving after their first successful harvest.

SERVES 6 Ⓥ

225 g/8 oz prepared shortcrust pastry (see page 199)
750 g/1½ lb pumpkin, peeled and deseeded
25 g/1 oz margarine (or butter)
2 eggs, lightly beaten
125 g/4 oz soft brown sugar
1 tsp ground ginger

½ tsp ground cinnamon
grated rind and juice of ½ lemon
125 ml/4 fl oz semi-skimmed milk
3 tbsp single cream
walnut halves (optional)

Line a deep 25 cm/10 in flan dish with the pastry. Prick it lightly and leave it to chill for half an hour. Preheat the oven to 200°C/400°F/gas 6. Line the pastry with crumpled foil or paper and baking beans and bake it blind for 10 minutes; remove the foil or paper and beans and return the case to the oven for a further 5 minutes.

Meanwhile, cut the pumpkin into 3–4 cm/1½–2 in cubes and either microwave, or steam in a steamer or colander over a pan of boiling water, covered, until quite tender (about 25 minutes).

Purée the pumpkin in a food processor or pass it through a sieve (should make about 450 ml/¾ pt of purée). Cool; then beat in the butter, eggs, sugar, spices, lemon rind and juice, and the milk and cream. Spoon the mixture into the pastry case and garnish with walnut halves if liked. Return the pie to the oven and bake for 15 minutes, then reduce the heat to 180°C/350°F/gas 4 for another 30 minutes or until the filling is set and firm to the touch.

Serve it hot or warm, accompanied, perhaps, by a jug of pouring cream, fromage frais or Greek yogurt.

KILOCALORIES	345	SUGARS	22g
TOTAL FAT	18g	SODIUM	260mg
SATURATED FAT	6g	FIBRE	2g

BANANA-CAROB FLAN

Carob powder, extracted from the locust bean, is far healthier than chocolate made from the fatty cocoa beans, and makes a passable substitute. It is used to flavour the filling in this biscuit-crumb flan.

SERVES 4–6

175 g/6 oz digestive biscuits, crushed
75 g/3 oz margarine (or butter), melted

FILLING
300 ml/½ pt semi-skimmed milk
15 g/½ oz cornflour
25 g/1 oz carob powder
50 g/2 oz Demerara sugar (or honey)
25 g/1 oz margarine (or butter)
2 tsp powdered gelatine
2 large ripe bananas, mashed
150 ml/5 fl oz Greek yogurt (or whipping cream)

Mix the biscuit crumbs with the melted margarine or butter and press the mixture over the base and up the sides of a 22.5 cm/9 in flan dish.

Mix a little cold milk with the cornflour and carob powder. Add the sugar or honey and margarine or butter. Bring the mixture to the boil, stirring constantly, and cook it over gentle heat for 3–5 minutes. Remove from the heat and allow to cool slightly.

Dissolve the gelatine in a couple of tablespoonfuls of water in a small heavy-based pan, heating it until it becomes quite clear. Stir the gelatine into the warm carob custard, then set it aside to cool. Beat the

mashed bananas and half the yogurt or cream into the cooked mixture, spoon it into the flan dish and leave it to set for a couple of hours.

Use the rest of the yogurt or cream to decorate the edges of the flan; if liked, fill the centre with banana slices.

KILOCALORIES	480	SUGARS	26g
TOTAL FAT	28g	SODIUM	470mg
SATURATED FAT	7g	FIBRE	1.5g

SAUCER PANCAKES

Foil plates are ideal for oven-baked pancakes. Good sprinkled with lemon juice, they can also be topped with fresh raspberry purée.

SERVES 6 Ⓥ

300 ml/½ pt semi-skimmed milk
1 lemon
50 g/2 oz margarine (or butter)
50 g/2 oz caster sugar
2 eggs, beaten
50 g/2 oz plain flour, sifted
150 g/6 oz raspberries, fresh or frozen (optional)

Put the milk in a small pan with strips of lemon peel; bring the milk almost to the boil, then remove it from the heat and leave to infuse until cold.

Preheat the oven to 190°C/375°F/gas 5. Cream the margarine or butter with the sugar until the mixture is light and fluffy. Add half the beaten eggs and 2 tablespoonfuls of the flour. Beat in the remaining egg with a sprinkling of flour, then fold in the rest of the flour. Gradually strain the cold lemon milk into the batter and beat again. The batter may curdle, but this will not affect the finished result.

Oil six 13 cm/5 in foil saucers and divide the mixture between them. Bake them on the middle shelf of the oven for 15–20 minutes or until they are brown and fluffy.

Slide the pancakes on to individual serving dishes and top with a squeeze of lemon juice. Alternatively, reduce the raspberries to a purée in the blender, rub them through a sieve and serve as a topping.

KILOCALORIES	135	SUGARS	4g
TOTAL FAT	9g	SODIUM	120mg
SATURATED FAT	2g	FIBRE	1g

APPLE MOUSSE WITH CIDER CREAM SAUCE

Windfall apples are excellent for making into purées to store in the freezer.

SERVES 4 (V)

750 g/1½ lb cooking apples, peeled and cored
75 g/3 oz light brown sugar
200 ml/7 fl oz medium-dry cider
2 large egg whites
50 g/2 oz caster sugar

SAUCE
25 g/1 oz caster sugar
100 ml/4 fl oz medium-dry cider
150 ml/5 fl oz whipping cream

Cut the prepared apples into chunks and put them in a large pan with the brown sugar and cider. Simmer and stir gently until the sugar has dissolved; if necessary, increase the heat until the liquid has evaporated, leaving a smooth purée. Rub this through a sieve, and leave it to cool.

Whisk the egg whites until they are firm, then gradually beat in the caster sugar to make a fairly stiff meringue. Fold the meringue into the apple purée; spoon it into individual serving dishes and chill until required.

For the sauce, blend the cream with the sugar and cider and set it over gentle heat; do not let the sauce reach boiling point. Serve the warm sauce with the cold apple mousse.

KILOCALORIES	290	SUGARS	59g
TOTAL FAT	4g	SODIUM	70mg
SATURATED FAT	2g	FIBRE	3g

LEMON AND PEACH SHERBET

This cooling, refreshing sweet not only looks attractive, but is also totally fatless – ideal for slimmers and others on low-fat diets.
See illustration page 223.

SERVES 4

1 packet lemon jelly
1 tsp lemon peel, finely grated
1 can (450 g/15½ oz) peach slices, in natural juice
2 egg whites

2–3 drops lemon juice
8 strawberries

Break the jelly into cubes, put them in a small pan with 300 ml/½ pt boiling water and melt them over minimum heat, stirring all the time. Remove the pan from the heat.

Stir the lemon peel and the juice drained from the canned peaches into the jelly. Leave it in the fridge until it is just beginning to thicken and set; at this stage it will look like unbeaten egg whites. Remove from the fridge. Whisk the egg whites and 2–3 drops of lemon juice to a stiff snow.

Whisk the jelly mixture until foamy, then beat in about one-third of the egg whites. Gently fold in the remaining whites with a metal spoon. Reserve eight peach slices for decoration and divide the rest between four sundae glasses; mound the jelly foam on top and leave the sherbets to set in the fridge.

Just before serving, decorate with the remaining peach slices and halved strawberries.

KILOCALORIES	120	SUGARS	28g
TOTAL FAT	–	SODIUM	50mg
SATURATED FAT	–	FIBRE	1g

RHUBARB AND GINGER FOOL

Rhubarb has a natural affinity with ginger, which neutralises the oxalic acid.

SERVES 4 (V)

450 g/1 lb rhubarb, trimmed weight
1 tsp powdered ginger
75 g/3 oz brown sugar
450 ml/¾ pt custard (see page 200)
4 tbsp whipping cream (or Greek yogurt)
1 piece stem ginger, thinly sliced

Cut the washed rhubarb into 2–3 cm/1–1½ in lengths and put in a pan with 3 tablespoonfuls of water. Bring to the boil over medium heat, stirring until the juices start to run and come to the boil. Lower the heat and cover the pan; simmer slowly for 5–8 minutes or until the rhubarb has reduced to a pulp, still stirring to prevent it sticking.

Add the ginger and sugar to the rhubarb and continue stirring until the sugar has melted. Remove the pan from the heat and cool the mixture slightly; stir the custard into the rhubarb, incorporating it thoroughly. Allow to cool completely before spooning it into four sundae glasses. Chill for at least 3–4 hours, and preferably overnight, in the fridge.

To serve, whisk the cream until thick and mound it over the rhubarb fool; decorate with ginger slices.

KILOCALORIES	235	SUGARS	35g
TOTAL FAT	5g	SODIUM	140mg
SATURATED FAT	3g	FIBRE	1.5g

FRUIT SOUP

Scandinavian in origin, this soup can be served as a dessert, although in its native countries it is customarily served as a first course.

See illustration page 223.

SERVES 4 (V)

40 g/1½ oz quick-cooking tapioca
1.5 litres/2½ pt water
225 g/8 oz pitted prunes, roughly chopped
2 large apples, peeled, cored and diced
150 g/5 oz mixed dried raisins, apricots, peaches and pears, roughly chopped
2 bananas, thickly sliced
125 g/4 oz sweet cherries, fresh or *canned*
juice of a lemon
225 ml/8 fl oz unsweetened orange juice
*225 ml/8 fl oz unsweetened pineapple (*or *grape) juice*

Boil the tapioca in the measured water over gentle heat until semi-cooked (about 7–8 minutes). Add the prepared fruit and the fruit juices. Continue simmering, uncovered, for another 20 minutes or until the tapioca is cooked through and transparent and the fruit soft.

Serve hot or cold, with hot cinnamon toast (see below) or with freshly baked oatcakes (see page 240).

KILOCALORIES	430	SUGARS	96g
TOTAL FAT	1g	SODIUM	40mg
SATURATED FAT	–	FIBRE	8g

Cinnamon toast Spread four slices of hot wholemeal toast with 40 g/1½ oz margarine mixed with 2–3 tablespoonfuls of ground cinnamon and the grated rind of half a lemon. Cut the toast into fingers and serve at once.

BEST SEMOLINA PUDDING

Semolina pudding is every schoolchild's nightmare, but it need not be the stodgy porridge that passed for pudding at school dinners. It is best made a day in advance to allow time for the pudding to thicken.

SERVES 6–8 (V)

75 g/3 oz semolina, white or *brown*
600 ml/1 pt semi-skimmed milk
2 eggs, separated
75 g/3 oz caster sugar
juice of a lemon
few drops vanilla essence
*4–5 tbsp Greek yogurt (*or *single cream)*

SAUCE
*450 g/1 lb blackcurrants (*or *raspberries)*
(fresh or *frozen)*

Heat the milk gently in a heavy-based saucepan until hand-warm, sprinkle in the semolina and continue cooking, stirring all the time until the mixture comes to the boil. Reduce the heat and simmer, stirring often, for 7–10 minutes or until the semolina has thickened. Remove from the heat and leave to cool.

Stir the egg yolks, sugar, lemon juice, vanilla essence and yogurt or cream into the semolina. When the mixture has cooled to luke-warm, whisk the egg whites until they are stiff and fold them in with a metal spoon. Spoon the semolina into a serving dish and leave it in the fridge for several hours or overnight to set.

For the sauce, cook the fruit in the minimum amount of water until it is soft and the juices are running or make a purée by blending the berries in the liquidiser until smooth. Press the purée through a nylon sieve to get rid of the pips.

Pour the sauce into a bowl and serve as an accompaniment to the semolina pudding.

KILOCALORIES	190	SUGARS	20g
TOTAL FAT	6g	SODIUM	100mg
SATURATED FAT	3g	FIBRE	2g

Semolina is the Italian term for the large particles of endosperm which enclose the berries of durum wheat, beneath the outer bran layer. The grains cook to the consistency of porridge.

Set the shells on a grill pan covered with kitchen foil and place under high heat for a few minutes until the sugar has melted into the yogurt; cover the leafy parts with foil to prevent them getting singed. Serve at once.

KILOCALORIES	205	SUGARS	42g
TOTAL FAT	1g	SODIUM	50mg
SATURATED FAT	–	FIBRE	3g

APRICOT CROÛTONS

The French often use sweet brioche bread for croûtons, but wholemeal bread has a crunchier texture. Ripe apricots are preferable to dried.

SERVES 6 (V)

6 thin slices wholemeal bread
50 g/2 oz margarine (or butter)
12 ripe apricots (or 24 dried apricot halves)
50 g/2 oz light brown sugar

Preheat the oven to 165°C/325°F/gas 3. Spread the bread with the margarine or butter and arrange the slices on a buttered baking sheet. Cut fresh apricots in half and remove the stones. Arrange fresh or dried apricot halves on the bread, cut sides up, four to a slice. Sprinkle the sugar evenly over the apricots, and bake the croûtons on the middle shelf of the oven for 20–25 minutes or until the bread is crisp.

Serve hot, cut into triangles or squares.

KILOCALORIES	210	SUGARS	19g
TOTAL FAT	8g	SODIUM	260mg
SATURATED FAT	2g	FIBRE	4g

QUICK BLACK CHERRY STRUDEL

Strudel pastry, like filo, is not for the tidy-minded. It takes time and practice to achieve the characteristic paper-thin and mouth-watering result, though this recipe is a short-cut version.

SERVES 6 (V)

100 g/4 oz margarine (or butter)
150 g/6 oz plain flour, sifted
40 g/1½ oz caster sugar
3–4 tbsp skimmed milk
two cans (425 g/15 oz) black cherries,
stoned and preferably unsweetened

PINEAPPLE BRÛLÉE

Pineapples are probably the most popular of all fruit imported from the Tropics; they should be bought just ripe, when a fresh leaf can be pulled from the crown — underripe fruits will not mature, even at room temperature.

SERVES 4 (V)

2 small pineapples
3 tbsp white rum (or orange juice)
4 tbsp low-fat plain yogurt
3–4 tbsp soft brown sugar
grated rind of an orange

Trim any blemished leaves from the pineapples then, using a sharp knife, cut each fruit neatly in half. Loosen the flesh inside the shells with the tip of the knife, without piercing the skins. Scoop out the flesh, discard the hard cores and cut the pineapple into small cubes. Set the shells aside. Toss the flesh in the rum or orange juice and leave it to marinate in the fridge for at least 1 hour.

Just before serving, return the flesh and the juices to the pineapple shells, spoon the yogurt on top and sprinkle with the sugar mixed with grated orange rind.

100 g/4 oz curd cheese
25 g/1 oz chopped almonds
1 small egg, beaten
melted butter
flaked almonds (optional)
icing sugar (optional)
arrowroot

Rub the margarine into the flour until the mixture has the texture of fine breadcrumbs, stir in the sugar and mix with enough milk to form a stiff dough. Leave it to rest and chill in the fridge for at least 1 hour.

Drain the cherries (save the juice for the sauce). Beat the curd cheese until quite soft, mix in the chopped almonds and egg to give a spreading consistency. Preheat the oven to 200°C/425°F/gas 7.

The difficult part is the rolling out of the pastry. Ideally, use a large tea towel, floured just enough to prevent the pastry sticking to it. Roll the pastry as thinly as possible to a large square or rectangle – it should be so thin as to be almost transparent. Spread the curd cheese mixture over the pastry, leaving a clear 5 cm/2 in space at all four edges. Arrange the cherries over the cheese and moisten the edges with a pastry brush dipped in water.

Fold in the pastry edges and begin rolling the strudel, like a Swiss roll, using the cloth to ease the pastry into a neat even-shaped parcel. Seal the join with water and carefully ease the strudel roll on to a buttered baking sheet, join underneath, curving it into a horseshoe shape.

Brush the top of the strudel with melted margarine or butter and, if liked, dot it with a few almond flakes. Bake in the centre of the oven for about 25–30 minutes

or until golden-brown. Serve warm or cold, dusted, if liked, with icing sugar and accompanied by the cherry juice thickened to a sauce with arrowroot.

KILOCALORIES	405	SUGARS	35g
TOTAL FAT	20g	SODIUM	190mg
SATURATED FAT	5g	FIBRE	2g

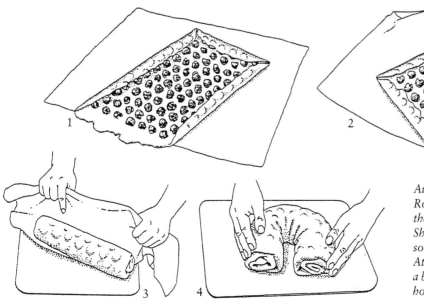

Austrian strudel pastry is difficult to handle. Roll it out on a large, floured towel, spread the filling over it and fold in the edges (1). Shape it into a roll by gently lifting the towel so that the pastry folds over on to itself (2). At the last turn, roll the strudel on to a baking sheet (3) and shape it into a horseshoe (4).

BANANA AND CAROB ICE-CREAM

Ice-cream does not necessarily have to contain milk or cream; in this recipe, bananas provide the base. For the best result, freeze ripe, peeled bananas in largish chunks and add them frozen to the liquidised mixture.

SERVES 4–6 Ⓥ

5-6 stoned dates
175 ml/6 fl oz water
pinch salt
75 g/3 oz cashew nuts (unsalted)
2 tbsp carob powder
1½ tsp vanilla essence
4 ripe bananas, frozen

Put the dates in the liquidiser, with the water, salt, cashew nuts, carob powder and vanilla. Blend until the mixture is smooth, then gradually add the bananas.

Pour the ice-cream mixture into a lidded plastic container and freeze it until solid. Thaw slightly in the fridge before serving. Alternatively, simply chill the banana mixture without freezing it and serve it as soft ice-cream.

KILOCALORIES	245	SUGARS	27g
TOTAL FAT	11g	SODIUM	230mg
SATURATED FAT	3g	FIBRE	2g

CAROB FLAN

This flan is made with wholemeal flour and polyunsaturated margarine, with a filling of cashew nuts flavoured and sweetened with dates and carob powder.

SERVES 6 Ⓥ

150 g/5 oz fine wholemeal flour
pinch salt
75 g/2½ oz white vegetable fat
4 tbsp iced water (approx)

FILLING
75 g/3 oz unsalted cashew nuts
1 tsp vanilla essence
475 ml/16 fl oz water
3–4 tbsp arrowroot
125 g/4 oz stoned dates
3 tbsp carob powder

Sift the flour and salt into a mixing bowl. Rub in the fat until the mixture has the consistency of fine breadcrumbs. Add enough iced water to form a soft dough. Wrap it in polythene and chill it in the fridge for at least 2 hours.

Preheat the oven to 220°C/425°F/gas 7. Roll out the pastry on a lightly floured surface, to a 30 cm/12 in wide circle and use it to line a 23 cm/9 in flan dish. Prick the pastry base and bake it blind for 12–15 minutes or until firm and light golden. Cool the flan case on a wire rack.

For the filling, put the cashew nuts, vanilla essence and half the water in a liquidiser and blend until smooth. Add the remaining water, the arrowroot and the dates, a few at a time. Blend for 1–2 minutes, then transfer the mixture to a pan and bring it to the boil over gentle heat, stirring until it thickens.

Remove the pan from the heat and blend in the carob powder mixed with a little water. Spoon the filling into the flan case and leave it to set in the fridge.

KILOCALORIES	340	SUGARS	8g
TOTAL FAT	19g	SODIUM	260mg
SATURATED FAT	5g	FIBRE	3g

RHUBARB ICE-CREAM WITH GINGER

Ideally, use the new season crop of deep rose-pink rhubarb, which gives this ice-cream a wonderful colour and flavour.

SERVES 4 Ⓥ

750 g/1½ lb young rhubarb
100 g/4 oz caster sugar
2 cm/1 in piece root ginger, peeled and crushed
300 ml/½ pt whipping cream

Trim, wash and cut the rhubarb into 3–4 cm/1½–2 in chunks, and put them in a stainless steel pan with the sugar and crushed ginger. Mix them thoroughly, then cover the pan and cook over fairly high heat for about 4–5 minutes. Stir from time to time to prevent the fruit sticking to the pan. Allow the rhubarb to cool before puréeing it in a food processor.

Whip the cream until stiff; fold it into the rhubarb

purée and spoon the mixture into one or two plastic containers; cover and leave to freeze. Transfer the container(s) to the fridge about 45 minutes before serving to allow the ice-cream to soften a little.

Serve topped with a little chopped stem ginger and with ginger biscuits or brandy snaps.

KILOCALORIES	390	SUGARS	30g
TOTAL FAT	30g	SODIUM	40mg
SATURATED FAT	18g	FIBRE	2.5g

EVE'S PUDDING

This is an old English recipe, traditionally made with apples, hence the name. Other fruits can replace or be mixed with apples – pears, plums and greengages.

SERVES 4 ⓥ

450 g/1 lb cooking apples (or *pears*)
50–75 g/2–3 oz soft brown sugar
2 tbsp water
100 g/4 oz margarine (or *butter*)
100 g/4 oz caster sugar
few drops almond essence
2 eggs
100 g/4 oz self-raising flour, sifted

Peel, core and slice the apples or pears (or a mixture of the two). Arrange them in layers in 1.5 litre/2½ pt buttered pie dish, sprinkling each with a little brown sugar. Add the water.

Preheat the oven to 190°C/375°F/gas 5. Cream the margarine or butter and sugar with almond essence until the mixture is light and fluffy. Beat in the eggs, one at a time, and finally fold in the flour.

Spoon this sponge mixture over the fruit and bake in the lower half of the oven for 30 minutes. Reduce the heat to 160°C/325°F/gas 3 for a further 15 minutes or until the sponge and the fruit are cooked through.

Serve hot with custard or low-fat plain yogurt.

KILOCALORIES	515	SUGARS	56g
TOTAL FAT	23g	SODIUM	330mg
SATURATED FAT	5g	FIBRE	2.5g

ⓥ This symbol denotes a recipe suitable for vegetarians.

MELON SORBET

Basically, a sorbet consists of frozen fruit juice or purée suspended in a sugar syrup. The airy texture derives from stiffly beaten egg whites.

SERVES 4 ⓥ

1 melon
2–3 knobs stem ginger, finely chopped
100 g/4 oz caster sugar
250 ml/8 fl oz water
1 tbsp ginger wine (or *Kirsch* or *white rum*)
2 egg whites

Cut the melon into quarters, scoop out the seeds and cut away the peel; dice the flesh, which should weigh approximately 450 g/1 lb. Purée the melon flesh in a liquidiser and fold in the stem ginger.

Bring the sugar and water to the boil over gentle heat; simmer for a few minutes, then add the wine, Kirsch or white rum and simmer for another minute. Set the sugar syrup aside to cool.

Beat the syrup into the melon purée and spoon the mixture into a lidded plastic container; place in the freezer until the contents are mushy and crystals have formed round the edges (about 2 hours). Scoop the melon mixture into a chilled bowl and whisk it thoroughly to break up the crystals. Fold in the stiffly beaten, dry egg whites and return the sorbet to the container; freeze for several hours until firm.

Half an hour before serving, remove the sorbet from the freezer and let it 'come to' in the fridge before scooping it into individual glasses.

KILOCALORIES	195	SUGARS	45g
TOTAL FAT	–	SODIUM	110mg
SATURATED FAT	–	FIBRE	2g

Water ices, the classic Italian *granite*, consist of simple sugar syrups flavoured with fruit-juice or coffee concentrates. They do not incorporate egg whites, and the ice crystals which form during freezing are broken down less frequently than in sorbets. This results in a more granular texture. Water ices are often served between courses as palate cleansers.

Please see the introduction for a full explanation of the nutritional factboxes.

Apple Crêpes

This easy pudding is quickly made from thin, freshly baked or freezer-stored pancakes. They should be almost transparent but do not have to be perfectly round in shape.

SERVES 4 Ⓥ

50 g/2 oz plain flour
pinch of salt
1 egg
300 ml/½ pt semi-skimmed milk
margarine (or *butter* or *vegetable oil*)
2 medium-sized cooking apples, peeled, cored and thinly sliced
2 tbsp brandy
2 tbsp caster sugar

Sift the flour and salt into a bowl, and break the egg into a well in the centre. Gradually beat in the milk until the batter is thin and smooth.

Melt a small knob of butter in a small frying-pan over high heat. Ladle in enough batter just to cover the base. Cook the pancake until the underside is dappled, then turn it and cook the other side. Continue until all the batter is used up.

Butter a baking sheet that will fit under the grill. Fold the pancakes in half and arrange them well spaced on the sheet; cover them with a single layer of apple slices. Turn the grill to high. Sprinkle brandy and caster sugar over the apples and place the baking sheet under the hot grill until the sugar caramelises, and the edges of the pancake and apple slices are beginning to catch. Keep them warm while the remaining pancakes are finished in the same way.

Serve warm with cream, low-fat plain yogurt or ice-cream.

KILOCALORIES	155	SUGARS	15g
TOTAL FAT	3g	SODIUM	170mg
SATURATED FAT	1g	FIBRE	1g

Kiwi Fruit in Wine Jelly

Imported in quantity from New Zealand, kiwi fruit used to be known as Chinese gooseberries. Egg-shaped and encased in a thin brown and hairy skin, the bright green flesh and juicy taste of kiwi fruit slightly resembles that of gooseberries. Refreshing on their own, kiwi fruit also combine well with fruit and vegetable salads; they also contain as much vitamin C as lemons (see also table opposite). They are ready for eating when just soft to the touch and will ripen at room temperature. Leaf gelatine produces a more sparkling jelly than powdered gelatine.

SERVES 4

3 kiwi fruit, peeled
10 sheets leaf gelatine (or *3 tsp powdered gelatine)*
450 ml/¾ pt medium-dry or *sweet white wine*
juice of a lime
kumquats (optional)

Soak leaf gelatine in a bowl of cold water for 15 minutes to soften it; wring it out loosely, place it in a small bowl with 3 tablespoonfuls of water and set in a pan of gently simmering water until melted. Alternatively, dissolve the powdered gelatine in 4 tablespoonfuls of hot water.

Stir the dissolved gelatine into the wine, add the strained lime juice and mix thoroughly. Pour one third of the liquid into a shallow, 23 cm (9 in) ring mould rinsed in cold water and leave in the fridge to set. Meanwhile, cut the kiwi fruit into very thin slices.

Brush half the kiwi fruit slices with a little liquid jelly and arrange them over the set jelly; carefully spoon over another third of the jelly and return the mould to the fridge. When set, repeat with the remaining fruit slices and jelly. Leave for several hours to set completely.

To serve, unmould the jelly, dipping the mould briefly in hot water and inverting it on to a serving dish. Pile small whole kumquats into the open centre and serve with a bowl of low-fat plain yogurt.

KILOCALORIES	115	SUGARS	8g
TOTAL FAT	–	SODIUM	30mg
SATURATED FAT	–	FIBRE	1g

Comparative vitamin C contents for fruit and vegetables (per 100 g/4 oz)

Guavas	230 mg
Blackcurrants	200 mg
Strawberries	77 mg
Kiwi fruit	59 mg
Lemons	58 mg
Oranges	54 mg
Limes	46 mg
Gooseberries	26 mg
Potatoes (new)	9 mg
Potatoes (old)	6 mg

MILK CHOCOLATE MOUSSE WITH CINNAMON CREAM

———— • ————

This rich, rich pudding is something to indulge in when caution is thrown to the wind.

SERVES 4 Ⓥ

125 g/4 oz milk chocolate
15 g/½ oz margarine (or butter)
4 eggs, separated
2 drops lemon juice (or vinegar)
2 tbsp Greek yogurt
2 tbsp double cream
2 tsp Demerara sugar
cinnamon

Break up the chocolate and put it with the margarine or butter into a basin set over a pan of hot water; stir occasionally until the chocolate has melted. Add the egg yolks, one by one, and mix thoroughly with the chocolate mixture.

Whisk the egg whites with the lemon juice or vinegar until they form a snow. Beat about one third into the chocolate mixture, then lightly fold in the remainder with a metal spoon. Divide the mousse between four sundae glasses and chill for at least 4 hours.

Whip the cream until thick; stir in the Demerara sugar, and heap the cream up on top of the mousse. Sprinkle lightly with cinnamon and serve.

KILOCALORIES	375	SUGARS	22g
TOTAL FAT	28g	SODIUM	160mg
SATURATED FAT	14g	FIBRE	–

DUTCH APPLE PUDDING

———— • ————

Many Dutch desserts, cakes and teabreads are characterised by spices, nuts and raisins, a legacy from the spice trading days with the East Indies.

SERVES 4–6 Ⓥ

450 g/1 lb cooking apples, peeled, cored and diced
1 egg, beaten
50–75 g/2–3 oz caster sugar
50 g/2 oz plain flour
1 tsp baking powder
¼ tsp ground cinnamon
¼ tsp salt
25–50 g/1–2 oz chopped walnuts

Preheat the oven to 180°C/350°F/gas 4. Mix the apples with the beaten egg and the sugar. Sift the flour, baking powder, cinnamon and salt together, and fold with the nuts into the apple mixture. Spoon the mixture into a shallow, greased ovenproof dish, about 20 cm/8 in in diameter, and bake in the oven for 25 minutes or until the pudding is well risen.

Serve the pudding hot with ice-cream or Greek yogurt.

KILOCALORIES	210	SUGARS	24g
TOTAL FAT	8g	SODIUM	20mg
SATURATED FAT	1g	FIBRE	2g

YOGURT CAKE

———— • ————

Yogurt stabilised with bicarbonate of soda gives a light and fluffy texture to this wholemeal dessert cake. It is best served and eaten on the day of baking.

SERVES 6 Ⓥ

275 g/10 oz plain wholemeal flour
3 tsp baking powder
4 eggs, separated
225 g/8 oz molasses sugar
100 g/4 oz margarine (or butter), melted
pinch of bicarbonate of soda
225 ml/8 fl oz low-fat plain yogurt
2 tbsp honey
cinnamon
50 g/2 oz flaked almonds, toasted

Preheat the oven to 190°C/375°F/gas 5. Sift the flour and baking powder together. Whisk the egg yolks until thick and creamy. Fold in the sugar and butter and again whisk thoroughly, then fold in the flour. Mix the bicarbonate of soda with the yogurt and fold it into the mixture. Finally, whisk the egg whites until they are just stiff and fold them in with a metal spoon.

Spoon the mixture into a well-greased shallow cake tin about 28 × 18 cm/11 × 7 in and bake for 35 minutes or until it is golden-brown. Leave the cake to cool in the tin. Transfer it to a serving plate, spread the honey on top and sprinkle with cinnamon and almonds. Serve the cake cut into slices.

KILOCALORIES	545	SUGARS	11g
TOTAL FAT	23g	SODIUM	250mg
SATURATED FAT	5g	FIBRE	5g

CIDER SYLLABUB

— · —

An old English dessert, at its best made a day in advance to give the flavours time to mature. Fairly rich, it is suitable after a light main course.

SERVES 4 Ⓥ

150 ml/¼ pt medium-sweet cider
2 tsp lemon peel, finely grated
2 tbsp lemon juice
75g /3 oz caster sugar
150 ml/¼ pt double cream, chilled
150 ml/¼ pt Greek yogurt, chilled

Pour the cider into a bowl and add the lemon peel and juice, then stir in the sugar until it has dissolved. Cover the bowl and leave the cider to infuse at room temperature for about 3 hours.

Stir the Greek yogurt and cream into the cider and whisk the mixture until it is thick and forms soft peaks. Spoon the syllabub into four stemmed glasses and chill for at least 8 hours.

Serve the syllabub on its own or accompanied by crisp brandy or ginger snaps.

KILOCALORIES	300	SUGARS	23g
TOTAL FAT	21g	SODIUM	40mg
SATURATED FAT	13g	FIBRE	–

BREAD-AND-BUTTER PUDDING

— · —

This popular nursery pudding is often made with slices of buttered white bread, but a thinly sliced currant loaf or leftover currant buns or brioches give additional flavour and need little butter. It makes all the difference if the pudding can stand for at least 1 hour while the custard soaks into the bread before baking.

SERVES 4 Ⓥ

1 small fruit loaf, thinly sliced
25 g/1 oz margarine (or *butter*)
25 g/1 oz currants (or *dried peel* or
a mixture of the two)
4 small eggs
600 ml/1 pt semi-skimmed milk
nutmeg (or *cinnamon*)

Butter a 1 litre/1½ pt ovenproof pie dish and fill it with alternate layers of fruit loaf and dried fruit; butter

the bread for the top layer and arrange it buttered side up. Beat the eggs thoroughly and warm the milk slightly, then beat the eggs into the milk, season to taste with nutmeg or cinnamon and pour the custard over the bread. Leave the pudding to soak for at least an hour.

Preheat the oven to 180°C/350°F/gas 4, with a roasting tin half filled with water set on the middle shelf. Place the pie dish in the tin and bake for about 50 minutes or until the custard is set and golden-brown. Serve at once.

KILOCALORIES	315	SUGARS	19g
TOTAL FAT	14g	SODIUM	320mg
SATURATED FAT	4g	FIBRE	–

FRUIT CHEESECAKE

— · —

This cheesecake is based on low-calorie cottage cheese and agar-agar.

SERVES 6

1 litre/1¾ pt pineapple juice
2½ tbsp agar-agar flakes (see glossary)
2 tbsp powdered gelatine
4–5 bananas, sliced
175 g/6 oz low-calorie cottage cheese (or *quark*)
175 ml/6 fl oz skimmed milk
125 g/4 oz strawberries, sliced

Bring 700 ml/1¼ pt of the pineapple juice to the boil. Add the agar-agar flakes and stir until they have dissolved, then stir in the powdered gelatine and set the mixture aside. Put the bananas and the remaining pineapple juice in a liquidiser and blend until creamy; fold them into the gelatine mixture.

Liquidise the cottage cheese or quark with the milk until it has the texture of whipped cream; fold it into the half-set banana mixture and add the strawberries. Spoon the cheesecake into a 23 cm/9 in china flan dish, first rinsed with cold water, and leave it to set and chill in the fridge.

Serve the cheesecake cut into portions.

KILOCALORIES	450	SUGARS	102g
TOTAL FAT	1g	SODIUM	150mg
SATURATED FAT	–	FIBRE	1g

STRAWBERRY CHEESECAKE
— • —

This simple cheesecake is suitable for freezing, without the decoration of whole strawberries or small chunks of fresh pineapple and angelica or sprigs of mint.

SERVES 8–10

225 g/8 oz digestive biscuits
100g /4 oz margarine (or butter), melted
50 g/2 oz sugar (optional)

FILLING
½ lemon jelly block
225 g/8 oz cream cheese
150 ml/5 fl oz fromage frais
juice and rind of a lemon
strawberries for decoration

Preheat the oven to 190°C/375°F/gas 5. Crush the biscuits to fine crumbs, and mix them thoroughly with the butter and sugar in a bowl. Line a 25 cm/10 in loose-bottomed cake tin, or a flan dish, with the crumb mixture, pressing it down firmly and raising it slightly round the sides. Bake the biscuit crust in the centre of the oven for 12 minutes, then leave it to cool.

For the filling, dissolve the jelly tablets in 150 ml/5 fl oz of hot water. Leave it to cool and meanwhile cream the cheese until smooth and lightly whip the fromage frais. As the jelly reaches setting point, fold in the cream cheese, fromage frais and the lemon rind and juice. Spoon the filling into the baked crumb case and place in the fridge for 1–2 hours to set.

Decorate the cheesecake with whole or halved strawberries, complete with hulls for a pretty effect.

Half the quantity of biscuit crust can also be used for individual cheesecakes, pressed into eight to ten patty tins. Allow them to cool after baking before setting them in paper cases and filling them with the cheese mixture.

KILOCALORIES	370	SUGARS	15g
TOTAL FAT	27g	SODIUM	320mg
SATURATED FAT	10g	FIBRE	1g

Honey Most honeys are pure, but some varieties are blends. During storage, honey granulates easily, but becomes runny again if the jar is stood in a pan of water over gentle heat.

APRICOT WHIP
— • —

Easily made, this airy whip is suitable for a dinner party, to follow a substantial main course.

SERVES 4–6 Ⓥ

125 g/4 oz dried apricots
2 tbsp honey
125 ml/4 fl oz Greek yogurt
125 ml/4 fl oz whipping cream
¼ tsp vanilla essence
175 g/6 oz stoned dates, chopped
125 g/4 oz chopped hazelnuts

Put the apricots and honey in a pan with just enough water to cover them. Bring gently to the boil and simmer, uncovered, for 10–20 minutes. Drain the apricots and leave them to cool for a few minutes before chopping them finely.

Whip the cream, if used, with the vanilla; fold in the apricots and dates, and most of the hazelnuts into the yogurt and/or cream mixture. Spoon into four individual sundae glasses and chill for at least 1 hour.

Just before serving, sprinkle the remaining hazelnuts on top.

KILOCALORIES	400	SUGARS	32g
TOTAL FAT	28g	SODIUM	50mg
SATURATED FAT	8g	FIBRE	4g

Right *In the foreground is apricot whip, at the back fruit soup and lemon and peach sherbet.*

BAKING

Soft white bread was for centuries regarded as the prerogative of the well-to-do, while for the lower classes the daily bread was dark in colour and coarse in texture. Nowadays, wholemeal bread is recommended by nutritionists and it is the fibre content of the wholemeal bread which makes it preferable to white, for although the milling process in the case of white flour removes the outer bran layer and the wheatgerm, these must by law be added to the milled flour.

In protein and fat content there is barely any difference between white, wheatmeal and wholemeal, but the amounts of dietary fibre in wholemeal bread exceed those of white bread, with wheatmeal falling between the two.

Most bread goes stale or mouldy within five to seven days – home-made more quickly still. In general, store bread in loosely wrapped polythene at room temperature. Don't store bread in the fridge; the best place is in the freezer, where baked loaves will keep for up to four weeks.

FLOUR

For all baking purposes wheat flour is used (sometimes in conjunction with rye and oatmeal for additional flavour).

Wholemeal flour This is obtained from wholemeal grains with nothing added or removed. It has a high proportion of bran, is therefore difficult to aerate and produces a close-textured bread which rises little.

Wheatmeal flour This is unbleached and is the best for pastry and cake-making. It can be used for bread-making if the flour is milled from strong wheat and not soft.

Granary flour Granary is wheatmeal with the addition of malted barley, wheat or rye flakes to give extra flavour and nutty texture.

White flour This is available as plain (ordinary), strong (or bread) and self-raising flour. Plain is milled from soft wheat; it holds air well from the creaming of fat and the beating of eggs and is best for cake-making and for biscuits, which require a short texture. Strong white flour is the traditional flour for bread-making; it is milled from hard (usually durum wheat) and soft wheat. Self-raising flour is milled white flour with the addition of raising agents of cream of tartar and bicarbonate of soda.

RAISING AGENTS

Yeast is composed of microscopic living organisms which ferment and expand upon exposure to warm liquids and to the sugary starches present in flour. Fresh baker's yeast is available from health-food shops and bakers; it should be putty-coloured and firm. Store, covered, in the fridge for up to two weeks. It should be allowed to 'come to' and be steeped in tepid water before use. Dried yeast should be used according to packet instructions.

Test a rising dough by pressing it with a finger; if the dent springs back after the touch, the rising procedure is incomplete. Kneading dough can be done by hand or with an electric mixer or food processor. Proving, also known as the second rising, is where the dough is kneaded for a second time after the initial rising to knock out any air bubbles and to ensure an even texture. Shape the dough, place the loaves on baking trays and leave in a warm place till doubled in size.

Baking powders, which are used in the raising of cakes and biscuits, contain bicarbonate of soda, a substance that reacts with cream of tartar to release effervescent gases which cause the cake mixture to rise when exposed to oven temperatures.

FATS

Fat, in the form of lard, white vegetable fat, oil, butter or margarine, is sometimes added to enrich yeast doughs.

Butter and polyunsaturated margarine have similar calorific contents (around 740 calories per 100 g) and amounts of fat (80 g per 100 g weight); however, polyunsaturated margarine has only 20 g of saturated fat compared with 55 g present in butter.

CAKES

Few of us now eat cakes every day, though they are undoubtedly a treat when we do indulge. And the damage can be mitigated if they are not filled or topped with cream, chocolate, icing, candied or glacé fruit. Instead, try using thick yogurt or low-fat soft cheese flavoured with lemon or orange rind, or substitute puréed fruit for jam. Cocoa powder has fewer calories than drinking chocolate or chocolate.

Wholewheat flour can replace some of the white flour to increase fibre and improve flavour – a little extra liquid will be required. Cakes can be tested to see if they are ready by inserting a skewer into them; if it comes away clean, not sticky, the cake is ready.

COFFEE LOAF

— • —

This cross between a cake and a teabread may be served sliced, plain or buttered.

MAKES A 900 g/2 lb LOAF (V)

225 g/8 oz self-raising flour
100 g/4 oz margarine (or butter or white vegetable fat)
100 g/4 oz soft brown sugar (or Demerara sugar)
100 g/4 oz currants
25 g/1 oz cut mixed peel
50 g/2 oz shelled pecans (or walnuts), chopped
2 eggs, beaten
2 tbsp coffee essence (or strong black coffee)
3–4 tbsp semi-skimmed (or skimmed) milk

Preheat the oven to 180°C/350°F/gas 4. Grease and line a 900 g/2 lb loaf tin with buttered greaseproof paper. Sift the flour into a bowl and rub in the fat until the mixture resembles fine breadcrumbs. Stir in the sugar, currants, peel and pecans or walnuts, then add the eggs, coffee essence and sufficient milk to give a soft dropping consistency.

Spoon the mixture into the tin, level the top and bake in the centre of the oven for 1–1¼ hours or until well risen. If the top browns too quickly, cover it with a sheet of greaseproof paper.

Cool the loaf on a wire rack.

[Nutritional values are per slice; roughly 25 slices per loaf.]

KILOCALORIES	110	SUGARS	8g
TOTAL FAT	5g	SODIUM	80mg
SATURATED FAT	1g	FIBRE	0.5g

FRUITY TEA RING

— • —

This yeasted pastry bread, richly flavoured with spices and currants, can be served without butter or margarine.

MAKES 1 RING (V)

225 g/8 oz strong plain white flour
1 tsp caster sugar
15 g/½ oz fresh yeast (or 1 tbsp dried yeast)
100 ml/4 fl oz warm semi-skimmed (or skimmed) milk
pinch salt
50 g/2 oz margarine (or butter or white vegetable fat)
½ beaten egg
75 g/3 oz soft brown sugar (light or dark)
2 tsp ground mixed spice (or 1½ tsp ground ginger)
100 g/4 oz currants

Put 65 g/2½ oz of the flour and the sugar in a large bowl with the fresh or dried yeast and the milk. Mix lightly and leave for about 20 minutes or until frothy. Sift the remaining flour with the salt and rub in half the fat. Add the egg, and the flour mixture, to the yeast batter and mix to a fairly soft dough.

Turn out on a lightly floured surface and knead until smooth and even, about 10 minutes by hand or 3–4 minutes in an electric mixer. Shape into a ball, place in a large, lightly oiled polythene bag and leave to rise in a warm place for about 1 hour or until doubled in size. Knock the dough back and knead it for about 2 minutes, until smooth and elastic.

Roll the dough out to an oblong about 30 × 23 cm/12 × 9 in. Melt the remaining fat and brush it all over the dough; sprinkle it with the brown sugar, the spice and the currants. Starting from the long edge roll the dough up like a Swiss roll and shape it into a ring, sealing the ends together; place the ring on a greased baking sheet. Using a pair of well-oiled scissors, cut triangular slashes about two-thirds of the way through the dough at 2.5 cm/1 in intervals. Carefully fold the tips of the cuts slightly up and backwards.

Preheat the oven to 190°C/375°F/gas 5. Cover the ring lightly with oiled polythene and leave it in a warm place for about 30 minutes or until well risen. Bake the ring in the centre of the oven for 25–35 minutes or until well risen and golden brown. Remove the ring to a wire rack and leave to cool.

[Nutritional values are per slice; roughly 13 slices per ring.]

KILOCALORIES	145	SUGARS	12g
TOTAL FAT	4g	SODIUM	70mg
SATURATED FAT	1g	FIBRE	0.5g

HONEY BUNS

—— • ——

These spongy buns can be baked in advance and stored for about 1 week in an airtight container.

MAKES 12 Ⓥ

50 g/2 oz margarine (or butter)
50 g/2 oz white vegetable fat
75 g/3 oz light soft brown sugar
1 large egg, beaten
2 tbsp clear honey
175 g/7 oz plain flour
½ tsp bicarbonate of soda

Cream the fats together until well blended, then beat in the sugar until the mixture is fluffy; beat in the egg and clear honey. Sift the flour and bicarbonate of soda together and work this into the mixture. Cover and chill it until firm.

Preheat the oven to 180°C/350°F/gas 4. Roll the dough into balls about the size of a walnut and set them well apart on greased baking sheets. Bake in the oven for about 12 minutes or until the buns are well-risen. Leave them to cool on a wire rack.

KILOCALORIES	155	SUGARS	10g
TOTAL FAT	7g	SODIUM	80mg
SATURATED FAT	2g	FIBRE	0.5g

CIDERED TEABREAD

—— • ——

A cut-and-come-again fruity teabread which remains moist for several days.

MAKES A 900 g/2 lb LOAF Ⓥ

350 g/12 oz mixed dried fruits (raisins, dates, figs, sultanas, mixed peel)
300 ml/½ pt medium-sweet cider
275 g/10 oz self-raising flour
50 g/2 oz walnuts, chopped
175 g/6 oz soft light brown sugar
grated rind of 1 orange
2 large eggs, beaten

Chop the dried fruit and leave to soak in cider for at least 3 hours, preferably overnight. Grease and line a 900 g/2 lb loaf tin with buttered greaseproof paper.

Sift the flour into a bowl and mix in the walnuts, sugar and orange rind. Add the cidered fruit mixture and the eggs and mix thoroughly. Preheat the oven to

160°C/325°F/gas 3. Spoon the mixture into the prepared tin and bake in the centre of the oven for 1½–1¾ hours or until the teabread is well risen and golden-brown. Leave to cool on a wire rack.

[Nutritional values are per slice; roughly 26 slices per loaf.]

KILOCALORIES	125	SUGARS	17g
TOTAL FAT	2g	SODIUM	60mg
SATURATED FAT	–	FIBRE	1g

WHOLEMEAL MUFFINS

—— • ——

English muffins are yeast-raised and baked on a kind of griddle plate. American muffins, raised with baking powder, are quicker to make; they are excellent for freezing.

See illustration page 235.

MAKES 18 Ⓥ

275 g/10 oz wholemeal flour
2 tsp baking powder
2 tsp bicarbonate of soda
50 g/2 oz soft brown sugar
pinch salt
150 ml/5 fl oz semi-skimmed (or skimmed) milk
2 eggs, beaten
150 ml/5 fl oz vegetable oil

Preheat the oven to 200°C/400°F/gas 6. Put the flour in a bowl and sift in the baking powder, bicarbonate of soda, sugar and salt. Mix well. Blend the ~~treacle with the~~ milk ~~and add it~~, add with the eggs and oil, to the dry ingredients. Beat thoroughly.

Spoon the mixture into greased bun tins, to just below the rims, and bake the muffins in the centre of the oven for about 15 minutes or until well risen.

Cool on a wire rack and eat on the same day.

KILOCALORIES	150	SUGARS	5g
TOTAL FAT	9g	SODIUM	40mg
SATURATED FAT	–	FIBRE	1.5g

Right *(top right) Two savoury loaves, white with yeast extract and wholemeal with herbs, behind a crown-shaped milk loaf and soft bran baps. In the centre, a crusty wholemeal loaf next to granary twists and rolls; and in the foreground, pitta and glazed rye bread.*

WHOLEMEAL BREAD

—— • ——

This can be made with any of the plain brown bread flours, such as wholemeal, wholewheat and stone-ground. For a lighter loaf, replace one-third of the brown flour with strong white bread flour.

See illustration page 227.

MAKES A 900 g/2 lb LOAF (V)

675 g/1½ lb wholemeal (or wholewheat or other plain brown) flour
1½ tsp salt
1 tbsp caster sugar (optional)
25 g/1 oz white vegetable fat (or margarine)
25 g/1 oz fresh yeast (or 1 tbsp dried yeast, plus 1 tsp caster sugar)
450 ml/¾ pt warm water (approx)

Put the flour in a bowl, mix in the salt and sugar (if used) and rub in the fat. Blend the fresh yeast with all the water; if dried yeast is used, dissolve the sugar in the water, sprinkle the yeast on top and leave it in a warm place until frothy (about 10 minutes). Add the yeast to the dry ingredients and mix to a pliable dough which leaves the sides of the bowl clean; if necessary, add a little more water.

Turn out on a lightly floured surface and knead until smooth (about 10 minutes by hand or 3–4 minutes in an electric mixer fitted with a dough hook). Shape into a ball, place in a lightly oiled polythene bag and leave to rise in a warm place for about 1–1½ hours until doubled in size.

Remove the dough from the bag, knock it back to remove the air bubbles and knead it until smooth and even again (about 2 minutes). For a large loaf, knead and stretch the dough to an oblong shape the same width as the tin and three times as long; fold it into three, with the join underneath, and tuck in the ends. Smooth the top and place the dough in a well-greased 900 g/2 lb loaf tin.

Alternatively, divide the dough into two equal halves and shape to fit two greased 450 g/1 lb loaf tins. For cob loaves, shape the dough into two round balls, place them on greased baking sheets and flatten the tops slightly. Coburgs are made as cobs, but with a deep cross slashed in the top. For a bloomer, shape all or half the dough to an evenly thick baton by rolling the dough backwards and forwards with the palms of both hands. Tuck the ends underneath and place the loaf on a greased baking sheet. After the dough has proven, cut diagonal slashes along the top of the loaf.

Cover the tins or baking sheets with lightly oiled polythene and put them to rise in a warm place until the dough reaches the top of the tins or the loaves have doubled in size. Preheat the oven to 230°C/450°F/gas 8. Remove the polythene and either leave the loaves plain or brush them with lightly salted water for extra crispnes or with plain water and sprinkle with poppy seeds oatmeal or cracked wheat.

Bake in the centre of the oven, 30–40 minutes for loaves in tins, a little less for those on baking sheets. Cool on wire racks.

[Nutritional values are per slice; roughly 25 slices per loaf.]

KILOCALORIES	95	SUGARS	1g
TOTAL FAT	1g	SODIUM	130mg
SATURATED FAT	–	FIBRE	2.5g

RYE BREAD

—— • ——

This coarse-textured loaf is made with a sour dough to start the fermentation process. The 'starter' needs at least 24 hours before the bread can actually be made. The characteristic nutty texture comes from a proportion of coarse rye flour; if this is difficult to obtain, use rye flakes and grind them coarsely in a liquidiser.

See illustration page 227.

MAKES 2 (V)

STARTER DOUGH
150 g/5 oz coarse rye flour
150 g/5 oz fine rye flour
1 tsp caster sugar
300 ml/½ pt soured milk (or fresh semi-skimmed milk soured with 1 tbsp lemon juice)

SECOND DOUGH
125 ml/scant 5 fl oz warm water
1 tbsp black treacle
25 g/1 oz fresh yeast (or 1 tbsp dried yeast, plus 1 tsp caster sugar)
300 g/10 oz strong white flour
1½ tsp salt

GLAZE
2 tsp cornflour
100 ml/4 fl oz water (approx)

For the sour-dough starter mix the rye flours and sugar with the soured milk in a large bowl, cover and leave at room temperature for about 24 hours or until the dough is bubbling.

Blend the water with the treacle, crumble the fresh yeast into this mixture or sprinkle it with the dried yeast and sugar, together with 2 level tablespoonfuls of the white flour. Leave the mixture in a warm place for 10–20 minutes or until frothy. Sift the remaining white flour and salt and work it into the yeast batter, together with the starter dough. Mix to a firm, slightly sticky dough.

Turn the dough out on a floured surface and knead it until smooth and firm. Shape into a ball, place this in an oiled polythene bag and leave it to rise in a warm place for 1–1½ hours or until doubled in size. Knock the dough back and knead it again on a floured surface until smooth. Divide the dough into two, shaping them into batons or coburgs. Place them on greased baking sheets, cover with oiled polythene and leave until doubled in size. Heat the oven to 230°C/450°F/gas 8.

Meanwhile, make the glaze by blending the cornflour with the water and bringing it slowly to the boil, stirring continuously until the mixture has thickened and become opaque; leave to cool. Remove the polythene from the loaves and brush the tops with the glaze. Reduce the oven temperature to 200°C/400°F/gas 6, place the loaves in position immediately and bake for 30 minutes. Reduce the temperature to 150°C/300°F/gas 2, brush the loaves with more glaze and return them to the oven for 30 minutes. Glaze once more and bake for 2–3 minutes.

Cool on a wire rack.

[Nutritional values are per slice; roughly 12 slices per loaf.]

KILOCALORIES	200	SUGARS	4g
TOTAL FAT	1g	SODIUM	260mg
SATURATED FAT	–	FIBRE	4g

SAVOURY BREADS

For these loaves, the dough is rolled round a savoury filling which shows in an attractive pinwheel effect when the bread is sliced.

See illustration page 227.

MAKES 2 450 g/1 lb LOAVES Ⓥ

675 g/1½ lb strong white flour
2 tsp salt
15 g/½ oz white vegetable fat
15 g/½ oz fresh yeast (or 1 tbsp dried yeast,
plus 1 tsp caster sugar)
450 ml/¾ pt warm water (approx)

Sift the flour and salt into a bowl and rub in the fat. Cream fresh yeast with the water; if using dried yeast,

dissolve the sugar in the water, sprinkle the yeast on top and leave it in a warm place for about 10 minutes or until frothy. Add the yeast liquid to the dry ingredients and mix to a firm dough. Add a little extra flour if necessary, until the dough leaves the sides of the bowl clean.

Turn out on a floured surface and knead until smooth and elastic (about 10 minutes by hand or 3–4 minutes in an electric mixer). Shape into a ball, place it in a lightly oiled polythene bag and leave it to rise in a warm place for about an hour or until doubled in size.

Grease two 450 g/1 lb loaf tins. Cut the dough in half, knock it back and knead it for 2 minutes, then roll it out on a floured surface to a rectangle about 1 cm/½ in thick and as wide as the tin. Spread the dough with one of the fillings below, leaving a 2.5 cm/1 in plain margin all around. Beginning at the narrow end, roll the dough up loosely like a Swiss roll; place it in the tin. Smooth the top, cover the tin lightly with oiled polythene and leave the loaf to rise in a warm place until the dough reaches the top of the tin and springs back when lightly pressed. Preheat the oven to 230°C/450°F/gas 8. Bake in the oven for 25–30 minutes or until well browned and the base of the loaf sounds hollow when tapped.

Cool on a wire rack and eat fresh on the day of baking.

Fillings
Herbs Cream 50 g/2 oz butter or margarine with a good pinch of salt and pepper, ½–1 crushed garlic clove (optional), 3–4 tablespoonfuls of chopped fresh herbs. (110 calories a slice.)
Yeast extract Spread 2 tablespoonfuls of yeast extract over the dough. (100 calories a slice.)
Garlic Cream 75 g/3 oz butter or margarine with salt, pepper, grated rind of ½ lemon and 4 crushed garlic cloves. (120 calories a slice.)
Parmesan Cream 75 g/3 oz butter or margarine with salt, pepper, a good pinch of cayenne pepper, 2 teaspoonfuls of made mustard and 2 tablespoonfuls of grated Parmesan cheese. (100 calories a slice.)
Curry Cream 75 g/3 oz butter or margarine with 2 tablespoonfuls of grated raw onion, salt, pepper and 1–2 tablespoonfuls of curry powder. (115 calories a slice.)

[Nutritional values are per slice; roughly 13 slices per loaf.]

KILOCALORIES	95	SUGARS	1g
TOTAL FAT	1g	SODIUM	160mg
SATURATED FAT	–	FIBRE	1g

OATY DROP SCONES

Drop scones, known as pancakes in Scotland and pikelets in Wales, are traditionally cooked on a griddle. In these scones, oatmeal gives a different texture and black treacle extra flavour.
See illustration page 235.

MAKES 12–15 Ⓥ

50 g/2 oz self-raising flour
1½ tsp baking powder
pinch salt
50 g/2 oz fine oatmeal
1 tbsp Demerara (or soft brown) sugar
25 g/1 oz margarine (or butter or white vegetable fat)
1 tbsp black treacle (optional)
1 egg, beaten
125 ml/scant ¼ pt semi-skimmed (or skimmed) milk
vegetable oil for greasing griddle

Sift the flour, baking powder and salt into a bowl and stir in the oatmeal and sugar. Melt the fat and black treacle in a small pan, cool slightly before stirring it into the dry ingredients, with the egg and a little of the milk. Beat the mixture until smooth, gradually adding the rest of the milk.

Grease a griddle or large heavy-based frying-pan and heat until the fat gives off a faint blue haze; wipe off any excess fat. Drop tablespoonfuls of the batter on to the hot griddle and cook them gently for about 3 minutes on each side or until browned.

Keep warm, wrapped in a cloth, while cooking the remainder of the batter. Serve warm or cold, spread with butter and a preserve, if liked.

KILOCALORIES	85	SUGARS	3g
TOTAL FAT	5g	SODIUM	70mg
SATURATED FAT	1g	FIBRE	0.5g

GRANARY TWISTS

Granary flour is composed of malted wheat, rye flour and whole or cracked wheat grains. Use all granary flour or one-third strong white and two-thirds granary flour.
See illustration page 227.

MAKES 2 LARGE TWISTS Ⓥ

650 g/1½ lb granary bread flour
1 tsp salt

1 tsp caster sugar (optional)
25 g/1 oz white vegetable fat
25 g/1 oz fresh yeast (or 1 tbsp dried yeast,
plus 1 tsp caster sugar)
450 ml/¾ pt warm water (approx)

Put the granary flour in a bowl (if using part white flour, sift this and mix the two together), add the salt (and sugar) and rub in the fat. Cream the fresh yeast with the water; if using dried yeast, dissolve the sugar in the water, sprinkle the yeast on top and leave in a warm place for about 10 minutes until frothy. Mix the yeast with the dry ingredients to a firm dough.

Turn the dough out on a lightly floured surface and knead it until smooth and even – about 10 minutes by hand or 3–4 minutes in an electric mixer. Shape the dough into a ball, place it in a lightly greased polythene bag and leave it to rise in a warm place for about 1 hour or until the dough has doubled in size and springs back when lightly pressed. Knock the dough back, knead it for about 2 minutes or until smooth.

For large twists, divide the dough into two or three pieces and cut each of these in half; roll them into sausage shapes about 40 cm/16 in long. Pinch the ends of two dough sausages and twist and plait them round each other, pinching them together at the end. Place on greased baking sheets, cover with oiled polythene and leave them to rise in a warm place until doubled in size. Preheat the oven to 230°C/450°F/gas 8. Brush the tops of the loaves with milk if liked and bake for 20–25 minutes. Cool on wire racks.

Variation The dough can be used for ordinary or twisted rolls. Divide it into about 14 equal pieces and shape these either into plain rolls, or into twists as described above, rolling the sausages to a length of 20 cm/8 in. Bake for 15 minutes or until brown.

[Nutritional values are per large slice; roughly 8–10 slices per twist.]

KILOCALORIES	150	SUGARS	1g
TOTAL FAT	2g	SODIUM	140mg
SATURATED FAT	–	FIBRE	3g

SWEET SCONES

This traditional teabread appears in many forms, made variously with self-raising or plain flour (and baking powder), plain or flavoured with cheese, sweet spices, nuts, honey or sultanas. For savoury scones omit the sugar and sultanas and add herbs, yeast extract or grated low-fat cheese instead.

MAKES 10–12 Ⓥ

225 g/8 oz self-raising flour
pinch salt
75 g/3 oz margarine (or butter)
1½ tbsp caster sugar
40 g/1½ oz sultanas
1 small egg, beaten
65 ml/2½ fl oz buttermilk (or
low-fat plain yogurt)

Sift the flour and salt into a bowl, add the margarine, cut into small pieces, and rub it in until the mixture resembles fine breadcrumbs. Stir in the sugar and sultanas, add the egg and gradually enough of the liquid to give a smooth and firm dough which leaves the sides of the bowl clean.

Turn the dough out on to a lightly floured surface; shape and pat it flat rather than rolling it, to a thickness of 1–1.5 cm/½–¾ in. Preheat the oven to 220°C/425°F/gas 7–8.

Cut into 10–12 diamond shapes and lift them on to a greased baking sheet. The tops can be left plain or lightly brushed with milk or beaten egg. Bake in the centre of the oven for 10–12 minutes.

Cool on a wire rack; eat on the day of baking.

KILOCALORIES	145	SUGARS	5g
TOTAL FAT	6g	SODIUM	180mg
SATURATED FAT	1g	FIBRE	0.5g

PRUNE AND BRAN TEABREAD

Although a proprietary bran breakfast cereal can be used for this fibre-rich teabread, natural bran is preferable. Use pre-soaked prunes.

See illustration page 235.

MAKES A 450 g/1 lb LOAF Ⓥ

225 g/8 oz pitted prunes (or 175 g/6 oz stoned prunes)
75 g/3 oz natural bran
200 g/7 oz light soft brown sugar
300 ml/½ pt semi-skimmed (or skimmed) milk
175 g/6 oz self-raising flour
1 tsp baking powder
1 large egg, beaten

Stone the prunes if necessary, chop the flesh and put it in a bowl with the bran, sugar and milk. Mix well and leave to stand for at least 8 hours.

Sift the flour and baking powder together and add this, with the egg, to the prune mixture; blend thoroughly. Preheat the oven to 180°C/350°F/gas 4. Grease and line a 450 g/1 lb loaf tin with oiled greaseproof paper. Turn the dough into the tin and bake in the centre of the oven for 1¼–1½ hours or until well risen and firm to the touch.

Cool the bread on a wire rack before storing it, wrapped in foil.

[Nutritional values are per slice; roughly 13 slices per loaf.]

KILOCALORIES	160	SUGARS	25g
TOTAL FAT	1g	SODIUM	70mg
SATURATED FAT	–	FIBRE	3.5g

FIG TEABREAD

This teabread is reminiscent of the traditional parkins which were a strong feature of North England baking.

MAKES A 450 g/1 lb LOAF Ⓥ

225 g/8 oz plain flour
1 tsp baking powder
100 g/4 oz margarine (or butter or white vegetable fat)
100 g/4 oz dark soft brown sugar
100 g/4 oz figs, chopped
grated rind of a lemon
1 tsp bicarbonate of soda
6 tbsp semi-skimmed milk (approx)

Grease and line a 450 g/1 lb loaf tin or a 13–15 cm/5–6 in square cake tin with oiled greaseproof paper. Sift the flour and baking powder into a bowl, rub in the fat until the mixture resembles fine breadcrumbs. Stir in the sugar, figs and lemon rind until evenly blended. Dissolve the bicarbonate in 2 tablespoonfuls of the milk and add to the dry ingredients with sufficient extra milk to give a stiff dropping consistency.

Preheat the oven to 180°C/350°F/gas 4. Spoon the mixture into the tin and bake in the centre of the oven for 50–60 minutes or until the bread has risen and is just firm to the touch. Cool on a wire rack.

[Nutritional values are per slice; roughly 13 slices per loaf.]

KILOCALORIES	165	SUGARS	13g
TOTAL FAT	7g	SODIUM	70mg
SATURATED FAT	1g	FIBRE	1g

WHOLEMEAL SCONE ROUNDS
—— • ——

A versatile and economical scone recipe suitable for a variety of sweet and savoury flavours. Best served fresh, split and buttered, the scones can be refreshed in the oven if they are beginning to go stale.

MAKES 12 Ⓥ

175 g/6 oz wholemeal flour
175 g/6 oz self-raising flour
pinch salt
75 g/3 oz margarine (or butter)
25–40 g/1–1½ oz soft brown (or caster sugar)
50–75 g/2–3 oz sultanas (optional)
1 large egg, beaten
150 ml/¼ pt buttermilk (or semi-skimmed milk soured with 2 tsp lemon juice)
flour for dredging

Sift the flours and salt into a bowl and rub in the margarine until the mixture resembles fine breadcrumbs. Mix in the sugar and sultanas (if used), then add the egg and sufficient milk to form a fairly soft dough. Knead this lightly, then divide it in two and shape each piece into a round about 2.5 cm/1 in thick. Preheat the oven to 230°C/450°F/gas 8.

Place each scone round on a baking sheet dredged with flour, sprinkle more flour over the scone rounds and mark each into six wedges. Bake them in the upper part of the oven for about 15 minutes or until lightly browned.

Cool on a wire rack; break them apart before serving.

Variations Add the finely grated rind of a lemon or orange to the dry mixture.

For savoury scones, omit sugar and sultanas and replace with 1 tablespoonful of fresh herbs, or with a good pinch of mustard powder and 50 g/2 oz of finely grated mature Cheddar or 2 tablespoonfuls of grated Parmesan cheese. Savoury scones can be brushed with milk and sprinkled with coarse sea salt instead of flour before baking.

KILOCALORIES	180	SUGARS	9g
TOTAL FAT	6g	SODIUM	150mg
SATURATED FAT	1g	FIBRE	2g

Ⓥ This symbol denotes a recipe suitable for vegetarians.

LYNN'S BANANA BREAD
—— • ——

This cake-like loaf is a good addition to the children's lunch-box and actually improves by the second day. Some of the flour can be replaced with wholewheat flour for improved flavour and fibre.

See illustration page 235.

MAKES A 900 g/2 lb LOAF Ⓥ

65 g/2½ oz margarine (or butter or white vegetable fat)
150 g/5 oz caster sugar
2 eggs, beaten
200 g/7 oz plain flour
2 tsp baking powder
½ tsp salt
½ tsp grated nutmeg
3 bananas (approx 225 g/8 oz, peeled)
50 g/2 oz glacé cherries (optional)
50 g/2 oz walnuts, chopped
50 g/2 oz raisins

TOPPING
25 g/1 oz margarine (or butter)
40 g/1½ oz plain flour
25 g/1 oz brown sugar

Grease and line a 900 g/2 lb loaf tin with oiled greaseproof paper. Cream the fat with the sugar until light and fluffy; add the eggs and 1 tablespoonful of the flour. Beat thoroughly. Sift the remaining flour, baking powder, salt and nutmeg together and mash the bananas to a purée; sprinkle the washed, dried and chopped cherries with a little of the sifted flour. Fold the banana purée, cherries, walnuts and raisins into the cream mixture, mixing well. Fold in the sifted flour and spoon the mixture into the prepared tin.

For the topping, rub the margarine into the flour to a crumbly texture, fold in the sugar and spoon the topping over the banana mixture. Set the tin on the centre shelf of a cool oven and bake at 150°C/300°F/gas 2 for 1¼–1½ hours or until cooked through. Ease the bread carefully out of the tin and leave it to cool on a wire rack before slicing.

[Nutritional values are per slice; roughly 26 slices per loaf.]

KILOCALORIES	115	SUGARS	12g
TOTAL FAT	4g	SODIUM	70mg
SATURATED FAT	1g	FIBRE	0.5g

Sweet Teabread

A moist loaf which keeps well and is made with chunky marmalade and Brazil nuts. These can be replaced with equal amounts of chopped apples and raisins, dried chopped apricots and raisins or walnuts and chopped dates.

MAKES A 450 g/1 lb LOAF (V)

350 g/12 oz plain flour
4 tsp baking powder
pinch salt
100 g/4 oz soft brown sugar
100 g/4 oz marmalade
25 g/1 oz margarine (or butter), melted
1 egg, beaten
200 ml/7 fl oz semi-skimmed (or skimmed) milk
100 g/4 oz Brazil nuts, blanched and chopped

Sift the flour, baking powder and salt into a bowl; stir in the sugar and the marmalade. Blend the margarine with the egg and milk and work this into the flour mixture, followed by the nuts. Mix the dough thoroughly, adding a little more milk if necessary to give a soft dropping consistency. Preheat the oven to 180°C/350°F/gas 4.

Spoon into a greased 450 g/1 lb loaf tin, smooth the top and bake in the centre of the oven for about 1–1¼ hours. Cool on a wire rack, then wrap the teabread in kitchen foil and store for 24 hours before slicing it.

Serve plain or spread sparingly with low-fat spread.

[Nutritional values are per slice; roughly 13 slices per loaf.]

KILOCALORIES	220	SUGARS	15g
TOTAL FAT	8g	SODIUM	60mg
SATURATED FAT	2g	FIBRE	1g

Bread mixes Both brown and white bread mixes are readily available, with either yeast or baking powder as the raising agent. The packets give clear instructions and usually require only a liquid to be added to produce loaves of better flavour than shop-bought ones. Bread raised with baking powder has short keeping qualities. Bran bread and scone mixes also come in packets and will store, unopened, in a cool, dry place for several months.

Soda Bread

Soda bread is quickly made and has an excellent flavour and texture. It should be eaten fresh, preferably on the day it is baked.

MAKES 1 LOAF (V)

225 g/8 oz plain white flour
2 tsp bicarbonate of soda
2 tsp cream of tartar
½ tsp salt
225 g/8 oz wholewheat flour
50 g/2 oz white vegetable fat
300 ml/½ pt soured milk (or buttermilk or semi-skimmed milk soured with 1 tbsp lemon juice)

Dredge a baking sheet with flour and preheat the oven to 220°C/425°F/gas 7. Sift the white flour with the soda, cream of tartar and salt into a bowl and mix in the wholewheat flour. Rub in the fat until the mixture resembles fine breadcrumbs. Mix in sufficient soured milk to form a soft but manageable dough.

Turn out on a floured surface, shape into a round about 18 cm/7 in in diameter and set on the baking sheet. Dredge the top with flour (or brush it with water and sprinkle with cracked wheat or buckwheat); mark the bread into quarters with a sharp knife and bake in the centre of the oven for about 30 minutes or until well risen and golden-brown. Cool on a wire rack.

[Nutritional values are per slice; roughly 13 slices per loaf.]

KILOCALORIES	80	SUGARS	1g
TOTAL FAT	2g	SODIUM	60mg
SATURATED FAT	–	FIBRE	1g

Pitta

This type of slightly leavened bread is of Arab origin though associated with Greek cuisine. It has become popular as a versatile addition to soups, salads and dips, for picnics and all types of packed meals, including the school lunch-box.

See illustration page 227.

MAKES 8 Ⓥ

*450 g/1 lb strong white flour (or half wholemeal
and half white flour)*
300 ml/½ pt warm water (approx)
*15 g/½ oz yeast (or 2 tsp dried fresh yeast,
plus 1 tsp sugar)*
1 tsp salt
1 tbsp olive oil

Cream fresh yeast with half the water; for dried yeast, dissolve the sugar in half the quantity of water and sprinkle the yeast on top. Leave for about 10 minutes until frothy. Sift the flour and salt into a bowl, add the yeast liquid and mix to a dough with the remaining warm water mixed with the oil.

Turn out on a lightly floured surface and knead until smooth and elastic (8–10 minutes by hand or 3–4 minutes in an electric mixer). Place in a lightly oiled polythene bag and leave to rise in a warm place for about 1½ hours or until doubled in size. Knock the dough back to remove all air bubbles and knead it again until smooth. Divide it into eight equal pieces and shape or roll each into an oval approximately 25 cm/10 in long by 12.5 cm/5 in wide. Place the pittas on greased baking sheets, cover with sheets of oiled polythene and leave to prove in a warm place for about 30 minutes. Preheat the oven to 240°C/475°F/gas 9.

Bake the pittas near the top of the oven for 6–8 minutes or until they puff up and begin to colour. Remove them from the oven and wrap them immediately in tea towels and leave until they have collapsed.

Serve warm or hot.

KILOCALORIES	200	SUGARS	2g
TOTAL FAT	3g	SODIUM	250mg
SATURATED FAT	–	FIBRE	3.5g

BRAN BAPS

The addition of bran to a dough slows down the rising, but the resulting flavour and texture are well worth the extra time. Use coarse-wheat bran or a natural bran product. Some health-food shops stock a complete bran bread mix, ideal for these baps; they will freeze for up to 6 months.

See illustration

MAKES 10 ROLLS OR 2 BAPS Ⓥ

400 g/14 oz strong white flour
*15 g/½ oz fresh yeast (or 2 tsp dried yeast,
plus 1 tsp caster sugar)*
150 ml/¼ pt warm semi-skimmed milk
1 tsp salt
50 g/2 oz bran
50 g/2 oz white vegetable fat
190 ml/scant 7 fl oz warm water

Cream the fresh yeast with the milk; if dried yeast is used, dissolve the sugar in the milk, sprinkle the yeast on top and leave it in a warm place for about 10 minutes or until frothy.

Sift the flour and salt into a bowl, mix in the bran and rub in the fat. Add the yeast liquid and enough water to form a slightly soft dough. Knead this on a lightly floured surface until smooth and elastic – about 10 minutes by hand or 3–4 minutes in an electric mixer.

Shape the dough into a ball and place in a lightly oiled polythene bag. Leave it to rise in a warm place for 1–1½ hours until doubled in size. Turn the dough out on a lightly floured surface, knock it back and knead it until smooth. For two large baps, cut the dough in half, shape each piece into a ball, then roll it out to a circle approx 2.5 cm/1 in thick. Set on greased and floured baking sheets. Alternatively, divide the dough into ten pieces and shape them into balls before rolling them out to oval or round shapes about 1.5 cm ½ in thick. Place on greased and floured baking sheets. Cover the baps or rolls lightly with oiled polythene and leave them to rise in a warm place until doubled in size.

Preheat the oven to 220°C/425°F/gas 7. Remove the polythene and press the centres of the baps with three or four fingers to prevent blisters during baking, or prick them with a fork. Sprinkle lightly with flour and bake baps for 20–30 minutes, rolls for 15–20 minutes. Cool on a wire rack.

[Nutritional values are per roll.]

KILOCALORIES	190	SUGARS	2g
TOTAL FAT	5g	SODIUM	250mg
SATURATED FAT	1g	FIBRE	3g

Right *In the centre is chocolate cake with chocolate icing and nuts, flanked by apple fruit cake and on the left by oaty drop scones, wholemeal muffins and sliced prune and bran teabread. On the shelf below, Lynn's banana bread (left) and coconut and date streusel cake.*

MILK BREAD

Use semi-skimmed milk for the liquid content or half
whole milk and half water. This bread stays fresh for a
considerable time.
See illustration page 227.

MAKES 2 LOAVES Ⓥ

450 g/1 lb strong white flour
15 g/½ oz fresh yeast (or 1½ tsp dried yeast,
plus 1 tsp caster sugar)
450 ml/¾ pt semi-skimmed milk (or
milk and water mixed)
1½ tsp salt
225 g/8 oz wholemeal flour
50 g/2 oz margarine (or white vegetable fat)

Blend the fresh yeast with all the liquid; for dried yeast,
dissolve the sugar in the liquid, sprinkle the yeast over
the surface and leave in a warm place for about 10
minutes until frothy. Sift the white flour and salt into a
bowl, mix in the wholemeal flour and rub in the fat.
Add the yeast liquid and mix until it resembles a fairly
soft dough.

Knead on a lightly floured surface until smooth and
elastic (about 10 minutes by hand or 3–4 minutes in a
food processor). Shape into a ball and place in an oiled
polythene bag; leave it to rise in a warm place for
about 1 hour or until doubled in size. Remove the
dough from the bag, knock it back and knead once
more until smooth.

Grease a round sandwich tin, approximately 20 cm/
8 in in diameter; divide half the dough into 6–8 even
pieces and shape them into balls; set one in the centre
of the tin and arrange the others round it. Shape the
remaining dough into a baton, cob or large baps.

Cover lightly with oiled polythene and leave to rise
in a warm place until doubled in size. Remove the
polythene. Preheat the oven to 220°C/425°F/gas 7.
Leave the top plain or brush with beaten egg, sprinkle
with flour, poppy seeds, cracked wheat or oatmeal.
Bake in the centre of the oven for 30–40 minutes.
[Nutritional values are per slice; roughly 26 slices
per loaf.]

KILOCALORIES	140	SUGARS	2g
TOTAL FAT	3g	SODIUM	180mg
SATURATED FAT	1g	FIBRE	1.5g

Please see the introduction for a full explanation of the
nutritional factboxes.

NAAN

Naan is flat leavened bread, baked and eaten daily
throughout India. Traditionally, it is slapped on to the
sides of a very hot clay oven called a *tandoor* and
baked while something else is cooking.

MAKES 6 Ⓥ

450 g/1 lb plain white flour (not strong flour)
2 tsp caster sugar
150 ml/¼ pt warm semi-skimmed (or skimmed) milk
2 tsp dried yeast
½ tsp salt
1 tsp baking powder
2 tbsp vegetable oil
150 ml/5 fl oz low-fat plain yogurt, lightly beaten
1 large egg, beaten

Dissolve 1 level tablespoonful of the sugar in the warm
milk, sprinkle the yeast on top and leave it in a warm
place for about 10 minutes until frothy. Sift the flour,
salt and baking powder into a bowl, with the
remaining sugar. Add the yeast liquid, the oil, yogurt
and egg and mix to a pliable dough which leaves the
sides of the bowl clean. Turn the dough out on a
floured surface and knead until smooth and elastic
(about 10 minutes by hand, 3–4 minutes in a mixer).

Shape into a ball, place in an oiled polythene bag
and leave to rise in a warm place for about 1 hour or
until doubled in size. Preheat the oven to the hottest
possible (240°C/475°F/gas 9) and place a heavy baking
sheet in the oven. Set the grill to fairly hot.

Remove the dough from the polythene, knock it
back and knead until smooth, then divide it into six
equal pieces. Use one piece at a time, keeping the
remainder covered with the oiled polythene. Shape
each dough piece to a ball and roll it out to a tear-
shaped naan approximately 25 cm/10 in long and
12.5 cm/5 in at its widest. Carefully remove the hot
baking sheet from the oven and slap the naan on to it;
return it immediately to the hot oven for about
4 minutes until just beginning to brown.

Remove the baking sheet from the oven and set it
under the grill, 7.5–10 cm/3–4 in from the heat, for
about 30 seconds or until the naan has browned
slightly. Wrap the naan in a tea towel and keep it
warm while the other pieces of dough are baked in the
same way.

KILOCALORIES	340	SUGARS	6g
TOTAL FAT	7g	SODIUM	210mg
SATURATED FAT	–	FIBRE	2.5g

COCONUT AND DATE STREUSEL CAKE

— • —

This moist, coconut-flavoured cake looks attractive baked in a ring mould. To avoid turning the cake with its crumble topping upside down, use for preference a spring-release ring mould or tin with a removable base. See illustration page 235.

MAKES 1 CAKE Ⓥ

350 g/12 oz self-raising flour
pinch salt
200 g/8 oz margarine (or butter or white vegetable fat)
150 g/6 oz light soft brown sugar
100 g/4 oz unsweetened desiccated coconut
3 large eggs, beaten
2 tbsp semi-skimmed milk (approx)

TOPPING

40 g/1½ oz margarine (or butter)
50 g/2 oz plain flour, sifted
50 g/2 oz Demerara sugar
50 g/2 oz stoned dates, finely chopped
40 g/1½ oz walnuts, chopped
25 g/1 oz unsweetened desiccated coconut

Grease and flour a 24 cm/9½ in spring-release ring mould or a 20 cm/8 in deep cake tin. Sift the flour and salt into a bowl and rub in the fat until the mixture resembles fine breadcrumbs. Stir in the sugar and coconut, followed by the beaten eggs and sufficient milk to mix to a fairly stiff but dropping consistency. Spoon the mixture into the prepared tin and level the top. Preheat the oven to 180°C/350°F/gas 4.

For the topping, rub the fat into the flour and stir in the sugar, dates and nuts. Spread the crumble over the cake and sprinkle the coconut on top. Bake in the centre of the oven for about 1 hour or until the cake is well risen.

Cool the cake in the tin for 5 minutes, then unclip the spring and ease the cake on to a wire rack to cool completely.

[Nutritional values are per slice; roughly 20 slices per cake.]

KILOCALORIES	260	SUGARS	12g
TOTAL FAT	16g	SODIUM	195mg
SATURATED FAT	6g	FIBRE	1.5g

Ⓥ This symbol denotes a recipe suitable for vegetarians.

CHRISTMAS CAKE

— • —

This rich fruit cake improves with keeping, especially if the top is pricked closely with a skewer and 4 tablespoonfuls of brandy poured over it.

MAKES 1 CAKE Ⓥ

50 g/2 oz glacé cherries, quartered (optional)
175 g/6 oz raisins
175 g/6 oz currants
175 g/6 oz sultanas
50 g/2 oz ground almonds or
blanched almonds, chopped
100 g/4 oz mixed peel, chopped (optional)
225 g/8 oz margarine (or butter)
225 g/8 oz soft brown sugar
50 g/2 oz plain flour
1 tsp mixed spice
½ tsp ground nutmeg
175 g/6 oz wholemeal flour
4 large eggs, beaten
grated rind of an orange (or lemon)
2 tbsp orange (or lemon) juice
2 tbsp semi-skimmed milk

Grease and double line a 20 cm/8 in round cake tin with buttered greaseproof paper. Mix together the cherries, raisins, currants, sultanas, almonds and peel. Cream the fat and sugar until light and fluffy, and sift the plain flour and spices into a separate bowl; add the wholemeal flour. Beat the eggs into the creamed mixture, one at a time, following each with a tablespoonful of the flour; add the dried fruits, orange rind, fruit juice and milk and mix thoroughly. Preheat the oven to 150°C/300°F/gas 2.

Spoon the cake mixture into the tin and bake in the lower part of the oven for about 3¼ hours. Cover the top of the cake with foil or greaseproof paper if it browns too quickly.

Cool the cake in the tin set on a wire rack; turn it out when quite cold and store wrapped in paper and foil.

[Nutritional values are per slice; roughly 23 slices per cake.]

KILOCALORIES	250	SUGARS	30g
TOTAL FAT	11g	SODIUM	120mg
SATURATED FAT	2g	FIBRE	1.5g

Please see the introduction for a full explanation of the nutritional factboxes.

APPLE FRUIT CAKE

Windfall apples are ideal for this moist fruit cake. The flavour improves if the cake is stored in foil for a couple of days.
See illustration page 235.

MAKES 1 CAKE Ⓥ

100 g/4 oz plain flour
¼ tsp bicarbonate of soda
1 tsp mixed spice
½ tsp ground coriander
100 g/4 oz wholemeal flour
100 g/4 oz margarine (or butter)
150 g/6 oz light soft brown sugar
2 large eggs
125 g/5 oz each of currants and raisins
50 g/2 oz mixed peel (optional)
grated rind of a lemon
225 g/8 oz cooking apples, coarsely grated

Preheat the oven to 180°C/350°F/gas 4. Grease and line a 20 cm/8 in round, deep cake tin with buttered greaseproof paper. Sift the plain flour, bicarbonate of soda and spices into a bowl and mix in the wholemeal flour. Cream the fat and sugar in a separate bowl, beat in the eggs, one at a time, following each with a spoonful of the flour mixture. Fold in the remaining flour, the dried fruits, peel, lemon rind and the grated apples.

Spoon into the prepared tin, level the top and bake just below the centre of the oven for about 1¼ hours or until golden-brown. Remove from the oven and let the cake settle in the tin for about 10 minutes before turning it out on to a wire rack.

[Nutritional values are per slice; roughly 20 slices per cake.]

KILOCALORIES	160	SUGARS	20g
TOTAL FAT	5g	SODIUM	60mg
SATURATED FAT	1g	FIBRE	1g

CHOCOLATE CAKE

Traditionally flavoured with coffee essence and coated with chocolate icing, the richness of this cake can be tempered with orange juice in place of coffee.
See illustration page 235.

MAKES 1 CAKE Ⓥ

3 tbsp cocoa powder, sifted
4–5 tbsp hot water
150 g/6 oz margarine (or butter)
175 g/7 oz light soft brown sugar
3 large eggs
150 g/6 oz self-raising flour, sifted
grated rind of an orange
1 tbsp orange juice (or coffee essence)

CHOCOLATE ICING
100 g/4 oz plain chocolate, broken up (or chocolate dots)
50 g/2 oz margarine (or butter)
50 g/2 oz icing sugar, sifted
chopped nuts (optional)

Grease and line the base of two 20 cm/8 in round sandwich tins or one deep 20 cm/8 in round cake tin with buttered greaseproof paper. Dissolve the cocoa in the water and leave it to cool. Cream the margarine and sugar until light and fluffy; beat in the eggs, one at a time, following each with a tablespoonful of the flour. Beat in the cocoa mixture and fold in the rest of he flour, the orange rind and juice (or coffee essence.)

Preheat the oven to 180°C/350°F/gas 4. Divide the cake mixture evenly between the two tins or pour it into the large tin; level the top. Bake just below the centre of the oven, allowing 35–40 minutes for the two cakes, about 1 hour for the larger one. Turn out on to a wire rack and leave to cool.

For the icing, melt the chocolate in a small bowl set over a pan of hot water, then stir in the margarine until melted. Beat in the icing sugar until smooth; use a scant half to sandwich the cakes together, splitting the larger cake in half horizontally; spread the remainder over the top. As the icing sets make a swirling design with a round-bladed knife and decorate with chopped nuts if liked. For a healthier icing, omit the chocolate and cream the margarine and sugar together and beat in 1 tablespoonful of cocoa or carob powder. Use to fill the cake only.

[Nutritional values are per slice; roughly 8 slices per cake.]

KILOCALORIES	465	SUGARS	38g
TOTAL FAT	27	SODIUM	340mg
SATURATED FAT	8g	FIBRE	0.5g

BATTER GINGERBREAD

Gingerbread has one of the oldest traditions in British cookery, and appears as cakes or biscuits, flapjacks or parkin in numerous local recipes. Use a warm spoon to ensure a level spoonful of black treacle.

MAKES 1 CAKE Ⓥ

175 g/6 oz self-raising flour
2 tsp ground ginger
½ tsp mixed spice
50 g/2 oz margarine (or butter)
2 tbsp Demerara sugar
2 tbsp black treacle
2 large eggs
150 ml/¼ pt semi-skimmed (or skimmed) milk
1 tsp bicarbonate of soda

Place all the ingredients (except the milk and bicarbonate of soda) in a bowl, process them until well combined, then add the milk and bicarbonate. Continue to process for a few seconds until the mixture is bubbly. Preheat the oven to 180°C/350°F/gas 4.

Grease and line with buttered greaseproof paper a shallow 20 cm/8 in round cake tin or a 450 g/1 lb loaf tin; pour in the mixture. Level the top and bake in the centre of the oven for 1–1¼ hours or until the cake is well risen and firm to the touch.

Cool on a wire rack and store it for several days before serving.

[Nutritional values are per slice; roughly 13 slices per cake.]

KILOCALORIES	105	SUGARS	4g
TOTAL FAT	4g	SODIUM	100mg
SATURATED FAT	1g	FIBRE	0.5g

ORANGE MADEIRA CAKE

A classic madeira cake is flavoured with lemon rind and decorated with citron peel; this recipe uses orange rind as well.

MAKES 1 CAKE Ⓥ

150 g/6 oz margarine (or butter)
150 g/6 oz caster sugar
150g/6 oz S-R Flour
150g/6oz Plain Flour
3 eggs, beaten

grated rind of a lemon
grated rind of a medium-sized orange
1 tbsp lemon (or orange) juice
strips of candied citron peel (optional)

Grease and line a 20 cm/8 in round cake tin with buttered greaseproof paper. Cream the margarine and sugar until light and fluffy. Sift the two flours together in a separate bowl. Beat the eggs, one at a time, into the creamed mixture, following each with a spoonful of flour; fold in the remaining flour and the fruit rinds and juice, using a metal spoon. Preheat the oven to 160°C/325°F/gas 3.

Spoon the cake mixture into the prepared tin, level the top and arrange one or more thin slices of citron peel on top. Bake the cake in the centre of the oven for just over 1 hour or until well risen, firm and lightly coloured. Cook the cake in the tin for 5 minutes before turning it out on to a wire rack.

[Nutritional values are per slice; roughly 13 slices per cake.]

KILOCALORIES	210	SUGARS	12g
TOTAL FAT	11g	SODIUM	150mg
SATURATED FAT	3g	FIBRE	0.5g

ALL-IN-ONE FRUIT CAKE

This easily prepared fruit cake with a Demerara topping can be baked in a round tin, or as a slab cake.

MAKES 1 CAKE Ⓥ

225 g/8 oz self-raising flour
1½ tsp baking powder
1 tsp ground cinnamon
½ tsp each of ground nutmeg and ground ginger
175 g/6 oz soft margarine (or butter)
175 g/6 oz light soft brown sugar
100 g/4 oz currants
175 g/6 oz sultanas (or raisins)
50 g/2 oz mixed peel
grated rind of a lemon (optional)
3 eggs
3 tbsp semi-skimmed milk
Demerara sugar (optional)

Sift the flour, baking powder and spices into a bowl; add the margarine, sugar, dried fruits, peel, lemon rind (if used), eggs and milk. Mix the ingredients thoroughly and beat until smooth. Preheat the oven to 180°C/350°F/gas 4.

Spoon the mixture into a greased, 23 cm/9 in round cake tin lined with buttered greaseproof paper. Level the top and sprinkle it with Demerara sugar; bake just below the centre of the oven for 1–1¼ hours or until golden-brown and firm to the touch (cover the cake with greaseproof paper if the top browns too quickly).

Cool the cake in the tin for 5 minutes, then turn it out on to a wire rack and leave until cold.

[Nutritional values are per slice; roughly 10 slices per cake.]

KILOCALORIES	380	SUGARS	41g
TOTAL FAT	16g	SODIUM	270mg
SATURATED FAT	4g	FIBRE	1.5g

LEMON SPONGE CAKE

Softer in texture than a Victoria sponge, this cake is iced with a translucent lemon icing which soaks into the moist and fluffy sponge. It can be left plain or decorated with freshly grated lemon rind.

MAKES 1 CAKE (V)

100 g/4 oz margarine (or butter)
100 g/4 oz caster sugar
2 large eggs, beaten
2 tsp lemon rind, finely grated
150 g/5 oz self-raising flour, sifted
25 g/1 oz cornflour
½ tsp baking powder
150 g/6 oz icing sugar
4–5 tbsp lemon juice

Warm a large mixing bowl enough to soften the margarine without becoming runny. Beat it with the sugar and 1 teaspoonful of lemon juice, by hand or in an electric mixer, until light and fluffy. Gradually beat in the eggs and lemon rind, beating in a little of the sifted flour if the mixture begins to curdle. Preheat the oven to 190°C/375°F/gas 5.

Sift the cornflour, baking powder and half the icing sugar into the flour. Using a metal spoon, fold half of this into the creamed mixture, with 3 tablespoonfuls of lemon juice and finally fold in the remaining flour. Spoon the sponge mixture into a well-greased 20 cm/8 in cake tin, level the top and bake the cake on the middle shelf of the oven for 25–30 minutes or until it is well risen, golden and springy to touch.

Turn the cake out on a wire rack to cool. Mix the remaining icing sugar with the rest of the lemon juice

until it is thick enough to coat the back of a wooden spoon. Pour the icing over the cake, letting it flow down the sides.

[Nutritional values are per slice; roughly 12 slices per cake.]

KILOCALORIES	190	SUGARS	18g
TOTAL FAT	8g	SODIUM	130mg
SATURATED FAT	2g	FIBRE	0.5g

GINGERBREAD

Gingerbread made with oatmeal is common in the North of England and Scotland where it is often known as parkin.

MAKES 16 (V)

100 g/4 oz margarine (or butter)
100 g/4 oz black treacle
100 g/4 oz light soft brown sugar
100 g/4 oz plain flour
pinch salt
1½ tsp ground ginger
½ tsp mixed spice
100 g/4 oz fine oatmeal
1 large egg, beaten
4 tbsp semi-skimmed milk
½ tsp bicarbonate of soda

Grease and line an 18 cm/7 in deep, square cake tin with buttered greaseproof paper. Put the fat, treacle and sugar in a pan over gentle heat until melted and dissolved; allow it to cool slightly. Sift the flour, salt, ginger and spice into a bowl, add the oatmeal and mix well. Stir in the treacle mixture, egg and 3 table-spoonfuls of the milk. Blend the remaining milk with the bicarbonate of soda and add to the ingredients, beating them until smooth. Preheat the oven to 180°C/350°F/gas 4.

Pour the mixture into the prepared tin and bake in the centre of the oven for 50–60 minutes or until the gingerbread is firm to the touch. Cool on a wire rack, then wrap it in foil and store for 3–4 days before serving, cut into squares.

KILOCALORIES	140	SUGARS	11g
TOTAL FAT	6g	SODIUM	90mg
SATURATED FAT	1g	FIBRE	0.5g

GRANTHAM GINGERBREADS

These crisp, ginger-flavoured biscuits can also be made as spiced biscuits by substituting cinnamon and/or mixed spice for ginger.
See illustration page 243.

MAKES 30–40 Ⓥ

100 g/4 oz margarine (or butter)
100 g/4 oz caster sugar
100 g/4 oz light soft brown sugar
1 large egg, beaten
250 g/9 oz self-raising flour
1½ tsp ground ginger
Demerara sugar

Preheat the oven to 150°C/300°F/gas 2. Cream the fat until soft, add the sugars and beat thoroughly. Beat in the egg. Sift the flour and ginger together and add to the creamed mixture; knead it to a pliable dough. Roll into balls about the size of walnuts and place them on lightly greased baking sheets allowing plenty of space for them to spread.

Sprinkle each gingerbread nut with a little Demerara sugar and bake them towards the top of the oven for about 30 minutes. Remove from the oven and allow to settle for a few minutes before moving them to a wire rack to cool.

KILOCALORIES	75	SUGARS	8g
TOTAL FAT	3g	SODIUM	50mg
SATURATED FAT	1g	FIBRE	–

OATCAKES

Traditional Scottish oatcakes are the perfect accompaniment to a selection of cheeses served with celery sticks and radishes.

MAKES 16 Ⓥ

225 g/8 oz quick-cooking oats
75 g/3 oz plain flour
¼ tsp bicarbonate of soda
½ tsp salt
50 g/2 oz white vegetable fat (or butter), melted
hot water

Put the oats in a bowl and mix in the flour sifted with the salt. Make a well in the centre, pour in the melted fat and mix to a pliable dough with hot water. Roll the dough out fairly thinly on a working surface sprinkled with oats and cut it into circles round a saucer; divide each circle into four triangles. Heat the oven to 220°C/425°F/gas 7.

Lift the oatcakes on to ungreased baking sheets, sprinkle them with a little oatmeal and bake in the centre of the oven for 15 minutes. Cool on a wire rack.

KILOCALORIES	90	SUGARS	–
TOTAL FAT	4g	SODIUM	90mg
SATURATED FAT	1g	FIBRE	1g

BROWN SUGAR MERINGUES

Brown sugar gives these meringues a deliciously crunchy texture and tints them a pale coffee colour.
See illustration page 243.

MAKES 30 Ⓥ

50 g/2 oz light soft brown sugar
50 g/2 oz caster sugar
2 large egg whites

Line two baking trays with non-stick silicone paper. Sift the two sugars together. Whisk the egg whites to stiff peaks. Whisk in the sugars a little at a time, making sure the mixture is stiff before adding more.

Spoon small piles of meringue on to the prepared trays or spoon the mixture into a large piping bag fitted with a star or plain nozzle; pipe with whirls, fingers, stars or other shapes. Bake in a cool oven (110°C/225°F/gas ¼–½) for 1 hour. Reverse the baking trays in the oven and continue baking for a further hour or until the meringues have set.

Leave them to cool completely on the baking trays before storing.

KILOCALORIES	20	SUGARS	3g
TOTAL FAT	–	SODIUM	10mg
SATURATED FAT	–	FIBRE	–

DATE FLAPJACKS

Traditional flapjacks are made with rolled oats and syrup. Here they are flavoured with dates and lemon.
See illustration page 243.

MAKES 12 (V)

100 g/4 oz margarine (or butter)
2 tbsp clear honey
2 tbsp golden syrup
grated rind of ½ lemon
50 g/2 oz stoned chopped dates (or raisins or sultanas)
225 g/8 oz rolled oats

Preheat the oven to 190°C/375°F/gas 5. Grease a 20 cm/8 in shallow, square cake tin. Melt the fat in a pan, add the honey and syrup and heat through until runny. Remove from the heat, add the lemon rind and dates (or raisins or sultanas), followed by the oats; mix well.

Spoon the mixture into the tin, pressing it down evenly, especially in the corners. Bake in the centre of the oven for 25–30 minutes or until firm and golden-brown. Cool in the tin for a few minutes, then cut the cake into finger-sized bars. Leave them in the tin until quite cold before removing the flapjacks and breaking them into the bars.

KILOCALORIES	165	SUGARS	8g
TOTAL FAT	8g	SODIUM	90mg
SATURATED FAT	2g	FIBRE	1.5g

WALNUT FINGERS

Crisp thin biscuits with a nutty flavour and coffee glaze.
See illustration on page 243.

MAKES 32–36 (V)

100 g/4 oz plain flour, sifted
100 g/4 oz wholemeal flour
150 g/6 oz block margarine (or butter)
100 g/4 oz icing sugar, sifted
75 g/3 oz shelled walnuts, finely chopped
½ large egg white
2 tsp coffee essence (or strong black coffee)

Grease three baking sheets. Mix the two flours together in a large bowl and make a well in the centre. Cut the margarine or butter into small pieces and put them in the well with the icing sugar. Work the fat and sugar together with the fingertips and gradually incorporate the flour. Finally work in the walnuts and knead the dough until smooth. Wrap it in foil and chill for 30 minutes.

Roll out half the dough to a rectangle, approximately 5 mm/¼ in thick, and mark it all over into a criss-cross pattern with a sharp knife. Mix the egg white with the coffee essence and brush it liberally over the dough. Cut the dough into fingers, 7.5 × 2.5 cm/3 × 1 in and transfer them to the baking sheet. Preheat the oven to 190°C/375°F/gas 5.

Repeat the process with the rest of the dough and bake the biscuits for about 15 minutes. Cool the biscuits on a wire rack.

KILOCALORIES	75	SUGARS	3g
TOTAL FAT	5g	SODIUM	40mg
SATURATED FAT	1g	FIBRE	0.5g

PEANUT COOKIES

The flavour of peanut butter comes through strongly in these crisp cookies.

MAKES 15–18 (V)

50 g/2 oz peanut butter
50 g/2 oz margarine (or butter)
grated rind of ½ orange (or lemon)
40 g/1½ oz light soft brown sugar
½ large egg, beaten
40 g/1½ oz raisins, chopped
100 g/4 oz self-raising flour, sifted

Lightly grease two baking sheets. Put the peanut butter, margarine or butter, orange rind and sugar into a bowl and beat thoroughly until light and fluffy. Beat in the egg followed by the raisins. Finally add the flour and mix to a fairly firm dough. Shape this into walnut-sized balls and set them well apart on the prepared baking sheets. Preheat the oven to 180°C/350°F/gas 4.

Flatten each cookie slightly with a fork and mark the tops with a criss-cross pattern. Bake in the centre, or just below, of the oven for 15–20 minutes or until well risen and golden-brown. Cool on a wire rack.

KILOCALORIES	75	SUGARS	4g
TOTAL FAT	4g	SODIUM	60mg
SATURATED FAT	1g	FIBRE	0.5g

Opposite (top row) *Walnut fingers and Grantham gingerbreads, more gingerbreads and lemon shortbread bars above a row of gingerbread folk, and date flapjacks at the bottom. In the corners are brown sugar meringues.*

HAZELNUT FREEZER BISCUITS

Once prepared and shaped into a roll this biscuit mixture can be stored in the freezer; it can be sliced while still frozen.

MAKES 40–50 Ⓥ

200 g/7 oz margarine (or butter)
150 g/5 oz caster sugar
1 large egg, beaten
225 g/8 oz self-raising flour
75 g/3 oz hazelnuts, finely chopped

Cream the margarine and sugar, then gradually beat in the whisked egg. Sift the flour and fold this and the nuts into the creamed mixture. Shape it into a roll on a lightly floured surface, adding a little extra flour if necessary. Wrap the dough roll in greaseproof paper and chill in the fridge for 1 hour if is to be baked straight away; otherwise overwrap with foil and freeze.

Preheat the oven to 190°C/375°F/gas 5. Slice the dough roll thinly, setting the rounds on greased baking trays; bake near the top of the oven for about 10 minutes or until the biscuits are pale gold. Cool them on a wire rack.

KILOCALORIES	75	SUGARS	4g
TOTAL FAT	5g	SODIUM	60mg
SATURATED FAT	1g	FIBRE	0.5g

LEMON SHORTBREAD BARS

Although not true shortbread, these biscuits have a similarly short and crisp texture.
See illustration page 243.

MAKES 32 Ⓥ

125 g/5 oz soft margarine (or butter)
150 g/6 oz Demerara sugar
1 egg, beaten
225 g/8 oz plain flour
1 tsp baking powder
50 g/2 oz rolled oats
finely grated rind of a lemon

Cream the fat until soft, then beat in the sugar until fluffy; beat in the egg. Sift together the flour and baking powder and fold this into the creamed mixture, followed by the rolled oats and lemon rind. Work it by hand to a firm dough.

Shape into two 6.5 × 15 cm/2½ × 6 in blocks, wrap them in foil and chill in the fridge for 1–2 hours. Cut each dough block into 16 slices and place them on greased baking sheets. Preheat the oven to 190°C/375°F/gas 5.

Mark each bar with a criss-cross design and bake near the centre of the oven for 10–15 minutes. Cool on a wire rack.

KILOCALORIES	80	SUGARS	5g
TOTAL FAT	4g	SODIUM	30mg
SATURATED FAT	1g	FIBRE	0.5g

MINCEMEAT SQUARES

These small pastry-like squares have a spiced mincemeat filling. Alternatively, use puréed or sliced apple instead of mincemeat.

MAKES 12

225 g/8 oz self-raising flour
pinch salt
100 g/4 oz white vegetable fat, (butter or margarine)
100 g/4 oz light soft brown (or caster) sugar
1 large egg, beaten
2–3 tbsp semi-skimmed milk
6 tbsp mincemeat
grated rind of ½ lemon (or orange)
1 tsp mixed spiced
2 tbsp Demerara sugar (optional)

Lightly grease a shallow 20 cm/8 in square cake tin. Sift the flour and salt into a bowl and rub in the fat until the mixture resembles fine breadcrumbs; stir in the sugar. Add the egg and sufficient milk to mix to a fairly soft dough. Divide it in two and press one portion over the base of the tin. Top with the mincemeat and sprinkle with lemon or orange rind and spice. Preheat the oven to 190°C/375°F/gas 5.

Roll out the remaining dough to fit the tin; press it down over the mincemeat. Brush the top with milk and sprinkle with the Demerara sugar. Bake in the centre of the oven for 35–40 minutes.

Cool the pastry in the tin for 5 minutes, cut it into squares and leave them to cool in the tin.

KILOCALORIES	220	SUGARS	22g
TOTAL FAT	8g	SODIUM	200mg
SATURATED FAT	2g	FIBRE	0.5g

GINGERBREAD FOLK

Gingerbread stalls were formerly a feature of country fairs. In Germany and Austria gingerbread men are traditional Christmas decorations; they are threaded with ribbons and hung on the Christmas tree.

See illustration page 243.

MAKES 6 Ⓥ

150 g/5 oz plain flour
½ tsp baking powder
1 tsp ground ginger
3 tbsp golden syrup
50 g/2 oz sugar
50 g/2 oz margarine (or butter)
currants
silver balls

Sift together the flour, baking powder and ginger. Melt the syrup, sugar and margarine or butter in a pan over gentle heat, then stir the mixture into the dry ingredients. Use a wooden spoon at first, then form it to a firm but pliable dough with the hands. Let the dough cool slightly, then roll it out on a lightly floured board and cut it into the classic gingerbread shapes. Use currants for eyes and buttons on the larger figures, and coloured or silver balls on smaller ones. Preheat the oven to 180°C/350°F/gas 4.

Transfer the gingerbread to greased and lightly floured baking sheets and bake in the centre of the oven for about 10 minutes depending on the size. Cool on a wire rack.

KILOCALORIES	210	SUGARS	17g
TOTAL FAT	7g	SODIUM	80mg
SATURATED FAT	2g	FIBRE	1g

GLOSSARY OF FOOD TERMS

A

Adoo mirch – A spicy mixture popular in Gujarati cooking. Liquidise or process 50 g/2 oz fresh root ginger with 50 g/2 oz fresh green chillies (deseeded and chopped) and ½ teaspoonful of salt to a fine paste. Store in a covered container in the fridge for up to three weeks.

Agar-agar – A jellying substance obtained from seaweeds and preferred by vegans to gelatine (*qv*). Available from chemists and health-food shops as a powder or as flakes, and as the Japanese *kanten* in tablet or cake form. Agar-agar dissolves in boiling water, but should not be allowed to boil as it loses its ability to set. On average, 1 teaspoonful agar-agar will set 750 ml/1¼ pt liquid.

Ajowan seeds – Small, spicy and pungent seeds, with long keeping qualities, that are related to caraway and cumin; the flavour is strongly reminiscent of thyme.

Arrowroot – A highly starchy, fine-grained substance used for thickening fruit glazes, pie fillings and compotes. It is preferable to cornflour in that it lacks any flavour of its own and produces a clear uniform jelly.

Asafoetida – Strongly aromatic spice, added to vegetarian dishes for its digestive powers; use in minute quantities.

Asam (or asem) – See **Tamarind**

B

Baking blind Technique used when baking flans and open pies. Pastry is laid in a flan dish or tin and weighed down with baking beans or dried beans whilst being cooked on its own in the oven before a filling is added.

Barley flakes – Whole barley grains with the bran layer intact, rolled flat and used in muesli mixes.

Bean curd – See **Tofu**.

Blachan – See **Terasi**.

Bouquet garni – The classic French herb flavouring for stocks, sauces and soups consists of sprigs of fresh parsley and thyme, and a bay leaf tied together in a bunch; other aromatic herbs – basil, chervil, tarragon and rosemary – can be added to taste. Remove the bouquet before serving.

Bulghur – See **Cracked wheat**.

C

Candlenuts – See **Kemiri**.

Cardamom – An expensive, highly aromatic Eastern spice, best bought whole in the dried pods, or as seeds; usually creamy or pale green in colour. A traditional ingredient in garam masala (*qv*) mixtures. The related black cardamoms are larger, dark brown in colour, less aromatic but cheaper.

Carob powder – Product of the sweet pulp of the Mediterranean locust bean, used as a chocolate substitute.

Cellophane noodles – Sold dried, these are the product of soaked, ground and strained mung beans. Available from oriental stores.

Chickpea flour – See **Gram flour**.

Clarified butter – Rendered down butter that has had its impurities removed. To obtain 125 g/4 oz of clarified butter, melt 225 g/8 oz of salted butter in a small pan over gentle heat without stirring or browning. Let the butter come to a foam. Continue to cook gently until the foam subsides; remove from the heat and leave until the butter deposit has sunk to the bottom of the pan, leaving the clear liquid on top. Pour this carefully through muslin, taking care to leave the deposit behind. See also **Ghee**.

Coconut milk – Commonly used in Indonesian cookery. It consists of a mixture of water and oils extracted from the grated flesh. Do not allow recipes containing coconut milk to boil or they will curdle. Use within 24 hours. Coconut milk can be bought in supermarkets or be made using fresh, desiccated or creamed coconut. See page 111.

Cornflour – Pure starch substance derived from maize and used as a thickening agent. It creams easily with cold water to a smooth paste and is almost colourless at boiling point.

Cracked wheat (or **bulghur**) – Hulled wheat which is steamed until partly cooked, dried and then ground into three basic grades – coarse, medium and fine. Kibbled wheat is similar but has not been hulled before crushing and needs soaking before use.

Curry leaves – A spice flavouring in Indian vegetarian cookery. The leaves emit a strong curry aroma. Available fresh or dried from oriental stores and health-food shops.

D

Daikon – See **Radish, white.**

Dill weed The leaves of the dill plant. The pungent, warm taste is used to flavour fish dishes.

F

Fenugreek – Highly aromatic seeds used in Indian and some European cookery for their bitter properties.

Filo (phyllo) pastry – This pastry is paper-thin and is used in Greek cookery for both sweet and savoury dishes. It is a simple flour-and-water paste, worked so thin that it dries and breaks on exposure to air; it must be stored, wrapped in plastic, in the fridge.

Five spices – Spice compound used in Chinese dishes and consisting of anise, cloves, fennel, star anise and coriander.

G

Galangal (galingale) – See **Laos.**

Garam masala – A highly aromatic mixture (literally 'hot mixture') of six spices – black peppercorns, cloves, cinnamon, cardamoms (*qv*), cumin and bay leaves – used widely in Indian cookery.

Gelatine – Product derived from the bones of animals. It is used for setting liquids to jelly-like substances. Available as powders or transparent sheets or leaves, gelatine needs soaking before use in order to absorb water and swell; boiling, especially with acid liquids, reduces the gelling power. Setting properties are also affected by the brand of gelatine, the type of liquid, the time allowed for setting, the air temperature and the container. On average, 15 g/½ oz of powdered gelatine will set 600 ml/1 pt of liquid.

Ghee – Basically the Indian equivalent of clarified butter (*qv*), which is unsalted butter rendered down to purify it of sediment. Ideal for frying as it tolerates higher temperatures than ordinary butter without browning, and also has a longer storage life. Available from oriental stores and health-food shops.

Gram flour – Also known as besan, this high-protein flour is obtained from chickpeas and is widely used in Indian cooking.

H

Haloumi – A salty sheep's milk cheese of Syrian origin, matured in whey.

Hoisin sauce – Dark red and sweet Chinese condiment made from soya beans and flavoured with garlic and spices.

J

Jaggery – Also known as gur, this is a dark-coloured aromatic crude sugar from India, chiefly derived from palm sugar, though some cane sugar may form the base.

Juniper berries – From an evergreen shrub and widely used in Scandinavia for flavouring, marinating and pickling. The berries give a bitter-sweet flavour and are often associated with gin and cordials.

K

Kaffir lime leaves – Fresh or dried leaves from a citrus tree used to flavour Indonesian dishes, especially fish; available dried from oriental stores.

Kelp – Edible seaweed, sold dried. Nutritionally, kelp is a rich source of iodine; needs to be soaked and reconstituted before use.

Kemiri – Also known as candlenuts, these are rich in an oil so volatile that it burns readily, hence the name. The flavour is somewhat tart.

Kibbled wheat – See **Cracked wheat.**

L

Laos – Also known as galangal or galingale, this is a strongly flavoured spice obtained from the roots of a member of the ginger family. It is used sparingly to flavour oriental stews and curries and is very popular in Thai cookery.

Lemon grass – Used in Indonesian cooking to impart a lemon-like flavour. Available from oriental stores as dried grass blades or as a powder (sereh) and used in minute quantities for flavouring.

M

Mango powder – Sun-dried, unripe mangoes ground into powder and a popular flavouring in many Indian dishes.

Mei-Kuei-Lu wine – An expensive, highly aromatic and colourless Chinese spirit derived from rose petals.

Mooli See **Radish, white.**

O

Oils – Oils derived from the seeds of plants contain polyunsaturated fats in varying proportions, and while some are bland and therefore more suited to frying and general cooking, others have distinctive flavours which enhance and complement other foods. Olive oil is expensive, especially the best grade of unrefined extra 'virgin' oil; it also contains a high proportion of saturated fat. It is best used in dressings and mayonnaises and not recommended for frying as it has a low smoking point.

Cooking oils include sunflower, groundnut (peanut), corn and soya oils, all rather bland in flavour but capable of being heating to high temperatures without smoking; sunflower, soya and corn oils contain only small amounts of saturated fat, but groundnut oil has almost equal proportions of saturated and polyunsaturated fatty acids.

Speciality oils are always more expensive, notably safflower oil and the distinctive nutty sesame seed oil – a favourite for stir-fried dishes. Walnut and hazelnut oils are gourmet oils for salad dressings, while mustard oil is too pungent for anything but spicy Indian dishes. Coconut oil has a mild nutty flavour; it is not recommended for frying (it solidifies easily) and contains more saturated fat than butter. Blended vegetable oils are also available, generally based on rape-seed oil.

Oyster sauce – A Chinese condiment used as a dip and to flavour savoury dishes; thick and golden-brown, it is made from oysters cooked in soya sauce (*qv*).

P

Phyllo pastry – See **Filo pastry**.

Pomegranate seeds – Sweet varieties of the pomegranate make fine fruit desserts; the dried seeds used to flavour chutneys, stuffings and meat dishes in Indian and Middle Eastern cooking come from sour pomegranate varieties.

Proving – Also known as second rising (in bread-making): it is where the dough is kneaded for a second time after the initial rising to knock out any air bubbles and to ensure an even texture. Shape the dough, place the loaves on baking trays and leave in a warm place till doubled in size.

R

Radish, white – Also known as daikon and mooli; larger and longer than the related salad vegetable; used sliced, chopped or grated as a garnish for soups or fish, and in pickles and relishes.

Ricotta cheese – A soft fresh white cheese made with the whey of the milk and used in savoury and sweet dishes.

Rye flakes – Whole rye grains rolled and usually toasted to increase storage life; used as a breakfast cereal.

S

Salam leaves – Strongly aromatic leaves, used fresh or dried to flavour savoury Indonesian dishes.

Santen – See **Coconut milk**.

Sereh – See **Lemon grass**.

Shao-hsing wine – The traditional Chinese rice wine, used for cooking; similar to pale medium-dry sherry.

Shrimps, dried – Tiny shrimps, much used in Chinese cooking as a side dish or as a garnish to bland foods; rinse in cold water and soak for about 30 minutes.

Soya bean curd – See **Tofu**.

Soya flour – High-protein flour, low in starchy carbohydrates and used commercially as a dough improver.

Soya milk – Made from the protein-rich soya beans and thus containing polyunsaturated fat only; excellent substitute for those allergic to cow's milk.

Soya sauce – The best-known and most widely used by-product of the soya bean; the flavours are a blend of sweet, salty and meaty tastes and are derived from fermented soya beans mixed with ground wheat or barley. Many commercial brands are chemically fermented and artificially coloured and lack the authentic flavour. Numerous grades are available, from dense, dark and pungent to pale-coloured light soya sauces for delicate flavouring; the best are always those made by natural fermentation.

T

Tahini – An oily paste made from toasted sesame seeds. Used with chickpeas in the Greek and Middle Eastern dip, hummus.

Tamarind – Also known as asam or asem, the hard seed pods of the tamarind tree are much used in Indonesian cookery and impart a sour-fruity flavour. Tamarind pulp is sold in sticky blocks which must be softened to extract the juice. Break off a small knob and cover it with warm water (25 g/1 oz tamarind pulp will yield approximately 300 ml/ ½ pt tamarind water); when the water has cooled, squeeze and rub the pulp repeatedly to free fibres and the large seeds; rub the mixture through a sieve and reserve the water.

Terasi – Also known as blachan and an important flavouring in Far Eastern cookery. Made from salted and dried shrimps or prawns. Available as cakes, powders or pastes.

Tofu – Also known as bean curd or soya cheese and available in blocks from oriental stores or health-food shops. A bland, protein-rich food prepared from soya milk by coagulating the protein. Best used fresh.

V

Vinegar – Literally, soured wine produced by fermentation. Used in marinades, salad dressings, pickles and relishes as a preservative and for adding sharpness to bland foods. Wine vinegars come from soured red or white wines (or sherry) and these can further be flavoured with herbs (garlic, chilli, mint, tarragon, etc.) or with fruit (raspberry). Malt, cider and rice vinegars are made from fermented ale, cider and rice wine respectively.

W

Wheat flakes – Whole hulled grains, rolled flat and often dry-roasted in order to increase storage life.

Wheatgerm – The embryo wheat plant, removed from the grain before milling. Good sprinkled over breakfast cereal and plain yogurt or added to bread doughs. Once a packet is opened it should be stored in the fridge as it quickly goes rancid when exposed to the air.

Y

Yeast flakes – Dried flakes, the result of the fermentation process of baker's yeast, yielding a high-protein product with a distinct cheese flavour.

INDEX

Numbers in italic denote illustrations.

OVEN TEMPERATURES

VERY COOL	110°C/225°F/gas mark ¼
	120°C/250°F/gas mark ½
COOL	140°C/275°F/gas mark 1
	150°C/300°F/gas mark 2
MODERATE	160°C/325°F/gas mark 3
	180°C/350°F/gas mark 4
MODERATELY HOT	190°C/375°F/gas mark 5
FAIRLY HOT	200°C/400°F/gas mark 6
HOT	220°C/425°F/gas mark 7
	230°C/450°F/gas mark 8
VERY HOT	240°C/475°F/gas mark 9

FLUID MEASURES CONVERSION

METRIC	IMPERIAL	US
5 millilitres	1 teaspoon	1 teaspoon
15 millilitres	1 tablespoon	1 tablespoon
120 millilitres	4 fl oz	½ cup
150 millilitres	¼ pint (5 fl oz)	⅔ cup
225 millilitres	8 fl oz	1 cup
300 millilitres	½ pint (10 fl oz)	1¼ cups
450 millilitres	¾ pint (15 fl oz	2 cups
600 millilitres	1 pint (20 fl oz)	2½ cups
750 millilitres	24 fl oz	3 cups